LIFE CYCLE
COSTING
FOR
DESIGN
PROFESSIONALS

Life Cycle Costing: An economic assessment of competing design alternatives, considering all 'significant' costs of ownership over the economic life of each alternative, expressed in equivalent dollars.

Alphonse J. Dell'Isola, PE, CVS
Stephen J. Kirk, AIA, CVS

LIFE CYCLE COSTING FOR DESIGN PROFESSIONALS

Alphonse J. Dell'Isola, PE, CVS
Stephen J. Kirk, AIA, CVS

McGRAW-HILL BOOK COMPANY

New York   St. Louis   San Francisco   Auckland
Bogotá   Hamburg   Johannesburg   London   Madrid   Mexico
Montreal   New Delhi   Panama   Paris   São Paulo
Singapore   Sydney   Tokyo   Toronto

Library of Congress Cataloging in Publication Data

Dell'Isola, Alphonse J

    Life cycle costing for design professionals.

    Bibliography: p.
    Includes index.
    1.Building—Estimates.   2.Engineering economy.
I.Kirk, Stephen J., joint author.   II.Title.
TH435.D358   690′.068′1   80-21758
ISBN 0-07-016280-8

The editors for this book were **Joan Zselecsky** and **Virginia Blair,** the designer
was **Blaise Zito Associates,** and the production supervisor was **Thomas G.
Kowalczyk.** It was set in **Times Roman** by **University Graphics, Inc.**

Printed and bound by **Halliday Lithograph.**

This book is dedicated to the authors' wives and families who were so patient during the many months involved with the preparation of this text. As a "life cycle" investment, the proceeds from this book are being placed in educational trust funds.

Contents

Preface

The cost of ownership for facilities is rising at an ever increasing rate. Owners are having difficulty in both obtaining initial capital and affording to operate and maintain their facilities. Additional efforts are required to analyze these costs by the principal decision maker—*the design professional*. In addition, the energy situation has forced every decision maker to examine in greater detail the resulting impact of various courses of action.

As many have stated, the energy crisis, which is continuing to plague all industrialized nations, is an economic problem more than a lack of alternatives. In other words, given enough dollars, alternative fuel sources such as: solar, coal, shale oil, geothermal, hydroelectric, etc. could be substituted to satisfy our energy needs. The question is, "Which one(s) and how much investment?"

Designers are faced with a similar situation. The problem is not so much a lack of ideas; this is historically what designers are best at providing. The task facing them today is in dealing with *limited economic resources* in such a way that optimum proposals are selected and implemented.

The emphasis of this book then is to describe procedures for the designer to use in evaluating various energy and other life cycle ideas with respect to economics—and other noneconomic criteria.

The end result is an assessment of the consequences of various courses of action for an owner in such a way that all involved in the design process will make better decisions.

This book has been organized so that it may be used as a resource for the design professional in preparing a life cycle cost analysis during the design process. The book is organized to lead the designer through each step of the analysis. Examples and illustrations are provided to reinforce this process. The first five chapters, Introduction, Concepts, Economics, Life Cycle Estimating Procedures, and Formats, are intended to describe the various elements of the total process. Chapter 6, Design Methodology, places the earlier chapters into proper position with respect to the process. The remaining chapters, Case Studies, Other Uses, Summary and Conclusions, further illustrate examples and other applications of the technique of life cycle analysis.

Material has been provided in the appendixes to assist the designer in actual applications. Economic tables, format sheets, and selected life cycle data are provided. A sample scope of work for life cycle cost analysis has also been provided to assist the professional in negotiating with the client for additional design fees to perform the analysis. Excerpts of various governmental regulations further emphasize the importance of performing life cycle cost analyses.

A companion volume, entitled, the *Life Cycle Cost Data and Educational Supplement*, will be published with supporting life cycle costing data and an educational supplement to provide additional learning or teaching experience.

This book may also be used as a text for architects and engineers to learn the process using a practical text developed by practicing professionals. A Glossary allows designers to quickly look up key words used in life cycle costing. Finally, appropriate sources for additional information, organized by topic, are contained in the Bibliography.

This book may also be used in conjunction with related problem solving topics. These may include: Value Engineering, Engineering Economics, Cost Estimating, Systems Methodology, Energy Analysis and Professional Practice, etc. Chapters, as appropriate, may be read and studied to reinforce these topics.

ACKNOWLEDGMENTS

The authors would like to express their sincere appreciation to the many individuals of Smith, Hinchman & Grylls, Associates, including Michael Dell'Isola, who reviewed the early drafts of this book and offered their comments for improvement. The confidence provided by the American Consulting Engineers Council and the American Institute of Architects in allowing the authors to conduct life cycle costing training courses is also very much appreciated. The questions and discussions which ensued at each workshop by the design professionals in attendance allowed constant testing and evaluation of the techniques included in this book. Government agencies such as the National Aeronatics and Space Administration (NASA) and the Naval Facilities Engineering Command (NAVFAC) are thanked for their early enthusiasm with regard to LCC. Finally, appreciation is given to Mountain States Bell Telephone & Telegraph Company for its continuous support in allowing the authors to apply the techniques of life cycle costing to more than $200 million worth of new facilities.

CHAPTER ONE
INTRODUCTION

"When we mean to build,
We first survey the plot, then draw the model;
and when we see the figure of the house,
Then must we rate the cost of the erection;
which if we find outweighs ability,
What do we then but draw anew the model
In fewer offices, or at least desist
To build at all? . . ."

William Shakespeare
Henry IV, Part 2, I. iii, 1598.

BACKGROUND

The effective use of resources such as labor, money, time, energy, and building materials is becoming a matter of utmost concern to all segments of our socioeconomic system. Substantial quantities of these resources are committed by the architect and engineer through their design of facilities. In this era of rapidly rising prices for materials, escalating wages forced up by inflation, increasing energy costs, and congressional and presidential scrutiny of new construction and major repairs and alterations of federally funded facilities, owners are seeking every avenue to increase value and conserve resources.

In recent years, the initial costs of construction have been rising at an ever-increasing rate. As the rising curve of costs approaches the vertical, will anyone be able to afford to build—let alone to own and operate—a facility? Many in the construction industry face this crisis. As with initial costs, follow-on costs, such as maintenance and operations, have also escalated rapidly.

These events are even more evident at the level of family housing. A young family starting out in life finds that homes that sold for $30,000 ten years ago now sell for $60,000 or more. The down payment and closing costs reach well above $10,000. The economy has set up a sit-

uation where, because of construction costs, it is practically impossible for young couples to purchase homes.

What has happened to follow-on costs? Instead of buying a house, the family decides to rent an apartment. Apartments built as recently as 5 years ago are very energy-intensive—the monthly electric bill can amount to some $200. The family is caught between high initial costs and high operating costs.

On top of this, interest rates have gone from 6 percent to 16 percent in 10 years. Costs of financing for cars, houses, clothing, etc. multiply to create a situation of great concern for the future insofar as providing a desirable *quality of life* for human beings is concerned.

The Building Owners and Managers Association (BOMA) collects and shares its experience each year in regard to the costs of owning and operating commercial office buildings. Figure 1-1 graphically displays these costs for the past few years. To combat these trends, the technique of *life cycle costing* (LCC) is being promoted to satisfy the requirement for further design analysis.

Life cycle costing for the design professional can be defined as **"an economic assessment of competing design alternatives, considering all significant costs of ownership over the economic life of each alternative, expressed in equivalent dollars."** P. A. Stone, a British economist, applies the terminology "cost-in-use" and suggests that the technique is concerned with "the choice of means to a given end and with the problem of obtaining the best value for money for the resources spent."[1] In 1972 the U.S. Department of Health, Education, and Welfare summarized life cycle analysis as the systematic consideration of "cost, time and quality."[2] Life cycle costing most certainly ad-

1. P. A. Stone, *Building Design Evaluation: Costs-in-Use,* 2d ed., E. & F. N. Spon, London, 1975, p. 177.
2. *Life Cycle Budgeting as an Aid to Decision Making,* Building Information Circular, Department of Health, Education, and Welfare, Office of Facilities Engineering and Property Management, Washington, 1972, p. 1 (draft).

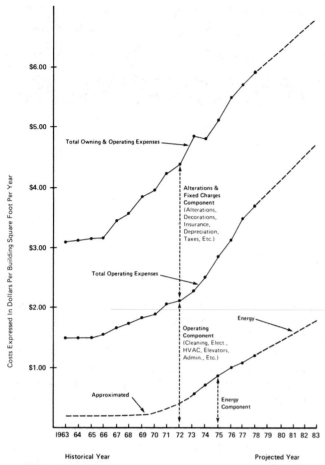

FIGURE 1-1
Historical life cycle costs of office buildings, national average.
(Source: BOMA Experience Exchange Report.)

dresses these as well as several other issues related to decision processes, analytic methods, data bases, and component performance.

Federal, state, and industrial clients have each issued LCC directives to the designers of their facilities. In 1977, President Carter established a goal of reducing energy consumption by 45 percent for all federally owned new buildings over their prior 1975 counterparts. The U.S. Congress, November 1978, established the National Energy Conservation Policy Act, which mandates that all new federal buildings be *life cycle cost effective* as determined by LCC methods prescribed by the legislation. Existing buildings are to be reviewed to improve their energy efficiency in general and to minimize their life cycle cost. Nebraska passed legislation in 1978 requiring a life cycle analysis for every state facility with a project cost over $50,000. Alaska, Florida, Massachusetts, Wisconsin, Texas, North Carolina, New Mexico, Washington, Maryland, Wyoming, Colorado, Illinois, and Idaho, among others, had similar legislation either in effect or pending in 1979. The General Services Administration (GSA) has developed elaborate procedures for predicting a facility's

total cost. The cities of Atlanta, Phoenix, and Chicago also require a life cycle analysis from their designers.

CLIENT DEMANDS

Clients are feeling the economic squeeze and reacting to it. With their costs compounded by the energy situation, *they are looking for design professionals with new skills.* They want facilities with the lowest possible first cost, energy consumption, maintenance cost, replacement cost, design and construction time, staffing cost, and financing cost, together with the longest serviceable life attainable within the other parameters, the highest possible quality, the best appearance, and the least taxes. How can proper decisions be made with all these parameters to consider? How has the profession historically made these decisions? The authors believe that design professionals have not completely fulfilled their responsibility to clients to consider all these factors in the design process. Also, owners have not been forceful enough in requiring and being willing to pay for these services. *Owners must provide the required fees and data and be prepared to become involved in the trade-off decisions necessary for final design selections.*

To ensure the most value for costs, design professionals must use a clearly defined methodology and have the tools necessary to develop the required data. Then, they should be prepared to estimate the fees for their services. Of the typical client demands all are measurable to some extent in dollars except quality and aesthetics, and even these can be evaluated given the functions required of the facility and a proper methodology. Chapter 6, "Design Methodology," outlines an approach for weighing these noneconomic criteria in the selection process.

DESIGN AND ENERGY CONSIDERATIONS

Design professionals must respond to owners' needs and demands. The designer today requires a methodology to analyze first cost, energy consumption, maintenance cost, replacement cost, financing, and so on—in short, a tool to look at *total cost.* This approach is necessary to determine if owners can afford not only the initial costs but also the follow-on costs. How many facilities has the typical design professional participated in where the owner was given an estimate for both the initial and annual costs? What training and expertise must the designer have to deal with these client needs?

There exists a hierarchy of objective or goal priorities, from the design professional's point of view, which are to be solved in any design. These can be related to Maslow's need-priority model[3] (Figure 1-2) which illustrates certain *basic physiological needs* that the designer must first satisfy for the client. These basic needs include such things as program and user requirements and cost and time constraints of the project. Once these have been fulfilled, the designer concentrates on the client's security and safety needs. The requirements of documents such as the building codes and regulations are reviewed and compared with the initial layout. Next, the designer must establish a design that has *social belonging.* In other words: Will the community appreciate and understand the design solution, and will the design receive peer designer acceptance?

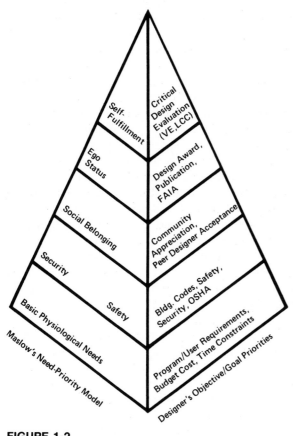

FIGURE 1-2
Priority pyramid.

These needs having been satisfied, the next block on the priority model relates to *ego status.* For an architect this might be a design award or being voted into the College of Fellows and entitled to use the designation FAIA (Fellow of the American Institute of Architects). For an engineer it might be a fellowship in an engineering society or recognition through publications and awards. However, there is one more need—that of *self-fulfillment.* That designers are beginning to recognize this is shown in their efforts to make postoccupancy evaluations.

3. Abraham Maslow, *Maslow's Hierarchy of Needs,* film, Salenger Educational Media, Santa Monica, Calif.

Can the design stand the test of time? This highest level of the pyramid, from the designer's point of view, can be described as the "critical design-evaluation" phase. To achieve success in this category, such things as LCC, value engineering, energy conservation, and postoccupancy evaluation need to be considered. How many design professionals are prepared to respond? Today, many owners are asking for these requirements. One of these owners is the Mountain States Telephone and Telegraph Company. In their planning of a number of proposed large facilities, they want to know not only what it will cost them to build these facilities, but also what the cost to maintain and operate them will be. What are the annual budgets for the facilities now being designed? How much will be spent in maintenance and operation? What will be the dollar cost for interest? *Getting involved in LCC is the first step toward finding the answers.*

Figure 1-3 represents the breakdown of the principal blocks of costs for a typical office facility. It is interesting to note the distribution: initial costs, 35 percent; maintenance and operations costs, 32 percent; and interest costs, 29 percent. In the figure no costs for employee wages have been included. Normally, the largest block of ownership cost is the initial cost. Therefore, the first requirement is to have a standard costing procedure and accounting method to properly define and collect initial costs. Together with this, there must be a procedure to define and collect costs for maintenance and operation and for other items such as interest. These procedures must be compatible with the standard costing system for initial costs. The effect of time on the value of money must be considered. Today's dollar is not equal to tomorrow's dollar. Money invested in any form earns, or has the capacity to earn, interest. This concept is discussed at length in Chapter 3, "Economics."

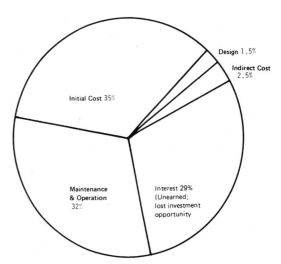

FIGURE 1-3
Total cost of ownership, typical office building.

What are some of the reasons owners have not always received optimum decisions from their agents? And, in particular, why has there been less-than-optimum decision making in some of the LCC done to date? The major reasons are lack of management and owner commitment, lack of ideas, lack of information, recurring circumstances, honest wrong beliefs, and habits and attitudes. If owners do not provide designers the opportunity or incentive to do LCC, it will seldom be done effectively. *Owners must require specific tasks using the methodology of LCC and be willing to provide additional funds to cover the efforts required from the designer.*

Who is providing designers with new ideas and better information to assure optimum decisions? The majority of new ideas come from manufacturers and suppliers. Yet many owners and designers actually discourage vendors' participation in the design process, to the point of not allowing them in the door. At a recent value engineering and LCC workshop held at an engineers' club, club rules did not allow vendors to participate. In addition, very few design firms have a person or a department appointed to assist manufacturers' representatives with new ideas. Seldom do firms conduct in-house seminars concerning the latest uses of new products. Coupled with this attitude toward vendors, little effort is spent to seek out top professionals from outside to bring in new ideas and more information. Yet, *if decisions are to be optimized and alternatives properly assessed, designers must continually seek out innovations and new product information.*

In addition, designers must overcome recurring circumstances, such as lack of time and lack of redesign funding, that almost always are present and cause poor decisions and unnecessary costs. Since these circumstances seem to follow a standard pattern, designers should either plan ahead knowing that the chance of their recurring is great or offset their impact by generating new solutions on existing projects for later application to follow-on designs.

Designers have to look for, question, challenge, and change honest wrong beliefs that tend to creep into any organization. Many designers are making decisions today that are based on what they think are the best alternatives. These alternatives may not, in fact, be the best ones. For example, many electrical engineers believe that only circuit breakers should be used for main switchgear. On the other hand, there is another generation of engineers who are switch- and fuse-oriented. Whose decision is optimal for a given project? One or the other has some honest wrong beliefs. Where are the quality assurance procedures in facility design similar to those used in the manufacturing process?

Designers must also review the habits and attitudes in their organizations to see which ones must be changed to improve decision making. Of prime concern is to try to achieve a positive approach to problem solving. A positive approach enhances optimum decisions, but a negative approach contributes to poor solutions. It can be guaranteed

that at the end of each year, the designers with positive attitudes toward new ideas will have made better decisions than designers who express only reasons why an idea won't work. *Remember, positive attitudes achieve positive results!*

HISTORICAL DEVELOPMENT OF LCC
Early Years, Engineering Economics

Written records pertinent to LCC are somewhat obscure. The first edition of *Principles of Engineering Economy* by Eugene L. Grant was published in 1930 and became the classic reference for all who dealt with the effects of engineering economics. One of the first government references to LCC was published in 1933 by the comptroller general of the United States. With regard to tractor acquisitions, the General Accounting Office (GAO) supported acceptance of bids predicated on the total cost to the government after 8000 hours of operations. Maintenance costs were included in the bid price. More than 25 additional rulings in the following years mandated LCC procurement for all types of equipment, culminating with the GAO report on LCC purchases for the Department of Defense published in 1973. During the decade 1940–1950 when material and labor shortages resulting from the war effort caused extensive searches for substitute materials and production procedures, Larry D. Miles originated the idea of Value Analysis or Value Engineering (VE) at the General Electric Company. As conceived, VE was much broader than life cycle analysis alone, incorporating functional studies along with a "total cost" concept.

The earliest proponent of VE for the construction industry was Alphonse J. Dell'Isola, who published an application guide in 1972. He was one of the first to observe and graphically display the relationship among decisions and their potential impact on total cost, pointing out that the initial planning and design choices have maximum effect on life cycle costs.

The years 1950–1960 were relatively static with regard to LCC development in the United States. During that period, however, P. A. Stone began his work in England at the Building Research Station, which, in the decade to follow, resulted in the publication of two major texts concerning cost-in-use.

The American Telephone and Telegraph Company (AT&T) published its first edition of *Engineering Economy* in 1952. (The most recent edition was published in 1977.) Its purpose was to bring under one cover, for designers' use, a discussion of the basic principles of engineering economy and to outline the techniques of making comparative cost studies. This document states:

It is the responsibility of the engineer to determine the plan which will meet the physical requirements in the most economical manner. . . .

In the telephone business (and other industry) . . . the company has not only the desire, but the obligation to provide service. Therefore the only engineering question is: How can good service be provided at the lowest over-all cost?

The importance of this is perhaps best described in the final sentence of this document: "The future success of a company rests largely on the quality of the engineering work done today."

Significance Recognized

In 1961, an important conference entitled "Methods of Building Cost Analysis" was sponsored by the Building Research Institute in Washington, D.C. The papers presented procedures for developing life cycle cost analyses for buildings, their enclosures, lighting and heating, ventilating, and air-conditioning systems. It was also during the early 1960s that an effort was undertaken by the Logistics Management Institute that led to publication in 1965 of a most influential report for the assistant secretary of defense. The document concluded that, had total life cycle costs been considered, many Department of Defense contracts would have been awarded to other than low bidders at considerable overall savings to the government. As a consequence, in 1970 the Department of Defense published the first in a series of three guidelines for LCC procurement. The initial requirement was a consideration of replacement cost in the purchase of certain items (replacement siding on family housing, solid-state 15-megahertz oscilloscopes, computers, etc.). The policy was reinforced in 1971 by Department of Defense directive 5000.1, which mandates LCC procurement for major systems acquisitions. The third instruction, *Life Cycle Costing Guide for System Acquisition,* was issued in 1973 and specified elementary-level life cycle analysis procedures. The first publication related to facilities was prepared by the Department of the Army, Office of Chief of Engineers, in 1971 but never officially issued. It contained general and specific procedures for long-term economic analysis of barracks, warehouses, and 32 other facility types.

In November 1972, the comptroller general of the United States issued one of the most exhaustive and devastating reports to date on the life cycle costs for U.S. hospital facilities. The objective of the effort, conducted by Westinghouse researchers, was to "study the feasibility of reducing the cost of constructing hospital facilities. . . ."[4] Existing hospitals throughout the United States were examined and tested against a variety of innovative design

4. *Study of Health Care Facilities Construction Costs,* Report to the Congress, Comptroller General of the U.S., November 1972.

and construction solutions. The conclusion: "GAO believes that life cycle cost analysis is essential in the planning and design of all hospital construction projects." It was further demonstrated that operation and maintenance costs for such facilities could equal the initial investment within 1 to 3 years. This gave some additional credibility to similar values produced earlier by the National Bureau of Standards, which suggested that capital costs represent less than 2 percent of a building's total life cycle cost.

The Department of Health, Education, and Welfare (HEW), at the request of the GAO's November 1972 report "Study of Health Facilities Construction Cost," sponsored an "Evaluation of the Health Facilities Building Process" dated March 31, 1973. The overall objectives of the study included the evaluation of existing processes for acquisition of those health facilities that are procured by federally assisted grant and loan programs. Special emphasis was placed on life cycle cost analysis and its impact on the procurement process.

Because of the interest generated by this document, another firm was commissioned to study LCC. The objective was to "bring the concept of life cycle budgeting and costing to bear on the process of planning, budgeting, designing, constructing, and operating health facilities." The result was a series of four volumes from 1975 to 1976 entitled *Life Cycle Budgeting and Costing as an Aid in Decision Making.*

While the activities described above were primarily the result of inflationary pressures and increasing technical sophistication of products and buildings (and thus, higher maintenance and operating costs), 1973 brought the Arab oil embargo and crystallized the "energy crisis."

In 1975 two major pieces of legislation, the Energy Policy and Conservation Act and the Energy Conservation and Production Act, reiterated the need for long-term analysis. Both have influenced procurement practices. Title III of the former provided $150 million to state governments in 1976 to develop statewide energy conservation plans. Building Energy Performance Standards (BEPS) became available in 1979 for implementation. Over half the states have enacted energy legislation based on groundwork by ASHRAE's (American Society of Heating, Refrigeration and Air Conditioning) standard 90–75, written in 1975, and virtually all others had legislation in progress or pending in 1980.

Procedures Developed

During the same period, the U.S. General Services Administration (GSA) began several fundamental projects to establish effective cost management and LCC. The UNIFORMAT framework for initial costs was published by GSA in 1975. It was an extension of a previous system developed for the American Institute of Architects and termed MASTERCOST. The framework was extended in an LCC study prepared for the University of Alaska in

1974. The Alaskan system provides a coordinated code of accounts for operation and maintenance expenditures and general equations for executing long-term cost analyses.

Two facility LCC systems have been completed by GSA. The first, entitled "Life Cycle Planning and Budgeting Model," which began in 1974, is a comprehensive, automated system designed to evaluate lease, construction, and renovation options to satisfy user-agency space requirements. It permits relatively nontechnical personnel to provide input about floor areas and functional requirements (for instance, for work stations). Based on existing federal standards and a series of quasi-engineering and other assumptions, it generates an anticipated building configuration. The configuration, transformed into UNIFORMAT categories, is then priced for capital, maintenance, and operation costs.

In 1974–1975, the second GSA system consisted of a unique bid package arrangement for buildings, which incorporated the concept of LCC. The systems portions of three Social Security payment centers were let for bid on a total cost basis. The entire project has yet to be completely evaluated; however, the designs have resulted in facilities with some of the lowest energy-consumption figures. Of course, many other systems procurement projects were executed during the late 1960s and early 1970s (School Construction Systems Development, for example). However, the GSA buildings were the first major facilities purchase using total costs as a bid criterion.

The Naval Facilities Engineering Command is testing an Economic Building Performance Model (EBPM), developed initially by Stephen J. Kirk, which projects initial and long-term costs for alternative design solutions for Naval facilities. The computer-based model evaluates initial costs and other owning and operating costs. This model has since been further refined and is discussed in greater detail in Chapter 5, "Formats." As for other governmental agencies, the Facilities Division of NASA had prepared but never officially issued a draft of a Guide Manual for LCC in 1978.

With regard to equipment purchases, the federal supply service (GSA) has adopted a life cycle procurement technique similar to that used by the Department of Defense. The entire procedure is described in a training manual published in 1977.[5] The methodology allows equipment and other purchases to be considered within a total cost context which includes acquisition costs, initial logistics, and recurring costs.

Energy Highlighted

The energy concerns described previously have also spawned numerous federal bills and within state legisla-

tures to encourage or mandate conservation. Legislation in several states has been designed to require LCC.

In 1974, Florida became the first state to formally adopt LCC and require consideration of initial, energy, operation, and maintenance costs as criteria for the design of buildings over 5000 square feet. All the other states mentioned previously include LCC as part of energy legislation, with the exception of Alaska, which passed a law in 1975 requiring LCC procurement of all public facilities. The Florida bill further stated that the State Department of Transportation and Public Facilities would "develop life cycle costs of public facilities of the State and those public facilities of political subdivisions of the State ..." and "develop life cycle methodologies for special purposes." The authors have prepared a booklet, *Life Cycle Cost Analysis,* designed for facilities procurement, for the state of Wyoming.

Since 1977 the Department of Revenue for the State of Illinois Capital Development Board has issued two request-for-proposal documents for the preparation of value analysis of conceptual design alternatives. This request for proposal (in Appendix A) includes requirements for life cycle cost analysis. A sample proposal for life cycle cost analysis services is also contained in Appendix A.

In April 1977, the American Institute of Architects (AIA) issued a formal set of guidelines for architects and engineering consultants electing to offer LCC as an additional service. The guide presents a method for computing the present value and uniform annual values for total building costs. It also recommends techniques for incorporating the results into the building decision process. The UNIFORMAT framework is offered as a vehicle for organizing both the required data and the analysis. The system is manual and requires a user to provide all cost and performance input data.

In addition, in conjunction with the American Consulting Engineers Council, AIA has sponsored LCC seminars.[6]

In the mechanical (energy) area in particular, a large number of energy analysis programs that incorporate long-term economic models are currently being utilized. Some examples are presented in Table 1-1. The economic portion typically involves the computation of maintenance costs, interest rates, and depreciation, and performance of a cash-flow analysis and rate-of-return evaluation. One of the first ones, developed by the Trane Company called the TRACE program, will forecast consumption values for alternative fuels applied to various building systems and generate cost estimates for initial investment, utilities, and annual owning expenditures. The results may be evaluated on a present-worth or uniform-annual-equivalent basis for HVAC systems.

5. *Life Cycle Costing Workbook: A Guide for the Implementation of Life Cycle Costing in the Federal Supply Services,* U.S. General Services Administration, Washington, 1977.

6. *ACEC/AIA Estimating Procedures for Life Cycle Costing,* Director of Professional Development and Meetings, 1155 15th Street, Washington, DC 20105.

TABLE 1-1
AUTOMATED ENERGY ANALYSIS MODELS

Program	Developer
Energy Analysis	
ESAS	Ross Meriwether & Associates
NECAP	National Aeronautics and Space Administration
TRACE	Trane Company
AXCESS	Electric Energy Association (now sponsored by the Edison Electric Institute)
E-CUBE	American Gas Association
BLAST	Corps of Engineers
CALCON I	California / ERDA
GATX	Postal Service
ESP-1	Automated Procedures of Engineering Consultants
MEDSI	Mechanical Engineering Data Services
ESOP	HUD-MIUS
VALUES	Veterans Administration
Predecessors to energy analysis	
POST OFFICE	National Postal Service (load calculation)
NBSLD	National Bureau of Standards (load calculation)

Public Law 95-619 established the National Energy Conservation Policy Act on November 9, 1978. This law mandates that all new federal buildings be *life cycle cost effective* as determined by methods prescribed by the legislation. In the design of new federal buildings, cost evaluation shall be made on the basis of life cycle cost rather than initial cost. For existing buildings, retrofit measures are to be taken to improve their energy efficiency in general and to minimize their life cycle cost.

Public hearings were held in May and June of 1979 regarding a proposal by the Department of Energy (44 FR 25366, April 30, 1979) that LCC analysis be required in all new construction or retrofitting projects in federal buildings. The proposal would require LCC methods to be used in early design and planning to determine which energy-saving investment to use. For existing buildings the proposed change would require retrofit investments to be ranked by cost savings. The aim, according to the Department of Energy, was to reduce consumption of fossil fuels through use of solar and other renewable energy sources.

The Department of Energy issued a final rule to establish a methodology and procedures to conduct life cycle cost analyses, January 23, 1980. This methodology involves estimating and comparing the effects of replacing building systems with energy-saving alternatives in existing federal buildings and of selecting among alternative building designs containing different energy-using systems for a new federal building.

Terotechnology

The British have actively engaged in LCC for some time and have coined a new term, *terotechnology,* defined as "a combination of management, financial, engineering, and other practices applied to physical assets in pursuit of economic life cycle costs." Terotechnology is a multidisciplinary approach to ensure optimum life cycle costs in the development and use of equipment and facilities. It includes the design of various assets with the objective of attaining the proper balance of performance, reliability, maintainability, supportability, quality, and related features. Terotechnology constitutes the cradle-to-grave management of resources in an efficient and effective manner, and includes functions in all phases of the life cycle—feasibility studies, research and development, design, production, operation, maintenance and logistics support, replacement, and disposal.

Terotechnology was developed in the early 1970s in response to the increasing problems of waste and the high costs of doing business. A committee for terotechnology was formed in the United Kingdom in April 1970 to establish terotechnology in British industry and commerce. The objective is to "bring together" existing capabilities and methods in a way that can be used to improve the management of physical assets. To encourage this effort, the British have established a National Terotechnology Centre for the promotion of these concepts and objectives.[7]

SUMMARY

Until recently, only initial-cost dollars have been of prime concern in the building cycle. Because of the continuing escalation of events, LCC techniques are being expanded. The process offers the owner the opportunity to impose limits and the designer thresholds to achieve. The establishment of energy budgets, maintenance targets, and other owning and operation constraints are now possible. As experience grows in these areas, more efficient performance from the facilities can be expected.

The best opportunity for saving life cycle dollars is in the earliest stages of design process. The theory, for the most part, is well established. Owners must take the responsibility for setting realistic goals in the planning and

---

7. Refer to the National Terotechnology Centre, Cleeve Road, Leatherhead, Surrey KT227SA, United Kingdom.

budgeting phase and giving assistance as necessary to designers, so that LCC does not become just another paperwork exercise. Owner personnel must become familiar with LCC procedures and be prepared to suggest areas for study to the designer. LCC should be done using value engineering reviews to develop design alternatives at the earliest possible stages of facility design so that any changes may be made with minimum effort and optimum effect.

LCC analysis can also be used in conjunction with the concept of zero-base budgeting originated by the federal government. Basically, zero-base budgeting provides minimum dollars (reviewed each year) required to procure and operate a given facility or program. LCC analysis allows reasonable comparisons of various facility program, acquisition, and operating costs well in advance of required funding. Various decision packages (minimum, current, and augmented) can be developed in response to functional requirements, quality, and standards of operation assumed.

Federal, state, and local governments, as well as industry organizations such as American Telephone and Telegraph and Owens Corning Fiberglas, are committed to providing facilities at the lowest total cost of ownership. This goal becomes realistically achievable through implementation of LCC during the planning and budget, schematic, and design-development stages of a project. As the English philosopher and economist, John Stuart Mill, asked in 1857, "Towards what ultimate point is society tending by its industrial progress? When the progress ceases, in what condition are we to expect that it will leave mankind?" The technique of LCC will aid designers to improve the use of our resources and, in the process, create a better environment.

CHAPTER TWO
CONCEPTS

"The architectural profession has been under severe pressure to find better overall answers to client demands for simultaneous handling of the intricate balance of time, quality and cost of projects. The ultimate goal is a facility that is delivered in the shortest possible time, at the lowest possible cost, with the highest possible quality and / or performance."

Philip J. Meathe, FAIA
Current Techniques in Architectural Practice
The American Institute of Architects, 1976.

DEFINITIONS

What is life cycle costing (LCC)? Basically, LCC is an economic assessment of an item, area, system, or facility, considering all the significant costs of ownership over its economic life, expressed in terms of equivalent dollars. LCC is a technique that satisfies the requirements of clients for adequate analyses of total costs.

A significant key to LCC is the economic assessment using equivalent dollars. For example, assume one person has $100 on hand, another has $100 promised 10 years from now, and a third is collecting $10 a month for 10 months. Each has assets of $100. However, are the assets equivalent in terms of today's purchasing power? The answer is not so simple because the assets are spread across different points in time. To determine whose assets are worth more, a baseline time reference must first be established. All monies are then brought back to the baseline, using proper economic procedures to develop equivalent costs. Design professionals normally choose between competing design alternatives. So, for design professionals, *life cycle costing is an economic assessment of design alternatives, considering all the significant costs of ownership over an economic life expressed in equivalent dollars.* It may also be used to assess the consequences of decisions already made and by owners for budgeting purposes.

For designers to perform a life cycle analysis, the owner must provide them with information regarding such things as the facility's economic life, the anticipated return on investment, and their financing costs, as well as noneconomic requirements.

From client to client, this information will vary greatly. As an example, assume an owner is planning to build a speculative apartment house. The federal government has set up an investment tax credit for this type of facility. However, it requires retention of property by the owner for a minimum of 10 years. The owner, in hiring a consultant to do LCC, would set a 10-year economic life, and would also state the minimum acceptable rate of return for the project to be economically attractive.

Suppose, on the other hand, the owner is a telephone company which will own and operate the facility from 40 to 100 years. In this example, the owner would require a permanent type of construction, normally with a 40-year economic life. These examples represent the extremes, but they illustrate that the economic information for LCC will vary from one client to the next.

The LCC definition states that all "significant costs of ownership" should be included. Figure 2-1 illustrates the types of costs that *may* be considered significant by the designer and client for an LCC study. These costs are organized so that they may be structured easily into an automated approach as experience is gained in the procedures. For clarification a brief discussion regarding these blocks of costs follows.

Initial costs include the owner's costs associated with initial development of a facility, including project costs (fees, real estate, site, and so on) as well as construction costs. Financing costs include the costs of any debt associated with the facility's capital costs. The category of operation (including energy) costs is used to keep track of such items as fuel and salaries required to operate the facility. Maintenance includes costs of the regular custodial care and repair, annual maintenance contracts, and sala-

9

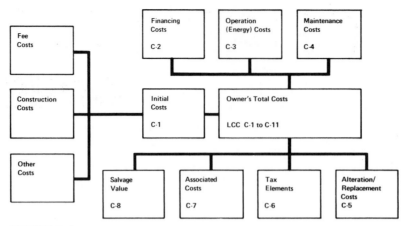

FIGURE 2-1
Life cycle cost elements.

ries of facility staff performing maintenance tasks. Usually replacement items less than $5,000 in value or having a life of less than 5 years are also included.

Alteration and replacement costs (block 5) requires a more detailed discussion. Alteration costs are those involved in changing the function of the space. For example, a facility is going to be built initially as an office building, but after 10 years the first floor area will function as a bank. The 10-year cost for conversion would be an alteration cost because of the change in the functional use of the space.

A replacement cost would be a one-time cost to be incurred in the future to maintain the original function of the facility or item. For example, assume the owner defines the LCC period as 40 years, and the design calls for a cooling tower on the roof. The useful life of a cooling tower is approximately 20 years, and the tower would have to be replaced at the end of that period. The cost involved is defined as a replacement cost—a future cost required to maintain the same function for which the facility was intended.

Block 6 includes those assignable costs associated with taxes, credits, and depreciation. These costs must be continually reviewed as tax laws change. For example, the recent investment tax credit for energy conservation has provided the impetus for many owners to consider adding energy-efficient features to their facilities. An accounting expense called *depreciation* is used to distribute the cost of capital assets, less salvage, for tax credit purposes. These tax elements are discussed at length in Chapter 4, "Life Cycle Estimating Procedures."

Associated costs include other identifiable costs not covered previously associated with a facility decision and may include functional use, denial of use, security, and insurance. Since the functional-use costs, when considered in an LCC, may be the most significant of all follow-on figures, they are discussed first. These costs include the staff, materials, etc., required to perform the function of organiza-

tion(s) using the facility or installation. As an example, suppose an LCC analysis is required for a branch bank. What is the function of the bank?—to service customers. Suppose there are two banks that have exactly the same initial costs. One bank can process 200 clients a day; the other can process only 150. Which is more cost-effective? The one that processes more customers. Functional-use costs for a branch bank would have to do with servicing customers. In life cycle analysis a cost difference or some other weight would have to be considered to take account of the diffence in capacity to provide the basic function of a facility. A hospital is another good example. The basic function of a hospital is to provide care. Suppose two hospitals are identical in costs and area; but, in one a doctor can get to a patient in half the time it would take in the other. The LCC would be tempered for the difference in functional-use cost.

Denial-of-use costs include the extra costs or lost income during the life cycle because occupancy or production is delayed as a result of a previous decision. As an example of denial-of-use costs, suppose that in making an alteration there are two approaches whose construction costs are the same. One alternative would require moving people out of the space for 6 months; the other alternative could be accomplished during nonworking hours. In the LCC the cost of not being able to use the space would have to be accounted for.

The associated cost effect of insurance was illustrated by a recent study of a food distribution warehouse. When different fire protection systems were examined, all costs were comparable except that one system had a lower annual insurance premium. The annual difference was accounted for in conducting the LCC.

Salvage value is the value (positive if it has residual economic value and negative if demolition is required) of competing alternatives at the end of the life cycle period. This cost can become quite important if one alternative requires a major replacement toward the end of its economic life. For example, two automobiles are being analyzed for purchase. The plan is to keep these cars for 4 years. It is estimated that one car will reach the end of 4 years without requiring any major motor repairs, but it will then need a major motor overhaul. The other car will require a new engine replacement at the end of the third year. As a result, the salvage value of the car with the recently installed new engine will be significantly higher. The same concept applies to building equipment.

LIFE CYCLE COSTING LOGIC

Within its more general definitions, LCC is not new. Many specific studies of facilities have had extremely large numbers of work hours devoted to answering the same life cycle cost questions. The difference between the majority of previous efforts and the approach outlined in this book is the establishment of a formal, consistent methodology.

This concept is central to LCC. It not only determines the ultimate validity of the answers developed, but it also lays the groundwork for future refinement of life cycle cost decision making.

A relatively simple methodology has been developed by the authors during the last few years. The best way to illustrate its simplicity is to use a hypothetical facility. For example, a hospital and its design team are considering two alternative nursing-station designs for each bed wing. One will cost far more to construct than the other because it relies more heavily on automated devices for patient monitoring and record keeping. The question is, however: does the saving in nursing salaries justify the increased facility cost?

Using life cycle cost methodology to obtain the answer is a process of several steps. First—to reduce the time and complexity of the analysis—those facility elements that will be the same in any of the options under consideration are identified and removed or fixed during the comparative analysis.

Next, the decision-making team isolates the significant costs associated with each alternative. The hypothetical automated solution in the above example has higher capital investment, operation, and maintenance costs but lower functional-use (nursing salary) costs. The costs isolated for each alternative must be grouped by year over a number of years equal to the economic life of the facility. Or, if more appropriate, grouped by time spans equal to the mode of user operation. In either case, probable replacement and alteration costs should be considered. A salvage value, if relevant, is also added for the end of the life cycle period.

All costs are converted to today's dollars by present-worth techniques using a reasonable discount factor (10

percent is used by some federal agencies, but many private owners use a higher rate). This discounting is done because a cost incurred in the tenth year of a facility's life is, of course, not the same present value as one incurred in the first year.

Finally, the team adds up the discounted costs and identifies the lowest-cost alternative. It may be necessary to make a sensitivity analysis of each of the assumptions to see if a reasonable change in any of the cost assumptions would change the conclusions. If it would, the probability of such an occurrence must be carefully weighed. If it appears that two or more events have roughly the same probability of occurrence, the option selected must reflect this. The final selection of an option will probably be based principally on cost, but the effect on total cost of any noneconomic factors will be factored in by the decision maker at the time of decision.

In summary, the methodology consists of identifying the significant costs associated with each alternative, adding each group of costs by year, discounting them back to a common base, selecting the lowest-cost alternative, and tempering final selection with noneconomic considerations. This process is illustrated in detail in the following chapters.

Most major facility decisions have life cycle cost implications. The question is which ones have the greatest impact. All projects are different, but a lesson learned from past construction cost control programs applies: in most cases, the early decisions are the most important in terms of the savings potential. For example, the decision on how many operating suites there will be in a hospital usually has far greater cost implications than has the detailed design for each suite. The selection of the type of HVAC system is more important than the choice of a manufacturer for the system selected. In both cases, the final choice theoretically could be made late in a project's development, but the cost penalty for making changes after the early sequences increases geometrically. This is illustrated in Figure 2-2, which indicates that the earlier the LCC, the greater the potential for cost reduction and the lower the cost to implement. When major document revisions are required, they negate the significant cost reduction potential.

Therefore, it is never too early to begin facility analysis in life cycle cost terms. There are many decisions with life cycle cost implications at every phase or decision point in the life of a project. Chapter 6 further discusses these study areas.

How would the flow of activities procede in a typical project? Figure 2-3 illustrates a recommended logic flow. The first requirement is the input data. It would normally consist of data such as (1) program and operational mode and (2) criteria and standards, quantities, and economic data such as taxes, investment tax credits, and interest rates. Next, input data for facility components such as ini-

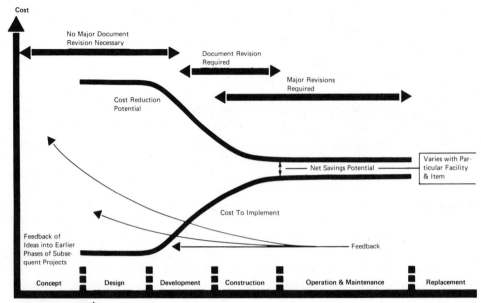

FIGURE 2-2
Phase cost reduction, facilities construction.

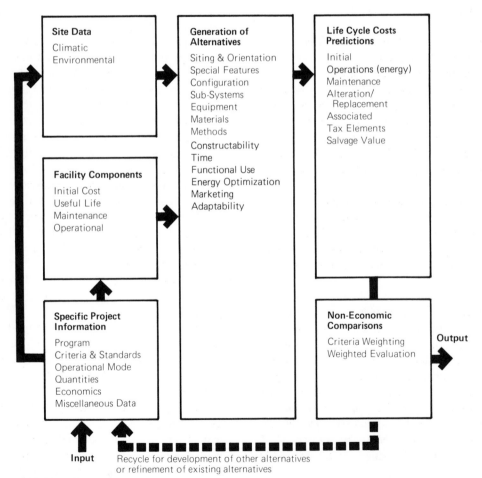

FIGURE 2-3
Life cycle costing logic.

tial cost, useful life, maintenance and operations, and site data such as climatic and environmental conditions would be collected. With these data, alternatives would be generated. This would be followed by the life cycle cost predictions. These predictions would be tempered by a noneconomic comparison before a final recommendation is developed.

Of the input data required, the specific project information and site data are usually easily accessible, but it is a different story for the facility components data. Where does a designer go to get data regarding useful life, maintenance, and operation costs—input needed to calculate roughly one-half of total costs? Few designers have had access to comprehensive data in these areas. The real problem is that there is not readily available a storage and retrieval format containing this data. This problem will be discussed in part in Chapter 4, "Life Cycle Estimating Procedures."

APPLICATION IN THE DESIGN PROCESS

As discussed previously, the greatest savings potential for a life cycle analysis occurs in the earliest stages of a project. Not only are the potential savings more significant, but the costs of making changes in the plans and specifications are much less. As the project gets into the construction and the owning and operation phases, the LCC value tends to become the feedback data for use in other projects. The major impact of LCC should occur in three phases: the concept, the preliminary design, and design development. Its influence during later phases should be more or less as a review and a validation of the assumptions made during these earlier phases. Study areas may include: facility versus other economic investment; new facility versus retrofit existing structure; high-rise versus low-rise construction; active/passive solar energy versus conventional HVAC; design layouts versus staffing efficiencies; spacial flexibility versus interior partitioning; natural lighting versus artificial means; native landscaping versus conventional landscaping; fire sprinkler systems versus insurance premiums; fixed partitions versus demountable partitions (tax credits); interstitial space versus floor-to-floor height; insulation and glazing versus energy requirements; fenestration and shading versus lighting requirements. (Source: "Life Cycle Costing: Increasingly Popular Route to Design Value," Stephen J. Kirk, *Architectural Record,* December 1979.)

There have been many cases in which LCC has been applied by only a single discipline. This has led to restrictive solutions. Figure 2-4 illustrates the design decision makers' influence on total building costs. It portrays the design process as a team involvement in which there are various disciplines making decisions in a discipline-ori-

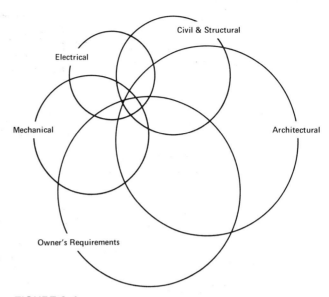

FIGURE 2-4
Decision maker's impact on total building costs, typical office building. Impact will vary by type of structure. *(From Alphonse J. Dell'Isola,* Valve Engineering in the Construction Industry, © *1975 by Litton Educational Publishing, Inc.)*

ented environment. One of the principal reasons for unnecessary initial costs has been the unidisciplinary approach used by designers. In too many cases the design has been dictated by the architect, to whose direction the other disciplines merely responded. A multidisciplinary approach to optimize the building as a system has produced more desirable results. What is disturbing is that to date there have been too many cases in which LCC has developed similar problems. The building industry is getting a discipline-oriented solution to an energy problem. Are the mechanical and electrical engineers getting even with the architects for their previous years of domination? There have been numerous examples of mechanical engineers, under the guise of energy conservation, designing their systems and telling everyone to design around those systems. The application of LCC has usually centered on the energy area, focusing on the mechanical engineering discipline. The result is an exaggerated energy orientation. It almost appears that the function of a facility in many instances is to conserve energy rather than to house people. *The best solutions will be developed only when all participants collaborate as a team and seek optimum solutions for the total problem.*

Example—Concept and Development

Figure 2-5, a chart prepared for a corporate client with large facilities to be located in several states, illustrates how LCC procedures can be integrated into the concept and development stages of the traditional design process.

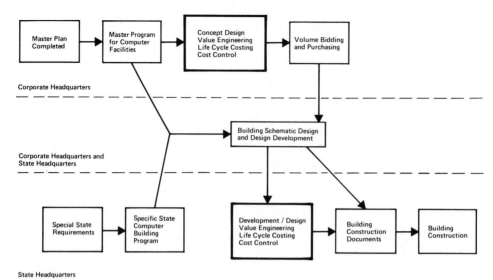

FIGURE 2-5
Integrated LCC design process.

For example, the concept design portion was broken down into a sequence of several events, which are presented in Figure 2-6. At the end of each event, starting with concept schematics, formal, concurrent reviews were held using the procedures outlined in this text. This series of reviews culminated with a formal 5-day workshop, which studied in depth such preselected items as exterior closure, computer room HVAC, emergency generators, fire protection, structural systems, and floor-to-floor height. Techniques of energy conservation, value engineering, LCC, and cost control were used during the week. Participants included representatives of the client, users of the facility, architect and engineer designers, and the staff of a value engineering and LCC consultant. *Implemented savings included over $4 million in first costs and $10 million in follow-on costs.* This process was then repeated during the development and design process focusing on more discrete building elements.

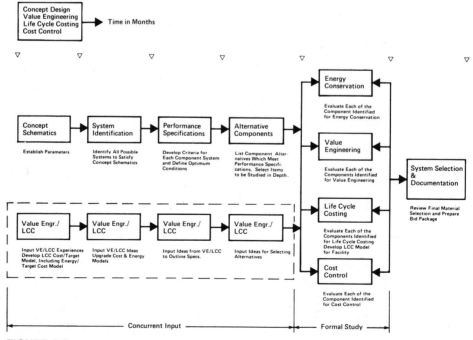

FIGURE 2-6
Integrated LCC concept design.

Example—Planning and Feasibility

LCC may also be used even sooner, during the predesign process. Examples include: site analysis (given use); use analysis (given site); impact analysis (given use and site); and land use programming (given impact).

To illustrate the potential benefit of an effective early-stage LCC study, the approach of the owner or builder of residential properties is cited. In most housing financial feasibility analyses, $1 taken out of operating expenses through better planning or design is equivalent to a $10 to $12 reduction in construction costs.

The size of most new facilities depends on the results of the project's financial feasibility analysis. The feasibility depends on a combination of the facility income, capital investment (including cost of debt service), and operating costs. A project becomes financially feasible when the owner can find the right balance between these three factors. In the equation, however, a reduction in capital investment cost of $1 for a facility, with borrowing at 8 percent, will increase a project's projected net annual income by only 8 cents. (See Appendix C, Table 3, "Periodic Payment (PP)": 40 years @ 8% interest, PP = 0.083860.) A reduction of $1 in operating costs, however, will increase net income $1. The difference is 12½ to 1. This type of analysis is very common in private real estate development.

It is often less difficult to take a dollar out of annual operating costs through better planning and design than it is to take it out of construction costs. When, in addition, the effect of every dollar of savings can potentially be multiplied by 10 or 12, annual costs are many times more important than a project's construction costs. With the large savings that can be achieved from life cycle reductions, the question is clearly not whether to, but how to, use LCC.

RELATIONSHIP TO OTHER PROGRAMS
Value Engineering

How does LCC relate to the value engineering (VE) concept, engineering economics, and noneconomic criteria? Figure 2-7 graphically portrays the interrelationship. At one end is the start of the design process, and at the other end is the ultimate design selection; between is the process. In developing the design selection, the basic site and facility program information is combined with the subsystems information to generate alternative solutions. It is in the generation of the alternative solutions that the VE methodology should be utilized. Because of its function analysis and creativity and brainstorming techniques, it is a powerful tool to assist in developing alternatives objectively.

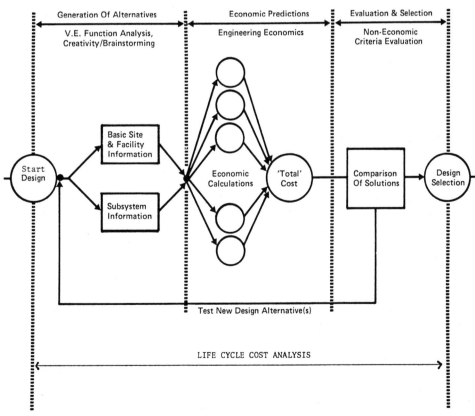

FIGURE 2-7
Interrelationship of LCC analysis and value engineering.

After developing alternatives the process becomes an economic exercise. At this point, LCC is performed on the alternatives using the principles outlined in engineering economics. The results are expressed as the total cost of each competing alternative.

In making an economic analysis, are designers required to take the lowest-cost alternative? Is the lowest-cost alternative always the optimum solution financially for the owner? There normally are noneconomic considerations such as politics, aesthetics, safety, and environment that have to be taken into account. Therefore, after the economically oriented exercise there must be an evaluation of noneconomic criteria. From this evaluation, a design selection is made. The objective of LCC analysis is an optimum solution not strictly based on costs. It must be emphasized that for this book, the whole process is defined as LCC analysis. LCC analysis proceeds from the start of the design process through to design selection.

Systems Approach

The *systems approach,* sometimes referred to as systems engineering, has been defined as "an inquiry to assist decision makers in choosing preferred further courses of action by systematically examining and reexamining the relevant objectives and quantitatively, where possible, the economic costs, effectiveness (benefits), and risks of the alternatives." True systems analysis is more a research or predesign strategy than a method or technique. It may be viewed as an approach to, or way of looking at, complex problems of choice under conditions of uncertainty.

The systems approach has been successfully used for problem solving in the development of military and space projects. It is also applicable to building problems, as they too are complex, involving the organization of many technologies, and require a multidisciplinary approach. The systems approach must logically be a complement to an LCC effort in the concept development phase of a facility.

The systems approach has two main features. Objectives or goals are stated clearly in terms of performance rather than prescriptions of a particular method. The advantage of employing performance terms is that it forces decision makers to make comparisons among alternative solutions. A sample performance requirement might be to limit energy consumption to 55,000 Btu per gross square foot per year.

The second feature of the systems approach is its emphasis on interrelationships within a system. For example, the traditional approach would be to analyze the economies of alternative exterior-wall systems to achieve the energy goal for a school and to separately analyze alternative structural system economies. The systems approach would consider the effect of the exterior-wall systems and the structural alternatives on each other and on the energy goal. The comprehensive view of the systems approach enables one to trace the effects of any set of choices and decisions on all other relevant decisions.

In the traditional process, the design of facility subsystems is often assigned to various design groups that work independently of each other. It is essential that a coordinating group or person, normally the architect, project manager, or construction manager, be assigned the task of assuring that the subsystems will work together. The combined output of these individual groups is a design reflecting emphasis on achieving functional compatibility and required performance with limited funds and time.

Integration of LCC analysis into the systems analysis effort contributes to the creation of an overall design having a life cycle cost consistent with the value of the system functions.

PROGRAM REQUIREMENTS

How should an organization start LCC planning? If owners or organizations are going to be serious about LCC, they should set up a comprehensive program at the beginning. It should be designed so that each year the program progresses one step further into a more refined LCC process. Eventually, a system should be created that will complete the circle, recycling LCC cost data from actual maintenance and operations to the early-stage design of new facilities.

How can this logic system be integrated into a working organization? Table 2-1 illustrates a master plan for the development of a comprehensive LCC system put together for a large government agency. This plan was set up for an estimated 5- to 10-year program. The chart is organized horizontally in accordance with the facility cycle, going from the early concept to design and development to construction to owning and operating. Vertically, the columns start from the present and go down to a future time. A 5- to 10-year cycle is envisioned.

As the chart indicates, the first step is to set objectives and issue initial guidance. Management must direct that LCC will be a part of the everyday decision-making process. The program should span all in-house activities and be built into all architectural and engineering contracts. In the early concept phase, notification should be given to all personnel, with procedures developed and defined in a convenient manual. In the design development phase, the recommended procedures should be reviewed and comments submitted, with seminars conducted for selected personnel. For the construction and owning and operating cycles, personnel should be notified about the intent to retrieve data. The first phase should take from 1 to 2 years. The next phase consists of applications, trials, and refinement, using manual methods. In the planning and budgeting phase, where gross cost or parameter costs are available,

TABLE 2-1
MASTER PLAN FOR DEVELOPMENT OF A COMPREHENSIVE LCC SYSTEM

Phase of development	Facility cycle ⟶			
	Concept	Design and development	Construction	Owning and operating
Problem definition and initial guidance	Develop manual method for LCC; notify field offices of LCC; test case applications	Review procedures and recommend LCC system; conduct seminars	Prototype LCC application	Field notification of intent to retrieve LCC data
Application trials and refinement	Review and revision of manual method; project application at headquarters, using manual LCC	Briefings and seminars and manual application on test cases.	Select trial project	Develop data system; preliminary collection from various sources
Development of LCC model	Develop computerized initial cost retrieval system	Trial project application using computer LCC model	Review contractor applications	Review of LCC data
Field office installation and application	Formalize historical LCC application for computer retrieval	Project application at all centers	Recommendations for field implementation	Continuing update and refinement of LCC data

Time ↓

manual methods should provide reasonable results. During this phase parameter estimates are developed. During design development, manual applications on test cases should be conducted. The next phase consists of the development of an automated LCC system, with the last phase centered on installation and application. Because of the limits on the number of variables that can be handled using manual procedures, consideration should be given to automated methods. To establish an idea of the magnitude of the problem, an analysis of a typical initial-cost data base was conducted. How many units of cost are there in an initial-cost data base for a construction project? One of the foremost cost data firms in the USA has 18,000 unit costs in its data base. How many items would the more complicated life cycle data base, including maintenance and operation, contain? Certainly at least 3 times the 18,000 initial unit-cost items. The only feasible approach to handling this volume of data is to use an automated system. It is recommended that LCC be done on a project basis with a concurrent effort devoted to developing a data system

under which some field response can be realized. The ultimate objective will be to have an LCC system with a good data base updated by actual construction costs and supported by actual data from the maintenance and operation personnel.

SUMMARY

In doing LCC, the ultimate objective is optimum design decisions. The goal can be achieved through an organized LCC analysis that will optimize the total cost of ownership and be tempered by noneconomic criteria. Owners must require specific efforts toward LCC and be willing to devote additional funds to these efforts. Designers must continually seek out new ideas and more information to meet the challenge. The ultimate objective should be the use of an automated system continuously updated and refined, using actual field data.

CHAPTER THREE
ECONOMICS

"I am disturbed when a consulting engineer tells me and my committee that he can make his life cycle cost figure come out any way he wants."

Senator Robert Morgan
Chairman, Senate Subcommittee on Buildings and
Grounds.

INTRODUCTION

Life cycle costing deals primarily with identifying, then assessing, the economic impacts of various alternatives over time. One must deal with both present and future costs in a way that will relate the two as a basis for making decisions. Today's dollar is *not* equal to tomorrow's dollar. Money invested in any form earns, or has the capacity to earn, interest. For example, $100 invested at 10 percent annual interest and compounded annually will grow to $673 in 20 years. In other words, it can be said that $100 today is equivalent to $673 at year 20 assuming an earning power of money to the investor of 10 percent per year.* A current dollar is worth more than the prospect of a dollar at some future time. The exact amount depends on the investment rate (cost of money) and the length of time. Inflation also changes the value of money over time; however, *constant* dollars are used in life cycle analysis.

DEALING WITH INFLATION

During the past several decades, inflation has been a significant factor in the rising costs of products and services

*See Appendix C, Table 1: Future investment total equal to

$$\frac{1}{\text{present worth}} \text{ or } \frac{1}{.1486} = \$673$$

and in reduction of the purchasing power of the dollar. Inflation is a continuing rise in general price levels caused by an increase in the volume of money and credit relative to available goods. Figure 3-1 graphically depicts inflation and its effect on the purchasing power of the dollar.

Gerald A. Fleischer and Arnold Reisman were pioneers in formally extending existing quantitative methods of economic evaluation to the arena of decision making in an economic age characterized by inflation. Their paper titled "Investment Decisions Under Conditions of Inflation," published in the *International Journal of Production Research* in 1967, discussed and developed models for use with differing rates of inflation.

During the past several years, inflation has escalated to alarming new heights. It is no wonder, then, that inflation should be considered in a life cycle study. However, the problem that creates inconsistencies in an analysis is not so much that future costs will be greater than today's costs, but the uncertainty about *how much* costs will increase, and what rate of inflation should be assumed as the analysis base.

The U.S. Office of Management and Budget (OMB) requires that all estimates of costs for each year of a planning (design) period be made in *constant dollars*, that is, in terms of the general purchasing power of the dollar at the time of decision making. Estimates may reflect changes in the *relative* prices of cost components, where there is reasonable basis for estimating such changes, but should not include any forecasted change in the general price level during the planning (design) period. This is the procedure recommended in this book for an analysis. The *differential rate* of inflation, or *escalation rate,* has been defined as "that rate of inflation above the general devaluation of the purchasing power of the dollar."

Cost escalation can have a profound effect on the financial performance of an alternative. This is especially true when the rate of cost increase is high (as has been seen

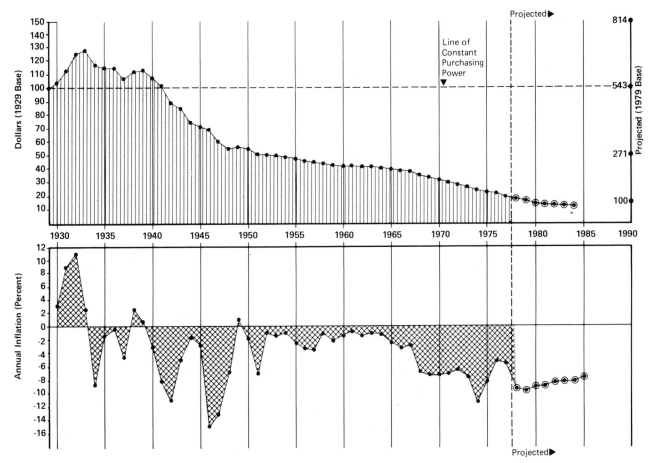

FIGURE 3-1
Inflation and the purchasing power of the dollar. *(Source: U.S. Department of Commerce,*
Implicit Price Deflator Index.)

with fossil fuel prices over the 1973–1980 period). Government agencies have made various estimates concerning fuel price increases relative to the overall economic price indices. Figure 3-2 presents an example of this information from the National Aeronautics and Space Administration (NASA).

The concept of differential cost escalation requires that variables be adjusted from today's-dollar purchasing levels only if they are above the *general economy inflation rate*. Nonescalation of these items and the corresponding effect upon the results may be included in the sensitivity analysis, which is explained later in this chapter. Formulas for dealing with differential escalation are also discussed later in the chapter.

In order to compare design alternatives, both present and future costs for each alternative must somehow be brought to a common point in time. Two methods are commonly used. Costs may be converted to today's cost (present worth) or, they may be converted to an annual series of payments (annualized). Either method will properly allow comparison between design alternatives. This book contains procedures, conversion tables, and examples for both methods.

PRESENT-WORTH METHOD

The present-worth method requires conversion of all present and future expenditures to a baseline of today's costs. Initial costs are already expressed in present worth. The following formulas are used to convert recurring and non-recurring costs:
Recurring costs (when $A = \$1.00$):

$$P = A \frac{(1 + i)^n - 1}{i(1 + i)^n} = PWA \qquad (1)$$

where i = interest rate per interest period (in decimals); minimum attractive rate of return

    n = number of interest periods

    P = present sum of money (present worth)

    A = end-of-period payment or receipt in a uniform series continuing for the coming n periods, entire series equivalent to p at interest rate i

PWA = present worth of an annuity factor
Nonrecurring costs (when $F = \$1.00$):

$$P = F \frac{1}{(1 + i)^n} = PW \qquad (2)$$

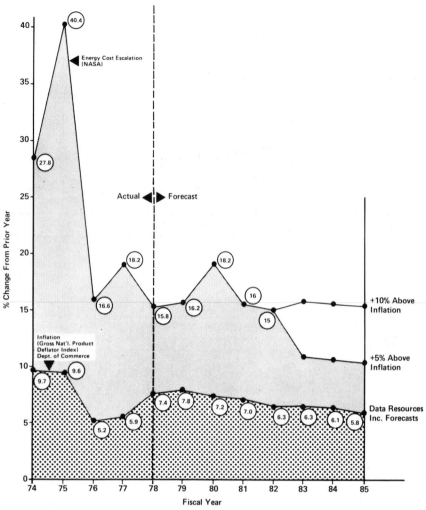

FIGURE 3-2
Energy cost escalation and inflation. *(Source: NASA, February 1979.)*

where F = sum of money at the end of n from the present date that is equivalent to P with interest rate i

PW = present-worth factor

To use these formulas the owner or designer must determine the rate of return. This interest rate is discussed later. The federal government through OMB circular A-94 (see Appendix B) has established 10 percent as the interest rate to be used in studies of this type, excluding the lease or purchase of real property.* The number of interest periods (n) or the life cycle period of the study is usually expressed in years. Normally, between 25 and 40 years are considered adequate for estimating future expenses. Differential escalation (that rate of inflation above the general economy) is taken into account for recurring costs, such as energy, by the following formula:

$$P = A \frac{[(1 + e)/(1 + i)]\ [(1 + e/1 + i)^n - 1]}{[(1 + e)/(1 + i)] - 1}$$

$$= PWA \tag{3}$$

where e = escalation rate

A = \$1.00

Economic tables exist for the many combinations of interest rates, interest periods, and discount rates. However, escalation tables are not available. Some calculators, such as the Texas Instruments Business Analyst and the Hewlett-Packard HP-22 business management calculators, have economic equations built in for quick calculation, but they do not deal with escalation. For reader convenience, a series of tables of escalated rates for selected interest rates are contained in Appendix C.

ANNUALIZED METHOD

The second method converts initial, recurring, and nonrecurring costs to an annual series of payments. It may be

---

* Public Law 96-294 of June 30, 1980 amended the National Energy Conservation Policy Act such that all energy-related LCC Studies shall use a 7-percent discount rate. Note: When $e = i$, $P = A \cdot n$

used to express all life cycle costs as an annual expenditure. Home payments are an example of this procedure; that is, a buyer opts to purchase a home for $439 per month (360 equal monthly payments at 10 percent yearly interest) rather than pay $50,000 one time, today. Recurring costs, as previously discussed, are already expressed as annual costs; therefore no adjustment is necessary. Initial and nonrecurring costs, however, require equivalent cost conversion. The following formulas are used for this conversion:

Initial costs:

$$A = P \left[\frac{i(1 + i)^n}{(1 + i)^n - 1} \right] = PP \qquad (4)$$

where A = annualized cost
P = $1.00
PP = periodic payment factor

Nonrecurring costs: Use Equation (2) to convert future expenditure to today's cost (present worth). Then use Equation (4) to convert today's cost (present worth) to an annual expenditure (annualized cost).

Since all costs are expressed in equivalent dollars, for both the present worth and the annualized methods, the life cycle cost is the *sum* of the initial, recurring, and nonrecurring costs (all expressed in equivalent dollars).

ECONOMIC TERMINOLOGY AND EXAMPLES
Discount or Interest Rate

Because calculation of present worth is often called "discounting," writers on economics frequently refer to an interest rate used in present-worth calculations as a *discount rate*. Any reference to the discount rate in the text means the minimum acceptable rate of return for the client for investment purposes, or the current prime or borrowing rate of interest. In establishing this rate, several factors must be considered. Is the project to be financed through borrowed money or from capital assets? Is the client a government agency or private industry? What is the rate of return for the industry before or after income taxes?

At times the owner may establish the minimum attractive rate of return based only on the cost of borrowed money. Although this view is particularly common in government projects and in personal economy studies, the same view may not be applicable to projects in competitive industry. Before an interest rate is established, the designer should consider the following:

1. Decisions made for competitive business enterprises are presumably made from the viewpoint of the owners of the enterprise. If the prospective return from investing borrowed funds in capital assets is just equal to the cost of the borrowed money, the owners will gain no advantage from borrowing. The prospective return needs to be greater than the cost of borrowed money to justify the risks and other disadvantages to the owners associated with fixed obligations to pay interest and repay principal at stated dates.

2. Even though it may *seem* as if certain types of assets can be financed entirely by borrowing (for example, certain equipment purchased on the installment plan), the amount of possible borrowing by any business enterprise depends on the amount of equity capital in the enterprise. Generally speaking, the cost of new capital to an enterprise ought to be viewed as a weighted average of the cost of borrowed capital and equity capital. This weighted average will nearly always be considerably higher than the cost of borrowed money.

3. In some types of loan transactions the risk of loss is recognized to be greater than in other types. The risk of loss influences the interest rate. Generally speaking, the poorer the credit rating of a borrower, the greater the interest rate one will have to pay. In a similar way the standard of attractiveness applied to proposals for capital expenditures in industry may be related to the estimated risk of loss.

4. Decisions in competitive business enterprises are presumably made from the viewpoint of the owners of the enterprise. Obviously it is to the owners' advantage to obtain the best possible rate of return *after* income taxes rather than *before* income taxes. When designers responsible for life cycle studies in competitive industry make studies before income taxes, the implication is that the same choices among alternatives would be after taxes as before taxes. However, there are instances where the best alternatives after income taxes are not the same as the best ones before income taxes. Usually this circumstance arises because of differences in the rate of write-off for tax purposes or differences in tax rates applicable to various investments.

Time Frames

Several time frames are used in an LCC analysis. First is the *economic* or *study period* used in comparing design alternates. The owner, not the designer, must establish this time frame. If the building life is considered as being forever, 25 to 40 years is long enough to predict future costs for "economic" purposes to capture the most significant costs. This is illustrated in Figure 3-3 by plotting an annual cost for 100 years discounted to present worth at a 10 percent interest rate. The area under the curve is the cumulative total present-worth cost of the system. Note that 80 percent of the total equivalent cost is consumed in the first 25 years.

A time frame must also be used for each system under analysis. The *useful life* of each system, component, or item under study may be the physical, technological, or economic life. The useful life of any item depends upon such things as: the frequency with which it is used, its age when acquired, the policy for repairs and replacements, whether preventive maintenance procedures are followed

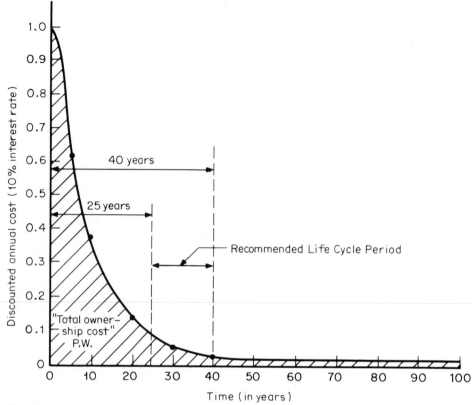

FIGURE 3-3
Recommended economic life cycle period.

as recommended by the manufacturer, the climate in which it is used, the state of the art, economic changes, inventions, and other developments within industry.

The *depreciation period* is a period selected that allocates the first cost of the system over the estimated useful life of the asset. This period is the basis for a deduction against income in calculating income taxes. There are several ways commonly used to distribute the initial cost over time, for example, straight line, sum of the years' digits, double declining balance, etc. The Internal Revenue Service (IRS) has established and made available certain guidelines for various system components.

The *amortization period* is the time over which periodic payments are made to discharge a debt. The period used is often arbitrary and is selected to meet the needs of the project. Financing costs are assessed during this period.

When evaluating alternatives with unequal useful lives during the economic life cycle period, a residual value must be established. The residual value is the estimated value of the system or component at the end of the economic life cycle or study period. This is commonly referred to as the *salvage value* of one alternative over another. The value of a system at the end of its useful life is normally equal to its scrap value less the cost incurred for its removal or disposal.

Present-Worth Example

Using the following product information, select between two alternative carpeting systems given a 10 percent interest rate and a 24-year life cycle study period. Recalculate the LCC using a 2 percent differential escalation rate for maintenance. Neglect the effect of overall inflation for other costs and assume replacement costs equal the initial costs.

	Prima carpet	X-Tendo carpet
Initial cost	$15.00/yd²	$10.00/yd²
Maintenance (annual)	1.50/yd²	2.00/yd²
Useful life	12 years	8 years

Neglect effects of inflation.

Solution:

Recurring cost (maintenance) expressed in present worth

$$P_{PC} = A \frac{(1 + i)^n - 1}{i(1 + i)^n}$$

$$= A \frac{(1 + 0.1)^{24} - 1}{0.1(1 + 0.1)^{24}}$$

$$= A \frac{9.8497 - 1}{0.1(9.8497)}$$

$$= A \frac{8.8497}{0.98497}$$

$$= A(8.9847)*$$

Prima carpet maintenance $= \$1.50(8.9847)$

Present worth, Prima carpet $\quad P_{PC} = \$13.48$

X-Tendo carpet maintenance $= \$2.00(8.9847)$

Present worth, X-tendo carpet $\quad P_{XC} = \$17.97$

Nonrecurring cost (carpet replacement) expressed in present worth P

$$= F \frac{1}{(1+i)^n}$$

X-Tendo carpet replacement year ($n = 8$)

$$= \$10 \frac{1}{(1+0.1)^8}$$

$$= \$10(.4665)$$

Present worth $= \$4.67$

Prima carpet replacement year ($n = 12$)

$$= \$15 \frac{1}{(1+0.1)^{12}}$$

$$= \$15(0.3186)$$

Present worth $= \$4.78$

X-Tendo carpet replacement ($n = 16$)

$$= \$10 \frac{1}{(1+0.1)^{16}}$$

$$= \$10(0.2176)$$

Present worth $= \$2.18$

The salvage value for both systems equals zero since they complete cycles at the end of the period.

The summary of life cycle (present-worth) costs is as follows:

Types of costs	Prima carpet	X-Tendo carpet
Initial cost	$15.00	$10.00
Maintenance (recurring) cost	13.48	17.97
Replacement (nonrecurring), year 8	0	4.67
Replacement (nonrecurring), year 12	4.78	0
Replacement (nonrecurring), year 16	0	2.18
Total life cycle present-worth costs	$33.26	$34.82

The Prima carpet would be selected on the basis of LCC.

Now, assuming maintenance costs rise at a differential escalation rate of 2 percent per year, recalculate the life cycle costs.

Solution:

Recurring cost escalating (maintenance) P expressed in present worth

$$P = A \frac{[(1+e)/(1+i)]\{[(1+e)/(1+i)]^n - 1\}}{[(1+e)/(1+i)] - 1}$$

$$= A \frac{[(1+0.02)/(1+0.1)]\{[(1+0.02)/(1+0.1)]^{24} - 1\}}{[(1+0.02)/(1+0.1)] - 1}$$

$$= A \frac{(0.92727)[(0.1633) - 1]}{(0.92727) - 1}$$

---

* This factor may be obtained from Table C-2 (10 percent interest, 24-year study period).

$$PWA = A \frac{0.77585}{0.072727}$$
$$= A (10.668)$$

Prima carpet maintenance $= \$1.50 (10.668)$
Present worth $P_{PC} = \$16.00$
X-Tendo carpet maintenance $= \$2.00 (10.668)$
Present worth $P_{XC} = \$21.34$

A summary of costs with maintenance escalations is as follows:

Types of costs	Prima carpet	X-Tendo carpet
Initial costs	$15.00	$10.00
Maintenance (escalated @ 2%/yr.)	16.00	21.34
Replacement, year 8	0	4.67
Replacement, year 12	4.78	0
Replacement, year 16	0	2.18
Total life cycle present-worth costs	$35.78	$38.19

In this case, the Prima carpet remains the lowest life cycle cost alternative.

Annualized Cost Example

Using the following information, select the most promising condenser using an 8 percent interest rate and a life cycle period of 18 years.

	Ferrous metal Condenser	Copper metal Condenser
Initial cost	$800.00	$950.00
Useful life	6 years	9 years
Operating cost per year	$50.00	$40.00

Neglect effects of inflation.

Solution:

Initial cost (expressed as annualized)

$$A_{fm} = P \frac{i (1 + i)^n}{(1 + i)^n - 1}$$
$$= P \frac{0.08 (1 + 0.08)^{18}}{(1 + 0.08)^{18} - 1}$$
$$= P \frac{0.08 (3.996)}{(3.996) - 1}$$
$$= P \frac{0.31968}{2.996}$$
$$= P (0.1067)*$$

Ferrous metal condenser initial cost, annualized $= \$800 (0.1067)$
Annualized cost $= \$85.36$

Copper metal condenser initial cost, annualized $= \$950 (0.1067)$
Annualized cost $A_{cm} = \$101.37$

Nonrecurring cost (condenser replacement) (present worth) $P = F \frac{1}{(1 + i)^n}$

then, annualized $A = P \frac{i (1 + i)^n}{(1 + i)^n - 1}$

Ferrous metal replacement, year 6 (present worth) $= \$800 \frac{1}{(1 + .08)^6}$
$= \$800 (0.6302)$
Present worth $= \$504.16$

Annualized ferrous metal replacement, year 6 $A = \$504.16 (.1067)$
Annualized cost $= \$53.79$

Copper metal replacement, year 9 (present worth) $P = \$950 \frac{1}{(1 + 0.08)^9}$
$= \$950 (0.5002)$
Present worth $= \$475.19$

Annualized copper metal replacement, year 9 $= \$475.19 (0.1067)$
Annualized cost $= \$50.70$

Ferrous metal replacement, year 12 (present worth) $= \$800 \frac{1}{(1 + 0.08)^{12}}$
$= \$800 (0.3971)$
Present worth $P = \$317.68$

Annualized ferrous metal replacement, year 12 $A = \$317.68 (.1067)$
Annualized cost $= \$33.90$

The salvage value for both alternates is equal to zero since their replacement cycle ends at the economic life.
A summary of life cycle (annualized) costs is as follows:

	Ferrous metal condenser	Copper metal condenser
Initial cost	$ 85.36	$101.37
Operating cost (recurring)	50.00	40.00
Replacement (nonrecurring), year 6	53.79	0
Replacement (nonrecurring), year 9	0	50.70
Replacement (nonrecurring), year 12	33.90	0
Total life cycle annualized costs	$223.05	$192.07

* This factor may be obtained from Table C-3 (8 percent interest, 18-year study period).

Based on life cycle costs the copper metal condenser should be selected.

OTHER ECONOMIC TECHNIQUES

The following economic techniques can be used in a life cycle study, depending on the client's requirements and special needs to understand the alternatives. With additional rules and certain mechanics, it is possible to perform a sensitivity analysis, determine the payback period, establish a breakeven point between alternatives, determine rates of return and extra-investment rate-of-return alternatives, perform a cash-flow analysis, and review the benefits and costs.

Certainty, Risk, and Uncertainty

Investment decisions may be made under assumed certainty, risk, or uncertainty. Decisions based on assumed certainty may be correct economic decisions, but they depend on things working out as planned. Decisions should be made in the light of calculated risks—gambling on the odds that the future will fulfill educated judgments. Decisions made with a full understanding of the uncertainties assume that the future may be different from what is anticipated and that the designer is aware of the effects that possible variations may have on the results predicted.

At this time, dealing with study uncertainties is more of an art than a science. There are some direct methods within easy reach of all designers. Beyond these, operations research and Delphi techniques are being developed into practical methods for dealing with uncertainty. Treatment of the latter is beyond the scope of this book. While there is much work yet to be done in this area, the following paragraphs discuss some of the concepts and methods that will enhance the value of study results in making economic decisions.

Sensitivity Analysis

When completing an LCC analysis, the designer may be very uncertain about a few key parameters because of inadequate input data, initial assumptions, accuracy of estimates, or any combination of factors. The basic questions are: (1) How sensitive are the results of the analysis to variations in these uncertain parameters? (2) Will these variations tend to justify the selection of an alternative not currently being considered? (3) How much variation in a given parameter is required to shift the decision to select alternative B rather than alternative A? The intent is to (a) determine the sensitivity of the results of the analysis to certain input parameters and (b) to assess the risk and uncertainty associated with a given decision, that is, the probability of making a wrong decision. In essence, the designer needs to address the "what if" questions in an attempt to minimize the risk associated with given decisions.

In accomplishing a sensitivity analysis, the designer may wish to establish a baseline of input parameters and then retest the alternatives while varying different key input parameters to determine the effect on the results. Variation may be accomplished by applying different multiple factors to the input parameter being tested. For example, the designer may wish to investigate the following:

1. Variation of the frequency of maintenance as a function of life cycle cost. For instance, multiple factors of 0.5 and 1.5 may be applied to the maintenance cost figure, with alternatives examined for each factor. Through the application of a series of multiple factors, the designer can assess the delta effects between any category and the total life cycle cost.

2. Variation of system operating time as a function of the equipment and facility use. Since system use varies considerably from one location to the next, or with different user organizations, it would be worthwhile to test this parameter in terms of life cycle cost.

3. Variation of assumed fuel escalation rates. Because of current market fluctuations, this may be the most significant single parameter for analysis.

4. Variation of the assumed discount rate as a function of life cycle cost. The selection of parameters to be tested for sensitivity relates directly to the high-cost categories and the major cost drivers (that is, the parameters with the greatest impact on cost). In each instance, the designer should be concerned with not only the delta effects of these variations on total life cycle cost, but the degree of variation that can occur without introducing any unnecessary risk in decisions pertaining to the selection of alternatives. The degree of variation that can be tolerated will relate directly to the accuracy of the input data necessary for the LCC analysis. If the allowable output variation is relatively small and the input data factors vary over a wide range, then the designer may wish to expend some additional effort to acquire better input data.

The sensitivity analysis can be extremely beneficial to the decision maker, and often conveys more information than any other single aspect of the overall LCC analysis. The designer can readily identify cause and effect relationships and predict trends, and is better prepared to respond to the "what if" questions.

Payback Period

One of the most used and misunderstood terms in engineering economics is that of the payback period. It is used to evaluate alternatives and project their savings over the number of years in which the initial extra expenditure is paid back. It is a figure most commonly used in the early stages of a design. The simple payback may be calculated by the following:

$$\text{Simple payback period} = \frac{\text{initial cost}}{\text{annual savings}} \quad (1)$$

The life expectancy is often ignored in the payback equation. Considering the realistic useful lives of systems can produce differing values. For this reason, all follow-on costs including replacement lives should be converted to an annualized cost savings before dividing into the initial-cost expenditure.

$$\text{Payback period(discounted)} = \frac{\text{initial cost}}{\text{annualized savings}} \quad (2)$$

Equation (2) provides a more realistic payback period for the alternatives being compared, considering the time value of money.

Breakeven Analysis

At times a choice exists between two alternatives, one of which may be more economical under one set of conditions and the other more economical under another set of conditions. By altering the value of one of the variables in the analysis and holding all the other points of difference between the two alternatives constant, it is possible to find a value for the variable that makes the two alternatives equally economical. This value is usually described as the *breakeven* point.

An example will illustrate how the breakeven analysis can be used. Given, for example, two alternative solutions where all costs are known and the discount rate has been established, it is possible to treat *time* as a variable, that is, to solve for the point on the time continuum at which one of the alternatives becomes more attractive than the other.

If lighting system A has an initial cost of $100,000 and an annual cost of $18,000 and lighting system B has an initial cost of $130,000 with an annual cost of $12,000; using a discount rate of 10 percent at which point on the time line does lighting system B (which is more expensive initially) become economically more attractive than system A?

Solution: First, determine the total present worths of the two lighting systems, set them equal to each other, and solve for the discount factors that make them equal. In this case it occurs when P_A equals P_B.
Total present worth P of system A:

$$P_A = \$100,000 + (\$18,000 \times PWA)$$

Total present worth of system B:

$$P_B = \$130,000 + (\$12,000 \times PWA)$$

Setting these two equal to each other and solving yields $PWA = 5.000$. Using the economic table for present worth of annuity and 10 percent discount rate, the PWA for 7 years is 4.868 and the PWA for 8 years is 5.335. The breakeven point, then, is just over 7 years, after which lighting system B becomes more economical. That time period may be considered the payback period for the extra $30,000 initial-cost investment associated with system B.

Figure 3-4 graphically portrays the costs associated with the lighting alternatives. As the illustration shows, the intersection of the two lines of annualized costs is the breakeven point. The graphical solution is much quicker for the analysis and better explains the process to a reader. However, it does not reflect the time value of money.

Rate of Return on Investment

From the discussions thus far, it can be seen that there are four variables used in an economic study:

$$
\begin{aligned}
i &= \text{discount rate} \\
n &= \text{time period} \\
P &= \text{present sum of money} \\
F &= \text{future sum of money} \\
A &= \text{annual sum of money}
\end{aligned}
\quad \right\} \quad \text{use any 2}
$$

In the sensitivity analysis these variables are changed to see if a decision changes. The calculation of the payback period shows the number of years to return the extra initial investment. In the breakeven analysis any one of the variables is altered to find a value that makes the alternatives equally economical. Rate of return on investment refers to variations in the established discount rate. If, for example, an owner plans to make an investment of funds to gain some form of return—for instance, annual energy savings—the rate of return can be calculated. What would be the expected rate of return for an investment of $100,000 today, with an energy savings of $15,000 annually, over a 15-year analysis period?

Setting the present-worth cost equal to the $15,000 annual savings,

$$P = A \times PWA$$
$$\$100,000 = \$15,000 \times PWA$$
$$PWA = 6.667$$

Referring to the economic tables in the Appendix C using a 15-year period, the PWA of 6.667 is somewhere between the PWA for 12 percent (6.811) and the PWA for 14 percent (6.142). Interpolating, it appears that the rate of return is approximately 12.5 percent.

In the example shown, an initial cost and a series of continuing benefits were involved. A rate of return from any series of costs and revenues over time can be determined by bringing all costs and revenues to their present worths, or to an equivalent annualized cost, and then solving for the discount rate. This may require a trial and error process of several iterations.

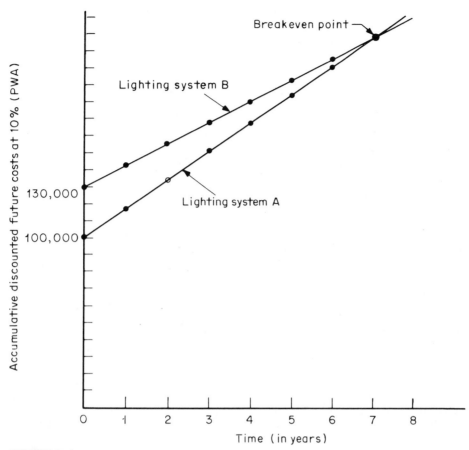

FIGURE 3-4
Breakeven analysis for lighting systems.

Rate of Return on Extra Investment

If two or more alternatives are being compared, it is possible to find the rate of return on the extra investment associated with the more expensive alternative without having to calculate the individual rates of return for each alternative.

Consider this situation: Plan A has an initial cost of $100,000 and a uniform annual cost of $15,000 per year. Plan B has an initial cost of $130,000, an annual cost of $12,000, and an estimated salvage value of $25,000 after 10 years. The life cycle is to be 10 years. What is the rate of return on the extra investment of $30,000 associated with plan B?

The methodology to be used parallels that used for the straight rate-of-return problem just shown: Find the total present worth of each alternative and solve for the discount rate that makes them equal.

Total present worth of plan A:

$$P_A = \$100,000 + (\$15,000 \times PWA)$$

Total present worth of plan B:

$$P_B = \$130,000 + (\$12,000 \times PWA)$$
$$- (\$25,000 \times PW)$$

Setting these two equal to each other and solving yields

$$(\$3,000 \times PWA) + (\$25,000 \times PW) = \$30,000$$

At this point, it is necessary to substitute trial PWA and PW factors for 10 years and various discount rates. Substituting, for example, factors for 10 years and 10 percent:

$$(\$3,000 \times 6.145) + (\$25,000 \times 0.3855) = \$28,073$$

These PWA and PW factors are not quite large enough to balance the equation. Trying the factors for a discount rate indicates that the answer is approximately 9.5 percent.

The mechanics are similar to those in the straight rate-of-return situation. Develop total present worths or equivalent uniform annual costs for both plans, set them equal to each other, and solve for the discount rate that makes them equivalent. This becomes the rate of return on the extra investment associated with the more expensive plan.

Calculating the rate of return on extra investment is always recommended when comparing various alternatives against investment goals. It may turn out that the most obvious alternative is not the one that best satisfies the investment objective.

TABLE 3-1

SUMMARY OF CASH FLOW EXAMPLE

Year	Cash outlay	Net income before taxes, depreciation	Depreciation charges	Net taxable income	Income taxes	Net income after taxes	Net cash flow	Discount factor* (present-worth factor for 10%)	Present value of net cash flow		
									10% rate	15% rate	20% rate
0	$120,000	0	0	0	0	0	($120,000)	1.000	($120,000)	($120,000)	($120,000)
1	0	$20,000	$15,000	$ 5,000	$ 2,500	$ 2,500	17,500	0.909	15,900	15,200	14,600
2	0	30,000	15,000	15,000	7,500	7,500	22,500	0.826	18,600	17,000	15,600
3	0	40,000	15,000	25,000	12,500	12,500	27,500	0.751	20,700	18,100	15,900
4	0	50,000	15,000	35,000	17,500	17,500	32,500	0.683	22,200	18,600	15,700
5	0	50,000	15,000	35,000	17,500	17,500	32,500	0.621	20,200	16,200	13,100
6	0	50,000	15,000	35,000	17,500	17,500	32,500	0.564	18,300	14,100	10,900
7	0	50,000	15,000	35,000	17,500	17,500	32,500	0.513	16,700	12,300	9,100
8	0	50,000	15,000	35,000	17,500	27,500	32,500	0.467	15,200	10,700	7,600
									$ 27,800	$ 2,200	($ 17,500)

*Factors for 15 percent and 20 percent not presented.

Cash-Flow Analysis

The discounted cash-flow approach should give results similar to the previous examples as long as the time value of money is considered. Cash flow, however, carries the procedure another step and provides the designer with a technique to incorporate variable annual expenditures, taxes, and depreciation. Chapter 4 contains additional information in this area.

The following example illustrates the process of cash-flow analysis: The system under consideration has a $120,000 initial cash outlay, a 10 percent discount rate, an amortization period of 8 years, and no salvage value. Straight-line depreciation is used for tax purposes. Income from the investment, after deducting property taxes, insurance, and maintenance, is $20,000 the first year; $30,000 for the second year; $40,000 for the third year; and $50,000 annually for the remaining 5 years. Table 3-1 shows the cash-flow analysis. The present-worth value is shown for the 10 percent discount rate with an income tax rate of 50 percent. In addition, the present value of net cash flow was calculated for the 15 percent and 20 percent rates. The 8-year present-value total at 10 percent equaled $147,800. This investment of $120,000 at the end of 8 years yielded a rate of return of about 15.1 percent (interpolating between the 15 percent and 20 percent cash-flow rates). If this is an acceptable return for the investor, the proposed system would presumably be approved.

Benefit/Cost Analysis*

Of the terms discussed, the origin of *benefit/cost analysis* is the clearest. It was created by Congress in the Flood Control Act of June 22, 1936. Congress stated that a project should be promulgated "if the benefits to whom-

ever they may accrue are in excess of the estimated costs." This became the foundation for the term *benefit/cost analysis*. Benefits could include such attributes as avoidance of property loss, improved property values, avoidance of loss of life, reduction of labor costs, improved business conditions, and other identifiable and quantifiable attributes. The reverse of benefits would be those hardship costs borne by a segment of the public because of a decision.

Since the decision has to be made on the basis of equivalency, it is necessary to quantify the projected costs as well as the benefits by the present-worth or annualized methods. A comparison of results expressed as a quotient or a difference indicates if the project is worthwhile. Benefit/cost analysis was intended to determine whether the public benefits, expressed in money, were greater than the cost of a project that would provide these benefits. It was not intended to discriminate between competing proposals for the solution of a problem.

Since the annualized and present-worth methods are appropriate tools for comparing alternative approaches, they can also test the viability of a project. The alternative that provides the best benefits/cost ratio is determined from this analysis. Using the engineering economics study technique to make the optimum economic selection as well expands the principal objective of the term's congressional definition.

SUMMARY

LCC is fundamentally intended to determine the expenses associated with various design alternatives using the concept of equivalent costs. However, there are other uses. It is not such a large step to consider using LCC in the context of more comprehensive benefits-and-costs studies. The economic section of the bibliography lists sources for further information.

* This ratio of present-worth savings to net present-worth costs is also known as the Savings/Investment Ratio (SIR).

CHAPTER FOUR
LIFE CYCLE ESTIMATING PROCEDURES

"Special efforts are required to gather and collect valid cost information for maintenance and operations. Currently, cost data are unavailable and unreliable. This is disturbing since these costs represent over 50% of the cost of ownership."

A. J. Dell'Isola
Value Engineering in the Construction Industry
1973.

INTRODUCTION

Estimating life cycle costs requires data and, at times, guesswork. *Analyzing* life cycle costs places a larger emphasis on procedures and technical skills and is intended to require less guesswork. Project decisions are made throughout the design process in an expanding fashion. On the other hand, accurate costs must be generated from a detailed cost base. This is illustrated in Figure 4-1. The level of decision making and the degree of information available determine what costing method is most appropriate. Systems costs, based on earlier projects or predefined subsystems of usual types of construction, provide the link between detailed costs and early stage estimates.

The clustering of cost items into systems becomes even more significant when estimates are prepared at budget and early design stages. *Systems costing* allocates funds to the various functional areas of a facility and allows the designer to make early cost comparisons among alternatives. When life cycle data is provided, a total cost analysis is possible. A clearly defined accounting framework is required to adequately relate LCC costs from project inception through occupancy.

This chapter outlines techniques that simplify assessment of the economic impact of design alternatives. Estimating procedures for initial costs; energy and operating costs; maintenance; alterations and replacements; taxes,

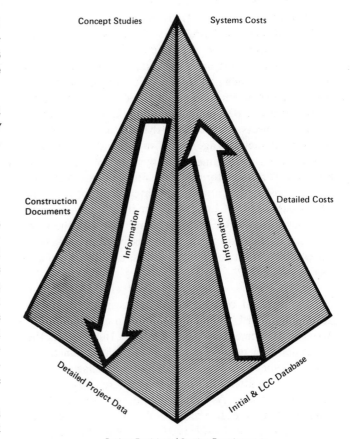

FIGURE 4-1
Project development decisions and their costing requirements.

credits, and depreciation; and associated costs are discussed.

ESTIMATING FRAMEWORK

A standard accounting system is one of the fundamental components of any cost control and estimating system.

29

The system serves several purposes:

1. It allows cost data from different stages in project development to be related uniformly and consistently.

2. It provides a frame of reference within which cost data may be collected.

3. It provides a checklist for estimating and for referencing specifications.

4. It facilitates communications among all members of a project team.

5. It allows study teams' designers and consultants to quickly identify and focus on high-cost areas.

6. It provides a basis for gathering life cycle costs.

The need for a consistent framework becomes even more important when the system is fully automated.

For designers, the standard base is the 16-division Uniform Construction Index (UCI), recently updated and renamed "MASTER FORMAT," which parallels the Construction Specification Institute (CSI) format. This format is now widely used as a data communication medium in the building industry; specifications, product data, project management systems, etc. are commonly structured around it. Because it resembles the form by which building projects are procured (that is, the familiar subtrade or contract package), it is also used intermittently as a cost control and estimating framework. While this format may be suitable for use at the final design stages, and during construction, it is inadequate during budget and early design. The UCI system is heavily product- and materials-oriented, which does not relate well with the kind of decisions that are made at the early design stages—whether to build two or three stories, use 30-foot or 60-foot bay sizes, etc.

For some years, managers involved with design-phase construction cost control problems have realized the inadequacy of the UCI and have moved to develop systems based on an elemental format. This approach involves the separation of a building into its component or functional parts, elements, or subsystems (terminology varies widely), in an attempt to relate these more closely to the language of design. As a consequence, several forms have proliferated—for example, those of Progressive Architecture, of the State University Construction Fund (New York), and of Boston Schools. In addition, many consultants have developed their own formats.

Responding to the inadequacy of the UCI, the GSA in 1973 issued a draft outline of the Uniform Building Component Format (UNIFORMAT). Concurrently, the American Institute of Architects (AIA) began development of the MASTERCOST system, intended to be a national building cost data bank.

Because the two formats were similar, GSA and AIA merged the UNIFORMAT and MASTERCOST classification systems. The various levels of detail and their relationship with UCI divisions are presented in Figure 4-2.

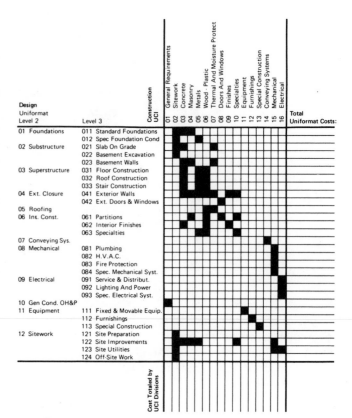

FIGURE 4-2
Relationship between UNIFORMAT and the Uniform Construction Index (UCI).

The significance of this organization will be further explained as part of the discussion on initial costs, which follows.

INITIAL COSTS

Initial costs are the owner's costs associated with the initial development of a facility and project support (fees, land, interest, etc.) as well as construction costs. These costs are often referred to as *first costs*. Cost items associated with the initial development of the facility may include design, consulting, legal, and other professional fees; construction costs, including all furnishings; equipment; land costs; and construction phase financing. As debt incurred to finance the initial costs is amortized, the amortization payments represent the financing costs considered as an annual charge.

Decisions based on the initial investment cost of a facility are familiar to all designers. The percentages of such costs are illustrated for a typical office building by Figure 4-3. The following brief examples, however, illustrate the relationship of first cost to life cycle cost:

● The selection of cooler, but more expensive, light fixtures that will reduce the size and energy requirement of the proposed HVAC system.

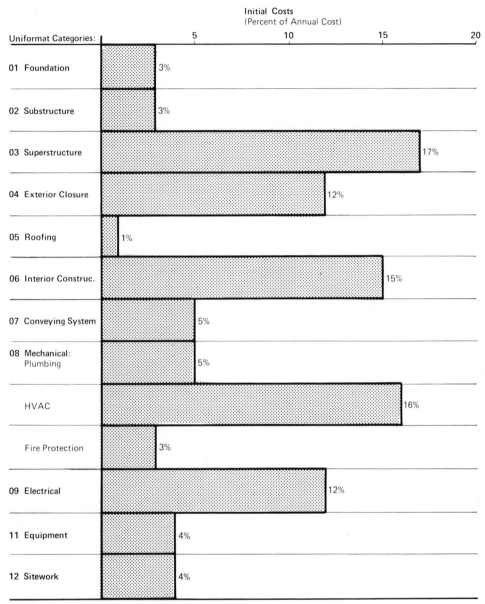

FIGURE 4-3
Relative cost impact of initial cost, typical office building.

- The purchase of additional land to permit the facility to be limited to a single story thus eliminating all first and life cycle costs associated with vertical transportation.

Budget Phase

Budget and conceptual estimates may be prepared using single-unit costs based on broad-accommodation parameters, for example, cost per student or per hospital bed and cost per square foot of gross floor area or cubic foot of building volume. Efficiency ratios and conversion factors for transforming net to gross floor areas, together with the cost per square foot of net usable area, are also useful in preparing estimates.

This information can be expanded to costs per square foot of functional activities programmed for each space, for example, cost per square foot of wet laboratories versus that for offices and secretarial spaces. These costs are also tempered by the basic criteria and design parameters of the building systems and components to be selected. Costs are then organized into a systems format such as UNIFORMAT.

Design Phase

In the early design phase, it is normal to utilize cost information based on the elements for each building subsystem, for the preparation of cost estimates. For example, the comparison between steel and concrete frames in terms of the project's scope and characteristics can be determined from previous experience on similar structures regardless of programmatic requirements. This is true for most of the major subsystems such as HVAC, electrical distribution, lighting, and plumbing.

As design progresses, more detailed elemental subsystem cost information is required. This cost information allows selection of components and the system specifications, which can later be used for the preparation of more detailed estimates. Because of the more detailed estimate, the designer is in a better position to control costs by suggesting changes in the project should the estimate indicate costs in excess of the budget.

As part of the construction documents, it is normal to use composite unit rates for construction components, assemblies, and systems for the preparation of more detailed cost estimates. Detailed unit rates are often required at this point for prebid estimates, final cost checks, and verification of contractor's breakdowns used as a basis for negotiations of contractor bid costs.

Such data is widely available and is published in various forms. It is sometimes difficult to accept this cost information, considering the time elapsed between its preparation and distribution. More seriously, there are gaps in the type of cost information required during the early stages of design. A workable system of retrieving and recycling cost data from one project to another is necessary to provide the basic framework for estimating construction costs in the early development stages.

When the system for estimating construction costs is materials-oriented rather than component- or system-oriented, its application can become cumbersome. Effective cost control procedures, regardless of the type of construction, require a framework based on functional or elemental parts of a building that perform similar functions. These parts are referred to as subsystems, functional components, elements, features, assemblies, etc. A time-consuming task for the designer is the conversion of typical construction trade costs into an elemental (systems) form of breakdown. To simplify this process, forms have been developed to organize and re-sort trade costs into the UNIFORMAT structure. The following example illustrates how this may be done.

Example—Estimate Organized into Systems

Figure 4-4 provides a gross area analysis of a two-story

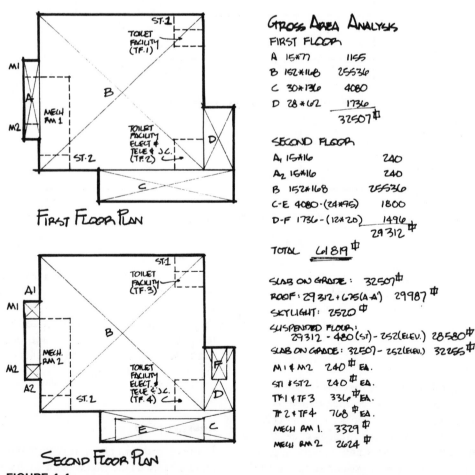

FIGURE 4-4
Computer processing center, gross area analysis.

computer processing center as interpreted from schematic design documents.

Using the cost estimate prepared for the project, the cost estimate summary was completed, with the results displayed in Figure 4-5. In order to accumulate these UCI-oriented costs according to systems (UNIFORMAT), each item within the 16 divisions is categorized according to its UNIFORMAT element assignment.

Figure 4-6 illustrates the cost summary matrix for the computer processing center estimate. In addition a cost model (shown in Figure 4-7) can easily be prepared to facilitate further LCC analysis. (Further discussion of the cost model is contained in Chapter 6, "Design Methodology.")

Once costs are redefined in this manner, meaningful information is illustrated for all phases from preplanning through design. For comparative purposes, costs expressed per unit of floor area are normally satisfactory. In addition, elemental unit costs are important in supplementing the cost per square foot of floor area. Each element should carry a specific elemental quantity; for example, exterior-wall costs should be expressed as "square feet of exterior wall area" to provide an average unit cost for that particular element.

There is an advantage in having a large number of such cost analyses for cost planning and estimating buildings in the early development phases. Cost data accumulated from one building or building type may be readily transferred to a different building type providing performance criteria are similar. Thus, a structural system for a given span, for given loads and heights, and for similar seismic conditions may be transferred from an office building to a university classroom, class-laboratory building, or similarly structured facility.

The inclusion of the following is essential in reporting data on a facility and in developing a building cost file:

1. Elemental categories for cost analysis; their description and units of measurement, and data arranged into a graded series with summaries of costs at different levels of aggregation. Shown in Figure 4-8, "Cost Control and Estimating System," are costs arranged into major groups. The objective is to create a list of elements that can serve as a reasonable standard for a wide variety of building types.

2. Floor areas and volumes must be calculated, based on a standard set of rules of measurement to ensure that the derived unit rates are consistent from project to project.

Project _COMPUTER PROCESSING CENTER_   Gross SF _61,819_ Date _1-79_

Div.	Item Description	Uniformat Element Assignment	Estimated Cost	Cost Per GSF
1.	General Requirements (Total)		345,000	5.58
	a. Mobilization Expenses	(1001)	10,000	
	b. Job Site Overhead	(1002)	125,000	
	c. Demobilization	(1003)	5,000	
	d. Main Office Expense & Profit	(1004)	205,000	
	e. Site Contractor Overhead & Profit	(12A)		
2.	Site Work (Total)		118,000	1.91
	a. Clearing & Demolition	(121)	4,000	
	b. Grading & Earthwork (site)	(121)	24,500	
	c. Excavation & Backfill (foundations)	(011)	2,000	
	d. Excavation & Backfill (basement)	(022)		
	e. Fill Below Grade Slab	(021)	6,500	
	f. Pile Foundation & Caissons	(012)		
	g. Shoring	(022)		
	h. Underpinning & Dewatering	(012)		
	i. Site Drainage & Utilities	(123)	32,000	
	j. Foundation & Underslab Drainage	(021)		
	k. Paving, Landscaping & Site Improvements	(122)	49,000	
	l. Off-Site Work (Railroad, Marine Work & Tunnels)	(124)		
	m. Other			
3.	Concrete (Total)		235,000	3.80
	a. Conc. Forms & Reinf (Foundations)	(011)	30,500	
	b. Conc. Forms & Reinf (Slab on Grade)	(021)	34,500	
	c. Conc. Forms & Reinf (Basement Walls)	(023)		
	d. Conc. Forms & Reinf (Floor & Supporting Frame)	(031)	40,000	
	e. Conc. Forms & Reinf (Roof & Supporting Frame)	(032)	35,000	
	f. Conc. Forms & Reinf (Exterior Walls)	(041)	85,000	
	g. Conc. Forms & Reinf (Int. Walls, Non-Load Brg.)	(061)		
	h. Conc. Forms & Reinf (Site Work)	(123)		
	i. Concrete Finishes (Exterior Walls)	(041)	10,000	
	j. Concrete Finishes (Interiors)	(062)		
	k. Concrete Finishes (Site Work)	(122)		
	l. Precast Concrete (Exterior Wall Panels)	(041)		
	m. Precast Concrete (Floor & Supporting Frame)	(031)		
	n. Precast Concrete (Roof & Supporting Frame)	(032)		
	o. Precast Concrete (Site Work Components)	(122)		
	p. Other			

FIGURE 4-5   (a)

Cost estimate summary comparing trade (UCI) and systems (UNIFORMAT). (_a_) Division 1-3; (_b_) division 4-6; (_c_) division 7-9; (_d_) division 10-14; (_e_) division 15-16.

Div.	Item Description	Uniformat Element Assignment	Estimated Cost	Cost Per GSF
4.	Masonry (Total)		105,000	1.70
	a. Masonry Foundations	(011)		
	b. Masonry Basement Walls	(023)		
	c. Masonry Exterior Walls	(041)	40,000	
	d. Masonry Interior Walls (Floor Supporting)	(031)		
	e. Masonry Interior Walls (Roof Supporting)	(032)		
	f. Masonry Interior Partitions (Non-Load Bearing)	(061)	25,000	
	g. Interior Paving & Finish	(062)	40,000	
	h. Exterior Paving & Masonry (Site Work)	(122)		
	i. Other			
5.	Metals (Total)		372,000	6.02
	a. Structural Steel in Foundations	(012)		
	b. Structural Steel Framing (Floor Supporting)	(031)	140,000	
	c. Structural Steel Framing (Roof Supporting)	(032)	100,000	
	d. Metal Joists & Decking (Floor Construction)	(031)	42,000	
	e. Metal Joists & Decking (Roof Construction)	(032)	45,000	
	f. Metal Stairs	(033)	16,000	
	g. Misc. & Ornamental Metal (Building Exterior)	(041)	4,000	
	h. Misc. & Ornamental Metal (Building Interior)	(062)	5,000	
	i. Misc. & Ornamental Metal (Site Work)	(122)		
	j. Other		20,000	
6.	Wood & Plastics (Total)		38,000	0.53
	a. Rough Carpentry (Framing & Decking — Floors)	(031)	3,000	
	b. Rough Carpentry (Framing & Decking — Roof)	(032)	2,000	
	c. Rough Carpentry (Exterior Wall)	(041)	5,000	
	d. Rough Carpentry (Partitions, Non-Load Bearing)	(061)	10,000	
	e. Rough Carpentry (Roof Other Than Framing & Decking)	(05)		
	f. Heavy Timber & Prefab Wood (Floor Supporting)	(031)		
	g. Heavy Timber & Prefab Wood (Roof Supporting)	(032)		
	h. Exterior Wood Siding & Trim	(041)		
	i. Fin Carpentry Millwork & Cabinet Work	(063)	13,000	
	j. Wood Paneling	(062)		
	k. Wood Stairs	(033)		
	l. Plastic Fabrications	(063)		
	m. Other			

FIGURE 4-5 *continued*   (b)

Div.	Item Description	Uniformat Element Assignment	Estimated Cost	Cost Per GSF
7.	Thermal & Moisture Protection (Total)		142,000	2.30
	a. Water & Dampproofing (Slab on Grade)	(021)		
	b. Water & Dampproofing (Basement Walls)	(023)		
	c. Water & Dampproofing (Exterior Walls)	(041)	19,000	
	d. Thermal Insulation (Foundation & Slab)	(021)		
	e. Thermal Insulation (Exterior Walls)	(041)	9,000	
	f. Thermal Insulation (Roof)	(05)	27,000	
	g. Roofing Shingles & Tiles	(05)		
	h. Shingles on Exterior Walls	(041)		
	i. Preformed Siding & Panels	(041)		
	j. Preformed Roofing	(05)		
	k. Membrane Roofing, Traffing Topping	(05)	54,000	
	l. Sheet Metal & Roof Accessories	(05)	2,000	
	m. Skylights	(05)	30,000	
	n. Sealants & Calking	(041)	1,000	
	o. Other			
8.	Doors & Windows (Total)		66,500	1.08
	a. Exterior Doors & Frames	(042)	4,000	
	b. Exterior Windows & Curtain Walls	(042)	14,000	
	c. Interior Doors & Frames	(061)	14,000	
	d. Exterior Glass & Glazing	(042)		
	e. Interior Glass & Glazing	(061)	22,000	
	f. Hardware & Specialties (Exterior)	(042)	1,500	
	g. Hardware & Specialties (Exterior)	(061)	11,000	
	h. Other			
9.	Finishes (Total)		95,000	1.54
	a. Lath & Plaster (Exterior)	(041)		
	b. Lath & Plaster (Interior)	(062)		
	c. Gypsum Wallboard	(062)	20,000	
	d. Tile & Terrazzo	(062)	11,000	
	e. Acoustical Ceilings & Treatment	(062)	46,000	
	f. Wood Flooring	(062)		
	g. Resilient Flooring	(062)		
	h. Carpeting	(062)		
	i. Exterior Coatings	(041)		
	j. Interior Special Flooring & Coatings	(062)		
	k. Interior Painting & Wall Covering	(062)	18,000	
	l. Other			

FIGURE 4-5 *continued*   (c)

Div.	Item Description	Uniformat Element Assignment	Estimated Cost	Cost Per GSF
10.	Specialties (Total)		360,000	5.82
	a. Chalkboards & Tackboards	(063)		
	b. Compartments & Cubicles	(061)		
	c. Signs & Supergraphics	(063)		
	d. Movable & Demountable Partitions	(061)		
	e. Lockers	(063)		
	f. Toilet, Bath, Wardrobe Accessories	(063)	4,000	
	g. Sun Control Devices	(041)		
	h. Access Flooring	(062)	350,000	
	i. Miscellaneous Specialties	(063)	6,000	
	j. Flagpoles	(122)		
	k. Other			
11.	Equipment (Specify)	(111)		
12.	Furnishings (Specify)	(112)		
13.	Special Construction (Specify)	(113)		
14.	Conveying Systems		102,000	1.65
	a. Elevators, Dumbwaiters & Lifts	(07)	102,000	
	b. Moving Stairs & Walks	(07)		
	c. Conveyors, Hoists, Etc.	(07)		
	d. Pneumatic Tube Systems	(07)		
	e. Other			

FIGURE 4-5 _continued_ (d)

Project _COMPUTER PROCESSING CENTER_ Gross SF 61,819 Date 1-79

Div.	Item Description	Uniformat Element Assignment	Estimated Cost	Cost Per GSF
15.	Mechanical		542,000	8.77
	a. Exterior Mechanical (to 5 ft. of bldg)	(123)	19,000	
	b. Water Supply & Treatment	(081)	36,000	
	c. Waste Water Disposal & Treatment	(081)	52,000	
	d. Plumbing Fixtures	(081)	30,000	
	e. Fire Protection Systems & Equipment	(083)	65,000	
	f. Heat Generation Equipment	(082)	20,000	
	g. Refrigeration	(082)	20,000	
	h. HVAC Piping, Ductwork & Terminal Units	(082)	210,000	
	i. Controls & Instrumentation	(082)	60,000	
	j. Insulation (plumbing)	(081)	4,000	
	k. Insulation (HVAC)	(082)	26,000	
	l. Special Mechanical Systems	(084)		
	m. Other			
16.	Electrical		227,000	3.11
	a. Utilities & Serv. Ent. to 5 ft. of Bldg.	(123)	1,000	
	b. Substations & Transformers	(091)	3,000	
	c. Distribution & Panel Boards	(091)	45,000	
	d. Lighting Fixtures	(092)	60,000	
	e. Branch Wiring & Devices	(092)	80,000	
	f. Special Electrical Systems	(093)	20,000	
	g. Communications	(093)	18,000	
	h. Electric Heating	(093)		
	i. Other			
	Total Construction Costs		2,792,500	44.36
	Contingency @ 10 %		279,250	4.44
	Escalation @ 11 %		331,892	5.37
	Construction @ Bid Date		3,340,592	54.17

FIGURE 4-5 _continued_ (e)

Project _COMPUTER PROCESSING CENTER_

Gross Square Footage (GSF — Note 1) _61,819_   Bid Date _10-79_ Date _1-79_

Element (Levels 2 & 3)	Estimated Cost ($)	Cost Per GSF	%	Element Quantity	Unit	Cost Per Elem. Qty.
01 Foundation	32,500	0.53	1.2	32,507	SF[2]	1.00
011 Standard Foundations	32,500	0.53	1.2	32,507	SF[2]	1.00
012 Special Foundation Cond.					LS	
02 Substructure	41,000	0.66	1.5	32,507	SF[2]	1.26
021 Slab on Grade	41,000	0.66	1.5	32,507	SF[2]	1.26
022 Basement Excavation					SF[2]	
023 Basement Walls					SF[3]	
03 Superstructure	423,000	6.84	15.4	61,819	SF[4]	6.84
031 Floor Construction	225,000	3.64	8.2	29,312	SF[5]	7.68
032 Roof Construction	182,000	2.94	6.6	32,507	SF[6]	5.60
033 Stair Construction	16,000	0.26	0.6	8	LANDING	2000
Total Structural (01-03)	496,500	8.03	18.1	750,000	CF[13]	0.66
04 Exterior Closure	192,500	3.11	7.0	14,927	SF[7]	12.90
041 Exterior Walls	173,000	2.80	6.3	14,711	SF[8]	11.76
042 Exterior Doors & Windows	19,500	0.31	0.7	216	SF[9]	90.29
05 Roofing	113,000	1.83	4.1	32,507	SF[6]	3.48
06 Interior Construction	615,000	9.95	22.4	208,000	SF[10]	2.96
061 Partitions	102,000	1.65	3.7	30,000	SF[11]	3.40
062 Interior Finishes	490,000	7.93	17.9	178,000	SF[12]	2.75
063 Specialties	23,000	0.37	0.8	208,000	SF[10]	0.11
07 Conveying Systems	102,000	1.65	3.7	6	LANDING	17000
Total Architectural (04-07)	1,022,500	16.54	37.3	750,000	CF[13]	1.36

Notes:

1. Facility gross square footage as per AIA/GSA.
2. Footprint area at grade level.
3. Area of basement walls below grade.
4. Total area suspended floor and roof structure.
5. Area of suspended floors.
6. Area of roof structure.
7. Total exterior area (walls, doors & windows).
8. Area exterior wall (above grade).
9. Area of exterior doors and windows.
10. Total area finished (including partitions).
11. Area of partitions (excl. openings).
12. Total area finished (excl. partitions).

FIGURE 4-6
Cost summary matrix based on GSA/AIA UNIFORMAT.

Calculations should be made for the gross floor area of buildings, using the industry standard "AIA Method of Measurement." The building volume measurement also provides the opportunity to translate costs into dollars per cubic foot. The ratio of gross floor area to volume provides the average floor-to-floor heights, useful in interpreting unit cost data. (See Figure 4-9 for a graphical presentation of the "AIA Method of Measurement.")

Until working drawings and specifications are completed and detailed estimates are to be prepared, the form of analysis just discussed will save time and give the designer an efficient system of pricing.

Parameter Estimating

A second method of estimating costs, called Parameter Costs of Buildings, was developed by _Engineering News-Record_. The data are derived from contractor-reported actual costs and are published in detail for each project. Figure 4-10 illustrates a typical report.

Parameter costs are useful in developing feasibility studies, calculating preliminary budgets, aiding design decisions, assisting in value engineering, determining and checking bids, and simplifying cost control. Given an approximate building configuration, designers use building parameters to prepare a preliminary estimate for a build-

Project _COMPUTER PROCESSING CENTER_

Gross Square Footage (GSF — Note 1) _61,819_   Bid Date _10·79_ Date _1·79_

Element (Levels 2 & 3)	Estimated Cost ($)	Cost Per GSF	%	Element Quantity	Unit	Cost Per Elem. Qty.
08 Mechanical	523,000	8.46	19.1	750,000	CF[13]	0.70
081 Plumbing	122,000	1.97	4.4	69	FIXT[14]	1768
082 HVAC	336,000	5.44	12.3	450	TONS[15]	746
083 Fire Protection	65,000	1.05	2.4	55,000	SF[16]	1.18
084 Special Mechanical Systems					LS	
09 Electrical	226,000	3.66	8.3	300	KVA[17]	753
091 Service & Distribution	48,000	0.78	1.8	300	KVA[17]	160
092 Lighting & Power	140,000	2.26	5.1	607	FIXT[14]	231
093 Special Electrical Systems	38,000	0.62	1.4		LS	
10 General Conditions & Profit	345,000	5.58	12.6			
1001 Mobilization Expenses	10,000	0.16	0.4			
1002 Job Site Overhead	125,000	2.02	4.6			
1003 Demobilization	5,000	0.08	0.2			
1004 Office Expense & Profit	205,000	3.32	7.5			
11 Equipment						
111 Fixed and Movable Equip.						
112 Furnishings						
113 Special Construction						
Total Building (01-11)	2,613,000	42.27	95.3	750,000	CF[13]	3.48
12 Site Work	129,500	2.09	4.7	105,000	SF[18]	1.23
12A Overhead & Profit				"	SF[18]	
121 Site Preparation	28,500	0.46	1.0	"	SF[18]	0.27
122 Site Improvements	49,000	0.79	1.8	"	SF[18]	0.47
123 Site Utilities	52,000	0.84	1.9	"	SF[18]	0.49
124 Off-Site Work				"	SF[18]	
Total Construction (01-12)	2,742,500	44.36	100	750,000	CF	3.66
Contingency @ 10 %	274,500	4.44				
Escalation @ 11 %	331,842	5.37				
Construction @ Bid Date	3,348,592	54.17				

Notes:

13. Total enclosed facility volume (CF).
14. Total number of fixtures.
15. Combined total of [heating (Btu/hr) & cooling (Btu/hr)] ÷ 12,000 Btu/ton.
16. Total area.
17. KVA demand, equivalent to transformer rating.
18. Gross site area.

FIGURE 4-6 _continued_

ing. In addition, costs of alternatives may be derived with the aid of parameters.

For example, to estimate using the parameter method, the total cost of a specific work item such as foundation construction is divided by a physical parameter (measure) such as the basement area. The resulting figure is used to estimate the cost of a similar work item in another building. Ideally, the other building should be in the same geographical area; however, this not required. The estimate may be transformed for use in other areas and updated by applying ENR's _20 Cities Building Cost Index_ series for the appropriate relationships.

Sources of Information

Estimated prices for various materials and operations are contained in various unit price publications. Costs are reasonably detailed, and the books are often marketed to contracting and subcontracting firms as well as to the design professions.

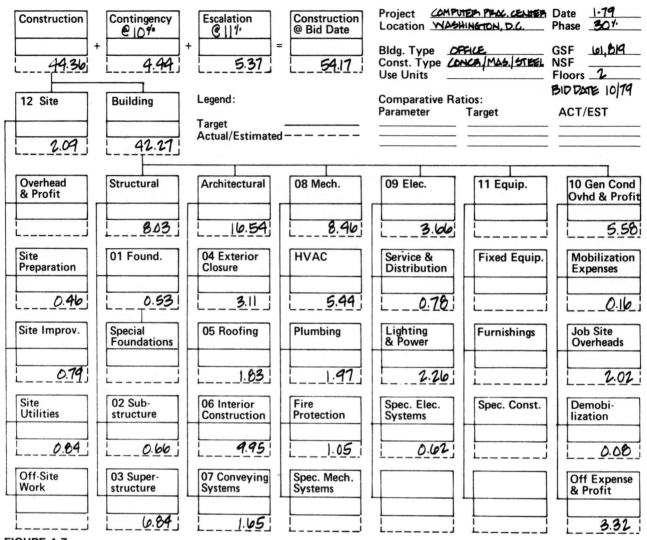

FIGURE 4-7
Cost model, computer processing center.

Among the best known of at least a dozen of these books is *Building Construction Cost Data,* published by Robert Snow Means Company, Inc., of Kingston, Massachusetts. Another is the *Dodge Manual for Building Construction Pricing and Scheduling,* a publication of McGraw-Hill Information Systems Company of New York City, produced in cooperation with Wood & Tower, Inc. A third is the *Building Cost File* published by Van Nostrand Rheinhold on a four-regional basis.

Such volumes are useful sources of detailed construction cost information and can be helpful in preparing estimates once design documentation is developed to the point that an accurate quantity survey can be made.

Value appraisal manuals are published mainly for the appraisal profession to assist in the preparation of replacement cost estimates for existing structures. They also achieve a steady sale within the construction industry as

they offer possibilities for producing preliminary cost estimates from minimum details. All supply regional cost modifiers to adapt base costs to a specific locality, and some issue special residential building valuation manuals.

One of a number in common circulation is the *Marshall Valuation Service,* published by Marshall and Swift Publication Company of Los Angeles. Released in three volumes, *Boeckh Building Valuation Manual* is the work of the American Appraisal Company of Milwaukee, with a bimonthly *Building Cost Modifier* available. McGraw-Hill also publishes a manual called *Dodge Cost Calculator and Valuation Guide,* with quarterly supplements.

The only extensive feedback of actual building costs marketed in the United States comes from McGraw-Hill as part of the Dodge construction contract reporting operation. As soon as a contract award becomes known, a questionnaire is mailed to the project architect in an at-

LEVEL 2	LEVEL 3	LEVEL 4
01 FOUNDATIONS	011 STANDARD FOUNDATIONS	0111 Wall Foundations
		0112 Col. Foundations & Pile Caps
	012 SPEC FOUNDATION COND	0121 Pile Foundations
		0122 Caissons
		0123 Underpinning
		0124 Dewatering
		0125 Raft Foundations
		0126 Other Spec Foundation Cond
02 SUBSTRUCTURE	021 SLAB ON GRADE	0211 Standard Slab on Grade
		0212 Structural Slab on Grade
		0213 Inclined slab on Grade
		0214 Trenches, Pits & Bases
		0215 Foundation Drainage
	022 BASEMENT EXCAVATION	0221 Excavation for Basements
		0222 Structure Fill & Compact
		0223 Shoring
	023 BASEMENT WALLS	0231 Basement Wall Construction
		0232 Moisture Protection
		0233 Basement Wall Insulation
03 SUPERSTRUCTURE	031 FLOOR CONSTRUCTION	0311 Susp Basement Floor Const
		0312 Upper Floors Construction
		0313 Balcony Construction
		0314 Ramps
		0315 Special Floor Construction
	032 ROOF CONSTRUCTION	0321 Flat Roof Construction
		0322 Pitched Roof Construction
		0323 Canopies
		0324 Special Roof Systems
	033 STAIR CONSTRUCTION	0331 Stair Structure
04 EXT CLOSURE	041 EXTERIOR WALLS	0411 Exterior Wall Construction
		0412 Exterior Louvers & Screens
		0413 Sun Control Devises (Ext)
		0414 Balcony Walls & Handrails
		0415 Exterior Soffits
	042 EXT DOORS & WINDOWS	0421 Windows
		0422 Curtain Walls
		0423 Exterior Doors
		0424 Storefronts
05 ROOFING		0501 Roof Coverings
		0502 Traf Topng & Paving Membr
		0503 Roof Insulation & Fill
		0504 Flashing & Trim
		0505 Roof Openings
06 INT CONST	061 PARTITIONS	0611 Fixed Partitions
		0612 Demountable Partitions
		0613 Retractable Partitions
		0614 Compartments & Cubicles
		0615 Int Balustrades & Screens
		0616 Interior Doors & Frames
		0617 Interior Storefronts
	062 INTERIOR FINISHES	0621 Wall Finishes
		0622 Floor
		0623 Ceiling Finishes
	063 SPECIALTIES	0631 General Specialties
		0632 Built-in Fittings
07 CONVEYING SYS		0701 Elevators
		0702 Moving Stair & Walks
		0703 Dumbwaiters
		0704 Pneumatic Tube Systems
		0705 Other Conveying Systems
		0706 General Construction Items
08 MECHANICAL	081 PLUMBING	0811 Domestic Water Supply Sys
		0812 Sanitary Waste & Vent Sys
		0813 Rainwater Drainage Sys
		0814 Plumbing Fixtures
	082 H.V.A.C.	0821 Energy Supply
		0822 Heat Generating System
		0823 Cooling Generating System
		0824 Distribution Systems
		0825 Terminal & Package Units
		0826 Controls & Instrumentation
		0827 Systems Testing & Balancing
	083 FIRE PROTECTION	0831 Water Supply (Fire Protect)
		0832 Sprinklers
		0833 Standpipe Systems
		0834 Fire Extinguishers

LEVEL 2	LEVEL 3	LEVEL 4
	084 SPEC MECHANICAL SYST	0841 Special Plumbing Systems
		0842 Spec Fire Protection Sys
		0843 Misc Spec Sys & Devices
		0844 Gen Const Items (Mech)
09 ELECTRICAL	091 SERVICE & DISTRIBUT	0911 High Tension Service & Dist
		0912 Low Tension Service & Dist
	092 LIGHTING AND POWER	0921 Branch Wiring
		0922 Lighting Equipment
	093 SPEC ELECTRICAL SYST	0931 Communications & Alarm Sys
		0932 Grounding Systems
		0933 Emergency Light & Power
		0934 Electric Heating
		0935 Floor Raceway Systems
		0936 Other Spec Sys & Devices
		0937 General Construction Items
10 GEN COND OH&P		1001 Mobilization & Init Expenses
		1002 Site Overheads
		1003 Demobilization
		1004 Main Off Expense & Profit
11 EQUIPMENT	111 FIXED & MOVABLE EQUIP	1111 Built-in Maintenance Equip
		1112 Checkroom Equipment
		1113 Food Service Equipment
		1114 Vending Equipment
		1115 Waste Handling Equipment
		1116 Loading Dock Equipment
		1117 Parking Equipment
		1118 Detention Equipment
		1119 Postal Equipment
		1120 Other Specialized Equipment
	112 FURNISHINGS	1121 Artwork
		1122 Window Treatment
		1123 Seating
		1124 Furniture
		1125 Rugs, Mats & Furn Acces
	113 SPECIAL CONSTRUCTION	1131 Vaults
		1132 Interior Swimming Pools
		1133 Modular Prefab Assembles
		1134 Special Purpose Rooms
		1135 Other Special Construction
12 SITE WORK	121 SITE PREPARATION	1211 Clearing
		1212 Demolition
		1213 Site Earthwork
	122 SITE IMPROVEMENTS	1221 Parking Lots
		1222 Roads, Walks, Terraces
		1223 Site Development
		1224 Landscaping
	123 SITE UTILITIES	1231 Water Supply & Dist Sys
		1232 Drainage & Sewage Systems
		1233 Heating & Cooling Dist Sys
		1234 Elec Dist & Lighting Sys
		1235 Snow Melting Systems
		1236 Service Tunnels
	124 OFF-SITE WORK	1241 Railroad Work
		1242 Marine Work
		1243 Tunneling
		1244 Other Off-Site Work

FIGURE 4-8
Cost control and estimating system based on GSA UNIFORMAT and AIA MASTERCOST.

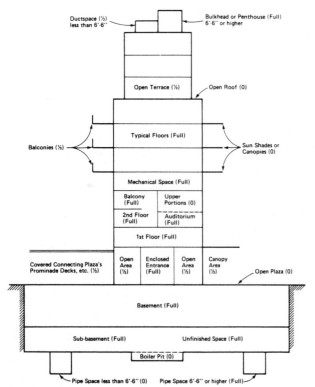

FIGURE 4-9
Example of gross floor area method of measurement.

tempt to collect basic data on the building relating to award cost, floor area, outline specifications, and some other details. This approach produces information on a considerable number of buildings, for which a rudimentary form of cost analysis can be prepared and is published in an manual called the *Dodge Digest of Building Costs and Specifications,* with semiannual supplements. No evaluation of the data is made, but it serves as a check of early square-footage estimates.

As an important part of Dodge Building Cost Services, McGraw-Hill, in conjunction with Wood & Tower, initiated publication in 1975 of an annual building cost and assembly manual that offers composite unit rates suitable for use in preliminary estimating stages. Called *Dodge Construction Systems Costs,* it is based on an elemental method that varies somewhat from the UNIFORMAT categories.

The Robert Snow Means Company also has an early-stage systems pricing book, which is a very useful guide for making design assumptions and pricing the results. There are a few sources of intermittent building cost information, including a series initiated by *Progressive Architecture* in 1973 under the heading *P/A Building Cost File.* As previously discussed, *Engineering News-Record* for many years has published a parameter cost series giving trade cost analyses of several projects in its quarterly cost issue.

On the West Coast, the monthly *Architectural Design*

Cost and Data produces anywhere from three to six building cost analyses on a trade basis, together with building descriptions, articles, and advertisements. Some of the case studies are incorporated in the *Preliminary Cost Guide* published by Architectural Data Corporation of Pasadena, California. In addition, Lee Saylor of Walnut Creek, California, issues a unit cost file.

Several cost consultants offer computerized estimating systems, some of which are specifically designed to assist architects and owners with early cost estimates. They usually contain extensive cost data bases, but such information is seldom marketed separately from the cost estimating services provided by cost consultants. One of the oldest, by William Orr of Fort Worth, Texas, is a system based on estimating parameters that are essentially the same as the building elements listed in the UNIFORMAT elemental breakdown. A considerable amount of development continues to be done in this area. The firm of Smith, Hinchman & Grylls Associates, Inc., together with the associate firm of Comprehensive Management Services, Inc., (CMSI) have developed an automated cost estimating system, which will be available for use by others in mid-1981 (McAuto Computer Network). This system, through a series of "work packages," simplifies quantity takeoffs to provide more *market analysis* time for the estimator. The automated system will use the R. S. Means Building Construction Cost Data for pricing information. All cost estimating, whether manual or automated, relies on historical data and experience in one form or another, the collection and retrieval of which is a costly but essential process.

Summary

Most cost estimating of construction projects to date has been trade-oriented. Certainly, the ability to modify design and to substitute materials and specifications are key tools in overall cost control. The elemental analysis system provides a more meaningful approach at the early stages.

Designers are called on continually to offer greater cost control services and information, and the degree of liability assumed in so doing cannot be underestimated. The use of elemental estimating techniques can expand capabilities to deal with problems in this area and provide information for earlier decision making. The availability of a broad data base and improved cost control procedures for capital costs and other life cycle costs will have tremendous impact in the coming years.

ENERGY AND OPERATING COSTS

Until the past few years, most [owners] have not been too concerned about getting maximum exchange for their energy dollars because of the abundance or relatively low cost of fuel and power. . . . Value engineered en-

	Courthouse	Church	Medical facility—ambulatory care
Type of Building	Courthouse	Church	Medical facility—ambulatory care
Location	Savannah, Ga.	Fond du lac, Wisconsin	Dayton, Ohio
Construction start complete	Oct. '76/Sept. '78	Oct. '77/June '78	Nov. '76/Feb. '78
Type of owner	Public	Private	Private
Frame	Reinf. concrete	Laminated wood	Precast concrete
Exterior walls	Precast	Load-bearing brick	Masonry
Special site work	—		
Fire rating	Fire resistive	Fire resistive	1-A

PARAMETER MEASURES:

	Courthouse	Church	Medical facility
1. Gross enclosed floor area	142.636 sf	16,000 sf	109,000 sf
2. Gross area supported (excl. slab on grade)	122,512 sf	16,000 sf	109,000 sf
3. Total basement floor area	20,412 sf		
4. Roof area	20,063 sf	16,000 sf	109,000 sf
5. Net finished area	561,072 sf	48,000 sf	482,000 sf
6. No. of floors including basements	7	1 ea	1
7. No. of floors excluding basements	1	1 ea	
8. Area of face brick	—	9,500 sf	34,500 sf
9. Area of other exterior wall	45,822 sf		
10. Area of curtain wall incl. glass		—	—
11. Store front perimeter	120 lf	78 lf	40 lf
12. Interior partitions	20,975 lf	460 lf (masonry/wood)	9,400 lf
13. HVAC	604 tons	36 tons	500 ton
14. Parking area	—		242,500 sf

OTHER MEASURES:

	Courthouse	Church	Medical facility
Area of typical floor	20,063	16,000 sf	109,000 sf
Story height, typical floor	12 ft	10 to 26 ft.	13 ft, 4 in.
Lobby area	4,691 sf	1,240 sf	9,600 sf
No. of plumbing fixtures	184	22 ea	216
No. of elevators	6	—	—

DESIGN RATIOS:

	Courthouse	Church	Medical facility
A/C ton per building sq ft	.0042	0.0023	0.0046
Parking sq ft per building sq ft	—		2.22
Plumbing fixtures as per building sq ft	.0013	0.0014	0.0020

TRADE	Code	Unit	Parameter Cost: Cost	Total Cost: Amount	%	Code	Unit	Parameter Cost: Cost	Total Cost: Amount	%	Code	Unit	Parameter Cost: Cost	Total Cost: Amount	%
General conditions and fee	1	sf	4.11	586.593	10 8	1	sf	5.73	91,600	12 45	1	sf	6.57	716.400	9 5
Sitework (clearing and grubbing)	3	sf	0.80	16,280	0 3	1	sf	0.11	1,800	0 2	1	sf	0.04	4.500	0 1
Utilities	1	sf	—	—	—	1	sf	0.53	8.400	1.1	1	sf	1.67	182.500	2 4
Roads and walks	3	sf	1.70	34.788	0.6	5	sf	0.17	8.000	1.1	1	sf	0.25	27.300	0 4
Landscaping	3	sf	1.61	32.930	0.6	5	sf	0.11	5.500	0.8	1	sf	0.64	69.600	1 0
Excavation	3	sf	2.35	48.045	0.9	2	sf	1.77	28.300	3.9	1	sf	1.95	212.200	2 8
Foundation	3	sf	2.48	50.604	0.9	2	sf	1.63	26.100	3.6	1	sf	0.21	23.400	0 3
Caissons and pilings	—	—	—	—	—	2	sf	0.65	10.500	1.4	1	sf	1.35	147.000	1 9
Formed concrete	1	sf	6.11	872.101	16 1	2	sf	0.38	6.000	0.8	1	sf	2.89	315.500	4 2
Exterior masonry	—	—	—	—	—	8	sf	7.58	72.000	9.8	8	sf	6.60	227.700	3 0
Interior masonry	5	sf	0.09	48.950	0.9	8	sf	6.11	58.000	7.9	—	—	—	—	—
Stone, granite, marble	1	sf	0.13	18.605	0.3	—	—	—	—	—	—	—	—	—	—
Structural steel	—	—	—	—	—	2	sf	1.01	16.100	2.2	—	—	—	—	—
Misc. metal, incl. stairs	1	sf	0.47	66.613	0.1	—	—	—	—	—	1	sf	1.09	118 700	1 6
Ornamental metal	—	—	—	—	—	—	—	—	—	—	—	—	—	—	—
Carpentry	1	sf	0.14	20.037	0 4	1	sf	1.78	28.500	3.9	1	sf	0.53	57.800	0 8
A/C enclosures	—	—	—	—	—	—	—	—	—	—	—	—	—	—	—
Waterproofing and dampproofing	1	sf	0.21	29.269	0.5	4	sf	0.08	1.300	0.2	1	sf	0.13	14.600	0 2
Roofing and flashing	4	sf	0.98	19.745	0.4	4	sf	1.67	26.800	3.6	4	sf	1.26	137.500	1 8
Metal doors and frames	5	sf	0.10	55.958	1.0	1	sf	0.54	8.600	1.2	5	sf	0.16	78.400	1 0
Metal windows	5	sf	0.10	56.093	1.0	1	sf	0.22	3.500	0 5	1	sf	0.34	36.700	0 5
Wood doors, windows, and trim	5	sf	0.08	47.051	0.9	1	sf	0.13	2.100	0.3	5	sf	0.07	35.000	0 5
Hardware	5	sf	0.11	63.300	1.2	1	sf	0.48	7.600	1.0	5	sf	0.11	52.900	0 7
Glass and glazing (total)	1	sf	0.12	17.746	0.3	1	sf	0.31	500	0.1	5	sf	0.14	65.400	0 9
Store front and lobby	11	lf	251.80	30.216	0.6	11	lf	76.92	6.000	0.8	11	lf	1,105.00	44.200	0 6
Curtain wall	11	lf	2,589.96	310.795	5.8	11	lf	66.66	5.200	0.7	—	—	—	—	—
Lath & plaster	5	sf	0.01	2.859	0.1	—	—	—	—	—	5	sf	0.09	41.000	0 5
Drywall	5	sf	0.81	451.684	8.4	1	sf	0.19	3.100	0 4	5	sf	0.46	220.700	2 9
Tile work	5	sf	0.04	24.477	0.5	1	sf	0.29	4.700	0.6	5	sf	0.02	9.300	0 1
Terrazzo	—	—	—	—	—	—	—	—	—	—	—	—	—	—	—
Acoustical ceiling	1	sf	0.62	89.113	1.7	4	sf	0.18	2.900	0.4	4	sf	0.90	98.500	1 3
Resilient flooring	1	sf	0.34	47.780	0.9	1	sf	0.07	1.100	0.2	1	sf	0.47	51.000	0 7
Carpet	1	sf	0.26	37.113	0.7	1	sf	0.84	13.400	1.8	1	sf	0.81	88.400	1 1
Painting	5	sf	0.05	29.082	0.5	1	sf	0.31	4.900	0.7	5	sf	0.25	121.000	1 6
Toilet partitions	1	sf	0.05	6.980	0.1	1	sf	0.04	600	0.1	1	sf	0.05	5.600	0 1
Special waste treatment	—	—	—	—	—	—	—	—	—	—	—	—	—	—	—
Venetian blinds	1	sf	0.07	10.271	0.2	—	—	—	—	—	1	sf	0.03	3.300	0 1
Special equipment	1	sf	0.13	18.046	0 3	1	sf	0.45	7.200	1 0	1	sf	4.08	445.000	5 9
Elevators	1	sf	2.00	285.707	5.3	—	—	—	—	—	—	—	—	—	—
Plumbing	1	sf	1.87	267.778	4.9	1	sf	5.71	91.400	12 4	1	sf	5.10	555.900	7 4
Sprinklers	—	—	—	—	—	—	—	—	—	—	—	—	—	—	—
HVAC	13	ton	3.66	772.443	14 3	13	ton	in plumbing			1	sf	12.67	1.381.800	18 3
Electrical: contracts	1	sf	1.31	522.295	9.6	1	sf	2.97	47.500	6 5	1	sf	8.01	872.700	11 5
fixtures	1	sf	1.31	186.656	3.5	—	—	—	—	—	1	sf	2.08	227.000	3 0
Miscellaneous trades	1	sf	1.62	230.607	4.3	4	sf	2.25	107.800	14 6	1	sf	6.23	678.600	9 0
Parking: Outside, enclosed	—	—	—	—	—	—	—	—	—	—	—	—	—	—	—
Open, paved	—	—	—	—	—	—	—	—	—	—	1	sf	1.83	200.000	2 6
TOTAL	1	sf	37.92	5.408.610	100	1	sf	46.00	736.000	100	1	sf	69.42	7.567.100	100

(a) includes laminated beams & deck. $71,000: millwork & casework. $19,800: sheet metal and skylight. $17,000 (b) includes graphics. $19,430, lightweight roof deck $19,436. millwork & casework. $47,246. jury & judges chair. $42,600: speciality modules. $33,923 and misc. trades. $67,972. (c) includes hospital & laboratory equip., $207,000: hospital casework. $238,000. (d) includes precast frame & deck, $396,000, skylight & space frame, $191,700.

FIGURE 4-10
Example parameter costs. *(Reprinted from Engineering News-Record, June 21, 1979, Copyright, McGraw-Hill, Inc., all rights reserved.)*

ergy provides an organized approach that assures total energy sensitivity during the design process.

Bernard Stainton, "VEE: Value Engineered Energy," *Plant Engineering,* March 22, 1979.

Energy consumption represents approximately $1.00 to $1.50 per square foot per year of annual life cycle costs of a typical office facility. As discussed earlier, operating costs include all energy-consuming elements of a facility. These normally fall into the categories of heating, cooling, ventilation, lighting, domestic hot water, and other miscellaneous loads. This section addresses various estimating methods, energy-modeling techniques, and energy-savings opportunities.

Figure 4-11 illustrates the relative cost impact of energy on the various UNIFORMAT system categories of a typical office facility. For example, this chart shows that the structure's exterior closure influences about 9.5 percent of the total energy consumed in a facility because of the heat gain and loss through the skin system. Lighting is the most significant influence, contributing as much as 48 percent from direct lighting energy and the indirect influence of additional heat in the space, which must then be cooled.

Resources to meet the human comfort needs include the building itself, the energy used, and the skills at hand to operate the building. A shortage in one area may be made up for by an abundance in another. Thus, a lack of energy can be compensated for by more skillful operation or an improved building. Efficient energy use should not and need not be achieved at the expense of comfort.

Efficient energy use incorporates some or all of the following approaches:

- Collecting the natural energy (heat, light, nocturnal cooling, air movement) that flows through a building, and storing it for use when needed (such as storing in the floor mass the abundant solar heat that comes through a south-facing window).
- Conserving collected energy (as by double-glazing a south-facing window).
- Using waste heat from building processes, building equipment, and power-generating equipment.
- Using renewable energy sources that function independently of the building design (such as active solar heating and cooling, solar energy from photovoltaics, wind, and geothermal and tidal energies).
- Efficiently converting nonrenewable energy sources into forms required by the building (such as carefully selected furnaces and chillers).[1]

1. Sizemore, Clark, & Ostrander, *Energy Planning for Buildings,* American Institute of Architects, 1979.

Energy-Estimating Methods

The designer must estimate the energy consumption of many types of equipment. Some equipment always operates at the same energy consumption rate. The energy consumption is found by multiplying the consumption rate by the hours of operation. Other equipment operates at variable rates. At least four estimating methods are available:

- Equivalent full-load hours.
- Degree days.
- Hour-by-hour.
- Outside temperature bins.

The *equivalent full-load hour method* calls for judgment, project information, and data from previous projects to estimate the equivalent number of full-load hours of operation per month for each item of equipment. These hours are multiplied by the hourly full-load rate of energy consumption. This yields the required energy consumption. The estimate is improved by using average-load efficiency instead of full-load efficiency of the variable-load equipment items. Still, accuracy of the results depends mainly on the user's judgment. This method is best for estimating consumption of items such as elevators and office equipment. In HVAC energy estimating, it is useful for making quick, early-stage estimates.

The *degree-day* method is also common in early-concept design work, chiefly for heating season estimates. It establishes a base temperature, usually 65°F, below which the building begins to require heating. Heating requirements are calculated for a 24-hour design-load heating period. The results are divided by the difference between the 65°F base temperature and the outside heating design temperature to obtain the Btu requirements per degree day. This value is multiplied by the number of monthly or annual degree days from weather data. These loads are then divided by the furnace efficiency to estimate the energy consumed to meet the load. This is an empirical method based on statistical samples of large numbers of buildings, with no assurance of accuracy when applied to a specific project.

Most HVAC systems are designed to handle extreme heating and cooling weather conditions which occur less than 5 percent of the time. The remaining 95 percent of the time they operate less efficiently at part loads, with the average load at about 30 percent. A system that is highly efficient at full load is not necessarily efficient at reduced load. A thorough HVAC energy estimate should be "dynamic" so it can evaluate system performance over a full range of likely operating conditions. Dynamic analysis methods include the *hour-by-hour* and *bin* methods.

The *hour-by-hour* method computes the instantaneous building load, residual stored loads, and resulting HVAC system performance separately for each of the year's 8760 hours. It then adds them to obtain monthly and yearly

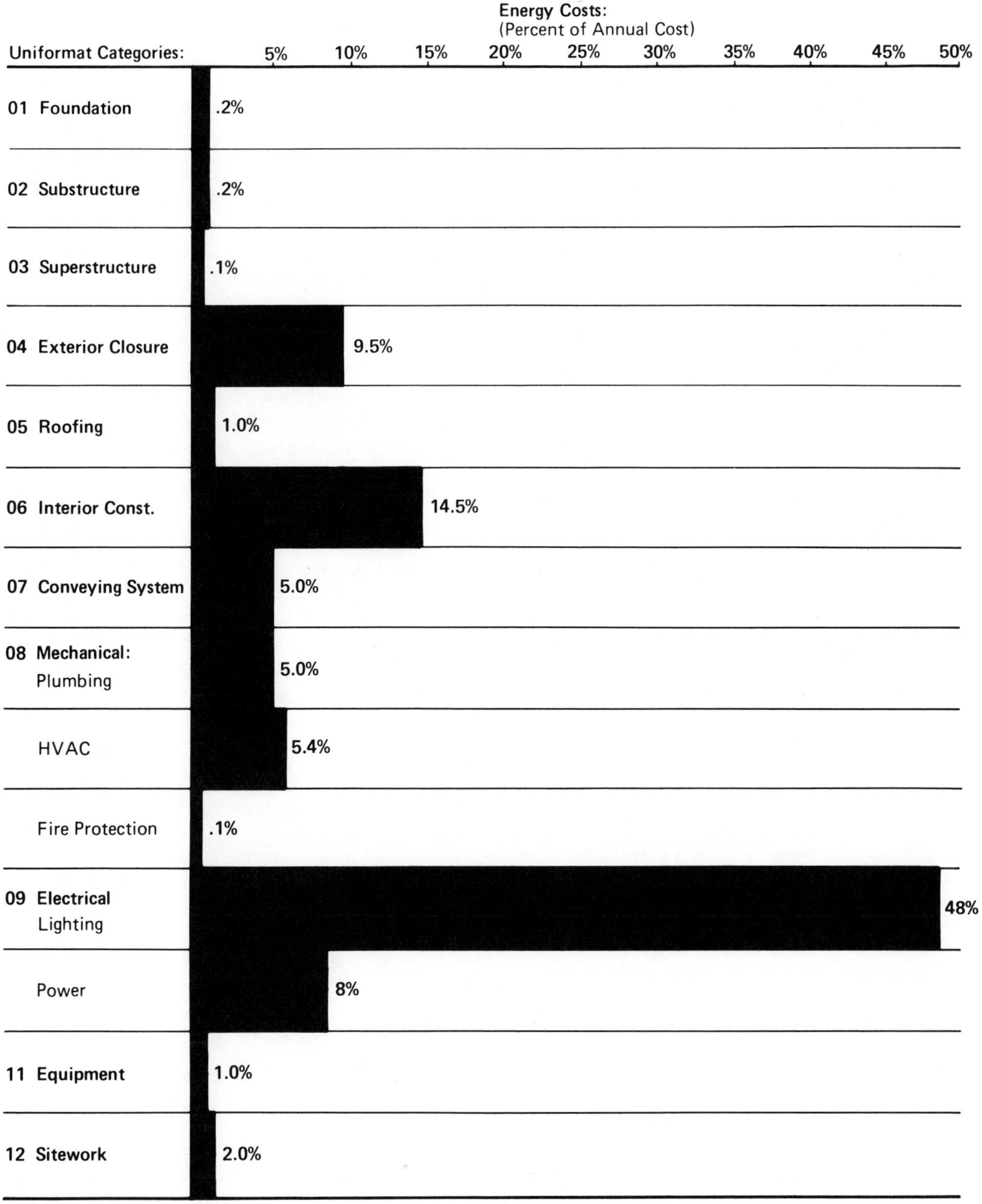

Energy Costs:
(Percent of Annual Cost)

Uniformat Categories:

01 Foundation	.2%
02 Substructure	.2%
03 Superstructure	.1%
04 Exterior Closure	9.5%
05 Roofing	1.0%
06 Interior Const.	14.5%
07 Conveying System	5.0%
08 Mechanical: Plumbing	5.0%
HVAC	5.4%
Fire Protection	.1%
09 Electrical Lighting	48%
Power	8%
11 Equipment	1.0%
12 Sitework	2.0%

FIGURE 4-11
Relative cost impact of energy.

consumption. Maximum demand (rate of energy use) is found by identifying the hour with the highest use. Building heat storage and temperature swing can also be simulated. Because of the amount of data handled, hour-by-hour analyses are often done by computer.

A modified hour-by-hour analysis may be done for one or more typical days of each month. The results for each day are multiplied by the number of assumed typical days to obtain the monthly energy consumption. This averaging, however, reduces the accuracy of the estimate by eliminating extremes of weather conditions, and solar and internal loads.

The *outside-temperature-bin* (a temperature bin is a range of outside temperatures, usually in 5°F increments) method is based on the principle that the load on an HVAC system is related to outside temperature. Like the typical-day-per-month, hour-by-hour method, it uses an averaging process and is therefore less correct than the true full-year hour-by-hour method. It does take into account internal loads, energy use created by patterns of operation and occupancy, and varying solar loads. The HVAC energy consumption at a few outside temperatures is calculated and the consumption at other temperatures and conditions is extrapolated. The bin method includes four steps:

- Plotting the energy profile (a graph of energy consumption versus outside temperature).
- Finding the number of hours in each outside temperature bin.
- Determining energy consumption for each temperature bin.
- Totaling energy consumption for bins.

A separate peak demand estimate is required if utility demand charges are to be estimated.

Computer programs are available using the hour-by-hour method; the typical-day-per-month, hour-by-hour method; and the bin method. They vary widely in ability to give accurate results for a particular situation. A program may provide an adequate solution for one situation and an inadequate solution for a different type of building or HVAC system. The inherent accuracy of a computer program depends on:

- Method of analysis, with the true hour-by-hour method having an advantage.
- Accuracy of load estimating. Many of the load-estimating methods incorporated into computer programs were developed to conservatively predict maximum design-load conditions, and are inaccurate in estimating part-load conditions.
- Accuracy of system response and equipment performance. Many programs are weak and inflexible in

this area. There are at least a dozen types of variable-air-volume systems available, yet most computer programs are unable to distinguish one from another.

Computers are able to manipulate a great number of weather conditions and perform a large number of error-free calculations. However, the program logic is frequently hidden, or described in such a manner as to make it difficult for the user to understand, resulting in possible misapplication of the program.

In the case of energy analysis, *accuracy* is a relative term that is virtually impossible to measure. There are always differences in use and occupancy, hours of building systems operations, control-point settings, building and system maintenance conditions, and actual and estimated weather conditions, which both create and explain differences between actual and estimated energy consumption. Annual energy estimates for the same building, using the popular computer programs, will vary as much as 30 percent.

The designer should be able to prepare analyses using both manual and computer methods. Simple preliminary analyses can usually be done more quickly and with less expense using a manual method. A manual analysis may be the only accurate alternative for unusual situations or for systems that have not been adequately programmed for computer use. The computer is the best choice for presenting a final polished analysis, especially if many alternatives are involved.

Energy Performance Standards

To better target energy performance standards for new buildings, the U.S. Department of Housing and Urban Development assigned the AIA Research Corporation the task of establishing a baseline of current practice. This baseline may be used for the evaluation of alternative systems to be used in new buildings. It was established by estimating the energy consumption of recent residential and nonresidential buildings from building design data. These Building Energy Performance Standards (BEPS), at the time of publication, were being reviewed by the Department of Energy for possible required use by the nation.[1]

The energy performance of buildings is a function of their physical characteristics, intended use, and climatic conditions. In order to calculate the annual energy consumption of the designed buildings, it was necessary for the research group to classify the variations in building type and climate across the country, define data requirements, identify a building sample, collect data on building

[1] *Federal Register*, Vol. 44, No. 230, Nov. 28, 1979, Department of Energy, Proposed Rule Energy Performance Standards for New Buildings.

designs, and employ consistent methods to calculate the energy performance from the several buildings.

Because of differences in design and construction practices and data availability buildings were divided into two major groups for data collection and data analysis. Nonresidential building types included commercial and multifamily high-rise residential construction. Residential building types included single-family homes, low-rise multifamily housing, and mobile homes.

The development of an adequate climatic classification system for data collection depended on isolating the climatic variables affecting energy consumption. Yet it was not possible to judge the variables' effect on energy use without building energy performance data for comparison.

An a priori climatic classification system for stratification of the building sample was constructed by the study group. This ensured that the locations chosen for data collection encompassed the range of climatic variation across the country. The following stratification based on

combinations of heating degree days and cooling degree hours was developed for the selection of data collection locations.

A revised system of heating and cooling degree-day regions (Figure 4-12) for data analysis and the tabulation of survey findings was developed by substituting more current cooling degree days for the cooling degree hours used for sample stratification.

1.	<2000 CDD >7000 HDD	5.	<2000 CDD 0–2000 HDD
2.	<2000 CDD 5500–7000 HDD	6.	>2000 CDD 0–2000 HDD
3.	<2000 CDD 4000–5500 HDD	7.	>2000 CDD 2000–4000 HDD
4.	<2000 CDD 2000–4000 HDD	CDD: Cooling degree day HDD: Heating degree day

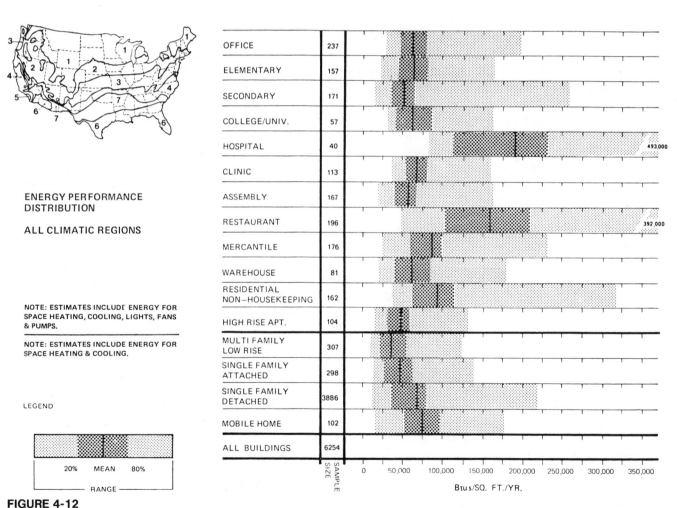

ENERGY PERFORMANCE DISTRIBUTION

ALL CLIMATIC REGIONS

NOTE: ESTIMATES INCLUDE ENERGY FOR SPACE HEATING, COOLING, LIGHTS, FANS & PUMPS.

NOTE: ESTIMATES INCLUDE ENERGY FOR SPACE HEATING & COOLING.

LEGEND

20% MEAN 80%

RANGE

Building Type	Sample Size
OFFICE	237
ELEMENTARY	157
SECONDARY	171
COLLEGE/UNIV.	57
HOSPITAL	40
CLINIC	113
ASSEMBLY	167
RESTAURANT	196
MERCANTILE	176
WAREHOUSE	81
RESIDENTIAL NON-HOUSEKEEPING	162
HIGH RISE APT.	104
MULTI FAMILY LOW RISE	307
SINGLE FAMILY ATTACHED	298
SINGLE FAMILY DETACHED	3886
MOBILE HOME	102
ALL BUILDINGS	6254

Btus/SQ. FT./YR.

FIGURE 4-12
Energy performance distribution, all climatic regions. (*Source: Energy Performance Standards for New Buildings, Phase I, AIA Research Corp. and Dept. of Energy, Jan. 12, 1978.*)

The intent of the building survey was to collect data on the most current design practices in order to calculate the energy performance of buildings. Actual buildings on which construction began in 1975 and 1976 were selected as the appropriate building population, from which the survey sample was chosen. These buildings represented the first generation of buildings designed since the 1973 oil embargo for which complete design data were available.

Use of design data from the sample buildings was appropriate for the study, since the performance standards would be used at the design rather than the operational stage. The design data accurately represent the variables within the control of the designers of actual buildings that, as designs, have satisfied their clients' functional and economic requirements.

The primary consideration in selecting a data analysis tool was that it produce accurate and reasonably precise estimates of energy performance from the sample buildings, using data that was readily available and practical to collect from building designers. A modified version of the AXCESS energy analysis computer program was selected as the tool to estimate the energy consumption of the sample buildings. This program met both the technical evaluation criteria and the resource constraints of the project. By assuming standard values for selected variables for each building type and using simplified building modeling techniques, it was possible to limit requirements for the survey form to 100 to 125 data points per building.

Figure 4-12 is a graphic presentation of the national summary statistics for nonresidential and residential performance estimates. The graph summarizes estimates of the designed energy performance of actual buildings throughout the continental United States on which construction began in 1975 and 1976. They are the result of processing data from 1661 nonresidential and 4593 residential data collection forms, representing 1661 nonresidential and high-rise apartment buildings and 344,529 low-rise residential units.

The estimates for nonresidential and high-rise apartment buildings include energy for space heating and cooling, lights, pumps, and fans. They do not include energy required for hot water; vertical transportation; or equipment such as computers, typewriters, and ovens; or process energy required for manufacturing and production. The estimates for low-rise residential buildings include energy for space heating and cooling but not for hot water. All the estimates represent energy use within building boundaries.

Standard operating and occupancy profiles were assumed for each building type in order to provide a consistent basis for comparison. (For example, office buildings were assumed to be occupied 9 hours per day and their heating and cooling equipment operated 10 hours per day, 5 days a week.)

Since the sample buildings were designed after the oil embargo of 1973, it is reasonable to expect that energy conservation was a more important criterion in their design than in the generation of buildings immediately preceding them. For instance, a preliminary analysis of the building characteristics of one building type, office buildings, has indicated higher thermal resistance values and lower installed lighting values than for pre-1974 buildings.

Figure 4-13 contains a series of bar charts indicating the relative percentage of each of the four energy end-use components measured by the phase I analysis: lighting, heating, cooling, and fans. These charts assist designers to proportion energy budgets for a given region of the country according to energy needs.

Energy Data for Analysis

The specific data and quantities for an energy estimate will vary from project to project. However, the information required may be organized into three types: building, environment, and mode of operation. The building data includes items such as:

- Floor areas and locations and uses for air-conditioned and heated spaces and nonconditioned spaces.
- Glass areas, including skylights; their orientation and shading (note type of glass and operation of windows).
- Wall and roof surface areas, thermal resistance, and weight (in the case of massive buildings).
- Building orientation, configuration, and solar access.
- Drawings, equipment schedules, and specifications for mechanical system design and distribution layout, including control diagrams for operation modes.
- Electrical drawings and reflected ceiling plans for lighting layout and fixture type and quantity.

Environmental or weather data for the project may be obtained from the local office of the National Weather Service, the Environmental Data Service of the National Oceanic and Atmospheric Administration (NOAA), U.S. Department of Commerce. Monthly heating and cooling degree days may also help in a comparison with similar buildings in other areas. Utility costs should be obtained from the utility company(s) to make energy source comparisons. Both energy peak demand and billing demand costs should be determined.

The designer must know how and when each piece of equipment is to be operated. Information should be gathered from the client to establish:

- Building operating hours (weekend, weekday).
- System and equipment control schedules.
- Control set points such as discharge air tempera-

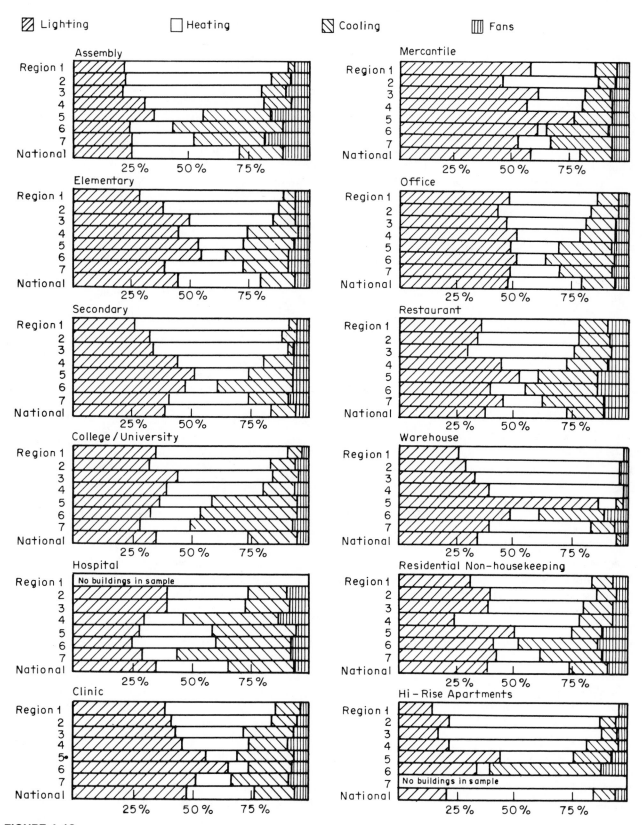

FIGURE 4-13

Energy end-use components. (Based on *Phase II Report for Development of Energy Performance Standards for New Buildings,* Task Report: Commercial and Multifamily Residential Buildings, HUD/DOE Report, January 1979.)

tures, chilled water temperatures, and freeze protection temperatures.

- Rooms, such as computer facilities, requiring special temperature control.
- Quantities of exhaust, outside ventilation, and air movement.

Information used in the analysis must be accurate, and any assumptions regarding use and operation must be documented. For instance, if HVAC equipment is assumed to operate 18 hours a day, 7 days a week, but really operates 12 hours a day, 5 days a week, then calculations will be very inaccurate. If cooling is assumed to operate an indoor temperature of 78°F but really operates at 72°F, results again will be misleading. If there are operable internal shading devices, are they to be taken as open, closed, or 50 percent closed?

If the building's energy use and costs during a specific year's operation are to be compared with actual records, it is important to specify the years, since weather, operations, use characteristics, and energy costs differ with various base years. All data must be related to the base year selected.

Energy Modeling*

Since energy consumption represents a major portion of total facility life cycle costs, a tool is required to assess the effect of energy reduction techniques. Depending on the progress of a facility design, the energy-modeling concept can be used to develop a basic energy budget or to indicate areas where potential energy savings exist. Unlike the cost model, the energy model uses energy units (EU) instead of dollars. These energy units can be translated into dollars, depending on the specific fuel chosen.

The energy model can be produced from a detailed energy analysis as well as from basic performance assumptions. The level of detail should be consistent with the amount of information available and the purposes intended. Since, in most cases, the results of the model will be used to make comparisons, the accuracy of calculations need only be sufficient to assure accuracy of comparison.

Figure 4-14 presents an example of an energy model produced for a utility company service center and used in a recent study. After projected consumption was examined, each area was studied in regard to potential energy savings. The target value (upper figure in each block) represents an optimum consumption that should meet requirements. A comparison between the target value and estimated value indicates where energy-saving potential exists. In this case, some 50 percent potential savings exist in the heating systems for shops and warehouses.

*This technique was first formally introduced by Bernard Stainton and Alphonse Dell'Isola in *Consulting Engineer*, August 1978, p. 76.

Several basic formats for developing an energy model exist. However, it must be understood that, unlike the cost model, no general-purpose energy model has yet been developed that covers all cases for all facilities. The following set of procedures is intended to provide a guideline and checklist for use in the preparation of an energy model. Generally, energy consumption for a facility will fall into the following major categories:

Heating, Cooling, & Ventilation: The ASHRAE Systems Handbook, Chapter 43, provides an excellent guide for the analysis of heating and cooling energy consumption. Appendix D, Tables D-1 to D-5, contains information excerpted from the ASHRAE guide and other reference material useful for estimating heating and cooling energy. It should be noted that other more exacting methods, such as the bin method or computerized techniques, are available. Use of such techniques is recommended when a more detailed analysis is required.

Lighting: Appendix D, Tables D-6 to D-8 provides basic data for estimating lighting levels and energy required for those levels for various types of fixtures. Table D-6 can be used for gross estimates.

Power: Power use varies significantly from facility to facility. A useful guideline is 0.25 watts per square foot for office structures to as high as 1 watt per square foot for specialty facilities (labs, etc.). Computer facilities, for example, may run as high as 10 to 50 watts per square foot for computer equipment areas.

Domestic Hot Water, Equipment, and Miscellaneous: Appendix D, Table D-9, presents basic guidelines for estimating hot water, equipment, and other loads. It should be noted that in many facilities domestic hot water energy use is the highest single item. Pump energy can be calculated by using the formulas in Table D-10.

General: The accuracy of the above estimate guidelines depends on a sound assessment of building occupancy schedules and use. Appendix D, Tables D-11 and D-12, provides heating values for various fuels and a list of energy conversion factors. Metric conversion factors are contained in Table D-13. Refer to the bibliography ("Estimating") for other sources of information helpful in determining energy consumption for various facilities.

Once the energy estimate has been made and the cost estimate prepared, one last step must be completed. The energy consumed should be reorganized into the UNIFORMAT systems categories. To assist in this process, refer back to Figure 4-13. The intent of this adjustment is to allocate energy loss to those areas controllable by the various disciplines. For example, heat loss and heat gain through the exterior closure and roof is most directly influenced by architectural decisions. Therefore, this portion of the energy consumed directly as a result of heat loss and gain is apportioned from the heating and cooling energy blocks. The HVAC category should include only the energy lost because of that equipment's inefficiency. It may

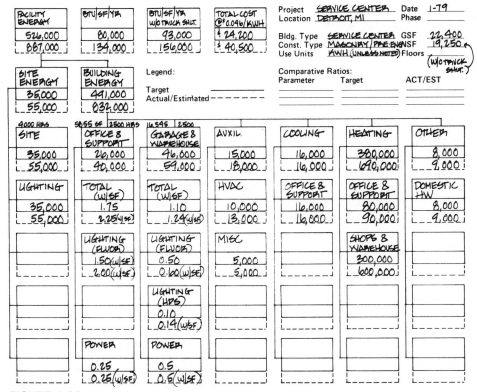

FIGURE 4-14
Energy model, service center.

also include those secondary pieces of equipment, such as cooling towers and pumps, used to produce cooling and heating.

Opportunities for Savings

The designer should review calculated loads from the analysis, as well as the relationships among the loads and between loads and the system response. Final results of energy performance calculations of themselves will not help in the absence of a broad understanding of the building's energy performance. It is essential that the designer note the key variables that determined the building's energy use during the energy analysis.

While opportunities for improvement may come from any source, the biggest ones will emerge from methodically reviewing the analysis. This is done by means of a series of questions, which will vary from one project to another. First the owner's concerns should be arranged in order of priorities. Then the factors that influence these concerns should be identified in order of their importance.

The designer must ask questions such as:

1. What is the owner's primary concern?
2. What determines the building's power or energy costs?

3. What modifications can be made to reduce consumption of the most significant item?

4. To which factors is the building's energy consumption sensitive?

Summary

This section was prepared to provide the designer with a basic look at the concepts and concerns that enter into an energy-estimating effort. The procedures remain essentially the same, whether it is a new or a retrofit life cycle study effort.

MAINTENANCE COSTS
Significance and Opportunities for Savings

Of the categories of life cycle costs, energy has received the most attention during the past several years. From the standpoint of owner cost impact, however, maintenance is usually the more significant cost item of an LCC study. The maintenance category alone averages in a typical office building approximately $1.50 to $2.50 per gross square foot per year. Ironically, this is just the cost that has received the least research and documentation for designers' use. This book presents in Appendix E a summary of maintenance data for typical kinds of construction.

What then is maintenance? Maintenance has been defined to include the costs of regular custodial care and repair, annual maintenance contracts, and salaries of facility staff performing maintenance tasks. Replacement items of less than $5,000 in value or having a life of less than 5 years are included as a part of maintenance. Thus, tasks such as replacing light bulbs and repainting are listed under the maintenance category.

Special care should be taken that system comparisons are based on comparable levels of maintenance. Estimates and data must refer to a uniform, optimum maintenance level. Much of the available historic data is not usable because one owner may be maintaining a facility in mint condition while another may permit considerable deterioration.

Some of the decisions with major maintenance implications are the following:

1. The choice of exterior and interior finishes—for example, the selection of high-quality surfaces that do not require painting or other recurring maintenance.

2. Selection of light fixtures, floor covering materials, and other interior elements with minimum routine repair and replacement requirements.

3. The decision whether to plan for and implement a preventive maintenance program, which can have implications for selection of the facility's equipment.

4. Whether to do most or all maintenance with full-time staff or to contract for the service.

Many of the individual elements that make up a facility have a shorter life cycle than that planned for the entire facility. As a result, replacement costs can become a major consideration in the evaluation of alternative items of equipment and other limited-life building elements.

For better understanding of the breakdown of maintenance costs with respect to design systems, Figure 4-15 provides an approximate percentage of annual costs for each of the UNIFORMAT level 2 categories discussed earlier. It can be seen that interior construction and mechanical systems have the most significant effect on maintenance costs. Designers must be especially careful when making decisions in these areas to consider the influence of maintenance on life cycle costs.

The opportunities for creative design for maintainability are enormous. Edwin Feldman, in his book entitled *Building Design for Maintainability,* points out that for most buildings maintenance costs will equal the original cost of construction (in undiscounted dollars) in as little as two or three decades. He also points out that, typically, architects, engineers, management, and interior decorators "just don't seem to care." This apparent lack of interest is perhaps because there has not been enough exposure to the economic importance of the subject; or perhaps too many people do not realize that an opportunity to minimize maintenance costs does indeed exist.

The greatest possible return on the maintenance dollar can be achieved when these costs are included in LCC analyses during the design stages of a facility. It is recommended that maintenance personnel, as well as the owner, work with the architect, engineers, and interior decorator in selecting materials and surfaces. Some architectural firms have already made moves in the direction of obtaining recommendations on maintainability and even of advising their clients on proper procedures.

Maintainability is an inherent characteristic of system design and installation that is concerned with ease, economy, safety, and accuracy in the performance of maintenance actions (that is, scheduled and unscheduled maintenance). Feldman defines it as "a characteristic of design and installation which is expressed as the probability that an item will be retained or restored to a specified condition within a given period of time when maintenance is performed in accordance with prescribed procedures and resources."

Estimating Methods and Maintenance Data

Maintainability can be specified, predicted, and measured. The primary measures of maintainability are a combination of maintenance times, supportability factors, and projected maintenance cost. Although this book does not attempt to provide statistical measures of accuracy for the data included, the following discussion of maintenance measures is appropriate.

The most common measures applicable in LCC are described below:

1. Mean time between maintenance (MTBM) is a function of both scheduled and unscheduled maintenance, and represents the average time between maintenance actions for a specified period or for the life cycle.

2. Mean preventive maintenance time (MPMT) is the mean (or average) elapsed time required to perform preventive or scheduled maintenance of an item. This may include servicing, inspection, calibration, and overhaul and can be accomplished when the system is in full operation or could result in downtime.

3. Mean active maintenance time (MAMT) is the mean elapsed time to perform scheduled (preventive) and unscheduled (corrective) maintenance.

As the state of the art develops for design application of maintenance cost, units of measure will greatly assist in more accurate predictions. To the extent possible, the information contained in Appendix E presents an approximation of the MTBM. The cycle for maintenance action can be expressed in days, weeks, quarters, etc. All maintenance actions can be expressed in work hours or work minutes to completion of the task described. To better understand what information is contained in this book, a dis-

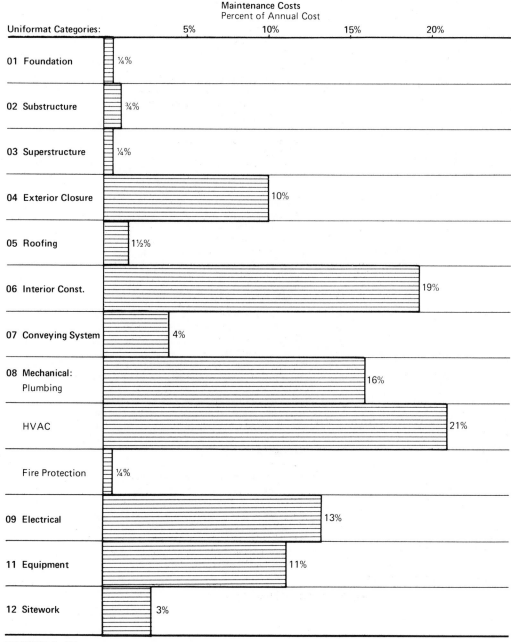

Maintenance Costs
Percent of Annual Cost

FIGURE 4-15
Relative cost impacts of maintenance.

cussion of each of the data items and its meaning follows. Appendix E contains maintenance item descriptions, annual labor, material, and equipment costs for a variety of construction systems.

Because maintenance labor costs amount to 80 to 90 percent of the total maintenance cost for a particular item, proper definitions of various building owning and operating labor trades with their corresponding duties have been prepared and are presented as Figure 4-16. These responsibilities vary somewhat from location to location. Trade unions specify the responsibility for the various building

maintenance tasks, and they should be consulted if there are uncertainties.

In Figure 4-17 labor units have been translated into 1979 costs. Four cities (Chicago, San Francisco, Denver, and New York) were selected to represent a cross section of the country. Costs were obtained for each of the building maintenance trades. The base wage, fringe benefits, and total hourly wage are shown. The average wage, including fringe benefits, for all four cities has been calculated from this data. To this average has been added the cost of supervision and overhead (30 percent assumed).

Trade	Duties
Janitorial	• Vacuuming — horizontal and vertical, nonindustrial-type
	• Spot interior glass washing
	• Dusting
	• Sweeping and dry mopping sporadic
	• Trash removal — desk-type wastebaskets — empty and light containers — filled bags to designated spot on floor
	• Cleaning of ashtrays
	• Spot cleaning of walls sporadic
	• Damp wiping
	• Mirror and brightwork
	• Policing of corridors and washrooms
	• Regular towel and supply service from storage areas — hand carried or small lightweight carts
	• Wet mopping (sporadic)
	• Night washroom sanitation (sporadic)
	• Manual scrubbing (sporadic)
	• Clean up after construction, painting, and repair jobs
	• Furniture washing and polishing
	• Metal washing and polishing
	• Exterior policing including hosing and sweeping of sidewalks
	• Carpet and furniture shampooing — manual
	• Washroom sanitation
	• Cleaning light fixtures
	• Cleaning venetian blinds — washing drapes
	• Operating Industrial-type vacuum cleaners and wet pickup machines
	• Wet mopping
	• Floor-type interior and exterior power machines and related wet mopping
	• Marble maintenance, exclusive of washing
	• Metal refinishing
	• Snow removal
	• Washing and polishing of vertical surfaces, baseboards, and ceilings
	• Incinerators, balers and compactors
	• Moving furniture and setting up for special events
	• Removal of old carpet
	• Loading and unloading of trucks, dock work, and moving supplies to and from storage areas
	• General handiwork

FIGURE 4-16
Building owning and operating labor trades.

The total labor cost to the owner is presented in the final column of Figure 4-17. This is the figure used to calculate annual item maintenance costs.

The maintenance required for each building item is described on the standard life cycle data sheets. Labor units, if known, are also listed as a part of this description, for example, minutes per quarter, hours per month. All maintenance figures as well as other data are in terms of the unit of measure listed beside the item description. Depending on the nature of the building item, there may be one or more maintenance tasks described. The intent is to present as much information concerning the maintenance of a particular item as possible to assist the designer in estimating the specific project. Maintenance costs, expressed in annual dollars, are presented next to the maintenance description. Labor hours, etc. are translated into yearly dollars per unit of measure. Maintenance material costs are listed adjacent to the labor cost column. Figures are provided to reflect the costs for minor replacement parts, expendable supplies, and miscellaneous materials. Minor replacement parts include items such as filters, linkages, contacts, seals, and light fixture tubes. Expendable supplies include lubricants, cleaners, and polishers. Miscellaneous materials might include testing supplies, storage devices, waste receptacles, and maintenance logbooks.

Maintenance equipment costs, although minor when compared to other maintenance costs, have also been included as a separate cost category. Equipment required to

Trade	Duties
Janitorial (Special)	• High level work — 12 feet from floor level and over • Furniture crating and uncrating • Removal of tile affixed to floor • Moving and storing of construction equipment and material • Exterior metal refinishing — after one hour in one day — from first hour of work • Loading and unloading of trucks and dock labor — after two hours in one day — from first hour work • Moving furniture — after three hours in one day — from first hour of work
Operating Engineers (Stationary engineers)	Operating or assisting in operating: • Heating and ventilation equipment • Engines • Turbines • Motors • Combustion engines • Generators • Pumps • Air-compressors • Ice and refrigerating machines • Air-conditioning units • Fans • Siphons • Automatic and power-oiling pumps and engines • Operating and maintaining all instrumentation and appurtenances • Steam boilers • Handling, preparing and delivering fuel from storage • Operating repairs of all plants, machinery, and engines • Power plant equipment • Power driven engines connected with: . water treatment plants . garbage, sewage disposal plants . breweries and distilleries . office, municipal buildings . canneries and dairies . theatres . schools, hospitals . hotels and motels • Pumping and boosting stations • Operation of valves, gates, locks
Elevator operators	• Operating passenger elevators • Operating freight elevators

FIGURE 4-16 *continued*

perform maintenance tasks may be organized into three general categories: tools and devices, testing equipment, and miscellaneous equipment. The tools and devices category includes items such as hand tools, power tools, vacuum sweepers, floor scrubbers, and buffers. Under testing equipment, items such as electrical meters, pressure gauges, velocity meters, and refrigeration testing apparatus may be included. Finally, the miscellaneous equipment category includes items such as safety devices (hats, glasses, shoes), scaffolding, and window washing apparatus. Costs for equipment items are amortized over the equipment's useful life.

Descriptions of both the material and the equipment items for a particular life cycle data element are provided when these costs become a very significant part of the total maintenance cost. Each life cycle data item may have a figure listed for energy demand, expressed in energy units (EU). For example, an electric hot water generator that is 100 percent efficient and has a 100 gallon per hour recovery rate will have an energy demand of .22 kW per gallon (assuming 50°F incoming water temperature). If no energy demand exists, a not applicable (N/A) notation is listed. The energy demand figures are used to calculate the energy consumption that item requires for a specific pro-

Elevator Starters	• Starting and monitoring passenger elevators
	• Starting and monitoring freight elevators
Security	• Primary function — building security
	• Guarding lobbies
	• Making clock rounds, etc.
	• Excludes highly compensated loss prevention, detection and investigative employees and security personnel employed by building tenants

Maintenance Electricians — Maintain, repair, and replace:

- Electrical wiring
- Electrical appliances
- Electrical equipment of any nature
- Light and power wiring fixtures
- Electrical related:
  - sprinkler systems
  - temperature controls
  - refrigeration
  - escalators
  - conveyors
  - private telephone systems
  - air-conditioning equipment
  - tube systems
  - radio and public address systems
  - elevators
  - motor generators
- General electrical maintenance work
- Excludes major construction or repair work

Fixture Cleaners and Relampers	• Clean and maintain fluorescent fixtures
	• Clean and maintain incandescent fixtures
	• Lamping and relamping of fluorescent fixtures
	• Lamping and relamping of incandescent fixtures
Window Washers	• Clean and maintain exterior windows on both sides
Firemen and Oilers	• Assist the engineer on any high-pressure steam generating plant
	• Assist the engineer on any high-pressure hot-water heating plant
	• May include service to low-pressure plants

FIGURE 4-16 *continued*

ject. From knowledge of the operation of the facility and the fuel costs, an estimate of the annual operation costs may be made.

Updating Information

As with any cost information, these data will begin to age rather quickly. To assist the designer to estimate an escalation factor for a particular item, statistical cost increases have been obtained from the Building Owners and Managers Association International. Costs since 1974 for various cost categories are presented in Table 4-1. From this information and the percentage changes from year to year, a projection for the future was made. Using this information or similar data obtained from local conditions, the cost data presented in the remainder of this document may be escalated to the point of building occupancy. Figure 4-18 can assist the designer in this process.

Figure 4-18 contains factors for escalating life cycle costs to some future date. Once the future date has been established, it is a matter of selecting the escalation curve most appropriate for the cost item and reading the cost projection factor from the left column. For example, given the maintenance for a revolving door in 1979 of $40 per year and a 6 percent escalation rate, what would be the annual rate for 1983? Using Figure 4-18, follow the column for 1983 to the escalation curve marked 6%. Reading directly across to the left from the intersection of 1983 and 6% lines, the cost projection factor would be 1.26. Therefore, the estimated maintenance cost for 1983 would be:

$$\$40.00 \times 1.26 = \$50.40, \text{ or approximately } \$50.00$$

Trade/Wage ($/HR)	Chicago	San Francisco	Denver	New York	Average	Supervisor & Overhead 30% Assumed	Total Labor Cost (used in data)
Janitorial:							
Base wage	5.69	6.61	5.78	6.16			
Fringe benefits	1.37	2.79	1.30	1.34			
Total	7.06	9.40	7.08	7.50	7.76	2.33	10.09
Janitorial (Special)							
Base Wage	5.94	6.61	6.39	6.78			
Fringe Benefits	1.37	2.79	1.40	1.41			
Total	7.31	9.40	7.79	8.91	8.17	2.45	10.62
Operating Engineers							
Base wage	11.55	10.25	8.66	8.49			
Fringe benefits	2.41	2.10	1.80	1.86			
Total	13.96	12.35	10.46	10.35	11.77	3.53	15.30
Elevator Operators							
Basic wage	5.72	6.61	Not	6.16			
Fringe benefits	1.32	2.79	reported	1.34			
Total	7.09	9.40		7.50	8.00	2.40	10.40
Elevator Starters							
Base wage	6.07	6.83	Not	6.67			
Fringe benefits	1.34	3.01	reported	1.39			
Total	7.41	9.84		8.06	8.43	2.53	10.96
Security							
Base wage	4.92	Price	3.50	4.55			
Fringe benefits	1.25	varies	1.15	1.15			
Total	6.17		4.65	5.70	5.51	1.65	7.16
Maintenance Electricians							
Base wage	10.75	Included	8.52	8.73			
Fringe benefits	2.07	with	1.80	1.89			
Total	12.82	Engineers	10.32	10.62	11.25	3.38	14.62
Fixture Cleaners Relampers							
Base wage	8.30	Janitor's	Janitor's	Electricians			
Fringe benefits	1.81	responsibility	responsibility	& Janitor's			
Total	10.11			responsibility	8.87	2.66	11.53
Window Washers							
Base wage	6.40	Not	Not	8.73			
Fringe benefits	1.20	reported	reported	2.13			
Total	7.60			10.86	9.23	2.77	12.00
Firemen & Oilers							
Base wage	9.24	Not	Not	6.16			
Fringe benefits	1.85	reported	reported	1.34			
Total	11.09			7.50	9.30	2.78	12.08

FIGURE 4-17
1979 wages for building maintenance labor trades.

Summary

Maintenance costs are significant in any LCC analysis and should be included in all alternatives. As more research is done in this area, more confidence can be placed in the comparisons. In the interim, however, the data in this book can be used as a baseline and a structure for further recording of information.

TABLE 4-1

HISTORICAL AND PROJECTED LIFE CYCLE COST ESCALATION RATES

	1974		1975		1976		1977		1978	
	CPGSF*	% Change	CPGSF*	% Change	CPGSF*	% Change	CPGSF*	% Change	CPGSF*	% Projection per year
Cleaning	77.2	7.4	82.9	4.8	86.9	5.3	91.5	9.1	99.8	7
Electrical system	7.8	9.0	8.5	3.5	8.8	10.2	9.7	44.3	14.0	10
Combined HVAC	23.6	11.9	26.4	4.2	27.5	10.2	30.3	1.3	30.7	6
Elevators	17.9	6.1	19.0	5.3	20.0	6.5	21.3	8.0	23.0	7
General building	40.2	10.7	44.5	6.1	47.2	12.5	53.1	17.9	62.6	12
Energy	71.7	21.3	87.0	12.0	97.5	11.9	109.1	5.3	114.9	10
Total operating†	259.4	12.2	291.0	7.4	312.6	9.1	341.1	10.3	376.1	9
Insurance	4.8	2.1	4.9	20.4	5.9	18.6	7.0	15.7	8.1	14
Real estate taxes	123.2	5.5	130.0	6.5	138.5	1.2	140.2	−1.6	137.9	2
Total own/operating†	418.0	2.9	430.1	10.5	475.1	9.6	520.6	−3.0	504.8	5

*Cents per gross square ft.

†Includes costs not shown above.

SOURCE: *1979 Downtown and Suburban Office Building Experience Exchange Report,* Building Owners and Managers Association International, Washington, D.C.

ALTERATION AND REPLACEMENT COSTS

Alteration costs are those involved with changing the function of the space. For example, in an office space, if a tenant leaves, the owner must have the space redone to suit the functional requirements of the new tenant. Replacement costs are those expenses incurred by the owner to maintain the original function of the facility or space. Alteration costs in a typical office building can range from $.50 to $.75 per gross square foot of space per year. Replacement costs range from $.40 to $.60 per gross square foot per year.

Alteration Costs

Alteration costs may include the expenditures for anticipated modernization or the changing of a facility to provide a function not originally intended. Estimates of health facility alterations have ranged as high as 10 percent of the usable space per year. The typical figure is considerably lower, but even annual changes of only 1 percent can be a significant cost consideration. The relative cost impact of alterations for the various UNIFORMAT cost categories are approximately 72 percent for interior construction, 12 percent for HVAC, and 16 percent for electrical.

Even those facilities that do not anticipate high-cost alteration programs should consider whether the decision to minimize alterations will lead to inefficiency in space flexibility for the future. Thus, some evaluation of the probability of, need for, and extent of the future alterations should enter into a study. In a recent study of health facility costs, the General Accounting Office noted some general guidelines for hospitals relative to interstitial space and its effect on alteration costs:

- *Surgery*—disruption is totally intolerable and, although few major remodelings were recorded, interstitial space would be justified.
- *Radiology*—disruption is tolerated, and most changes are confined to small areas; therefore, interstitial space may not be needed.
- *Laboratory*—frequency of change is not high, but work usually involves plumbing and other mechanical systems. Laboratory activities are relatively tolerant to disruption. When large-scale remodeling does occur it is sufficiently extensive that interstitial space might cut costs and save time.
- *Emergency*—the infrequency of change, which is mostly small-area remodeling, as well as tolerance for disruption, does not justify using interstitial space.

Typical decisions that create alteration costs include the following:

1. Whether or not to plan for movable partitions, interstitial space, utilities in the exterior walls, knockout panels, and other design options that facilitate alterations.

2. Whether to build spare capacity into the mechanical or electrical systems to permit additional demands.

The establishment of an "alterability" factor for various building components helps to single out systems for trade-

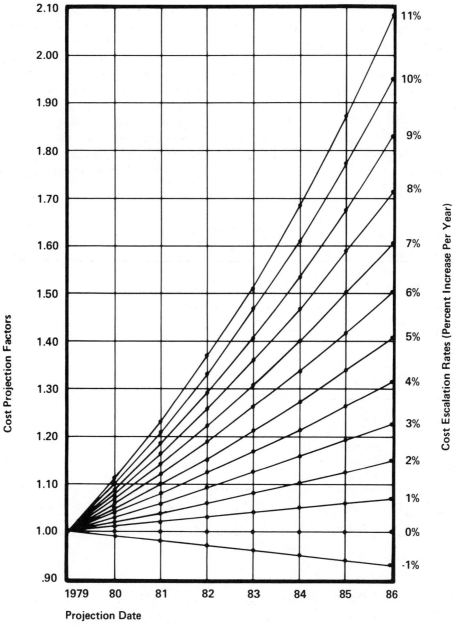

FIGURE 4-18
Factors for escalating life cycle costs.

offs. This factor might have a scale from 0 to 1, depending on the cost of altering the system. For example, for interior partitions this scale might be developed as in Table 4-2. Since a movable partition would cost very little to alter, it has been assigned an alterability factor of 0.1; and because a masonry partition would require total demolition and reconstruction at a new location, it has been assigned a factor of 1.0.

A given space or functional area may be assigned an alteration cycle. For example, an office rental space is known to change tenants every 6 years. Determining the annual cost of alteration thus becomes a matter of dividing the cost to alter by the alteration cycle.

TABLE 4-2
ALTERATION FACTORS: EXAMPLE

Interior partition	Alterability factor
Movable	0.1
Demountable	0.3
Gypsum board & metal stud	0.6
Masonry	1.0

Replacement Costs

Building replacement costs include the costs of replacing the many equipment or other facility elements with an estimated life cycle shorter than that planned for the entire facility. These costs can become a major consideration in the evaluation of alternative items of equipment and other limited-life building elements. Common limited-life elements found in facilities, as well as sample estimates of typical useful lives, are included in Appendix E.

Typical decisions based on replacement costs include:

1. Whether to specify short-life (but lower capital investment) building elements, such as rooftop HVAC units or shorter-life roofing materials.

2. Whether to specify short-life elements in areas that may undergo significant future alterations.

To help understand the breakdown of replacement costs with respect to design systems, Figure 4-19 provides an approximate percentage of annual costs for each of the UNIFORMAT categories for a typical office building. Replacement costs are most significant for interior construction and HVAC systems, each approximating 20 percent of the total replacement costs.

As discussed under maintenance, the performance of

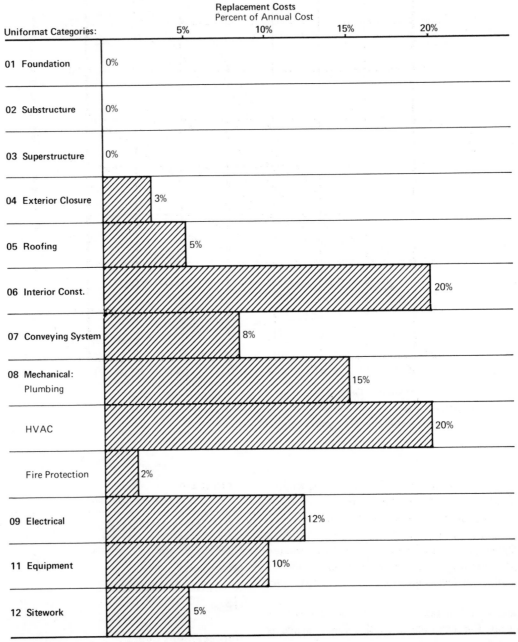

FIGURE 4-19
Relative cost impacts of replacements.

materials and systems can be specified, predicted, and measured. The life cycle data contained in Appendix E provides replacement cycle, or mean time between replacements (MTBR), for various materials and subsystems. The MTBR is the mean interval of time between item replacements due to either scheduled or unscheduled actions and usually generates space or repair part requirements.

Figure 4-20 presents various curves related to failure rates of components. The top curve illustrates a hypothetical distribution of failures. The normal distribution implies that 50 percent of similar items will fail at the mean life of the system. The lower curve illustrates that the failure rate has a lot to do with the running frequency of the system. As data is collected for various components, a more reliable data base may be developed taking into account differing modes of operation; high, normal, and low. The climatic conditions and functional applications will also vary the MTBR figures.

Appendix E contains selected sheets of replacement lives and percentages of replacement for a variety of construction systems. This information is contained in the last two columns of the data. The replacement life is expressed in years. This figure has been based in part on the historical physical life, the technological life, and the economic life of the given item. These figures are difficult to predict, and engineering judgment must be applied to adjust for owner operating and maintenance standards. The location of the facility, its relationship to others, and the microclimate will also affect the replacement life and must be taken into account.

The last column of the data in Appendix E, titled "percent replaced," refers to the percent of economic value of the item being replaced. If, for example, only a component of an item requires replacement at the year listed, that component's percent of the economic value of the total item cost, is listed. This allows the designer to estimate the cost of replacement of a particular item. For most cases in this document, 100 percent of the item is replaced at the year presented.

Summary

Alteration and replacement costs can amount to as much as $0.90 to $1.35 per gross square foot per year. In other words, these costs are as significant as energy consumption, and they approach the significance of maintenance costs. Therefore, designers should thoroughly analyze and estimate their effect.

TAXES, CREDITS, AND DEPRECIATION
Taxes

Private industries of all kinds are responsible for federal, state, and local income taxes. This cost burden can amount to as much as 50 percent of the profits of the industry. The federal government, through its income tax, is in essence a sharing partner with all profit-making organizations. Consequently, it has recognized that it should also share the expense of capital investment and does so through tax credits and depreciation allowances.

These tax-deductible expenses reduce the income subject to taxes or the tax itself, thus producing savings for the industry. Therefore, the expenses that provide tax credits or depreciation allowances may be stated in a life cycle analysis of alternatives as an after-tax equivalent cost. An alternative method lists the tax-deductible expenses as savings or as a benefit to the alternative that produced the tax allowance. For example, an industry paying 48 percent of its income in taxes would actually incur tax-deductible expenses at only 52 percent of their nominal cost.

Expenses that are tax-deductible include all maintenance and operating costs, insurance, and property taxes. State taxes are deductible expenses for federal income tax purposes. An allowance for depreciation of assets may also be deducted. Interest expense is deductible; however, it should not be included in a life cycle study because it is already taken into consideration when the discount rate is established.

This section discusses the effects of depreciation, energy, historic preservation, and investment tax credits during a design LCC evaluation. Methods of calculation and examples are provided to further explain how they may be considered for industrial clients.

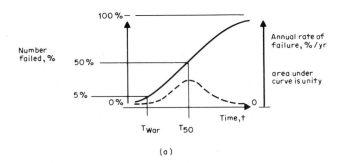

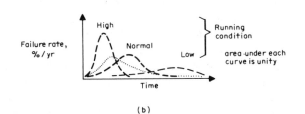

FIGURE 4-20
(a) Failure and failure rates. (b) Failure rates for various running conditions.

Credits

The Energy Tax Act of 1978 provides an energy investment credit of 10 percent for solar and wind energy property. An additional investment credit of 10 percent is permitted if the energy property also qualifies as regular investment credit property under existing law without considering the energy credit provisions. The Revenue Act of 1978 also liberalizes present laws dealing with the rehabilitation of existing structures.

In general, an industry is allowed a tax credit for investment in depreciable property with an estimated useful life of 3 years or more. The credit is applicable to:

1. Tangible personal property.

2. Elevators and escalators.

3. Other tangible property, including certain real property (except buildings and their structural components and land), if used as an integral part of manufacturing, production, or extraction, etc., or as a research or bulk storage facility for fungible commodities for these activities.

Thus, items such as demountable partitions, computer flooring, and special HVAC systems *may* be considered for investment tax credit if they are considered by the Internal Revenue Service (IRS) as an "integral part of the manufacturing ... process." This investment credit may be taken as a tax deduction in the year the asset is purchased.

For example, consider the following interior partition alternatives before and after tax consequences:

Alternative 1	Initial
Gypsum board on metal studs	$2.40/WSF
Alternative 2	
Demountable office partitions	$3.40/WSF

The gypsum board interior partition would be selected as the lowest cost alternative before tax credits are considered. However, assuming a 10 percent credit is allowed for the first year of the life cycle for the demountable partition (as shown in Table 4-3), the design selection based on LCC is reversed.

TABLE 4-3

	Alternative 1, gypsum partition	Alternative 2, demountable partition
Initial cost, per 1000 sq ft	$2400	$3400
Maintenance cost, present worth	800	100
Investment tax credit (10% of initial cost)	....	(340)
Total life cycle cost	$3200	$3160

The energy tax act allows a one-time 10 percent credit for certain "energy property" as defined by the IRS. This energy property falls into six categories:

1. Alternative energy.

2. Solar or wind energy.

3. Specially defined energy property.

4. Recycling equipment.

5. Shale oil equipment.

6. Equipment for producing natural gas from geopressured brine.

To qualify, the construction, reconstruction, or erection of the equipment must have been completed after September 30, 1978. Procedures for inclusion of the energy tax credit in a life cycle analysis are identical to the investment tax credit example.

The Tax Reform Act of 1976 and its incentives for rehabilitation provide a strong incentive to save historic property over the long term. While nearly everyone agrees that short-term tax advantages are provided, what about the economic benefits over the life of the building—after the protective first 5 years of tax shelter?

Facts were unavailable until a study by Stephen R. Weber of the National Bureau of Standards' center for building technology impartially analyzed the economics of the situation over a structure's life. In a report called "Historic Preservation Incentives of the 1976 Tax Reform Act: An Economic Analysis," he analyzes the economics of rehabilitation versus demolition from the perspective of LCC both before and after the enactment of the tax reform. He concludes that the tax act has "significantly affected the economic trade-off between rehabilitation and demolition" and that the economic advantages, even over the long term, are on the side of rehabilitation.

Under the act, the owner of a "substantially" rehabilitated historic building can depreciate the entire cost basis of the structure as though it were new, and rehabilitation expenditures may be amortized over 60 months rather than over the entire remaining life of the building. The act also penalizes demolition. Before the act was passed, the taxpayer could deduct demolition costs in the year in which they occurred and the remaining undepreciated basis of the building as current expenses, provided the property was not acquired for the purpose of demoliton. Now, demolition-related costs must be added to the value of the land, offering no tax benefits until the property is sold, at which time they can help reduce capital gains taxes. Another penalty involves depreciation, with the taxpayer permitted to use only the straight-line method.

Weber's focus is on the income tax effects of rehabilitation or redevelopment, and all other consequences of such decisions "are ignored by assuming that the before-tax costs of both options are equal." Only nonresidential buildings are considered; the possible effects of inflation are ignored.

Weber's LCC model, as he explains, calculates the sum of the following items: "(1) rehabilitation costs (or demolition and construction costs), minus (2) the present value of annual depreciation or amortization write-offs, plus (3) the present value of the capital gains taxes and recapture taxes due when the property is sold, and minus (4) the present value of the proceeds from the sale." Calculations are made for rehabilitation and for redevelopment both before and after the tax act.

Before the act was passed, rehabilitation was from 4 to 9 percent more costly than redevelopment; after the act, rehabilitation became from 13 to 28 percent less costly.

Potential investors and current owners of income-producing historic property "now have a strong incentive to consider rehabilitation as a serious alternative to demolition and redevelopment," Weber says.

Rehabilitation expenditures capitalized after October 31, 1978, on a building that has been in service for at least 20 years, qualify for the investment tax credit. Where there is progressive rehabilitation work, it appears that each major rehabilitation (for example, on separate floors) will be considered as a separate building and thus qualify. Expenditures for interior or exterior renovation, restoration, or reconstruction of a building qualify for the credit provided the improvements have a useful life of 5 years or more. Furthermore, the credit is available for all types of buildings used in business or productive activities except those used for residential purposes (tenants staying 30 days or more). The use of a building is determined on the basis of its use *after* rehabilitation. Thus rehabilitation of an apartment building into an office would make it eligible for the credit.

There are a few restrictions, however; the cost of acquiring, completing, replacing, or enlarging a building do not qualify. During the rehabilitation work, at least 75 percent of the walls must remain to qualify.

In another step towards liberalizing the list of various parts of a building eligible for the Investment Tax Credit the Senate Finance Committee Report listed the following items as being "tangible personal property" and thus not real property:

1. Special lighting to illuminate the exterior of a store.
2. False balconies and other exterior ornamentation.
3. Identity symbols, such as materials attached to the exterior or interior of a building or store, or signs (not billboards).
4. Floor coverings that are not an integral part of floors.
5. Carpeting.
6. Wall panel inserts, beverage bars, ornamental fixtures.
7. Artifacts, if depreciable.

8. Booths for seating.
9. Movable and removable partitions.
10. Large and small pictures of scenery, persons, and the like, which are attached to walls or suspended from the ceiling.

Because the tax situation is quite involved, it is suggested that the designer review all proposed LCC analyses with the clients' tax consultants before final design recommendations are made.

Depreciation

Investment in a facility is for a number of years. Profits are anticipated during this investment period. It would be incorrect to charge the cost of the facility entirely to operations for the first year and make no charge for the cost of the building for subsequent years. An expenditure that decreases in value with time must be apportioned over its life. The term to describe this loss in value is *depreciation*. Depreciation arises from two causes: wear and tear and obsolescence. Both are recognized by the IRS tax rules for depreciation. Because depreciation is a fundamental aspect of accounting and cost engineering, it should be considered in LCC analyses. There is an advantage in deferring taxes to later years because of the time value of money. An industry using depreciation, in theory, sets aside a fund to which payments are made so that the original investment can be restored when the item is worn out.

In order to mathematically consider depreciation in an LCC calculation, two items must be specified. First, the useful life of the system or components must be established. This may be accomplished through consultation with the IRS or the owner's tax consultant.

Second, the method of allocating the depreciation expense for each year of the life of the system must be determined. Three of the most commonly used methods accepted by the government include:

1. Straight line.
2. Declining balance.
3. Sum of the years' digits.

The owner may decide to depreciate each component of a facility using its own useful life, or the facility as a whole may be depreciated according to its useful life in years.

The straight-line method is the simplest for computing depreciation. Under this method, the cost of the system less its salvage value is generally deducted in equal amounts over the years of its estimated useful life. The depreciation for each year is determined by dividing the system cost (less salvage value) by the useful life. If, for example, an air-conditioning unit costing $36,000 will be depreciated over 10 years and has a salvage value of $6,000, the annual depreciation cost will be:

$$\frac{\text{First cost} - \text{salvage}}{\text{Useful life}}$$

$$= \frac{\$36,000 - \$6,000}{10 \text{ yr}} = \$3,000/\text{yr}$$

Assuming an industry pays 45 percent of its income in federal taxes, the annual life cycle tax benefit would be:

$$45\% \times \$3,000 = \$1,350$$

The government recognizes that most depreciation is not uniform and that a greater amount of depreciation may occur in the earlier than in the later years. To compensate for this, the declining-balance method was developed. Using this method, the depreciation taken each year is subtracted from the cost of the system before computing the next year's depreciation, so that the same depreciation rate applies to a smaller, or declining, balance each year. Thus, a larger depreciation deduction is taken for the first year and gradually smaller deductions in succeeding years.

The declining-balance depreciation rate is greater initially than the rate that would be used under the straight-line method. Under some circumstances, a rate as much as twice the straight-line method may be set. Double declining balance (twice the straight-line rate) is the maximum allowed under this method. In the previous example, the straight-line rate was 10 percent. Twice that amount would be 20 percent. Table 4-4 lists what would then be allowed for depreciation over the 10-year period.

Salvage value is not deducted from the cost of the system in determining the annual depreciation allowance. However, the system may not be depreciated below its reasonable salvage value. The remaining book value of $4,832 is considered salvage value. For tax purposes any variance from this value as salvage is considered either profit or loss.

The sum-of-the-years'-digits method also generates a much quicker depreciation than does the straight-line method. In general, a different fraction each year is ap-

plied to the system cost (less salvage value). The denominator of the fraction, which remains constant, is the total of the digits representing the years of estimated useful life of the system. For example, if the estimated useful life is 5 years, the denominator is 15; that is, the sum of $1 + 2 + 3 + 4 + 5$. To save time in arriving at the denominator, especially when an asset has a long life, square the life of the asset, add the life, and divide by 2. Thus, for air-conditioning system with a useful life of 10 years, the denominator would be $(10 \times 10) + 10$, giving

$$\frac{10^2 + 10}{2} = 55$$

The numerator of the fraction changes each year to represent the years of useful life remaining at the beginning of the year for which the computation is made. For the air-conditioning example, Table 4-5 lists what would be allowed for tax depreciation over the 10-year period.

Any other consistent method of computing depreciation, such as the sinking-fund method, may be used for federal income tax purposes. However, during the first two-thirds of the useful life of the system, the depreciation deductions under any such method must not result at the end of any tax year in accumulated allowances greater than the total that could have been deducted if the declining-balance method had been used. The limitations on the use of the declining-balance and sum-of-the-years'-digits methods apply equally to any consistent method other than the straight-line method.

Table 4-6 summarizes the three methods of calculating depreciation just discussed. The designer can easily see the relative benefits of different depreciation procedures. Using an assumed discount rate of 10 percent, the present worths of each of the depreciation methods have also been calculated. Figure 4-21 graphically portrays the discounted benefits of the depreciation methods.

In general, methods with accelerated depreciation show

TABLE 4-4

Year			Depreciation		Tax benefits	
1	(0.20)	($36,000)	=	$7,200 (0.45)	=	$3,240
2	(0.20)	(36,000 − 7,200)	=	5,760 (0.45)	=	2,592
3	(0.20)	(28,800 − 5,760)	=	4,608 (0.45)	=	2,074
4	(0.20)	(23,040 − 4,608)	=	3,686 (0.45)	=	1,659
5	(0.20)	(18,432 − 3,686)	=	2,949 (0.45)	=	1,327
6	(0.20)	(14,749 − 2,949)	=	2,359 (0.45)	=	1,062
7	(0.20)	(11,797 − 2,359)	=	1,888 (0.45)	=	849
8	(0.20)	(9,438 − 1,888)	=	1,510 (0.45)	=	680
9	(0.20)	(7,550 − 1,510)	=	1,208 (0.45)	=	544
10	(0.20)	(6,040 − 1,208)	=	966 (0.45)	=	435

TABLE 4-5

Year	Fraction		Depreciation	Tax benefits
1	$\frac{10}{55}$	($36,000 $-$ $6,000)	= $5,455	(0.45) = $2,455
2	$\frac{9}{55}$	($30,000)	= 4,909	(0.45) = 2,209
3	$\frac{8}{55}$	($30,000)	= 4,364	(0.45) = 1,964
4	$\frac{7}{55}$	($30,000)	= 3,818	(0.45) = 1,718
5	$\frac{6}{55}$	($30,000)	= 3,273	(0.45) = 1,473
6	$\frac{5}{55}$	($30,000)	= 2,727	(0.45) = 1,227
7	$\frac{4}{55}$	($30,000)	= 2,182	(0.45) = 982
8	$\frac{3}{55}$	($30,000)	= 1,636	(0.45) = 736
9	$\frac{2}{55}$	($30,000)	= 1,091	(0.45) = 491
10	$\frac{1}{55}$	($30,000)	= 545	(0.45) = 245

TABLE 4-6
COMPARISON OF DEPRECIATION METHODS

End of year	PW (10%) factor	Straight line		Double declining balance		Sum of the years' digits	
		Depreciation	PW	Depreciation	PW	Depreciation	PW
1	0.9091	$3,000	$ 2,727	$7,200	$ 6,546	$5,455	$ 4,959
2	0.8264	3,000	2,479	5,760	4,760	4,909	4,057
3	0.7513	3,000	2,254	4,608	3,462	4,364	3,279
4	0.6830	3,000	2,049	3,686	2,518	3,818	2,608
5	0.6209	3,000	1,863	2,949	1,831	3,273	2,032
6	0.5645	3,000	1,694	2,359	1,332	2,727	1,539
7	0.5132	3,000	1,540	1,888	1,969	2,182	1,120
8	0.4665	3,000	1,400	1,510	704	1,636	763
9	0.4241	3,000	1,272	1,208	512	1,091	463
10	0.3855	3,000	1,157	966	372	545	210
Total			$18,435		$23,006		$21,030
Tax benefit (45%)			$ 8,296		$10,353		$ 9,464

a higher present worth for the allowable depreciation costs, which is desirable because the owner has use of the capital for a longer time. However, the best method depends on the salvage value and the life of the asset.

Summary

As discussed, Congress changed the rules in 1978 as they relate to the Investment Tax Credit (ITC). However, it is

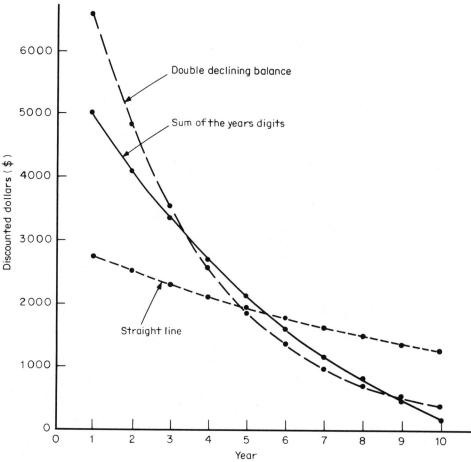

FIGURE 4-21
Graph comparison of depreciation methods.

still "the greatest economic stimulus in a generation." Why is it that, although the ITC has been 17 years in existence, American business is not taking full advantage of it? Most businesses, when building new or expanding old facilities, do not fully identify all the eligible property. A large number cannot properly segregate all costs of eligible property. Only a few "tax design" a new facility with the ITC in mind to minimize dual purpose property and thus increase the amounts of ITC property.

Today, in an inflationary economy when cash flow from depreciation and tax savings are more important than ever before, tax elements must be considered during design, using LCC procedures.

ASSOCIATED COSTS

Discussions thus far have focused on the following costs: first (initial), operating (energy), maintenance, alterations and replacements, and taxes, credits, and depreciation. But what about staff salaries (functional use), lost con-

struction time, denial of use, fire insurance, and a myriad of others? For example, few life cycle studies touch on personnel salaries—the largest area of expense associated with most facilities. In hospitals, this cost can exceed the initial cost of the facility in as little as 3 years after construction.

The following is a discussion of other life cycle cost items that may be significant in an analysis. Examples are also provided to further explain and justify their significance. The designer must take responsibility for inclusion of these costs, when a decision might switch from one alternative to another if they are considered.

Functional-Use Costs

Functional use includes costs of staff, materials, etc. required to perform the function of the organization using the facility. This is the largest single area of cost in most facilities. For example, a hospital's annual operating budget is often as much as 35 percent of the entire cost of buying or building the facility that houses these functions. It is also the least subject to cost scrutiny during the planning stage of many projects in spite of the significant impact that the facility can have on these costs.

One reason for this, of course, is that functional-use costs are among the most difficult to analyze. The qualitative parameters often make it difficult to quantify and compare alternative decisions. However, functional-use costs are so large that they should be considered in any comprehensive LCC analysis. Care must be taken, though, to compare costs at comparable performance levels.

Many facility decisions with functional-use cost implications can be analyzed. Typical decisions are the following:

1. Whether a reduction or redefinition of facility capability will be justified by a more economical life cycle cost level. For example, the decision made by many hospitals to build open-heart surgical capabilities had significant life cycle functional-use cost implications when they could not be fully supported through patient income. Other hospitals have built capabilities such as comprehensive emergency facilities, even though neighboring hospitals' facilities are adequate for the community's full needs. Many hospitals have been living with cost problems as a result of their failure to consider such factors.

2. Whether to select a design with higher construction costs but lower functional-use costs. For example, a recent hospital expansion design called for the construction of two new six-story nursing towers to be connected to a six-story existing facility. It was found that merely expanding the existing nursing units instead would cut the number of nursing stations in half and the required nursing staff by 30 percent.

3. Whether to provide services through contract, concessions, or facility staff. Such decisions as whether to have in-house laundries and food preparation, prepackaged pharmacies, and other support facilities have hinged on this issue.

4. Whether or not to build in greater staff efficiency at the price of higher operating costs. This is critical in such areas as the use of automated patient monitoring and diagnostic equipment.

Denial-of-Use Costs

Denial of use includes the extra costs occurring during the construction or occupancy periods, or both, because production (income) is delayed. This may be the result of process or a facility decision.

The major elements of denial-of-use costs are lost revenues and operating inefficiencies. Where the denial of use is attributable to a delay, there are also often considerable increases in construction costs because of inflation, increased interest rates, and other factors. There are also a number of nonquantifiable costs resulting from the non-availability of a facility, such as the loss of doctors or tenants who would otherwise plan to use it.

It is possible to allocate all aspects of denial-of-use costs to the other cost elements: operating inefficiencies to functional-use cost projections, increased cost escalation to initial costs, etc. Denial-of-use cost is really only the difference in total costs between two decisions that lead to different initial occupancy dates. In some analyses, however, the reason for keeping it as an identifiable cost element is to provide a single place for quickly summarizing all the cost implications of a decision that will increase the time required to achieve initial occupancy and start-up of the new facility. Often the major use of these data is to demonstrate to the facility decision maker the cost of delay. In addition, some typical decisions that hinge on this information include:

1. Whether or not to employ a construction manager and fast-track construction and thus reduce the time required to complete the facility.

2. Whether to spend the available funds to completely equip several departments and leave others as unfinished shell space until more funds are available or to partially equip all departments.

3. Whether or not to use public funding that requires a guaranteed maximum price, thus slowing down a fast-track project until the drawings are sufficiently detailed to obtain the guarantee.

4. Whether or not to delay construction while reapplying for permission from various agencies for additional space.

Other Costs

Other costs may include any identifiable expense related to a facility decision, not covered in the other categories; such as fire protection, utilities, security, waste disposal, insurance, and start-up.

The cost ramifications of facility decisions are only partially captured within the other cost categories. This special cost element calls for a compartment that accepts costs that cannot logically be put into one of the other categories. Its primary use is to accept quantified estimates of the costs of qualitative areas, such as aesthetics, patient convenience, comfort, safety, ecological impact, and increased usable space.

For example, if the design team has a strong preference for a particular exterior skin material, such as bronze-tinted glass, for aesthetic reasons, a special attempt should be made to put a dollar value on that choice to see if it significantly alters the LCC comparison. The regional planner deciding between a single central facility or several community facilities makes a similar attempt to quantify the value of the added patient convenience of the closer facilities.

In addition to the examples noted above, other typical decisions might be:

1. A value placed on the additional comfort created by designing extra HVAC capacity to meet the maximum load requirements, rather than a lower figure that would result in some discomfort several days per year.

2. A value placed on the increased safety achieved by installing smoke detectors, sprinklers, etc. not specifically required by the fire code.

3. A value placed on the added protection of a structural system that far exceeds minimum earthquake design code requirements.

Summary

There are many associated costs that *may* affect a life cycle study. These include functional use, denial of use, and other costs. These additional expenditures may range in significance from $.50 to $5.00 per gross square foot per year. The designer must take responsibility for inclusion of those items considered to be significant for the alternatives being evaluated.

CHAPTER FIVE
FORMATS

" . . . The object of the world of ideas is not the portrayal of reality—this would be an utterly impossible task—but rather to provide us with an instrument for finding our way about in this world more easily."

Hans Vailhinger
1876

INTRODUCTION

This chapter presents the recommended forms, materials, etc. necessary to perform a life cycle cost comparison. Both short and more detailed manual procedure formats are included for use. A brief discussion of evolving automated procedures for LCC is also included, and an economic building performance model is reviewed.

The quick or short-form procedure is used primarily in comparing specific facility components such as the type of HVAC system or various roofing materials. The detailed procedure allows a more comprehensive total facility analysis based on LCC.

MANUAL COMPONENT AND SYSTEM STUDY

The procedures outlined in this section are normally used when comparing items or component parts of a facility design. Both annualized and present-worth LCC conversions are discussed. Either procedure will arrive at the same economic solution. The present-worth method allows easier consideration of escalation, therefore it is more commonly used.

Both the forms used for comparison and the reference tables for cost conversions are outlined in the chapter. Reference economic tables are contained in Appendix C and blank worksheets are contained in Appendix F.

		Original	Alt. No. 1	Alt. No. 2
Collateral & Instant Contract Costs	**Initial Costs**			
	Base Cost	$816,000	$536,000	$738,000
	Interface Costs			
	a. Electrical	120,000	100,000	160,000
	b.			
	c.			
	Other Initial Costs			
	a. Owner-supplied equipment	64,000	64,000	2,000
	b.			
	c.			
	Total Initial Cost Impact (IC)	$1,000,000	$700,000	$900,000
	Initial Cost Savings			
Salvage & Replacement Costs	**Single Expenditures @ _____ Interest**			
	Present Worth			
	1. Year __8__ _____ Amount		200,000	
	PW = Amount x (PW Factor _.4665_) =		93,300	
	2. Year __10__ _____ Amount			20,000
	Amount x (PW Factor _.3355_) =			7,710
	3. Year __16__ _____ Amount	10,000	200,000	
	Salvage Amount x (PW Factor _.2176_) =	2,176	43,520	
	4. Year __20__ _____ Amount	(80,000)	(100,000)	(75,000)
	Amount x (PW Factor _.1486_) =	(11,890)	(14,860)	(11,145)
	5. Year _____ _____ Amount			
	Amount x (PW Factor _____) =			
	Salvage Amount x (PW Factor _____) =			

		Original	Alt. No. 1	Alt. No. 2
Life Cycle Costs (Annualized)	**Annual Owning & Operating Costs**			
	1. Capital IC x (PP _0.1175_) =	117,500	82,250	105,750
	Recovery __20__ Years @ __10__ %			
	Replacement Cost: PP x PW			
	a. Year 8 0.1175 x 93,300		10,960	
	b. Year 10 0.1175 x 7,710			910
	c. Year 16 0.1175 x 2,176 & 43,520	260	5,110	
	d. Year 20 0.1175x(11,890),(14,860)	(1400)	(1745)	(1310)
	e. Year 20 & (11,145)			
	Salvage:			
	2. Annual Costs			
	a. Maintenance	25,000	20,000	16,000
	b. Operations	30,000	35,000	25,000
	c.			
	d.			
	e.			
	3. Total Annual Costs	171,360	151,575	146,350
	Annual Difference (AD)		19,785	25,010
	4. Present Worth of Annual Difference		168,440	212,922
	(PWA Factor _8.5135_) x AD			

PP- Periodic Payment to pay off loan of $1.
PWA- Present Worth of Annuity (What $1 payable periodically is worth today).
PW- Present Worth (What $1 due in future is worth today).

Future Costs
Present Costs

FIGURE 5-1
Life cycle cost analysis, annualized-cost method—HVAC system.

Annualized Method

Figure 5-1, "Life Cycle Costing, Annualized," is the first method to be discussed. The form shown is broken down into three sections. Part 1 represents blocks of initial project or other capital investment costs. Part 2 lists all major replacement expenditures, which are taken back to present worth (discounted) using data from Table C-1. Part 3 takes all costs and equates them to a common baseline of annual cost. These costs are totaled and the annual differences converted to present worth. A hypothetical HVAC system example (Figure 5-1) is used to discuss procedures. The study team reviewed the original design and proposed two alternatives for satisfying the functions required.

The original design's initial cost is estimated to be $816,000; alternative system 1, $536,000; and alternative system 2, $738,000. These figures are entered under "base costs." Electrical connection costs total $120,000 for the original design, $100,000 for alternative 1, and $160,000 for alternative 2. Owner-supplied equipment is $64,000 for the original and alternative 1, and $2,000 for alternative 2. These initial costs are then totaled.

Next, replacement costs are entered. The original design incurs replacement costs of $10,000 at the sixteenth year. For alternative 1, substantial replacement costs of $200,000 will be incurred in the eighth and sixteenth years. For alternative 2, costs of $20,000 are estimated for the tenth year. Finally, the salvage value of each system (at the end of the life cycle period) is estimated. These amounts are discounted to determine the present worth. For example, the present worth of $200,000 due 8 years in the future is 0.4665 (Table C-1) times $200,000, or $93,-300. It must be pointed out that replacement costs used must be those costs (using today's dollars) estimated for the year indicated. In some cases this will require using present costs escalated for future price increases. However, the escalation should be limited to only the amounts of differential escalation over and above dollar devaluation. This must be done to keep all amounts in terms of a constant present-dollar purchasing power.

The first step in the third part is to amortize the initial costs, or to determine annual payment costs necessary to pay off a loan equaling the total initial costs. For this exercise, a life of 20 years at 10 percent interest is used. Table C-3 is entered under the interest rate across the 10-year line to find the periodic payment necessary to pay off a loan of $1—in this case, $0.1175 per year. Each total initial cost is multiplied by this factor to determine the annual capital recovery costs. For example, the annual cost required to recover the original cost of $1,000,000 over 20 years at 10 percent would be $117,500 per year.

The next step is to convert the replacement and salvage costs to a uniform series of payments. To do this, the present worth is amortized over the projected life. In the case of salvage value, the costs are negative, as indicated by the parentheses. For example, for alternative 1 the periodic payment necessary to pay off a loan of $93,300 is $93,300 times 0.1175 (Table C-3), or $10,960 per year.

After the annual impact of initial and replacement costs is determined, other annual costs, such as operation, maintenance, and taxes, are added. The total represents a uniform baseline comparison for the various systems over the

projected life at the selected interest rate. The annual differences are then determined and used for recommendations. In this example, alternative 2 resulted in the lowest annual owning and operating costs and would be recommended.

As added input, the present worth of the annual difference can be calculated. In this example, the present worth of the annual difference indicated for alternative 2 is the annual difference of $25,010 times the present worth of $1 payable annually (Table C-3), or 8.5135 × $25,010, which equals $212,922.

Present-Worth Method

As discussed in Chapter 3, "Economics," life cycle analysis can also be accomplished using the present-worth concept. The baseline of comparison becomes present-day value. Figure 5-2 shows life cycle cost analysis, present-worth method, using information from the previous example. The results validate conclusions developed using the annualized-cost method.

Impact of Escalation

There remains one area with significant effect on life cycle costs— escalation. As discussed in Chapter 3, LCC analysis should be in terms of constant dollars. For example, if the LCC is being conducted in 1982, then 1982 dollars in terms of purchasing power should be used throughout. However, with varying increases in all costs, especially with energy escalating at an ever-increasing rate, life cycle analyses that do not take account of differential escalation are questionable.

If rates of escalation are not constant but ever increasing, as illustrated in Figure 5-3, for the cost of energy since 1970, another approach is required. Tables C-4 to C-9 give the present worth of a present-day value of an escalating annual amount, starting at $1 per year at 6, 8, 10, 12, 15, and 20 percent interest rates. For example, Table C-6 indicates that, assuming an annual cost of $1 at 10 percent interest, nonescalating (0 percent column), the present worth of a 20-year cycle is $8.51. This equals the value used in the previous Figure 5-2 (present-worth factor of annual difference of 8.5135). Now, assuming that the annual amount will escalate differentially at 10 percent above dollar devaluation plus interest costs, the present worth of a 20-year cycle would be $20.00 (Table C-6). The impact of escalation on present worth would be ($20.00 − $8.51) or $11.49, or some 135 percent increase.

Applying this to the previous HVAC system, Figure 5-4 lists the calculations. For example, the present worths of all costs are listed as before, but operations costs are escalated (differentially) at 5 percent (12.72 versus 8.51) per year, while maintenance costs are escalated (differentially) at 3 percent (10.76 versus 8.51) per year.

		Original		Alternate No. 1		Alternate No. 2		Alternate No 3.	
Item: HVAC SYSTEM Life Cycle Period: 20 YEARS Date:OCT.1976		Estimated Costs	Present Worth	Estimated Costs	Present Worth	Estimated Costs	Present Worth	Estimated Costs	Present Worth
Collateral/Initial Costs	Base Cost _____		816,000		536,000		738,000		
	Interface Costs a. Electrical		120,000		100,000		160,000		
	b. _____								
	c. _____								
	Other Initial Costs a. Owner Supplied Equip.		64,000		64,000		2,000		
	b. _____								
	Total Initial Cost Impact (IC)		1,000,000		700,000		900,000		
Salvage & Replacement Costs	Single Expenditures @ 10% Interest 1. Year 8 PW Factor 0.4665			200,000	93,300				
	2. Year 10 PW Factor 0.3855					20,000	7,710		
	3. Year 16 PW Factor 0.2176	10,000	2,180	200,000	43,520				
	4. Year _____ PW Factor _____								
	5. Year _____ PW Factor _____								
	Salvage Yr. 20 PW Factor 0.1486	(80,000)	(11,890)	(100,000)	(14,860)	(75,000)	(11,145)		
	Total Present Worth		(9,710)		121,960		(3,435)		
Annual Costs	Annual Costs @ 10% Interest a. Maintenance Escal.Rate 0% PWA Factor 8.5135	25,000	212,841	20,000	170,270	16,000	136,275		
	b. Operations Escal.Rate 0% PWA Factor 8.5135	30,000	255,404	35,000	297,975	25,000	212,840		
	c. Others Escal.Rate _____ PWA Factor _____								
	d. Others Escal.Rate _____ PWA Factor _____								
	e. Others Escal.Rate _____ PWA Factor _____								
	Total Annual Costs		468,245		468,245		349,055		
	Total Present Worth Costs		1,458,535		1,290,205		1,245,620		
	Life Cycle (PW) Savings				168,330		212,915		

PW — Present Worth   PWA — Present Worth Of Annuity

FIGURE 5-2
Life cycle cost analysis, present-worth method—HVAC system.

If the annualized method is used, the annual sum for maintenance may also be increased by a factor to account for the escalated amount. This factor can be developed by multiplying the present worth, escalated figure (Tables C-4 to C-9), by the annualized factor in Table C-3 (periodic payment). For example, the factor for 3 percent, as in the previous example, would be 10.764 (Table C-6) times 0.11746 (Table C-3) = 1.264. The operation cost factor for 5 percent would be 1.494.

LCC General-Purpose Worksheet

Figure 5-5 is a general-purpose LCC worksheet for a more detailed system analysis using present worth. This form is also useful as a summary sheet for individual items or component analyses. As an example of its use, a computer center HVAC system comparison is shown.

MANUAL TOTAL FACILITY ANALYSIS

This section provides the material necessary to prepare an LCC analysis for facilities in more detail. Standard format sheets have been developed so that required calculations can be performed more easily. The first form is "data required for life cycle cost estimating." This form is a compilation of required data, including economics, facility and site and climate information. The forms are organized into six major categories: (1) structural, (2) architectural, (3) mechanical, (4) electrical, (5) equipment, and (6) site work. These forms follow the UNIFORMAT cost structure. One form has been devoted to each category with the exception of architectural, which has two. An LCC summary form is used to total this information for comparison of design alternatives. An original design and up to three design alternatives may be considered.

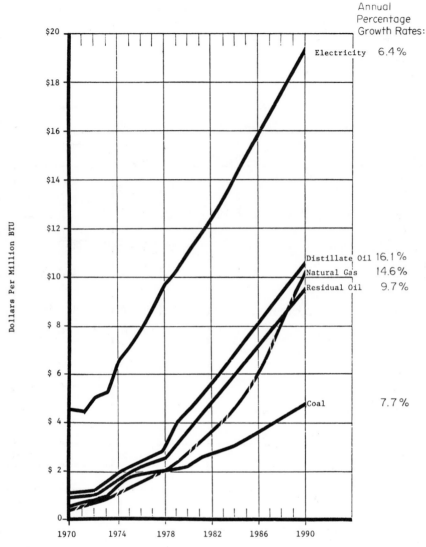

FIGURE 5-3
Historical and projected fuel prices, 1970–1990 (taxes included). *(Source: Allen Ferree, American Natural Resources System, Detroit, Michigan, 1979.)*

Instructions for Completing Forms

These eight forms provide a step-by-step manual system for calculating the significant life cycle costs of the more usual types of facility construction.

For forms 1 to 7, levels 2 and 3 of UNIFORMAT have been used to organize calculations. Life cycle costs that pertain to a particular building system are listed on the appropriate form. Each block should be completed as required, beginning with the initial cost of the system. Additional lines have been provided to include other significant items under each category. Each estimated cost should be converted to present-worth costs. Next, the present-worth costs in each category are totaled and entered on the appropriate line. The total of all present-worth costs is entered on the last line of the form. This process is repeated for each design alternative.

Form 8, the LCC summary, summarizes all the life cycle costs predicted from the earlier sheets. The present-worth costs should be entered in the appropriate space for each design alternative. All of the costs should be totaled for each alternative. The "total facility" life cycle cost appears at the bottom of the form. Life cycle savings may then be identified for each alternative.

The following general instructions apply to forms 1 to 8:

1. The present-worth factor always equals 1 for initial costs. Therefore, the estimated cost and the present worth are the same and should be so entered.

2. Before the estimated annual expenditure is converted to present worth, determine if an escalation rate is appropriate. If an escalation rate is not necessary, refer to Table C-2, "Present Worth of Annuity," for conversion to present worth. Use the column with the corresponding discount rate. By knowing the building life, select the correct

Item: HVAC SYSTEM Date: Oct. 1976
Life Cycle Period: 20 Years

		Original		Alternate No. 1		Alternate No. 2		Alternate No. 3	
		Estimated Costs	Present Worth	Estimated Costs	Present Worth	Estimated Costs	Present Worth	Estimated Costs	Present Worth
Collateral/Initial Costs	Base Cost		816,000		536,000		738,000		
	Interface Costs a. Electrical		120,000		100,000		160,000		
	b.								
	c.								
	Other Initial Costs a. Owner Supplied Equip.		64,000		64,000		2,000		
	b.								
	Total Initial Cost Impact (IC)		1,000,000		700,000		900,000		
Salvage & Replacement Costs	Single Expenditures @ 10% Interest								
	1. Year 8 PW Factor 0.4665			200,000	93,300				
	2. Year 10 PW Factor 0.3855					20,000	7,710		
	3. Year 16 PW Factor 0.2176	10,000	2,180	200,000	43,520				
	4. Year PW Factor								
	5. Year PW Factor								
	Salvage Yr. 20 PW Factor 0.1486	(80,000)	(11,890)	(100,000)	(14,860)	(75,000)	(11,145)		
	Total Present Worth		(9,710)		121,960		(3,435)		
Annual Costs	Annual Costs @ 10% Interest								
	a. Maintenance Escal.Rate 3% PWA Factor 10.764	25,000	269,100	20,000	215,280	16,000	172,224		
	b. Operations Escal.Rate 5% PWA Factor 12.718	30,000	381,540	35,000	445,130	25,000	317,950		
	c. Others Escal.Rate PWA Factor								
	d. Others Escal.Rate PWA Factor								
	e. Others Escal.Rate PWA Factor								
	Total Annual Costs		650,640		660,410		490,174		
	Total Present Worth Costs		1,640,930		1,482,370		1,386,739		
	Life Cycle (PW) Savings				158,560		254,191		

PW — Present Worth PWA — Present Worth Of Annuity

FIGURE 5-4
Life cycle cost analysis, present-worth method—HVAC system (with escalation).

Study Title: __COMPUTER CENTER - HVAC__
COMPUTER SPACE = 60,000 S.F.
Discount Rate: __10%__ Economic Life: __40 YEARS__

		Original Describe: ALL AIR SYSTEM S.C. DE·HUMIDIFIER WITH MECHANICAL REFRIGERATION		Alternative 1 Describe: PRIMARY AIR SYS. 100% ROOM RECIRC WITH MECH. AND NON·REFRIG COOL		Alternative 2 Describe:		Alternative 3 Describe:	
		Estimated Costs	Present Worth	Estimated Costs	Present Worth	Estimated Costs	Present Worth	Estimated Costs	Present Worth
Initial Costs									
	A. HVAC SYSTEM INCLUDING CHILLED WATER GEN.		3,396,660		1,666,896				
	B. ELECTRICAL INSTALLATION (DIFFERENCE)		15,000						
	C. WATER TREATMENT		6,000						
	D. MECHANICAL EQUIP. ADDITIONAL SPACE REQ'D								
	E. 10,800 SF @ $15.00/SF		162,000						
	F.								
	G. SUBTOTAL		3,579,660		1,666,896				
	H.								
	I.								
	J. Contingencies 15 %		730,250		340,046				
	K. Escalation 18 % + DESIGN & O.H. = 36%		1,288,677		600,082				
	Total Initial Cost		5,598,587		2,607,024				
Operations (Annual)		Diff. Escal. Rate	PWA W/Escal.						
	A. ELECTRICAL ENERGY 6% 20.478	542,244	11,104,068	352,620	7,220,952				
	B. WATER TREATMENT 1% 10.853	4,500	48,834	120	1,302				
	C. WATER 1% 10.853	4,482	48,642	120	1,302				
	D.								
	E.								
	F.								
	Total Annual Operations Costs		11,201,544		7,223,556				
Maintenance (Annual)		Diff. Escal. Rate	PWA W/Escal.						
	A. HVAC SYSTEM, FANS, DAMPERS 3% 13.654	6,000	81,924	12,000	163,848				
	B. S.C. DE·HUMIDIFIERS 3% 13.654	6,000	81,924	–	–				
	C. CHANGE FILTERS 3% 13.654	1,500	20,478	2,100	28,668				
	D.								
	E.								
	F.								
	G.								
	Total Annual Maintenance Costs		184,326		192,516				
Replacement/Alterations (Single Expenditure)		Year	PW Factor						
	A. S.C. DE·HUMIDIFIER NOZZLES 15 .2393	15,000	3,588						
	B. S.C. DE·HUMIDIFIER NOZZLES 30 .0573	21,000	1,200						
	C. S.C. DE·HUMIDIFIER PUMPS 15 .2393	9,600	2,292						
	D. S.C. DE·HUMIDIFIER PUMPS 30 .0573	15,600	894						
	E. S.C. DE·HUMIDIFIER ELIMIN. 25 .0922	120,000	11,064						
	F. HVAC FANS 20 .1486	420,000	62,412	90,000	13,374				
	G. HUMIDIFIERS 15 .2393			60,000	14,358				
	H. HUMIDIFIERS 30 .0573			90,000	5,154				
	I.								
	J.								
	Total Replacement/Alteration Costs		81,450		32,886				
Tax Elements		Diff. Escal. Rate	PWA W/Escal.						
	A.								
	B.								
	C.								
	D.								
	E.								
	F.								
	G.								
	Total Tax Elements								
Associated (Annual)		Diff. Escal. Rate	PWA W/Escal.						
	A. FILTERS, HI·CAP & FLAT 4% 15.495	18,000	278,910	6,000	92,970				
	B.								
	C.								
	Total Annual Associated Costs		278,910		92,970				
	Total Owning Present Worth Costs		11,746,230		7,541,928				
Salvage At End Of Economic Life		Year	PW Factor						
	Building (Struc., Arch., Mech., Elec., Equip.) 40 .022	130,908	(2,874)	48,000	(1,056)				
	Other 5% OF INITIAL COST								
	Sitework								
	Total Salvage		(2,874)		(1,056)				
	Total Present Worth Life Cycle Costs		17,341,943		10,147,896				
	Life-Cycle Present Worth Dollar Savings		–		7,184,047				

PW — Present Worth   PWA — Present Worth Of Annuity

FIGURE 5-5

Life cycle costing estimate, general-purpose worksheet—HVAC, computer facility.

factor. Multiply this factor by the estimated annual expenditure. Enter the computed amount in the present-worth column.

For example, the table indicates that, assuming an annual cost of $1 per year at 10 percent interest, nonescalating (0 percent), the present worth of a 20-year cycle is $8.51. This equals the value used in the previous table (present-worth factor of annual difference of 8.5135). Now, assuming that the annual amount will escalate differentially at 10 percent as the effect of interest cost, the present worth of a 20-year cycle would be $20.00. The cost of escalation in present worth would be $20.00 − $8.51 ($11.49), which equals a 135 percent increase.

3. To obtain the present worth of each replacement element, refer to Table C-1, using the column with the corresponding discount rate. By knowing the building life, select the correct factor. Multiply this factor by the estimated replacement cost and enter the value in the present-worth column.

4. To obtain the present worth of the projected salvage value, refer to Table C-1, using the column with the corresponding discount rate. By knowing the building life, select the correct factor. Multiply this factor by the estimated salvage value. Enter the computed amount in the present-worth columns.

5. Yearly domestic hot water energy cost estimation. (See Appendix D.)

6. Yearly heating energy cost estimation. (See Appendix D.)

7. Yearly cooling energy cost estimation. (See Appendix D.)

8. Yearly lighting energy cost estimation. (See Appendix D.)

9. List costs estimated from the previous seven forms.

10. Include mobilization and initial expenses, site overheads, demobilization, and main office expense and profit.

11. Calculate the difference between this design's and the design alternative's life cycle costs. Enter this figure in the appropriate space.

Sample Project Application—Visitors' Information Center

This hypothetical example more fully illustrates the application of LCC to total facility analysis. This example and the alternatives selected use the structural, architectural, mechanical, electrical, and summary forms. Blank forms have also been included for equipment and site work. As the designer becomes more familiar with LCC, the significance of the various items listed on the forms will become more obvious.

Original Design: The sample project application is a visitors' information center. It is a one-story building of 10,680 gross square feet. This facility is in addition to an existing structure. The walls of the new construction consist of 8-inch load-bearing concrete masonry units (CMUs) with vermiculite insulating fill. The roof is steel framed with bar joists. The building is both heated and cooled. To further describe the design, a floor plan (Figure 5-6) and building section (Figure 5-7) are shown. The typ-

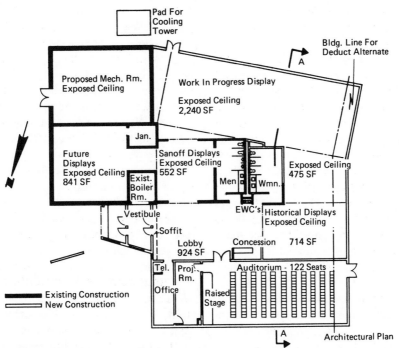

Scale — 1/8″ = 1′-0″

FIGURE 5-6

Original design layout, visitors' information center.

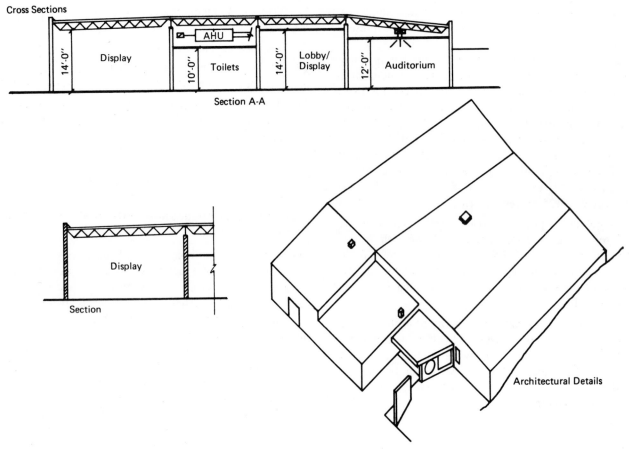

FIGURE 5-7
Original design, visitors' information center—cross sections and details.

ical wall section consists of an 8-inch CMU wall filled with vermiculite insulation with a gypsum wallboard interior. Three alternatives have been created to illustrate application of the LCC forms.

Alternative 1: An architectural change of the exterior-wall system was first examined. The proposed wall system consisted of a 4-inch brick wall, an air space, 1-inch rigid insulation, and 6-inch CMU backup. The thermo-transmittance (U) factor of the original design was 0.11 Btu/(hr)(ft²)(°F). The proposed wall system has a U-Factor of 0.05 Btu/(hr)(ft²)(°F). Because of the added thickness of the wall system, a structural change to the foundation wall is also necessary. The new foundation wall thickness is 12 inches instead of the previous 8 inches. The original design dictated that the 8-inch CMU be painted every 5 years. The new design will have no maintenance costs associated with it. The economic results of the proposed changes are reflected in the completed LCC forms.

Alternative 2: Next, it was suggested that solar collectors be used as part of the mechanical system for the building. The original mechanical system entailed an electric chiller for cooling the building and an oil-fired boiler system for space heating and domestic hot water. These systems would remain, but they would only be backup support as necessary for the solar energy system. A sketch of the proposed solar collector system is shown in Figure 5-8.

Alternative 3: Finally, an electrical change to the original design is examined. The lighting level in the original layout was considered to be excessive for the functions to be taking place in the visitors' information center. The original design consisted of an average of 3 watts per square foot of lighting over the entire floor area. This alternative reduced the level to 2 watts per square foot. Because of this lighting level decrease, the size of the cooling equipment could also be reduced. A reduction of 1 watt per square foot lighting load equals a 10,680 watt or 33,-535-Btu reduction in the building load that must be cooled. This is approximately a 3-ton decrease in the overall size of the cooling system. The LCC savings are reflected in alternative 3 of the completed forms.

Completed Life Cycle Estimates: The input LCC data and assumptions are contained on the completed first form (Figure 5-9). The life cycle analysis of the original and all three design alternatives are presented in Figures 5-10 thru 5-14. A summary of the results of the LCC

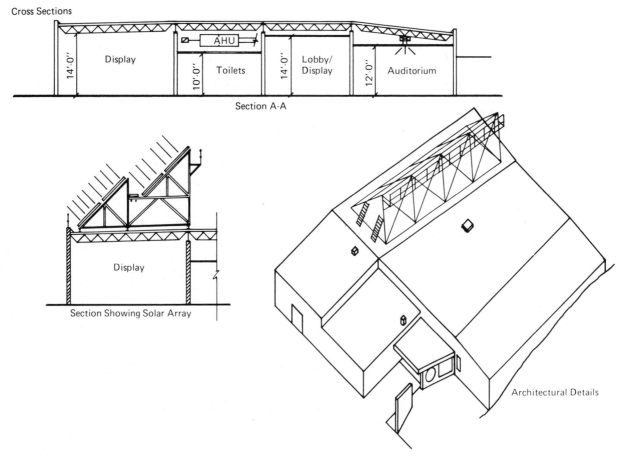

Cross Sections

Section A-A

Section Showing Solar Array

Architectural Details

FIGURE 5-8
Alternative, visitors' information center—solar collector.

analysis is contained in Figure 5-15. In this example, only alternative 3 creates life cycle savings. The remaining two forms, for equipment and for site, are presented as Figure 5-16 and Figure 5-17.

AUTOMATED TOTAL FACILITY ANALYSIS
Economic Building Performance Model[*]

An economic building performance model (EBPM) has been developed to predict more rationally the economic consequences of various decisions made in the design process. This life cycle computer model enables architects and engineers to quickly evaluate the performance of various building design alternatives over the lifetime of the facility. The EBPM combines economic theory with simplistic prediction algorithms concerning initial cost, fuel consumption, maintenance, building alterations, subsystem replacements, and fire protection. The intent of the model

is to provide the designer with comparative economic information about competing design alternatives in the early stages of design when it can be most advantageous.

Structure and Data Base: The EBPM is generally organized utilizing the cost control and estimating system framework known as UNIFORMAT. Currently, the data base contains over 1300 predefined subsystems, which range from concrete foundations to elements such as steam boilers, electrical service entries, and waste handling equipment.

Examples of the types of data contained in the subsystem base include initial cost, thermo-transmittance factor (U factor), maintenance cost useful life, fire protection factor, and equipment energy. A portion of this information, when combined with a few additional variables about the climate, fuel costs, people load, etc., allows calculation of energy consumption for heating, cooling, lighting, and equipment in the facility. Other information, concerning repair, cleaning, and servicing, allows the model to estimate the total maintenance costs. Knowing the useful life of the various subsystems makes calculation of replacement costs possible. Knowing the flexibility of interior subsystems allows prediction of alteration costs (those ex-

[*]Original authorship by Stephen J. Kirk as a part of architectural master's thesis, 1974.

Type	Variable Symbol	Nomenclature	Units Of Measure	Reference	Design Quantities Original *10,680 G.S.F. 8" CMU, STL. Frame bldg.*	Alternative 1 *Ext. Wall & Fndtn. Change to 4" Dk 9½" CMU*	Alternative 2 *Solar Collectr. System Addition to Orig. HVAC*	Alternative 3 *Reduction in Lighting Level from 3 to 2 Watt*
Economic	AA	Building Economic Life	Years		25	25	25	25
	AB	Project Discount Rate	% Of Cost		10%	10%	10%	10%
	AC	Escalation Rate/Yr.—Labor & Materials	% Of Cost		10%	10%	10%	10%
	AD	Escalation Rate/Yr.—Heating Fuel	% Of Cost		9%	9%	9%	9%
	AE	Escalation Rate/Yr.—Cooling Fuel	% Of Cost		5%	5%	5%	5%
	AF	Escalation Rate/Yr.—Lighting Fuel	% Of Cost		5%	5%	5%	5%
	AG	Escalation Rate/Yr.—Domestic Hot Water Fuel	% Of Cost		9%	9%	9%	9%
	AH	Escalation Rate/Yr.—Maintenance	% Of Cost		2%	2%	2%	2%
	AI	Escalation Rate/Yr—Associated Costs	% Of Cost		2%	2%	2%	2%
Facility	BA	Gross Area Of Building	Sq. Ft.	Sketch	10,680	10,680	10,680	10,680
	BB	Normal Building Population	Each	Project	40	40	40	40
	BC	Required Lighting/Year	Hours	Project	2,190	2,190	2,190	2,190
	BD	Average Amount Of Lighting Power Required Over Floor Area	Watt/Sq. Ft.		3	3	3	2
	BE	Domestic Hot Water Boiler Energy Required/Gallon Heated	Btu/Gal.	Manuf.	292	292	292	292
	BF	Domestic Hot Water Usage/Year	Days	Project	365	365	365	365
	BG	Daily Hot Water Gallons/Person	Gallon		3	3	3	3
	BH	Estimated Hourly Heating Load	Btu/HR	ASHRAE	250,000	235,000	250,000	261,000
	BI	Estimated Hourly Cooling Load	Btu/HR	ASHRAE	420,000	412,000	420,000	384,000
	BJ	Air Conditioning Power Per Design Ton	KW		261	261	261	239
					420,000	420,000	420,000	384,000
Site & Climatic	CA	Area Design Cost Factor	N/A		1.00	1.00	1.00	1.00
	CB	Fuel Costs — Heating	$/Million Btu		7.14	7.14	7.14	7.14
	CC	Fuel Costs — Cooling	$/KWh		.035	.035	.035	.035
	CD	Fuel Costs — Domestic Hot Water	$/Million Btu		7.14	7.14	7.14	7.14
	CE	Fuel Costs — Lighting	$/KWh		.035	.035	.035	.035
	CF	Equiv. Full Load Hrs. A.C. Equip. Per Year	Hr.		2050	2050	2050	2050
	CG	Heating Degree Days	Day °F		4000	4000	4000	4000
	CH	Summer Inside Design Temperature	°F		80°	80°	80°	80°
	CI	Winter Inside Design Temperature	°F		72°	72°	72°	72°
	CJ	Summer Outside Design Temperature	°F		95°	95°	95°	95°
	CK	Winter Outside Design Temperature	°F		10°	10°	10°	10°

FIGURE 5-9
Data required for life cycle estimating of visitors' information center.

penses in future years necessary to change the function of the interior spatial layout).

Depending on the nature of the project and the client involved, other life cycle costs may be calculated. Such items as fire protection, financing costs, salvage costs, taxes, depreciation, and tax shelter advantages may be considered.

Before a fair comparison can be made between the design alternatives, all future expenditures must be converted to a common year or baseline to account for the time value of money. The EBPM uses present-worth cost conversion for each year of the building's projected economic life.

Application Requirements: Most information for the model can be obtained from the designer's knowledge of the project and conventional single-line sketches of floor plans, elevations, etc. The designer identifies the subsystems required from a catalog listing, entering only the

Structural Life-Cycle Cost Estimate
(Foundations, Substructure, Superstructure)

		Original 10,680 6.S.F., 8" CMU, STL Frame Bldg.		Alternative 1 Exterior Wall Fndtn. change to 4"brk. 76" C.M.		Alternative 2 Solar Collector System Addition to Original HVAC		Alternative 3 Reduction in Lighting Level from 3 to 2 watt S.F	
		Estimated Costs	Present Worth	Estimated Costs	Present Worth	Estimated Costs	Present Worth	Estimated Costs	Present Worth
Element			1						
01 Foundations									
	011 Standard Foundations	6,750	6,750	8,225	8,225	6,750	6,750	6,750	6,750
	012 Special Foundations	N/A		N/A		N/A		N/A	
02 Substructure									
	021 Slab On Grade	8,980	8,980	8,980	8,980	8,980	8,980	8,980	8,980
	022 Basement Excavation	N/A		N/A		N/A		N/A	
	023 Basement Walls	N/A		N/A		N/A		N/A	
03 Superstructure		N/A		N/A		N/A		N/A	
	031 Floor Construction								
	032 Roof Construction	20,510	20,510	20,510	20,510	20,510	20,510	20,510	20,510
	033 Stair Construction	N/A		N/A		N/A		N/A	
Total Initial Cost			36,240		37,715		36,240		36,240
Annual Costs @ 10 % Discount Rate Escal. Rate 2 % PWA (With Escal.) Factor 11.0			2						
01 Foundations									
	A. Inspection	25	275	25	275	25	275	25	275
	B. Routine Repair, Moistureproofing, Resealing	100	1,100	100	1,100	100	1,100	100	1,100
	C.								
02 Substructure									
	A. Inspection	50	550	50	550	50	550	50	550
	B. Routine Repair, Moistureproofing, Resealing	150	1,650	150	1,650	150	1,650	150	1,650
	C. Painting, Touch-up, Routine Refinishing	50	550	50	550	50	550	50	550
	D.								
03 Superstructure									
	A. Inspection	25	275	25	275	25	275	25	275
	B. Arch. II-Finishes								
	C. Painting, Touch-up, Routine Finishing	150	1,650	150	1,650	150	1,650	150	1,650
	D.								
Total Annual Maintenance Costs			6,050		6,050		6,050		6,050
Single Expenditures @ ___ % Discount Rate Item Replaced: Year: PW Factor:			3						
	A.	N/A		N/A		N/A		N/A	
	B.								
	C.								
	D.								
Total Replacement Costs			0		0		0		0
Annual Costs @ 10 % Discount Rate Escal. Rate ___ % PWA (With Escal.) Factor ___			2						
	A.	N/A		N/A		N/A		N/A	
	B.								
	C.								
Total Annual Associated Costs			0		0		0		0
Final Value @ 25 Year PW Factor .0923			4						
01 Foundations		0	0	0	0	0	0	0	0
02 Substructure		0	0	0	0	0	0	0	0
03 Superstructure		10,000	(923)	10,000	(923)	10,000	(923)	10,000	(923)
Total Salvage Value			(923)		(923)		(923)		(923)
Total Present Worth Costs			41,367		42,842		41,367		41,367

Row labels (left margin): Initial Costs · Maintenance Costs · Replacement Costs · Associated Costs · Salvage Value · LCC

PW — Present Worth   PWA — Present Worth Of Annuity
*Any Structural Impact Has Been Included On Mechanical Form.

FIGURE 5-10
Structural life cycle cost estimate for visitors' information center.

code number and the quantity. Additional variables entered include the project discount rate, the economic life of the facility, and the project's geographic location. Because most of the data necessary to predict the life cycle costs are contained in the data base, the designer can very quickly perform the life cycle analysis.

Architectural Life-Cycle Cost Estimate
Part I (Exterior Closure, Roofing)

Handwritten annotations in column headers:
- Original: 10,680 b.S.F., 8" CMU, STL. Frame Bldg.
- Alternative 1: Ext. Wall ? Fndtn. Change to 4" brick 4" CMU
- Alternative 2: Solar Collector System Addition to Original HVAC
- Alternative 3: Reduction in Lighting Level From 3 to 2 watts S.F.

		Original Estimated Costs	Original Present Worth	Alternative 1 Estimated Costs	Alternative 1 Present Worth	Alternative 2 Estimated Costs	Alternative 2 Present Worth	Alternative 3 Estimated Costs	Alternative 3 Present Worth
Initial Costs	**Element**								
	04 Exterior Closure								
	041 Exterior Walls	18,490	18,490	33,400	33,400	18,490	18,490	18,490	18,490
	042 Exterior Doors And Windows	3,850	3,850	3,850	3,850	3,850	3,850	3,850	3,850
	05 Roofing								
	0501 Roof Coverings	7,480	7,480	7,480	7,480	7,480	7,480	7,480	7,480
	0502 Traffic Toppings & Paving Membranes	N/A		N/A		N/A		N/A	
	0503 Roof Insulation & Fill	5,340	5,340	5,340	5,340	5,340	5,340	5,340	5,340
	0504 Flashings & Trim	1,790	1,790	1,790	1,790	1,790	1,790	1,790	1,790
	0505 Roof Openings	N/A	–	N/A	–	N/A	–	N/A	–
	Total Initial Cost		36,950		51,860		36,950		36,950
Maintenance Costs	Annual Costs @ 10 % Discount Rate Escal. Rate 2 % PWA (With Escal.) Factor 11.0								
	04 Exterior Closure								
	A. Cleaning Windows, Spandrels	40	440	40	440	40	440	40	440
	B. Routine Erection Of Screens, Awnings	N/A		N/A		N/A		N/A	
	C. Touch-Up, Resealing, Routine Refinishing	5	55	5	55	5	55	5	55
	D. Routine Replacement Of Glazing, Panels	5	55	5	55	5	55	5	55
	E.	–	–						
	05 Roof								
	A. Inspection	10	110	10	110	10	110	10	110
	B. Routine Maintenance Of Roof Surface	300	3,300	300	3,300	300	3,300	300	3,300
	C. Cleaning Gutters, Drains	100	1,110	100	1,110	100	1,100	100	1,100
	D. Resealing, Skylight Repairs								
	E. Parapet Repointing	100	1,100	100	1,100	100	1,100	100	1,100
	F.								
	Total Annual Maintenance Costs		6,160		6,160		6,160		6,160
Replacement Costs	Single Expenditures @ 10 % Discount Rate								
	Item Replaced: Year: PW Factor:								
	A. Exterior Restoration 20 .148644	6,000	892	1,000	149	6,000	892	6,000	892
	B. Exterior Painting 7 .613158	3,500	1,746	0	0	3,500	1,746	3,500	1,746
	C. Roof Covering 15 .239392	5,000	1,197	5,000	1,197	5,000	1,197	5,000	1,197
	D. Painting, Reflashing 15 .239392	1,500	369	1,500	369	1,500	369	1,500	369
	E. Exterior Paint 14 .263331	4,500	1,185	0	0	4,500	1,185	4,500	1,185
	F. Exterior Paint 21 .135131	5,500	743	0	0	5,500	743	5,500	743
	Total Replacement Costs		6,172		1,706		6,172		6,172
Associated Costs	Annual Costs @ 10 % Discount Rate Escal. Rate 2 % PWA (With Escal.) Factor 11.0								
	A.	500	5,500	500	5,500	500	5,500	500	5,500
	B.	1,000	11,000	1,000	11,000	1,000	11,000	1,000	11,000
	C.								
	Total Annual Associated Costs		16,500		16,500		16,500		16,500
Salvage Value	Final Value @ 25 Year PW Factor .0923								
	04 Exterior Closure	(3,000)	(277)	(3,000)	(277)	(3,000)	(277)	(3,000)	(277)
	05 Roof	0	0	0	0	0	0	0	0
	Total Salvage Value		(277)		(277)		(277)		(277)
LCC	**Total Present Worth Costs**		65,505		75,948		65,505		65,505

PW — Present Worth   PWA — Present Worth Of Annuity

FIGURE 5-11
Architectural life cycle cost estimate, Part 1.

Architectural Life-Cycle Cost Estimate
Part II (Interior Construction, Conveying Systems)

Original: 10,680 b.S.F., 8" CMU, STL. Frame Bldg.

Alternative 1: Exterior Walls Foundation Change to 4" Brk & 6" CMU

Alternative 2: Solar Collector System Addition to Original HVAC

Alternative 3: Reduction in Lighting Level From 3 to 2 watt /S.F.

		Original Estimated Costs	Original Present Worth	Alt 1 Estimated Costs	Alt 1 Present Worth	Alt 2 Estimated Costs	Alt 2 Present Worth	Alt 3 Estimated Costs	Alt 3 Present Worth
Element			1						
06	Interior Construction								
061	Partitions	8,900	8,900	8,900	8,900	8,900	8,900	8,900	8,900
062	Interior Finishes	11,360	11,360	11,360	11,360	11,360	11,360	11,360	11,360
063	Specialties	4,400	4,400	4,400	4,400	4,400	4,400	4,400	4,400
		—							
07	Conveying Systems								
0701	Elevators	N/A		N/A		N/A		N/A	
0702	Moving Stair & Walks	N/A		N/A		N/A		N/A	
0703	Dumbwaiters	N/A		N/A		N/A		N/A	
0704	Pneumatic Tube Systems	N/A		N/A		N/A		N/A	
			—		—		—		—
Initial Costs — Total Initial Cost			24,660		24,660		24,660		24,660

Annual Costs @ 10 % Discount Rate
Escal. Rate ___ % PWA (With Escal.) Factor ___

		Original Est	Original PW	Alt1 Est	Alt1 PW	Alt2 Est	Alt2 PW	Alt3 Est	Alt3 PW
A.	Salaries (Operation, Etc.)	N/A		N/A		N/A		N/A	
B.	Elevator Energy Cost	N/A		N/A		N/A		N/A	
C.	Moving Stairs & Walks Energy Cost	N/A		N/A		N/A		N/A	
D.	Dumbwaiter Energy Cost	N/A		N/A		N/A		N/A	
E.	Pneumatic Tube System Energy Cost	N/A		N/A		N/A		N/A	
F.		—	—	—	—	—	—	—	—
G.		—	—	—	—	—	—	—	—
Operation Costs — Total Annual Operation Costs			0		0		0		0

Annual Costs @ 10 % Discount Rate
Escal. Rate 2 % PWA (With Escal.) Factor 11.0

		Original Est	Original PW	Alt1 Est	Alt1 PW	Alt2 Est	Alt2 PW	Alt3 Est	Alt3 PW
06	Interior Construction								
A.	Cleaning & Dusting Partitions, Chalkboards	500	5,500	500	5,500	500	5,500	500	5,500
B.	Maintenance Of Operable Partitions	N/A		N/A		N/A		N/A	
C.	Carpet Cleaning, Sweeping	N/A		N/A		N/A		N/A	
D.	Tile. etc., Floor Cleaning & Sweeping	5,000	55,000	5,000	55,000	5,000	55,000	5,000	55,000
E.	Stair Cleaning (If No Arch. Finish, Use Struc. Form Plan)	1,000	11,000	1,000	11,000	1,000	11,000	1,000	11,000
F.									
07	Conveying Systems								
A.	Preventative Maintenance, Inspection	N/A		N/A		N/A		N/A	
B.	Routine Cleaning	N/A		N/A		N/A		N/A	
C.	Repair, Adjustment	N/A		N/A		N/A		N/A	
D.			—		—		—		—
E.		—	—	—	—	—	—	—	—
Maintenance Costs — Total Annual Maintenance Costs			71,500		71,500		71,500		71,500

Single Expenditures @ 10 % Discount Rate

Item Replaced:	Year	PW Factor	Original Est	Original PW	Alt1 Est	Alt1 PW	Alt2 Est	Alt2 PW	Alt3 Est	Alt3 PW
A. Motors, Lifts	N/A		N/A		N/A		N/A		N/A	
B. Interior Painting	6	.564474	2,000	1,129	2,000	1,129	2,000	1,129	2,000	1,129
C. " "	12	.318631	2,500	797	2,500	797	2,500	797	2,500	797
D. " "	18	.179859	3,000	540	3,000	540	3,000	540	3,000	540
Replacement Costs — Total Replacement Costs				2,466		2,466		2,466		2,466

Annual Costs @ 10 % Discount Rate
Escal. Rate 2 % PWA (With Escal.) Factor 11.0

	Original Est	Original PW	Alt1 Est	Alt1 PW	Alt2 Est	Alt2 PW	Alt3 Est	Alt3 PW
A.	500	5,500	500	5,500	500	5,500	500	5,500
B.	—	—	—	—	—	—	—	—
C.	—	—	—	—	—	—	—	—
Associated Costs — Total Annual Associated Costs		5,500		5,500		5,500		5,500

Final Value @ 25 Year PW Factor .0923

	Original Est	Original PW	Alt1 Est	Alt1 PW	Alt2 Est	Alt2 PW	Alt3 Est	Alt3 PW
06 Interior Construction	10,000	(923)	(10,000)	(923)	10,000	(923)	10,000	(923)
07 Conveying Systems	N/A		N/A		N/A		N/A	
Salvage Value — Total Salvage Value		(923)		(923)		(923)		(923)
LCC — Total Present Worth Costs		103,203		103,203		103,203		103,203

PW — Present Worth   PWA — Present Worth Of Annuity

FIGURE 5-12
Architectural life cycle cost estimate, Part 2.

Mechanical Life-Cycle Cost Estimate

		Original $16,680 S.F., 8" CMU, STL. FRAME BLDG.		Alternative 1 EXTERIOR WALL & FOUNDATION CHANGE TO 4" BRK. & 6" CMU.		Alternative 2 SOLAR COLLECTOR SYSTEM ADDITION TO ORIGINAL H.VAC		Alternative 3 REDUCTION IN LIGHTING LEVEL FROM 3 to 2 WATT S.F.	
		Estimated Costs	Present Worth	Estimated Costs	Present Worth	Estimated Costs	Present Worth	Estimated Costs	Present Worth
Initial Costs	**Element**		1						
	08 Mechanical Systems								
	081 Plumbing	11,748	11,748	11,748	11,748	11,748	11,748	11,748	11,748
	082 Heating, Ventilation, & Air Conditioning	68,020	68,020	68,020	68,020	71,020	71,020	62,000	62,000
	083 Fire Protection	N/A		N/A		N/A		N/A	
	084 Special Mechanical Systems (SOLAR)	N/A		N/A		110,000	110,000	N/A	
		–	–	–	–	–	–	–	–
	Total Initial Cost		79,768		79,768		182,768		73,748
Operation Costs	**Annual Costs @ 10 % Discount Rate**		2						
	Escal. Rate NOTED % PWA (With Escal.) Factor NOTED								
	A. Salaries (Operation, Etc.) 20% ; 11.0	1,000	11,000	1,000	11,000	2,000	22,000	1,000	11,000
	B. Domestic Hot Water Energy Cost 9% ; 22.0	78	1,716	78	1,716	6		78	1,716
	C. Heating Energy Cost 9% ; 22.0	2,226	48,972	2,100	46,200	1,113	24,486	2,275	50,050
	D. Ventilation Energy Cost	N/A		N/A		N/A		N/A	
	E. Air Conditioning Energy Cost 5% ; 14.0	1,097	15,358	1,050	14,700	1,097	15,358	1,000	14,000
	F. Pumps, Motors, Etc. Energy Cost 5% ; 14.0	1,467	20,538	1,467	20,538	1,467	20,538	1,467	20,538
	G. Fire Protection Energy Cost 5% ; 14.0	50	700	50	700	50	700	50	700
	H.	–	–	–	–	–	–	–	–
	I.	–	–	–	–	–	–	–	–
	Total Annual Operation Costs		98,284		94,854		83,082		98,004
Maintenance Costs	**Annual Costs @ 10 % Discount Rate**		2						
	Escal. Rate 2 % PWA (With Escal.) Factor 11.0								
	08 Mechanical Systems								
	A. Plumbing & Sewage Cleanout/Repair	60	550	50	550	50	550	50	550
	B. Domestic H.W. System Repair, Adjust.	100	1100	100	1100	100	1100	100	1100
	C. HVAC Preventative Inspection, Testing	100	1100	100	1100	100	1100	100	1100
	D. Routine Cleaning: Ducts, Plenums	100	1100	100	1100	100	1100	100	1100
	E. Routine Cleaning: Boilers, Controls	200	2200	200	2200	200	2200	200	2200
	F. Repair Heating System	200	2200	200	2200	200	2200	200	2200
	G. Repair Ventilation System	100	1100	100	1100	100	1100	100	1100
	H. Repair Air Conditioning System	200	2200	200	2200	200	2200	200	2200
	I. Adjust Controls & Instrumentation	50	550	50	550	50	550	50	550
	J. Routine Replace Filters, Insulation	100	1100	100	1100	100	1100	100	1100
	K. HVAC System Balancing	100	1100	100	1100	100	1100	100	1100
	L. Fire Protection System Cleaning	N/A		N/A		N/A		N/A	
	M. Fire Protection System Repair	N/A		N/A		N/A		N/A	
	N. SOLAR COLLECTOR SYSTEM INSPECTION	N/A		N/A		500	5,500	N/A	
	O. " " " REPAIR	N/A		N/A		645	7,095	N/A	
	Total Annual Maintenance Costs		14,300		14,300		26,895		14,300
Replacement Costs	**Single Expenditures @ ___% Discount Rate**		3						
	Item Replaced: Year: PW Factor:								
	A. H.W. Boiler								
	B. Pumps, Motors								
	C. Control System								
	D. 13 .289664	N/A		N/A		2,500	724	N/A	
	E.								
	F.								
	Total Replacement Costs		0		0		724		0
	Annual Costs @ ___% Discount Rate								
	Escal. Rate ___% PWA (With Escal.) Factor ___								
	A.								
	B.								
	Total Annual Associated Costs								
Salvage Value	**Final Value @ 25 Year PW Factor .0923**								
	08 Mechanical System	(20,000)(	1,846)	(20,000)(	1,846)	(40,000)(	3,692)	(19,000)(	1,764)
	Total Salvage Value		(1,846)		(1,846)		(3,692)		(1,764)
LCC	**Total Present Worth Costs**		190,506		187,076		289,777		184,298

PW — Present Worth   PWA — Present Worth Of Annuity

FIGURE 5-13

Mechanical life cycle cost estimate.

Electrical Life-Cycle Cost Estimate

	Original 10,680 G.S.F., 8" CMU, STL. FRAME BUILDING		Alternative 1 EXTERIOR WALL & FOUNDATION CHANGE TO 4" BRK & 6" CMU		Alternative 2 SOLAR COLLECTOR SYSTEM ADDITION TO ORIGINAL H.V.A.C.		Alternative 3 REDUCTION IN LIGHTING LEVEL FROM 3 TO 2 WATT/ S.F.	
	Estimated Costs	Present Worth	Estimated Costs	Present Worth	Estimated Costs	Present Worth	Estimated Costs	Present Worth

Element

Initial Costs

	Estimated	Present Worth	Estimated	Present Worth	Estimated	Present Worth	Estimated	Present Worth
09 Electrical								
091 Service & Distribution	2,670	2,670	2,670	2,670	2,670	2,670	2,670	2,670
092 Lighting & Power	32,040	32,040	32,040	32,040	32,040	32,040	25,000	25,000
093 Special Electrical System (SMOKE DETECTORS)	2,136	2,136	2,136	2,136	2,136	2,136	2,136	2,136
	—	—	—	—	—	—	—	—
Total Initial Cost		36,846		36,846		36,846		29,806

Operation Costs

Annual Costs @ _10_ % Discount Rate
Escal. Rate _5_ % PWA (With Escal.) Factor _14.0_

	Estimated	Present Worth	Estimated	Present Worth	Estimated	Present Worth	Estimated	Present Worth
A. Salaries (Operation, Etc.)	50	700	50	700	50	700	35	490
B. Lighting Energy Cost	2,243	31,402	2,243	31,402	2,243	31,402	1,550	21,700
C. Communications/Alarm Energy Cost	N/A	N/A	N/A	N/A	N/A	N/A	N/A	N/A
D. Emergency Light/Power Energy Cost	N/A	N/A	N/A	N/A	N/A	N/A	N/A	N/A
E. Electric Heating Energy Cost	N/A		N/A		N/A		N/A	
F.	—	—	—	—	—	—	—	—
G.								
Total Annual Operation Costs		32,102		32,102		32,102		22,190

Maintenance Costs

Annual Costs @ _10_ % Discount Rate
Escal. Rate _2_ % PWA (With Escal.) Factor _11.0_

	Estimated	Present Worth	Estimated	Present Worth	Estimated	Present Worth	Estimated	Present Worth
A. Inspection, Testing, & Maint. Of Safety	100	1,100	100	1,100	100	1,100	100	1,100
B. Relamping And Routine Replacement	250	2,750	250	2,750	250	2,750	100	1,100
C. Repair Communications/Alarm System	100	1,100	100	1,100	100	1,100	100	1,100
D. Repair Electric Heating System	N/A		N/A		N/A		N/A	
E. SMOKE DETECTOR SYSTEM INSPECTION	100	1,100	100	1,100	100	1,100	100	1,100
F.	—							
Total Annual Maintenance Costs		6,050		6,050		6,050		6,050

Replacement Costs

Single Expenditures @ _10_ % Discount Rate

Item Replaced: Year: PW Factor:

	Estimated	Present Worth	Estimated	Present Worth	Estimated	Present Worth	Estimated	Present Worth
A. Distribution System								
B. Lighting System								
C. Commun./Alarm								
D. Emergency Generator								
E. Elec. Heat Equip.								
F.								
G.								
H.								
Total Replacement Costs		0		0		0		0

Associated Costs

Annual Costs @ _10_ % Discount Rate
Escal. Rate ___ % PWA (With Escal.) Factor ___

	Estimated	Present Worth	Estimated	Present Worth	Estimated	Present Worth	Estimated	Present Worth
A.								
B.								
C.								
Total Annual Associated Costs		0		0		0		0

Salvage Value

Final Value @ _25_ Year   PW Factor _.0923_

	Estimated	Present Worth	Estimated	Present Worth	Estimated	Present Worth	Estimated	Present Worth
09 Electrical	(10,000)	(923)	(10,000)	(923)	(10,000)	(923)	(7,000)	(646)
Total Salvage Value		(923)		(923)		(923)		(646)

LCC

Total Present Worth Costs		74,075		74,075		74,075		56,410

PW — Present Worth   PWA — Present Worth Of Annuity

FIGURE 5-14

Electrical life cycle cost estimate.

Life-Cycle Cost Estimate Summary

	Original 10,680 G.S.F., 8" CMU, STL. Frame Bldg.		Alternative 1 Exterior Wall: Fndtn Change to 4"Brk.½6" CMU		Alternative 2 Solar Collector System Addition To Original H.V.A.C.		Alternative 3 Reduction In Lighting Level from 3 to 2 watt/S.F.	
	Estimated Costs	Present Worth	Estimated Costs	Present Worth	Estimated Costs	Present Worth	Estimated Costs	Present Worth
Initial Costs								
Planning, Design, Special Studies Fees								
Structural	36,240	36,240	37,715	37,715	36,240	36,240	36,240	36,240
Architectural (Parts I & II)	61,610	61,610	76,520	76,520	61,610	61,610	61,610	61,610
Mechanical	79,768	79,768	79,768	79,768	82,768	82,768	73,748	73,748
Electrical	36,846	36,846	36,846	36,846	3,846	36,846	29,806	29,806
General Conditions & Profit ___% (If Approp.)	34,650	34,650	36,000	36,000	40,000	40,000	32,000	32,000
Equipment								
Sitework								
Other								
Contingencies ___%	24,900	24,900	25,700	25,700	27,000	27,000	23,700	23,700
Escalation ___%	8,200	8,200	8,700	8,700	9,000	9,000	8,100	8,100
Total Initial Cost		282,100		301,249		393,464		266,204
Operations								
Architectural (Part II)	0	0	0	0	0	0	0	0
Mechanical	5,918	98,284	5,745	94,864	6,721	83,082	4,745	98,004
Electrical	2,293	32,102	2,293	32,102	2,293	32,102	1,585	22,190
Equipment								
Sitework								
Other								
Total Annual Operations Costs		130,386		126,966		115,184		120,194
Maintenance								
Structural	550	6,050	550	6,050	550	6,050	550	6,050
Architectural (Parts I & II)	7,060	77,660	7,060	77,660	7,060	77,660	7,060	77,060
Mechanical	1,300	14,300	1,300	14,300	2,445	26,895	1,300	14,300
Electrical	550	6,050	550	6,050	550	6,050	460	5,060
Equipment								
Sitework								
Other								
Total Annual Maintenance Costs		104,060		104,060		116,065		103,070
Alterations								
Item(s) Altered / Year / PW Factor								
A.	0	0	0	0	0	0	0	0
B.								
C.								
D.								
Total Alteration Costs								
Replacement								
Structural	0	0	0	0	0	0	0	0
Architectural (Parts I & II)	33,500	8,638	15,000	4,171	33,500	8,638	33,600	8,638
Mechanical	0	0	0	0	2,500	724	0	0
Electrical	0	0	0	0	0	0	0	0
Equipment								
Sitework								
Other								
Total Replacement Costs		8,638		4,171		9,362		8,638
Financing Costs								
Functional Use Costs								
Denial Of Use Costs								
Associated								
A. Fire Protection	1,000	11,000	1,000	11,000	1,000	11,000	1,000	11,000
B. Security	1,000	11,000	1,000	11,000	1,000	11,000	1,000	11,000
C.								
D.								
E.								
Total Annual Associated Costs		22,000		22,000		22,000		22,000
Total Owning Present Worth Costs		265,084		257,187		262,601		253,902
Salvage								
Building (Struc., Arch., Mech., Elec., Equip.)	(53,000)	(4,892)	(53,000)	(4,892)	(73,000)	(6,738)	(49,000)	(4,523)
Other								
Sitework								
Total Salvage Value		(4,892)		(4,892)		(6,738)		(4,523)
Total Present Worth Life Cycle Costs		542,292		553,544		649,327		514,583
Life-Cycle Present Worth Dollar Savings				(11,252)		(107,035)		27,709

FIGURE 5-15

Life cycle cost estimate summary.

Equipment Life-Cycle Cost Estimate

	Original		Alternative 1		Alternative 2		Alternative 3	
	Estimated Costs	Present Worth	Estimated Costs	Present Worth	Estimated Costs	Present Worth	Estimated Costs	Present Worth
Initial Costs — Element 11 Equipment 111 Fixed And Movable Equipment____ 112 Furnishings____ 113 Special Construction____ **Total Initial Cost**								
Operation Costs — Annual Costs @____% Discount Rate Escal. Rate____% PWA (With Escal.) Factor____ A. Salaries (Operation, Etc.)____ B. Food Service Equip. Energy Cost____ C. Vending Equip. Energy Cost____ D. Waste Handling Equip. Energy Cost____ E. ____ F. ____ G. ____ **Total Annual Operation Costs**								
Maintenance Costs — Annual Costs @____% Discount Rate Escal. Rate____% PWA (With Escal.) Factor____ A. Inspection And Testing Of Equipment____ B. General Cleaning, Dusting Of Equip.____ C. Repair Food Service Equipment____ D. Repair Vending Equipment____ E. Repair Waste Handling Equipment____ F. ____ G. ____ **Total Annual Maintenance Costs**								
Replacement Costs — Single Expenditures @____% Discount Rate Item Replaced: Year: PW Factor: A. ____ B. ____ C. ____ D. ____ **Total Replacement Costs**								
Associated Costs — Annual Costs @____% Discount Rate Escal. Rate____% PWA (With Escal.) Factor____ A. ____ B. ____ C. ____ **Total Annual Associated Costs**								
Salvage Value — Final Value @____Year PW Factor____ 11 Equipment____ **Total Salvage Value**								
LCC — **Total Present Worth Costs**								

PW — Present Worth   PWA — Present Worth Of Annuity

FIGURE 5-16
Equipment life cycle cost estimate.

Examples of the types of projects to which the EBPM has been applied include office buildings, maintenance shops, a veterans hospital, and bank buildings. By making design trade-offs, certain features may be substituted for others, which are then tested. Questions such as whether the project should have a longer-lasting roof, a higher-quality boiler, more landscaping, or more exterior exposure can all be systematically evaluated.

Because of the increasing complexity and number of considerations faced by the designer, additional tools are necessary. The design professional using EBPM can compare the total cost of ownership of competing design alternatives and thereby better satisfy the client's needs.

To test the model just described, a 200-bed health care facility to be constructed by a large government agency was examined. Preliminary design drawings were reviewed

Sitework Life-Cycle Cost Estimate

	Original		Alternative 1		Alternative 2		Alternative 3	
	Estimated Costs	Present Worth	Estimated Costs	Present Worth	Estimated Costs	Present Worth	Estimated Costs	Present Worth

Element
 12 Sitework
   121 Site Preparation_____
   122 Site Improvements_____
   123 Site Utilities_____
   124 Off-Site Work_____
 	
   Real Estate_____
 Total Initial Cost								

Annual Costs @____% Discount Rate
 Escal. Rate____% PWA (With Escal.) Factor_____
   A. Salaries (Operation, Etc.)_____
   B. Lighting Energy Cost_____
   C. Snow Melting System Energy Cost_____
   D._____
   E._____
 Total Annual Operation Costs								

Annual Costs @____% Discount Rate
 Escal. Rate____% PWA (With Escal.) Factor_____
   A. General Site Cleaning_____
   B. Landscaping Maintenance_____
   C. Snow & Ice Removal (Parking, Walks)_____
   D. Relamping And Routine Replacement_____
   E._____
   F._____
 Total Annual Maintenance Costs								

Single Expenditures @____% Discount Rate
 Item Replaced: Year: PW Factor:
   A. Trees, Shrubs_____
   B. Parking Pavement_____
   C._____
   D._____
   E._____
 Total Replacement Costs								

Annual Costs @____% Discount Rate
 Escal. Rate____% PWA (With Escal.) Factor_____
   A._____
   B._____
   C._____
   D._____
 Total Annual Associated Costs								

Final Value @____Year PW Factor_____ 12 Sitework_____ **Total Salvage Value**								
Total Present Worth Costs								

PW — Present Worth   PWA — Present Worth Of Annuity

FIGURE 5-17
Sitework life cycle cost estimate.

to identify constraints in achieving the required function at the lowest total cost of ownership consistent with desired performance (Figure 5-18). The initial design analysis was based on the data predicted by the model from the printout shown in Figures 5-19 through 5-20. As alternatives were proposed, the EBPM was used for evaluation against the initial design ("shown as Design Alternative 2 on the printout," Figure 5-22.)

Sample Project Application—Health Care Facility

Layout and Architectural Study: The original health care facility design consisted of four one-story 50-bed units connected by enclosed corridors to a central two-story support facility. A detailed functional requirements analysis was prepared to further understand and define the scope of the project. From space planning worksheets it

Health Care Facility

Data:
Initial Cost $ 6,505,000
Life Cycle Cost $ 13,471,000
Annual Energy   12,879 x 10^6 Btu

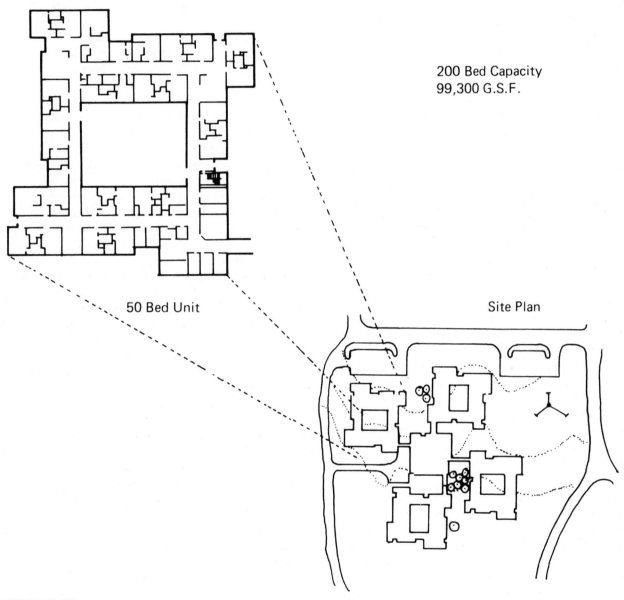

200 Bed Capacity
99,300 G.S.F.

50 Bed Unit

Site Plan

FIGURE 5-18
Health care facility, before LCC study.

was determined that a gross area of 18,000 square feet per 50-bed unit and 21,000 gross square feet for the support facility would satisfy the functions required. The health care facility was located on a sloping, wooded site to the east of the existing center.

Figure 5-19 shows the site and a typical 50-bed unit floor plan. The grades in the area of the site used dropped 20 feet from one side to the other. The grade change resulted in a two-story support facility with two units connecting to the lower level. The gross area of the project was approximately 99,300 square feet as follows: four 50-bed units at 19,000 square feet each, connecting corridors 1,500 square feet, and support facility 21,810 square feet.

As a result of the LCC layout study and life cycle analysis by the EBPM, a major redesign of the prototype 50-bed unit was recommended. Figure 5-20 illustrates the following features of the new design:

- Elimination of the courtyard with all rooms given a view.
- Relocation of the support services to the central core.
- Relocation of the bathrooms to the corridor side of the bedrooms.

The design also achieves the following beneficial results:

- Reduction of gross area by approximately 1000 square feet per 50-bed unit.
- Reduction of the length of exterior wall by approximately 450 linear feet.
- A more efficient arrangement of mechanical services.
- Less ground coverage, resulting in lower site development costs, loss of fewer trees, and improved site adaptability on a difficult site.
- Significant reduction in travel distance and improved function if the facility is altered in the future.
- Virtual elimination of connecting enclosed corridors.

As predicted by the EBPM, these items provide an initial savings of $515,000. It is further estimated that an additional savings of $75,000 will be realized from changes in site and connecting corridors. A one-level facility as shown provides an additional initial-cost savings of $50,000 in the central support facility.

Mechanical and Energy Study: The original HVAC system for the health care facility consisted of centralized dual electric rooftop packaged units located at the support facility, which, in turn, distributes chilled water to all bedroom units. High-pressure steam from an outside source is supplied to a centralized mechanical equipment room where it is converted to hot water for heating. Also, steam is redistributed to each 50-bed unit for domestic water heating.

Each 50-bed unit was provided with a 100 percent outside air supply rooftop air-handling unit with preheat,

cooling, and reheat coils, which condition ventilation air to each bedroom and corridor space. The ventilation air offsets the exhaust requirements for the bathrooms and toilets within the module. The bathroom air was exhausted to the atmosphere by exhaust fans, with no provisions for energy recovery.

Each 50-bed unit was provided with a perimeter fan coil to compensate for the external environmental changes and interior loads. Also, each exterior bathroom area was provided with a hot water converter heater, which was connected to the same forced hot water circulating loop serving the fan coil units. Domestic hot water was to be generated in each 50-bed unit on an individual basis with dual steam-to-hot-water converters.

For the required functions, the existing concepts appeared valid, although high in initial and operational cost. To reduce initial and life cycle costs, the mechanical team developed an alternative layout for the facility. The proposed HVAC system for the alternative layout was studied by the layout and architectural team for maximum cost optimization and energy conservation. The proposed system concept requires a centrally located mechanical equipment room within the support facility, where chilled water for cooling, hot water for heating, and domestic hot water are generated and circulated to all 50-bed units.

As a result of the new building layout and configuration, the exhaust system may be economically utilized for transfer of building heating and cooling energy to the outside ventilation air by means of a rotary enthalpy exchanger.

Also, to further minimize the outside air intake requirements, the air-conditioning units were arranged so as to simplify the system operation and maintenance. The air-conditioning units serve each bedroom unit with air to balance the bathroom exhausts and also serve the interior zone areas with conditioned air to satisfy the temperature needs. Air is recirculated from these areas. Four-pipe fan coil units are arranged to offset the outside environmental changes and satisfy the room temperature control requirements. All the mechanical team suggestions were tested and analyzed using the EBPM. The model predicted that in addition to the savings shown from architectural items, the initial cost of the health care facility would be reduced by $225,000. In energy savings potential alone the model predicted a 3,711 million Btu reduction per year. Life cycle cost savings amounted to over $400,000 present-worth dollars.

Conclusions: Because of the success achieved using both traditional and new tools and techniques, the health care facility has improved performance at a reduced total cost of ownership. With the increasing complexity and number of considerations faced by all design professionals, additional tools are necessary. The design professional, using EBPM, can compare the total cost of ownership of competing design alternatives and thereby better satisfy the client's needs.

SYSTEM NUMBER	BUILDING SYSTEM NAME AND DESCRIPTION	QUANTITY	UM	INITIAL COST/UM	MAINTENANCE COST/UM/YR	U-FACTOR	FIRE PRO FACTOR	EQ DAY/YR	ENERGY KW	ALTER COST	% COST REPLAC	LIFE
10113	12" RNF CONCRETE FOUNDATION WALL 2500# CONCRETE LOAD = 95 KIP/LF	5900.00	WSF	7.37	0.	0.	0.	0	0.	0.	100.	99
10121	12" THICK RNF CONCRETE SPREAD FOOTING 2 500# CONCRETE LOAD = 2.65 KIP/LF	2114.00	SF	2.32	0.	0.	0.0024	0	0.	0.	0.	99
10161	12" X 12" FORMED RNF CONC PIER 2500# CO NCRETE LOAD = 95 KIPS	108.00	LF	18.20	0.	0.	0.	0	0.	0.	100.	99
10172	14" RNF CONC SPOT FOOTING 2500# CONCRET E LOAD = 50 KIPS	340.00	SF	2.80	0.	0.	0.	0	0.	0.	100.	99
20103	12" X 18" RNF CONCRETE COLUMN	300.00	LF	22.00	0.	0.	0.0025	0	0.	0.	100.	99
30112	5" SLAB ON GRADE W/WWM, VAPOR BARRIER, & 4" FILL 3000# CONCRETE LOADING CAPA	19000.00	SF	1.28	0.	0.02	0.	0	0.	0.	100.	99
39010	VINYL ASBESTOS TILE FLOORING R = .06	16500.00	SF	0.62	0.62	0.	0.0024	0	0.	0.1	100.	20
40204	10" PRECAST HOLLOW CORE SLAB W/2" CONCR ETE FILL AND BUILT-UP ROOFING 4000# P	19500.00	RSF	4.45	0.	0.10	0.0025	0	0.	0.	15.	15
49103	ADD PER INCH - THICKNESS FOR RIGID INSU LATION R = 2.78	58500.00	SF	0.30	0.	0.	0.0049	0	0.	0.	100.	99
49201	SUSPENDED PLASTER CEILING R = .47	600.00	SF	3.07	0.06	0.	0.0080	0	0.	0.	100.	15
49204	24" X 48" EXPOSED GRID SUSPENDED ACOUSTICAL TILE CEILING	16500.00	SF	0.45	0.01	0.	0.0080	0	0.	0.	40.	10
50312	4" FACE BRICK VENEER W/6" CONCRETE BLOC K BACK-UP BEARING LOAD = 12 KIPS/LF	10200.00	WSF	6.12	0.01	0.15	0.0025	0	0.	0.	100.	99
	5/8" GYPSUM DRYWALL R = .11	10200.00	WSF	0.63	0.06	0.	0.	0	0.	0.	100.	30
	LED FOR CEILING		SF	0.30	0.	0.	0.0080	0	0.	0.	100.	99
111007	MODIFIER FOR STEAM HEAT EXCHANGER							0	0.	0.	100.	50
112020	RECIPROCATING CHILLER CENTRAL REFRIGERA TION SYSTEM	30.00	TON	221.00	5.00							
112045	AIR-COOLED CONDENSER FOR CENTRAL REFRIG ERATION SYSTEM	30.00	TON	370.00	5.00	0.	0.	0	0.	0.	100.	
112060	PUMPS, TANKS & SPECIALS FOR CENTRAL BOI LER HEATING SYSTEM	30.00	TON	25.95	5.00	0.	0.0025	125	0.230	0.	30.	10
112062	PUMPS FOR CENTRAL REFRIGERATION SYSTEM	30.00	TON	31.28	0.75	0.	0.0025	50	0.330	0.	10.	10
112064	PUMPS FOR CENTRAL REFRIGERATION SYSTEM A DD TO 112060 IF 2 PIPE OR NO CLNG TWR	30.00	TON	16.67	0.40	0.	0.0025	0	0.	0.	20.	10
112075	INSULATED HEATING PIPING TO AIR HAND- L ING UNITS OF CENTRAL BOILER SYSTEM	30.00	TON	154.60	0.15	0.	0.	0	0.	0.	10.	20
112077	INSULATED CHILLED WATER PIPING TO AIR H ANDLING UNITS OF CENTRAL COOLING SYST US	30.00	TON	185.13	1.85	0.	0.0025	0	0.	0.	100.	50
115034	MULTI-ZONE AIR HANDLING UNIT W/HW & CHW COILS, VIB MT, & AUTOROLL FILTER	30.00	TON	515.00	10.00	0.	0.0025	365	0.330	0.	10.	10
116020	LOW VELOCITY DUCT DISTRIBUTION & AIR DE VICES FOR AIR CONDITIONING SYSTEM	30.00	TON	368.01	3.28	0.	0.0025	0	0.	0.	10.	20
117020	FAN COIL TERMINAL UNIT	30.00	TON	465.00	5.00	0.	0.0025	175	0.230	0.	10.	5
118020	CONTROLS FOR CENTRAL PLANT AIR CONDI- T IONING W/MULTI-ZONE CHW COILS AHU	30.00	TON	235.00	1.78	0.	0.0025	0	0.	0.	100.	20
121010	COMBINATION 120/208 & 277/480-3 PHASE 4 WIRE GROUNDED ELECTRIC SERVICE EN- T	19000.00	SF	1.26	0.03	0.	0.0025	0	0.	0.	100.	16
126010	RECESSED FLUORESCENT LIGHTING	1.36	KW	1024.99	40.00	0.	0.0025	0	0.	0.	100.	25
126027	SURFACE MOUNTED INCANDESCENT LIGHTING	32.00	KW	600.00	48.41	0.	0.0024	0	0.	0.	30.	22
126060	EMERGENCY LIGHTING	19000.00	SF	0.10	0.	0.	0.0050	0	0.	0.	50.	15
129010	TELEPHONE CONDUIT & OUTLETS W/FISHWIRE	19000.00	SF	0.05	0.01	0.	0.0024	0	0.	0.	100.	50
129151	NURSES CALL SYSTEM (STUB-UP ONLY)	50.00	BED	65.00	0.01	0.	0.0025	0	0.	0.	0.	99
129300	FIRE DETECTION & ALARM SYSTEM	19000.00	SF	0.22	0.01	0.	0.0025	0	0.	0.	100.	25
129400	COMMERCIAL TELEVISION RECEPTION SYSTEM	19000.00	SF	0.17	0.	0.	0.0025	50	0.002	0.	50.	15
130100	KITCHEN EQUIPMENT - RANGE, SINK	3.00	EA	650.00	10.00	0.	0.0050	0	0.	0.	100.	14

FIGURE 5-19
Life cycle systems data for health care facility.

ECONOMIC BUILDING PERFORMANCE MODEL
DESIGN ALTERNATIVE 1
DATE 16 SEP 77

****** LIFE CYCLE BUILDING COST SUMMARY ******

A. THE INITAL COST FOR THE PROPOSED PROJECT IS   975958.89 DOLLARS

B. THE AVERAGE ANNUAL OWNING AND OPERATING COSTS ARE 162686.19 DOLLARS

        PROJECT DISCOUNT RATE (I) = 7.0 PER CENT
        PROJECT DESIGN TIME TO CONSTRUCTION = 0.90 YEARS
        PROJECT CONSTRUCTION TIME = 1.00 YEARS

C. SUMMARY OF YEAR BY YEAR ECONOMIC BUILDING PERFORMANCE:

END OF YEAR	ENERGY CONSUMPTION COSTS				ALTERATION COSTS	MAINTENANCE COSTS	REPLACEMENT COSTS	FIRE PROTECTION COSTS	COST SUMMARY	
	HEATING	COOLING	LIGHTING	EQUIP.					ANNUAL EXPENDITURE	PRESENT WORTH
0									24505.29	24505.29
1	5992.73	989.94	3171.48	9446.10	991.75	22338.71	0.00	1713.37	43652.34	40796.57
2	6412.22	1059.24	3393.48	10107.33	1065.22	22785.49	0.00	1747.64	45505.39	39746.17
3	6861.07	1133.38	3631.03	10814.84	1138.68	23241.20	0.00	1782.59	47464.12	38744.86
4	7341.35	1212.72	3885.20	11571.88	1212.14	23706.02	0.00	1818.24	49535.41	37790.33
5	7855.24	1297.61	4157.16	12381.91	1285.61	24180.14	2774.04	1854.61	54500.72	38858.26
6	8405.11	1388.44	4448.16	13248.64	1359.07	24663.74	0.00	1891.70	54045.81	36013.00
7	8993.47	1485.64	4759.54	14176.05	1432.53	25157.02	0.00	1929.54	56501.24	35186.13
8	9623.01	1589.63	5092.70	15168.37	1506.00	25660.16	0.00	1968.13	59102.00	34397.90
9	10298.62	1700.90	5449.19	16230.16	1579.46	26173.36	0.00	2007.49	61857.73	33646.50
10	11017.38	1819.97	5830.64	17366.27	1652.92	26696.83	28393.00	2047.64	93171.73	47363.78
11	11788.60	1947.37	6238.78	18581.91	1726.39	27230.77	0.00	2088.59	67876.01	32247.40
12	12613.80	2083.68	6675.50	19882.64	1799.85	27775.38	793.80	2130.36	71955.17	31948.95
		2229.54	7142.78	21274.43	1873.31	28330.89	0.00	2172.97	74647.38	30976.00
25	30397.91				2045.77	28897.51	4134.00	2216.43	82481.50	31987.74
26	32525.12	5372.84	17212.99	51268.07				2860.76	155212.09	56256.00
27	34801.88	5748.94	18417.90	54856.84	2901.80	37382.01	0.00		169165.53	25442.0
28	37238.01	6151.37	19707.16	58696.82	2975.26	38129.65	6318.00	2924.53	169165.53	
29	39844.67	6581.96	21086.66	62805.59	3048.72	38892.24	0.00	2983.02	172194.15	24204.09
30	42633.80	7042.70	22562.72	67201.98	3122.19	39670.09	196859.79	3042.68	379013.77	49789.94
31	45618.17	7535.69	24142.11	71906.12	3195.65	40463.49	0.00	3103.54	192769.12	23666.34
32	48811.44	8063.19	25832.06	76939.55	3269.11	41272.76	85226.40	3165.61	289311.01	33195.86
33	52228.24	8627.61	27640.31	82325.32	3342.58	42098.21	0.00	3228.92	216148.61	23178.63
34	55884.21	9231.55	29575.13	88083.09	3416.04	42940.18	0.00	3293.50	229012.66	22951.43
35	59796.11	9877.75	31645.39	94254.26	3489.50	43798.98	45529.55	3359.37	288261.41	26999.40
36	63981.84	10569.20	33860.56	100852.06	3562.97	44674.96	1571.40	3426.56	258936.57	22686.13
37	68460.57	11309.04	36230.80	107911.70	3636.43	45568.46	0.00	3495.09	272975.66	22331.82
38	73252.81	12100.67	38766.96	115465.52	3709.89	46479.83	0.00	3564.99	289630.77	22144.2
39	78380.50	12947.72	41480.65	123548.10	3783.35	47409.42	0.00	3636.29	307402.69	21965.46
40	83867.14	13854.06	44384.29	132196.47	3856.82	48357.61	278794.82	3709.01	605163.41	40413.03
TOTALS	1196359.	197627.	633139.	1885773.	96971.42	1349303.	1141756.	103491.	6531952.75	1370749.59

D. THE TOTAL COST OF THE PROPOSED PROJECT OVER ITS LIFE OF 40 YEARS IN PRESENT WORTH DOLLARS IS   2346708.50

E. THE ENERGY CONSUMED BY THIS DESIGN ON A YEARLY BASIS IS   2954. MILLION BTU

        HEATING ENERGY   =   996. MILLION BTU
        COOLING ENERGY   =   126. MILLION BTU
        LIGHTING ENERGY   =   404. MILLION BTU
        EQUIPMENT ENERGY =   1428. MILLION BTU

        HEAT RECOVERY DOLLAR SAVINGS PER YEAR =   0.

FIGURE 5-20
Life cycle building cost summary before study—typical 50-bed domiciliary unit of health care facility.

Health Care Facility

After Costs:
Initial $5,640,000
Life Cycle $11,651,000
Annual Energy   9168 x 10^6 Btu

Savings:
Initial $ 865,000
Life Cycle $ 1,820,000
Annual Energy   3711 x 10^6 Btu

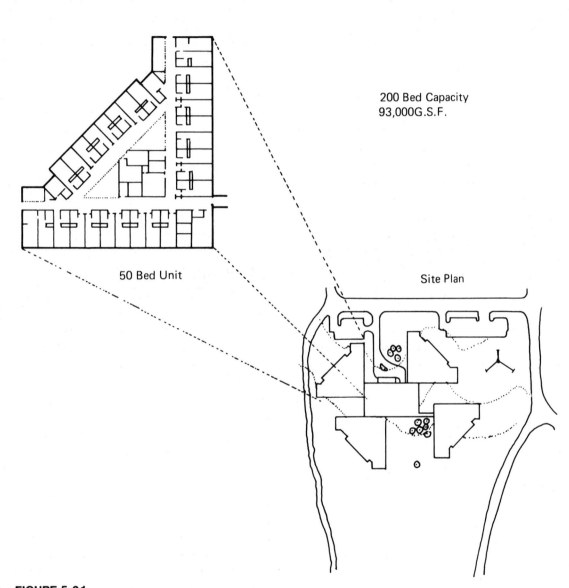

200 Bed Capacity
93,000 G.S.F.

50 Bed Unit

Site Plan

FIGURE 5-21
Health care facility after LCC study.

SUMMARY

This book recommends a format using the present-worth method. With increasing initial, maintenance, and operation costs, together with rising interest rates and escalating energy and labor costs, the concept of LCC for decision making has become increasingly important. No major decision pertaining to buildings that involves large follow-on costs should be made without using an LCC technique. This technique must be based on bringing all costs to a common baseline. The forms contained in this chapter assist the designer in this process.

ECONOMIC BUILDING PERFORMANCE MODEL
DESIGN ALTERNATIVE 2
DATE 16 SEP 77

****** LIFE CYCLE BUILDING COST SUMMARY ******

A. THE INITAL COST FOR THE PROPOSED PROJECT IS   821718.08 DOLLARS

B. THE AVERAGE ANNUAL OWNING AND OPERATING COSTS ARE 136693.81 DOLLARS

        PROJECT DISCOUNT RATE (I) = 7.0 PER CENT
        PROJECT DESIGN TIME TO CONSTRUCTION = 0.90 YEARS
        PROJECT CONSTRUCTION TIME = 1.00 YEARS

C. SUMMARY OF YEAR BY YEAR ECONOMIC BUILDING PERFORMANCE:

END OF YEAR	ENERGY CONSUMPTION COSTS				ALTERATION COSTS	MAINTENANCE COSTS	REPLACEMENT COSTS	FIRE PROTECTION COSTS	COST SUMMARY	
	HEATING	COOLING	LIGHTING	EQUIP.					ANNUAL EXPENDITURE	PRESENT WORTH
0									20632.47	20632.47
1	3081.91	730.78	3025.42	7953.89	1084.91	24745.46	0.00	1563.87	41101.32	38412.44
2	3297.64	781.93	3237.20	8510.66	1165.28	25240.36	0.00	1595.14	42662.94	37263.47
3	3528.48	836.67	3463.81	9106.40	1245.64	25745.17	0.00	1627.05	44307.57	36168.18
4	3775.47	895.23	3706.28	9743.85	1326.01	26260.07	0.00	1659.59	46040.49	35124.07
5	4039.75	957.90	3965.71	10425.92	1406.37	26785.28	2448.54	1692.78	50315.89	35874.53
6	4322.54	1024.95	4243.32	11155.74	1486.73	27320.98	0.00	1726.63	49794.15	33179.95
7	4625.11	1096.70	4540.35	11936.64	1567.10	27867.40	0.00	1761.17	51827.36	32275.48
8	4948.87	1173.47	4858.17	12772.20	1647.46	28424.75	0.00	1796.39	53973.85	31413.27
	5295.29	1255.61	5198.24	13666.26	1727.83	28993.24	0.00	1832.32	56240.96	30591.36
			5562.12	14622.89	1808.19	29573.11	23235.34	1868.97	81871.90	41619.52
22	12760.83	3029.00			1888.55	30164.57	0.00	1906.34	61169.01	29060.95
23	13654.09	3237.63	13403.85	35238.72			661.50	1944.47	64508.79	28542.67
24	14609.88	3464.27	14342.12	37705.63	2933.29			1987.36	66680.99	27670.24
25	15632.57	3706.77	15346.07	40345.02	3013.65	39801.51	147231.60			28626.47
26	16726.85	3966.24	16420.29	43169.18	3094.01	40597.54	0.00	2565.69	123445.7	
27	17897.73	4243.88	17569.71	46191.02	3174.38	41409.49	0.00	2617.00	129928.83	20909.49
28	19150.57	4540.95	18799.59	49424.39	3254.74	42237.68	6318.00	2669.34	143140.53	21528.65
29	20491.11	4858.81	20115.56	52884.10	3335.11	43082.44	0.00	2722.73	144154.75	20262.79
30	21925.49	5198.93	21523.65	56585.98	3415.47	43944.09	167927.83	2777.18	319883.15	42022.12
31	23460.27	5562.86	23030.31	60547.00	3495.83	44822.97	0.00	2832.73	160256.13	19675.12
32	25102.49	5952.26	24642.43	64785.29	3576.20	45719.43	81301.50	2889.38	250392.78	28730.34
33	26859.67	6368.91	26367.40	69320.26	3656.56	46633.82	0.00	2947.17	178497.23	19141.09
34	28739.84	6814.74	28213.12	74172.68	3736.93	47566.49	2604.00	3006.11	191116.98	19153.61
35	30751.63	7291.77	30188.04	79364.77	3817.29	48517.82	37046.05	3066.24	230226.31	22125.65
36	32904.25	7802.19	32301.20	84920.30	3897.65	49488.18	1309.50	3127.56	211853.18	18544.66
37	35207.54	8348.35	34562.28	90864.72	3978.02	50477.94	0.00	3190.11	222650.95	18214.81
38	37672.07	8932.73	36981.64	97225.25	4058.38	51487.50	0.00	3253.91	235553.12	18009.65
39	40309.12	9558.02	39570.36	104031.02	4138.75	52517.25	0.00	3318.99	249304.76	17814.07
40	43130.76	10227.08	42340.28	111313.19	4219.11	53567.60	195606.81	3385.37	459571.09	30690.33
TOTALS	615257.	145889.	603981.	1587875.	106080.48	1494675.	925616.	94461.	5488384.75	1190497.97

D. THE TOTAL COST OF THE PROPOSED PROJECT OVER ITS LIFE OF 40 YEARS IN PRESENT WORTH DOLLARS IS   2012216.05

E. THE ENERGY CONSUMED BY THIS DESIGN ON A YEARLY BASIS IS   2189. MILLION BTU

        HEATING ENERGY   =   552. MILLION BTU
        COOLING ENERGY   =   93. MILLION BTU
        LIGHTING ENERGY   =   386. MILLION BTU
        EQUIPMENT ENERGY =   1158. MILLION BTU

        HEAT RECOVERY DOLLAR SAVINGS PER YEAR = 900.00

FIGURE 5-22
Life cycle building cost summary after study—typical 50-bed domiciliary unit of health care facility.

CHAPTER SIX
DESIGN METHODOLOGY

"The greatest shortcoming in today's traditional approach to the design of facilities is the use of 'unidiscipline'-oriented decision making. This approach tends to sacrifice total system performance by maximizing subsystem performance. It results, in many cases, in failure to properly consider initial system and total life cycle costs."

A. J. Dell'Isola, Introduction,
Life Cycle Costing, ACEC/AIA Seminars
1978–1979.

INTRODUCTION

The following problem-solving methodology provides a vehicle to aid in decision making from inception to conclusion. Because it is an organized approach, it helps assure that proper consideration will be given to all the necessary facets of the design. Figure 6-1 divides an LCC analysis into four distinct sets of work elements:

1. Selection of study areas.
2. Generation of alternatives.
3. Design evaluation.
4. Design selection.

Each work element will be discussed at length in this chapter.

SELECTION OF STUDY AREAS

The selection process may be quite simple, as frequently there are many design questions concerning various facility trade-offs at design concept. Where no obvious areas

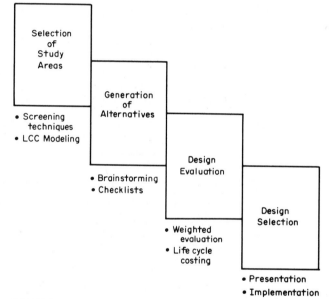

FIGURE 6-1
Steps in a life cycle costing study.

exist, a selection procedure is needed. A systematic selection procedure invariably results in a level of achievement surpassing that resulting from a random technique.

The selection of study areas is a management responsibility, which can be tempered with the advice and assistance of the designer using an in-house staff or consultant services. To be effective, management must be aware of the potential of the LCC technique, the capability of personnel, and the environment in which it must operate, and must take steps to fully utilize available resources.

Screening Techniques

LCC opportunity is enhanced through screening techniques because they create mainstream involvement of

LCC in the day-to-day business of design. One way for management to ensure results is to require systematic LCC in existing areas of opportunity before time becomes a critical factor. Some suggested study areas are listed in Figure 6-2. Selecting areas having the greatest savings potential with minimum input requires use of methods such as relative cost ranking and function analysis.

Relative Cost Ranking: In the relative cost ranking method, the estimated costs of the parts of subsystems are ranked from highest to lowest in terms of dollars per gross square foot of facility. Generally, potential improvement is greatest for those components with the highest total costs.

One means of developing the relative ranking is for the designer to apply *Pareto's law*. Pareto's law states, in essence, that the significant items in a given group are normally a relatively minor portion of the total number of items in the group. This law was developed at the end of the nineteenth century when Vilfredo Pareto, while studying the concentration of wealth and income in his native country (Italy), found that a very large percentage of the national income was concentrated in the hands of a very small percentage of the population.

With this method the LCC efforts would be focused on the small number of areas having the greatest costs. The reader must be cautioned that this method has certain

Areas of Study:	Conceptual	Schematic	Design Development
General Project Budget Layout Criteria & Standards	-Design Concepts -Program Interpretation -Site/Facility Massing -Access, Circulation -Project Budget -Design Intentions -Net to Gross Ratios	-Schematic Floor Plans -Schematic Sections -Approach to Systems Integration -Floor to Floor Height -Functional Space Relationships	-Floor Plans -Sections -Typical Details -Integrated Systems -Space Circulation -Specifications
Structural Foundation Substructure Superstructure	-Performance Requirements -Structural Bay Sizing -Framing Systems Exploration -Subsurface Conditions -Underground Concepts -Initial Framing Review -Structural Load Criteria	-Schematic Basement Plan -Selection of Foundation System -Structural System Selection -Framing Plan Outline -Sizing of Elements	-Basement Floor Plan -Key Foundation Elements, Details -Floor & Roof Framing Plans -Sizing of Major Elements -Outline Specifications
Architectural Exterior Closure Roofing Interior Construction Elevators Equipment	-Approach to Elevations -Views to/from Building -Roof Type & Pitch -Interior Design -Configuration of Key Rooms -Organization of Circulation Scheme -Need & Types of Vertical Circulation -Impact of Key Equipment on Facility & Site -Passive Solar Usage	-Concept Elaboration -Selection of Wall Systems -Schematic Elevations -Selection of Roof Systems -Room Design -Selection of Partitions -Circulation Sizing -Basic Elevator & Vertical Transportation Concepts -Impact of Key Equipment on Room Design	-Elevations -Key Elevation Details -Key Roofing Details -Initial Finish Schedules -Interior Construction Elements -Integration of Structural Framing -Key Interior Elevations -Outline Specification for Equipment Items
Mechanical HVAC Plumbing Fire Protection	-Basic Energy Concepts -Impact of Mechanical Concepts on Facility -Initial Systems Selection -Space Allocation -Performance Requirements for Plumbing, HVAC, Fire Protection	-Mechanical Systems Selection -Refinement of Service & Distribution Concepts -Input to Schematic Plans -Energy Conservation	-Detailed System Selection -Initial System Drawings & Key Details -Distribution & Riser Diagrams -Outline Specifications for System Elements
Electrical Service & Distribution Lighting & Power	-Basic Power Supply -Approaches to Use of Natural & Artificial Lighting -Performance Requirements for Lighting -Need for Special Electrical Systems	-Window/Skylight Design & Sizing -Selection of Lighting & Electrical Systems -General Service, Power & Distribution Concepts	-Detailed Systems Selection -Distribution Diagrams -Key Space Lighting Layouts -Outline Specification for Electrical Elements
Site Preparation Utilities Landscaping	-Site Selection -Site Development Criteria -Site Forms & Massing -Requirements for Access -Views to/from Facility -Utility Supply -Site Drainage	-Design Concept Elaboration -Initial Site Plan -Schematic Planting, Grading, Paving Plans	-Site Plan -Planting Plan -Typical Site Details -Outline Specification for Site Materials

FIGURE 6-2
Life cycle cost–study areas.

drawbacks. For example, there are often high-cost areas that do not have significant savings potential but which are also performing important functions. Cost ranking may be irrelevant in such cases. The function approach helps to avoid this potential problem.

Function Approach: The *function approach* is the fundamental ingredient of value engineering efforts. It is used to clearly define the purpose of every component, system, space, etc., of a facility. If costs or energy units or both are associated with functions (rather than with components or systems), it is easier to identify areas for improvement than it is when only case histories, involving similar functional requirements, are examined. Detailed discussions of the function approach are contained in the references listed in the value engineering bibliography at the end of this book.

The function is normally expressed by two words—a verb and its noun object. The verb answers the question "What does it do?" by defining the item's required action (it may generate, control, pump, emit, protect, transmit, etc.). The noun answers the question "What does it do it to?" by specifying what is acted upon (electricity, temperature, liquids, light, surfaces, sound, etc.). Whatever is specified must be measurable, or at least understood in measurable terms, since a value must be assigned to it during the later evaluation process of relating cost or energy units or both to function. For example, the function of a HVAC system "control environment" depends upon the specific user requirements involved, and can thus be determined.

Functions define a performance (task or aesthetic) feature that must be attained, as far as the user or owner is concerned, and reflect the primary reason for the existence of the item or the reason for which the owner is willing to pay. A function satisfies only user needs, not desires. A clear understanding of user need is necessary if an adequate definition of function is to be developed.

A function should be identified in the broadest possible terms to provide the most potential for improvement. This gives greater freedom for creativity in determining alternatives, and helps to overcome any preconceived ideas of the manner in which the function is to be accomplished. In a restricted sense, the function of food service in a building could be identified as "dispense food." A wider definition would be to indicate its function as "feed employees." This would provide many more choices beyond the normal use of a cafeteria in a building.

After a function description has been developed, an estimate of the target cost for performing each function may be determined. A *target cost* is defined as the lowest cost possible to accomplish the functions isolated. Also, it can be developed from the lowest cost previously experienced for similar functions. The target cost is compared with the estimate of the function's present cost. Large differences between the two indicate that the study should be pursued.

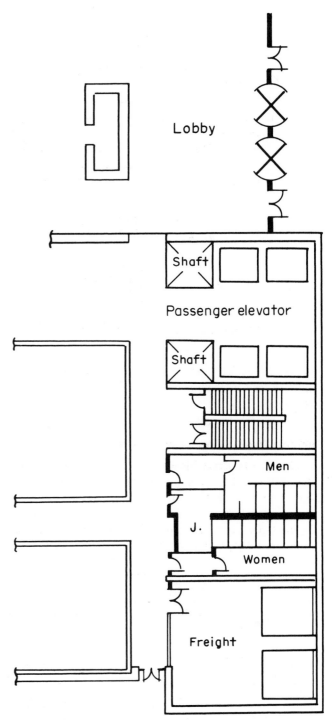

FIGURE 6-3
Floor plan.

Example: Figure 6-3 is a floor plan of elevators examined in a recent LCC study using the procedures just described. The components of the elevator system are listed on Figure 6-4, with their function(s), initial cost, and at times their life cycle costs. Each functional element is listed in descending order of initial or life cycle cost. Those functional element costs considered basic to the system are

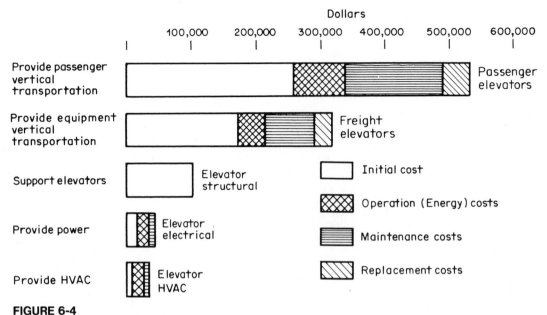

FIGURE 6-4
Elevator function analysis, costs expressed in present worth.

sometimes shaded in the graphical analysis. (See function analysis for Case Study 1, Chapter 7.) This is the associated target cost.

Models to Identify Areas of Study

Life Cycle Cost Model: Since costs are the foundation of an LCC study, a tool is needed to assemble total costs into units that can be quickly analyzed. For reference, a look at the manufacturing industry is warranted. Figure 6-5 is a general-purpose (life cycle) cost model used in the manufacturing industry. The model blocks out each

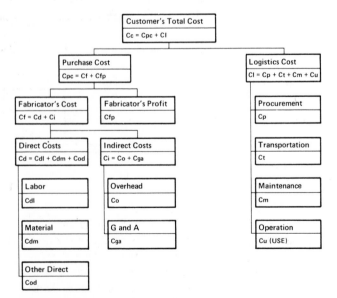

Formula: $C_c = [[(C_{dl} + C_{dm} + C_{od}) + (C_o + C_{ga})] + C_{fp}] + (C_p + C_t + C_m + C_u)$

FIGURE 6-5
General-purpose cost model.

major element in appropriate related cost areas of the customer's total cost. With this technique, a one-page visual analysis of the costs for the total system is possible.

The cost model concept can be applied to all types of facilities, including offices, health care, processing plants, and wastewater treatment facilities. The use of the cost model is a basic approach to the life cycle study, and so must reflect the best cost information available at the time of the study. The format of the cost model breakdown should reflect, as closely as possible, the functional requirement of the facility, and should be tied to a cost retrieval system for easy development and refinement. The general-purpose cost model has been expanded to include the cost target with the estimated costs. In study reviews, the team, augmented with specific cost expertise as required, develops costs they believe are the minimum possible for each block of the cost model. These target costs[1] are then summed. Blocks having the greatest differences between estimated and targeted costs are selected for study.

Example—Office Facility: Figure 6-6 illustrates the distribution of life cycle costs (present worth) for a hypothetical office building. The purpose of the life cycle cost model is twofold. First, the model graphically displays the types of costs (shown in Figure 6-7) that *may* be examined in the course of an LCC study. Second, the model, once completed, identifies high-cost areas that *should* be further analyzed. An inherent problem with using this type of model is that of acquiring data from similar projects with which to compare costs. Chapter 4, "Life Cycle Estimat-

1. Cost "target" as used here is equivalent to "worth," a value engineering term. At times the target value will be increased to a historical minimum value because of the overlap of functions the system is performing.

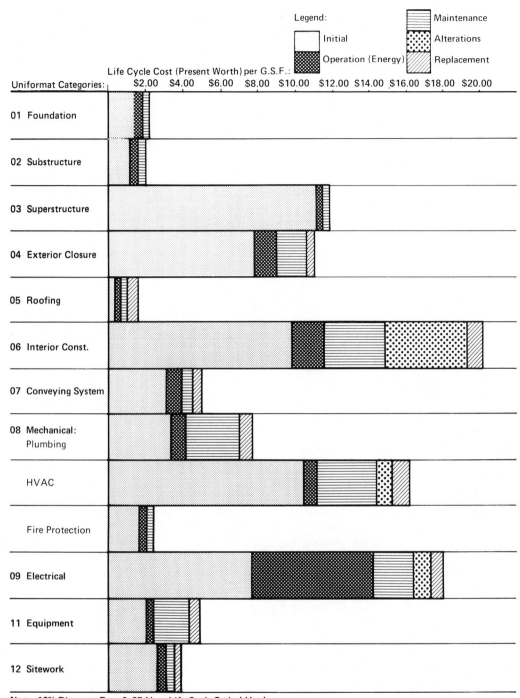

Legend:
Initial
Operation (Energy)
Maintenance
Alterations
Replacement

FIGURE 6-6
Life cycle cost distribution, present worth—typical office building.

ing Procedures," describes techniques for establishing these figures. Since not all blocks of life cycle costs are directly tied to components of a facility (for example, financing costs and functional-use costs), some may question the need or necessity for their determination. These costs could be classified as resultant costs because their final figure is usually directly related to the decisions made by the designer. They can be very significant and therefore should be estimated.

An additional aspect of the model is that it makes allowances for other identifiable life cycle costs for each specific application. Taxes, tax shelter figures, etc., may be included in the blocks as the user feels appropriate.

The costs to be included in the model may be either annualized costs for a specific item or they may be converted to present worth, today's value of all future costs. (See Chapter 3 for further discussion of annualized and present-worth costs.)

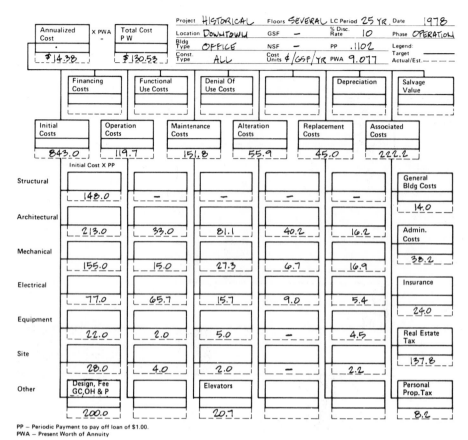

FIGURE 6-7
Life cycle cost model, historical average—office buildings. *(Source: BOMAI.)*

Figure 6-7 gives an example of the breakdown of life cycle costs incurred in the "historical average" office building. The information presented was obtained from the BOMAI (Building Owners and Managers Association International) "1979 Experience Exchange Report." All downtown office building experiences throughout the United States were averaged for the year 1978. The statistics shown illustrate the effect of the future costs of each of the building elements. Initial costs were converted to a uniform annual cost. The figure shows, for example, that annual maintenance costs amounted to $1.52 per gross square foot of building. Totaling all costs for the office facility, the annual cost approximates $14.38 per gross square foot.

Example—Shopping Center: A shopping center located in Sydney, Australia, was analyzed by a design team with the objective of minimizing life cycle costs. Figure 6-8 presents the LCC model that was prepared to identify high-cost areas. From this breakdown, it was readily determined that the finishes, structure, and services (mechanical, electrical, escalators) systems should be further analyzed. Note the relatively low cost of energy compared with the water costs. All costs are expressed in Australian dollars per square meter of floor area.

In the LCC review, the team, augmented with specific cost expertise as required, developed costs they believed were the minimum possible for each block of the model. These cost targets were added up and the results presented

in the upper portions of the model. Cost blocks with the greatest difference were then selected for study.

Example—Water Distribution System: To further illustrate the concept of LCC modeling, the design of a water distribution system for an industrial site is used. Figure 6-9 is the LCC model prepared from the initial concept for the use of cast iron ductile pipe. A cost estimate was prepared for the original design. These costs are presented in the LCC model as dollars per linear foot of pipe.

Annual costs for maintenance and operations (energy) were next estimated. Since the water distribution system required a continuous pump operation, the pumping condition was estimated as shown in Table 6-1.

Using the factors shown in Appendix C, the annual amounts were discounted to present worth. Next, replacement costs were estimated. These costs were based on the information given in Table 6-2. Using the discount tables in the Appendix, Tables C-1 and C-2, (a 10 percent discount rate and a 40-year life) these estimated costs were brought back to present worth and entered in the LCC model.

By using the LCC format indicated, it is possible to consider not only the effect of follow-on costs, such as maintenance and operations, but also the effect of the cost of money. Targets (the upper portions of the blocks) were established based on other water distribution systems providing similiar functions. The differences between the estimated costs and the target values indicate that significant savings (as much as 29 percent) are possible through the use of alternative piping systems.

Initial-Cost Model: Figure 6-10 is an initial-cost model of a 50-bed unit of a health care facility. As with the LCC model, costs may be assigned by UNIFORMAT functional area. From this cost model, the team selected the following cost block areas:

Structural	actual $ 7.75 versus target $ 6.50
Architectural	actual $17.03 versus target $13.75
Mechanical	actual $19.36 versus target $10.75
Electrical	actual $ 4.89 versus target $ 4.50
Equipment	actual $ 1.92 versus target $ 1.50

The areas having the greatest savings potential are architectural and mechanical, which would be the subject of in-depth studies.

Also, cost models can be used to establish cost targets for savings potential. For example, the total potential savings estimated for the areas isolated would be:

Structural: $7.75/ft^2 − $6.50/ft^2 × 17,450 ft^2 = $21,813
Architectural: $17.03/ft^2 − $13.75/ft^2 × 17,450 ft^2 = $57,236
Mechanical: $19.36/ft^2 − $10.75/ft^2 × 17,450 ft^2 = $150,244
Electrical: $4.89/ft^2 − $4.50/ft^2 × 17,450 ft^2 = $6,806
Equipment: $1.92/ft^2 − $1.50/ft^2 × 17,450 ft^2 = $7,329

Of the total building unit cost target ($978,596), the study isolated over $243,428 in initial-cost savings for one 50-bed unit, of which it would not be unreasonable to expect $150,000 in savings to be implemented in the final design. The costs used in this example were taken from the economic building performance model (EBPM), which was discussed in Chapter 5.

Energy Models: Since energy is a prime consideration of LCC, a way is needed to assemble total energy consumption into energy units (EU) for a selected period. For example, 1 year would provide a complete weather cycle that could be quickly analyzed. In energy modeling, energy reduction techniques are organized in a systematic application with respect to function. The only difference from a study of costs is that energy optimization rather than cost optimization is sought.

Energy units are used instead of dollars. The energy units can be translated into fuel costs for any type of fuel that may be economically viable for the project. Subsequently, the energy costs (or savings), other operating costs, and maintenance costs can be combined for use in the LCC analysis.

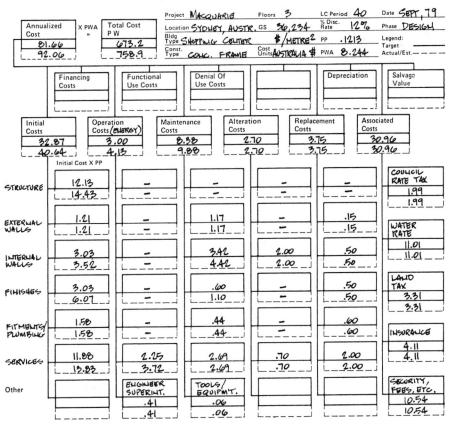

FIGURE 6-8
Life cycle cost model, shopping center.

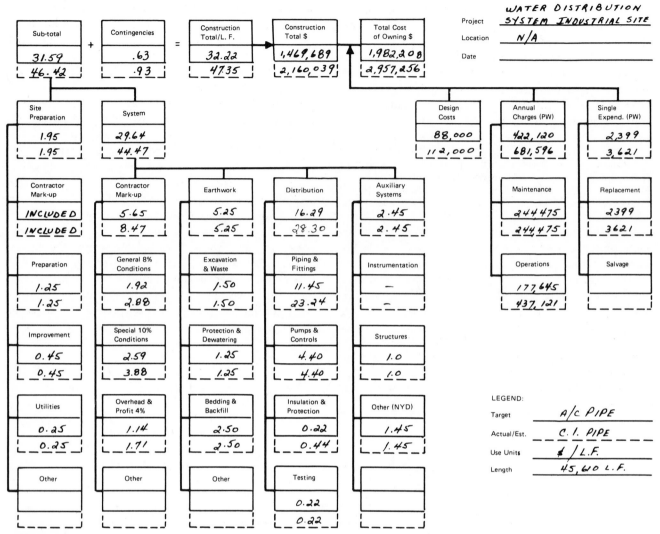

FIGURE 6-9
Life cycle cost model, water distribution system.

TABLE 6-1

Pump operation costs	
Pump	200 gal/min @ 125 lb/in² = 200-hp Motor
Operation	6000 hr
Operating Cost	200 hp × 0.745 × 6000 hr 894,000 kWh
Power	$.05/kWh
Total	$44,700/yr

System maintenance costs	
Staff	$15,000/yr
Vehicles	10,000/yr
Total	$25,000/yr

TABLE 6-2

COST OF REPAIRING LEAKS: 1 FOR EACH SIZE PIPE

Year	Cast Iron Pipe
1	N/A
5	$2657
10	3000
20	3750
30	4500

Experience has shown that significant LCC benefits are achieved through energy conservation. The energy model concept can be applied to all types of buildings and industrial processes and is equally useful for new or existing facilities. The use of the energy model is a basic approach to

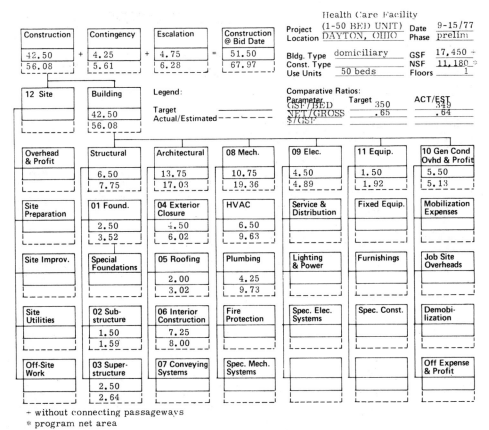

FIGURE 6-10
Cost model.

energy optimization and, therefore, must reflect the best energy use information available at the time of the study. Energy-estimating methods are discussed in Chapter 4 of this book.

Example—Health Care Facility: Figure 6-11 is an energy model developed for a health care facility, using Btu per square foot as the energy unit (EU). The format of the energy model breakdown should reflect as closely as possible the functional requirement of the facility with respect to operating hours and special process areas such as kitchens. The model should be tied to an energy use retrieval system for easy development and refinement.

The general-purpose energy model includes a target energy use estimate together with the actual energy consumption. The multidisciplinary team, augmented with specific energy-oriented expertise as required, develops the minimum energy consumption they believe possible for each block of the energy model. These estimates are based on previous energy studies, review of owner requirements, and creative thinking. The target energy is based on the simplest system to meet basic design objectives. Secondary energy function areas such as reheat (cooling for heat from lights) have little real value and should be targeted with that in mind. The energy use blocks are added to-

gether. The result is a basic energy model representing ideal energy consumption, which becomes an energy conservation target to compare with actual or projected energy use. Energy blocks having the greatest difference are then selected for in-depth study.

Example—Wastewater Treatment Plant: Figure 6-12 presents an energy model for a 10 million gallon day (MGD) wastewater treatment plant, using kilowatthours per million gallons per day and total electric and gas as energy units. Typical consumption ranges from 1000 to 5000 kilowatthours per million gallons per day depending on level of treatment and complexity.

GENERATION OF ALTERNATIVES

"Imagination is more important than knowledge." Albert Einstein

During this step, creative effort is focused toward the development of alternative means to accomplish the necessary functions. Consideration of alternative solutions

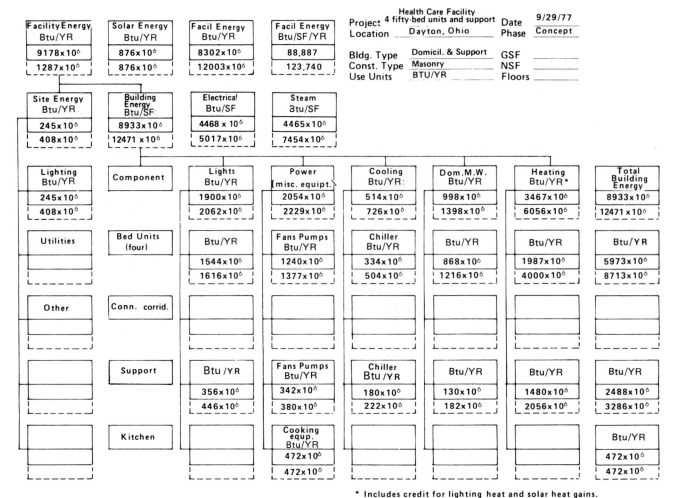

FIGURE 6-11
Energy model, health care facility. (Note Solar energy based on 4000 SF evacuated tube-type collector.)

should not formally begin until the problem is thoroughly understood and defined. All members of the study group should participate, for the greater the number of ideas conceived, the more likely that equally effective, less costly alternatives will be among them.

A proper frame of mind is important at this stage of the study; creative thinking must replace the conventional. The creative step answers the question, "What else will do?" Three techniques that will help answer this question are:

1. Simple comparison (with the study item): Conduct a thorough search for other systems, components, or facilities that are similar in at least one significant characteristic to the study area.

2. Function comparison (What are other means of performing the basic functions?): Conduct a creative problem-solving session in which known things are combined or rearranged in new and unusual ways, providing different ways of performing the basic function.

3. Challenge, create, and refine: challenge—question every aspect of the design; create—really reach for an unusual idea, another approach; refine—strengthen or add to an idea for performing the function in a new and unique manner.

Creativity

Creativity is the development of ideas that are new to the individual, although they are not necessarily new to someone else. It aids LCC by bringing one closer to discovering alternative designs that will accomplish the required functions.

There are two approaches to problem solving—the analytical and the creative. The analytical approach is substantially single in purpose. The problem is stated exactly. A direct approach to the solution is taken, proceeding through a step-by-step progression of experiments, evaluations, and mathematical manipulations to arrive at a sin-

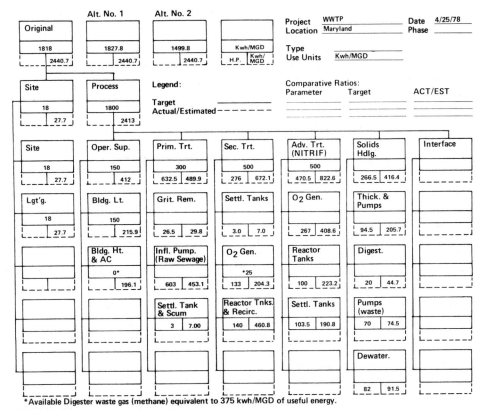

FIGURE 6-12
Energy model, wastewater treatment plant.

gle answer. The analytical problem frequently has only one workable solution. For example, finding the cause of failures is usually an analytical problem. One pursues the problem through a progression of suppositions to be proved or disproved by experiments, tests, and calculations until the problem is successfully narrowed to a single cause for each failure. Once the cause is ascertained, that problem is solved.

The creative process is that mental process in which past experience is combined and recombined (frequently with some distortion) to form new combinations that will satisfy some need. Another way of expressing it is: Creativity is the development of new ideas that will satisfy some expressed or implied need. Note that creative thinking must produce useful ideas, not just ideas. The daydreamer who produces ideas is not being creative because the ideas have no useful purpose. Everyone possesses to a greater or lesser degree creative capability, which can be improved through training and practice.

There are a number of creativity techniques available for problem-solving situations. Two of those more generally applicable to design include brainstorming and checklisting. Both techniques provide a method or procedure to help the designer generate more solutions to creative problems. These techniques provide formats for mental stimulation. It is necessary, during their use, to consciously think creatively.

Brainstorming

Brainstorming is a freewheeling type of creativity, usually done in a group. A typical brainstorming session takes place with four to six people sitting around a table and spontaneously producing ideas designed to solve a specific problem. During this session, no attempt whatsoever is made to judge or evaluate the ideas. Evaluation takes place after the brainstorming session has ended. Normally, a group leader will open the session by posing a problem. A secretary or tape recorder records each idea offered by the group. Before opening the session, the group leader will set the stage by reviewing the following group brainstorming rules:

1. Rule out criticism. Withhold adverse judgment of ideas until later.

2. Generate a large number of possible solutions; set a goal of multiplying the number of ideas produced in the first rush of thinking by 5 or 10.

3. Seek a wide variety of solutions that represent a broad spectrum of attacks on the problem.

4. Watch for opportunities to combine or improve ideas as they are generated.

5. Before closing the door on possible solutions, allocate time for subconscious operation on the problem while consciously performing other tasks.

The elimination of judgment from the idea-producing stage allows for the maximum accumulation of ideas. It prevents the premature death of a potentially good idea and conserves the time of the group of individuals working on the problem by preventing shifts from the creation of original ideas to the evaluation of the ideas. Consideration of all ideas encourages everybody to explore new areas, even those that seem impractical. This gives the opportunity to express thoughts to the innovator, who might be reluctant to voice them under ordinary conditions for fear of ridicule.

In addition to contributing ideas of their own, participants should suggest how ideas of others can be improved or how two or more ideas can be joined into still another idea. Two or more people working together under these ground rules can generate more ideas than one person working alone. This is mostly because ideas generated by various members of the group can be modified or improved upon and then offered as possible solutions to the problem. The efficiency of the group goes up as its size increases, until it reaches the point at which its operation becomes so cumbersome as to discourage some members' participation. The members of the group may be selected to represent different work backgrounds. Some should have a working familiarity with the subject under study. Group members need not all know one another before the session, but they should all come from equal levels with the organization to reduce the possibility of senior members exerting pressure or dominance on junior members.

The technique and philosophy of brainstorming can also be used by individuals to generate solutions to problems. However, this is not usually as productive as a group. It should be emphasized that brainstorming does not always give one the final problem solutions or ideas ready for immediate implementation. What one obtains are leads toward the final solution. Figure 6-13 summarizes the rules for brainstorming.

Checklisting: A checklist is an accumulation of points, areas, or possibilities serving to provide idea-clues or leads when compared against the problem or subject under consideration. The objective is to obtain a number of ideas for further follow-up and development. The checklist is one of the most commonly used aids in the search for new ideas. Checklists range from the specialized to the extremely generalized. Numerous publications exist to assist the designer with energy conservation ideas and are a form of checklist to simply remind the designer of key concepts that save energy.

Summary

Creative problem-solving techniques are the tools used to expand creative ability. They are techniques to empty the mind of habitual responses and force one to use words not normally used. The human mind is greater than the most elaborate computer in that it can store an almost infinite number of data; but unfortunately it can process and integrate only up to about seven bits of these data simultaneously. Because of this limitation, the previous rules are helpful in applying the creative approach to problem solving.

DESIGN EVALUATION

The purpose of this step is to select for further analysis and refinement the most promising alternatives from among those generated previously. During creativity there was a conscious effort to prohibit any judgmental thinking so as not to inhibit the creative process. Now the ideas must be critically evaluated. The first step in the evaluation of alternatives is to compare and rank the ideas. During the initial screening, the ideas are judged according to:

1. Ability to perform the function—ratings might be excellent, good, fair, and poor.

2. Ease of implementation, including cost and schedule—ratings might be:

   a. Simple idea: easy to implement.

   b. Moderately complex idea; moderately easy to implement.

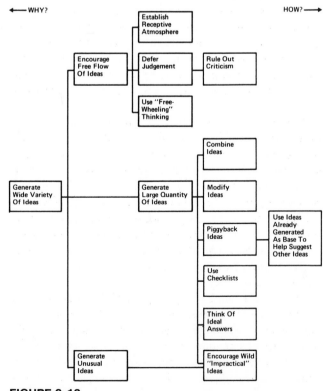

FIGURE 6-13
Rules of brainstorming.

c. Complex idea; difficult to implement.

3. Magnitude of savings (initial and life cycle).

Advantages and Disadvantages

Another step in the evaluation process is to judge, as objectively as possible, the advantages and disadvantages of each idea that survives the initial screening mentioned above. All surviving ideas should receive a preliminary evaluation. Figure 6-14 provides an example of idea comparison for alternatives, with a listing of the advantages and disadvantages. The initial analysis produces a shorter list of ideas, each of which has passed the evaluation standards set by the group. The selection should be based on an estimate of the relative life cycle cost reduction potential of the alternatives, and how well they satisfy the functions required.

The alternatives that remain are developed far enough to obtain more detailed cost estimates. Although the evaluation phase is the responsibility of the study group, others should be consulted for help in estimating the potential of these alternatives. Cost estimates must be as complete, accurate, and consistent as possible to minimize errors during the assessment of the alternatives.

Following are some of the questions that should be asked about each alternative:

1. Will the idea work? Can it be modified or combined?

2. What is the life cycle savings potential?

3. What are the chances for implementation? Will it be relatively easy or difficult to make the change?

4. Will it satisfy all the user's needs?

Weighted Evaluation

Consideration should next be given to factors that may be equal to or more important than costs alone. These non-economic criteria have, in the past, been evaluated primarily by intuition.

Simple decisions, involving an analysis of one or two criteria and a yes-no, either-or answer, can be reached quite easily. However, decisions more frequently require an analysis of several criteria, each carrying a given weight depending on the circumstances of the project. A decision maker learns to analyze choices with proper perspectives of all criteria. *Weighted evaluation* is a tool for complex decision making.

Weighted evaluation is a formally organized process for the selection of optimum solutions in areas involving several criteria. In the process, criteria are assigned differing values according to their potential effect on a project. The alternatives developed are then evaluated against these criteria. The alternative with the highest score is selected for implementation.

Idea	Advantages	Disadvantages	Estimated Potential Savings	
			Initial	Life Cycle
REMOVE TWO FREIGHT ELEVATORS, CONVERT ONE PASSENGER ELEVATOR TO FUNCTION FOR BOTH PASSENGERS AND FREIGHT.	LESS COST, ENERGY SAVINGS, IMPROVED MAINTENANCE	SOME INCREASE IN WAITING TIME, FREIGHT DELIVERY SCHEDULING	IMPROVED	IMPROVED
USE DUMBWAITER FOR FREIGHT REQUIREMENTS	DIRECT DISTRIBUTION OF PAPER TRANSPORT, LESS COST, ENERGY SAVINGS	MINOR RE-DESIGN	IMPROVED	IMPROVED
ONE CORE AREA FOR ALL 6 ELEVATORS	LAYOUT EFFICIENCY, SPACE REDUCTION	ELEVATORS - DUAL FUNCTIONS, FREIGHT DELIVERY SCHEDULING	IMPROVED	IMPROVED
SOLID STATE (SCR) CR ELEVATOR DRIVE IN LIEU OF MOTOR GENERATORS	ENERGY SAVINGS	NON-COMPETITIVE COST	INCREASE	IMPROVED

FIGURE 6-14
Idea comparison, elevators.

Weighted evaluation assures optimum decisions. Good decisions are made by placing the proper emphasis on all criteria. During evaluation it is important to discuss and weigh the following areas:

- Needs versus desires.
- Important versus unimportant.
- Design trade-offs versus required functions.

Procedure

The recommended procedure for weighted evaluation has been broken down into two processes, the *criteria weighting process* and the *analysis matrix*. The criteria weighting process is designed to isolate important criteria and establish their weights or relative importance. On the criteria scoring matrix all criteria important in the selection of alternatives are listed. Criteria are compared, one against another, this series of comparisons being the simplest way to achieve the evaluation.

One criterion may be more or less important, have more or less effect on required functions, or have more or less appeal. Normally, limiting the comparison to only two criteria eliminates the need for sophisticated measuring tools.

In comparing two criteria, preference for one over the other is scored according to its strength. (That is, 4—major preference, 3—medium preference, 2—minor preference, 1—no preference.) Scores are then tallied, the raw scores brought to a common base (10 is used for a normal evaluation), and the criteria and weights transferred to the analysis matrix.

In the analysis matrix, each alternative is listed and ranked against each criterion. The rank and weight of each constraint are multiplied and totaled. The alternatives are then scored for recommended implementation.

Example: Application

Figure 6-15 illustrates the use of the weighted evaluation for the selection of an elevator system for a small office facility. On the criteria scoring matrix five criteria considered important for evaluation are listed. Weights of criterion importance were determined through the use of the matrix. In this case, initial cost was considered the most important factor and assigned the weight of 10, with the other criteria ranked accordingly lower. Next, the team listed the criteria and weights and the alternative ideas selected and developed from the idea comparison sheet. The ranking and scoring indicated that the best idea was to use four passenger elevators one of which would serve for freight.

Performance Criteria

Table 6-3 illustrates a checklist of attributes that may be used as criteria in the evaluation of various systems ac-

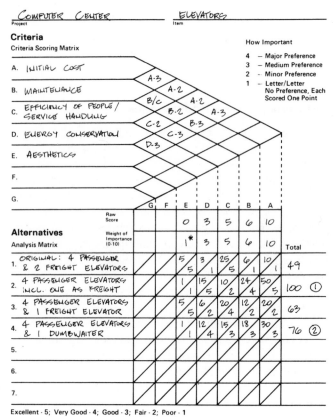

FIGURE 6-15
Weighted evaluation, elevators.

cording to the degree to which they are safe, functional, sensible, and practical. This checklist should be reviewed before a weighted evaluation is completed.

Life Cycle Costing

LCC procedures (using formats outlined in Chapter 5) are applied as required to those alternatives meeting the functional criteria. Initial, operations, maintenance, alterations and replacement, and other costs (including taxes, credits, and depreciation) considered significant by the team should be estimated. All assumptions about discount rate, life cycle study period, escalation rates, etc., should be clearly documented for future reference.

Sensitivity analysis should follow the LCC of the alternatives. Assumptions of highest risk and data items of significant magnitude should be varied to see what effect, if any, they may have on the final outcome of the economic evaluation.

The elevator system recommended by the weighted evaluation process is further analyzed to illustrate the concepts of LCC. Figure 6-16 presents the alternatives compared with the original design. Four passenger elevators with one used for freight appears to provide optimum value for the owner.

TABLE 6-3
PERFORMANCE CRITERIA CHECKLIST

Safety	Functional	Sensible	Practical
Life	Strength	Aesthetic	Cost
Flammability	Static	Arrangement	Initial
Smoke production	Dynamic	Composition	Operation
Toxicity	Wind	Texture	Maintenance
Radiation	Seismic	Gloss	Salvage value
Hazardousness	Thermal	Odor	Replacement
	Internal	Color	Depreciation
Property		Uniformity	
Fire endurance	Durability		Interface
Theft security	Impact resistance	Environmental	Fit
Vandalism security	Moisture resistance	Audibility	Attachment
Resistance to misuse	Thermal resistance	Frequency reverberation	Tolerances
Specific code restrictions	Corrosion resistance	Quality of illumination	Modularity
	Chemical resistance	Color rendition	Relocatability
	Weather resistance	Lack of glare, shadow,	Rotatability
	Surface stability (crack-, spall-,	reflection	Sequence of erection
	craze-, blister-,	Air cleanness	
	delamination-, chalk-, fade-	Air velocity, distribution	Service
	resistance)	Air temperature, moisture	Repairability
	Stain resistance	Touch	Interchangeability
	Absorbency		Accessibility
	Cleanability	Measurable	Replaceability
	Friability / frangibility	Levelness	Disturbance to other systems
	Abrasion resistance	Plumbness	and occupants
	Dimensional stability	Dimensions	Future extendability
	Cohesiveness	Volume	Modifiable in place
	Adhesiveness	Flatness	Adaptability at interface with
		Shape	other components
	Transmission	Weight	Replacement sequence
	Conductivity		Frequency of service
	Transparency	Physical	
	Permeability, (to light, sound,	Hardness	Source
	heat, air, radiation)	Ductility	Multiple source
		Malleability	Guaranteed source
	By-product emission	Resilience	Stability of producers
	Wastes	Elasticity	Dependability of energy
	Odors	Reflectance	source
	Dust	Toughness	
	Energy (sound, light, heat,	Brittleness	Personnel
	static electricity, radiation,	Density	Availability of maintenance
	vibration)	Viscosity	and repair personnel and
		Creep	facilities
	Dynamic	Coefficient of friction	Required education, trainability
	Force required to operate	Coefficient of expansion	of maintenance and repair
	Speed of operation		personnel
	Cycle time		Labor restrictions
	Vibration		

SOURCE: *CSI Manual of Practice*, vol. 2, 1975.

Before the lowest LCC alternative is recommended, problems relative to implementation should be anticipated and answers secured to as many such problems as possible. Conferences with specialists in areas such as the following are most helpful:

1. Installation.

2. Inspection.

3. Maintenance.

4. Procurement (purchasing).

5. Operations.

6. Materials.

7. Constructability.

At the conclusion of this step, one or more alternatives are recommended as the best value for implementation.

Study Title: CONVEYING SYSTEM: ELEVATORS (8 FLOORS)

Discount Rate: 10% Economic Life: 40 YEARS

	Original Describe: 4 PASSENGER & 2 FREIGHT ELEVATORS		Alternative 1 Describe: 4 PASSENGER ELEV. INCL. ONE AS FREIGHT (6000)		Alternative 2 Describe: 4 PASSENGER INCL. ONE AS FREIGHT + D.W.		Alternative 3 Describe:	
	Estimated Costs	Present Worth	Estimated Costs	Present Worth	Estimated Costs	Present Worth	Estimated Costs	Present Worth
Initial Costs								
A. PASSENGER ELEVATORS	260,000		195,000		195,000			
B. 6000 LB. PASSENGER ELEVATOR	–		85,000		85,000			
C. FREIGHT ELEVATORS	172,000		–		–			
D. DUMBWAITERS (D.W.)	–		–		22,000			
E. SHAFTS - STRUCTURAL	94,000		60,000		70,500			
F. PITS	8,000		5,500		6,000			
G. ELECTRICAL	15,000		10,000		10,500			
H. HEATING & VENTILATION	6,000		4,000		4,000			
I. SUB-TOTAL:	555,000		359,500		393,000			
J. Contingencies ___%								
K. Escalation 21%	116,000		75,000		82,000			
Total Initial Cost	671,000		434,500		475,000			

Operations (Annual) — Diff. Escal. Rate / PWA W/Escal.

	Diff. Escal. Rate	PWA W/Escal.	Est. Costs	Present Worth	Est. Costs	Present Worth	Est. Costs	Present Worth		
A. ENERGY - ELEVATORS (25 HP)	0%	9.779	12,220	119,500	8,140	79,660	8,140	79,660		
B. ENERGY - DUMBWAITERS (5 HP)	0%	9.779	–	–	–	–	611	5,975		
C.										
D.										
E.										
F.										
Total Annual Operations Costs				119,500		79,660		85,635		

Maintenance (Annual) — Diff. Escal. Rate / PWA W/Escal.

	Diff. Escal. Rate	PWA W/Escal.	Est. Costs	Present Worth	Est. Costs	Present Worth	Est. Costs	Present Worth		
A. CLEAN, ETC. ($350/ELEV.)	0%	9.779	2,100	20,536	1,400	13,691	1,400	13,691		
B. CLEAN, ETC. ($135/D.W.)	0%	9.779	–	–	–	–	135	1,320		
C. INSPECT, REPAIR ($450/STOP)	0%	9.779	21,600	211,226	14,400	140,818	14,400	140,818		
D. INSPECT, REPAIR D.W. ($170/S.)	0%	9.779	–	–	–	–	1,360	13,299		
E.										
F.										
G.										
Total Annual Maintenance Costs				231,762		154,509		169,128		

Replacement/Alterations (Single Expenditure) — Year / PW Factor

	Year	PW Factor	Est. Costs	Present Worth	Est. Costs	Present Worth	Est. Costs	Present Worth		
A. PASSENGER ELEVATORS	20	.1486	260,000	38,636	195,000	28,977	195,000	28,977		
B. 6000 LB. ELEVATORS	20	.1486	–	–	85,000	12,631	85,000	12,631		
C. FREIGHT ELEVATORS	20	.1486	172,000	25,559	–	–	–	–		
D. DUMBWAITERS	20	.1486	–	–	–	–	22,000	3,269		
E.–J.										
Total Replacement/Alteration Costs				64,195		41,608		44,877		

Tax Elements — Diff. Escal. Rate / PWA W/Esc.

	Diff. Escal. Rate	PWA W/Esc.								
A. NOT CONSIDERED										
B.–G.										
Total Tax Elements										

Associated (Annual) — Diff. Escal. Rate / PWA W/Esc.

			Est. Costs	Present Worth	Est. Costs	Present Worth	Est. Costs	Present Worth		
A. DENIAL OF USE COST - SPACE			N/A		4,800 SF	(216,000)	4,444 SF	(200,000)		
B. (8 FLOORS AT $45/SF)										
C.										
Total Annual Associated Costs			N/A			(216,000)		(200,000)		
Total Owning Present Worth Costs				415,457		59,777		99,640		

Salvage At End Of Economic Life — Year / PW Factor

	Year	PW Factor	Est. Costs	Present Worth	Est. Costs	Present Worth	Est. Costs	Present Worth		
Building (Struc., Arch., Mech., Elec., Equip.)	40	.022	(43,200)	(950)	(28,000)	(616)	(30,200)	(664)		
Other (10% OF INITIAL COST)										
Sitework										
Total Salvage				(950)		(616)		(664)		
Total Present Worth Life Cycle Costs				1,085,307		493,661		574,640		
Life-Cycle Present Worth Dollar Savings						591,899		510,867		

PW — Present Worth   PWA — Present Worth Of Annuity

FIGURE 6-16

Life cycle costing estimate in general-purpose worksheet.

106

Life Cycle Costing Summary

Computer Control
_____
Project

Elevators
_____
Item

_____
Team Members

_____
Team

_____
Team Members

_____
Date

Summary of Change (Study Area, Original & Proposed)

Study Area

This study concerned itself with vertical transportation and the functions to be performed. Over 800 personnel and large quantities of computer paper require vertical transportation daily.

Original

The original design contained 4 passenger elevators and two freight elevators. Using a traffic study prepared for the client and standard industry elevator criteria, the team established a requirement of 3.5 elevators for the personnel. Paper transportation could be handled in one of two ways. A passenger elevator could be sized for 6000-lb loads and used in offpeak personnel travel times. Or, a dumbwaiter could be used to directly transfer paper, etc., from storage to computer floors. Both of these suggestions were life-cycle costed.

Proposed

Using the criteria weighting process the following criteria were established to evaluate the various alternates with the original design: initial cost, maintenance, efficiency of people/service handling, energy conservation, and aesthetics. The 4 passenger elevator scheme with one rated for 6000 lb was judged by the team to be most desirable. In addition to energy and maintenance savings, the 4 versus 6 elevator scheme reduced each of the 8 floors of the facility by 600 SF.

Estimated Savings Cost Summary:

	Arch.	Struct.	Mech.	Elec.	Site	Total
Initial Cost Savings	236,500					236,500
Life Cycle Cost Savings (PW)						591,839
Annual Energy Savings (EU)						74,600 kWh

Percent Savings Initial _____ 35%

Percent Savings Life Cycle _____ 54%

Percent Savings Energy _____ 33%

FIGURE 6-17
Life cycle costing summary.

DESIGN SELECTION

"Man is so constituted as to see what is wrong with a new thing—not what is right. To verify this, you have but to submit a new idea to a committee. They will obliterate 90% of rightness for the sake of 10% wrongness. The possibilities a new idea opens are not visualized, because not one man in 1000 has imagination." Charles F. Kettering

Final selection is made from any surviving alternatives. The process involves not only detailed technical and economic testing but also consideration of the probability of successful implementation. The alternatives are investigated in sufficient depth to enable the development of specific recommendation(s) for implementation. To do this, the remaining alternative(s) should be subjected to:

1. Careful analysis, to ensure that the owner's and user's needs are satisfied.
2. A determination of technical adequacy.
3. The development of accurate estimates of costs, implementation expenses, and schedules—including schedules and costs for conducting all necessary tests.

The final step involves the actual preparation of the best alternative(s) and their presentation to those having the authority to implement the proposal(s). This is the last step in an LCC study. It usually includes:

1. Preparation and presentation of the LCC proposals.
2. Establishment of a plan of action that will assure implementation of the schedule.
3. Follow-up as required until the idea is implemented in the final design.
4. Validation of initial, energy, and other LCC savings once the facility is occupied.

Figure 6-17 illustrates an example LCC proposal for the computer facility, elevator scheme.

SUMMARY

The problem-solving methodology just explained can be applied to any item suitable for life cycle study. It provides a vehicle to carry the study from inception to conclusion. By an organized approach it assures that proper consideration has been given to all necessary facets of the study. The methodology divides the study into a distinct set of work elements. Judgment is required in determining the depth to which each step is performed. Organization for a multidisciplinary team study should take account of the resources available and the results expected. Typically, two major documents are produced: a report summarizing the results of the effort and a project book containing all the detailed backup information.

CHAPTER SEVEN
CASE STUDIES

"The primary criterion to be applied in a choice among alternative proposed investments in physical assets should be selected with the objective of making the best use of *limited resources*."

Grant and Ireson
Principles of Engineering Economy
1970, p.16.

INTRODUCTION

The previous chapters dealt primarily with the principles and concepts necessary as an introduction to life cycle costing. Although this information is an essential prerequisite, a good understanding of the subject area can be acquired only by application of these techniques to a project. The designer must develop cost and energy models, define cost estimating relationships, and determine specific components of cost to become familiar with LCC. Unless one actually gets involved at the detailed level, it is difficult (if not impossible) to adequately understand various system and component parameters and the interactions that occur. It is not sufficient to merely feed data into a computer model and observe the output without thoroughly understanding what takes place in the process. Once this understanding is attained, the computer model can be useful in facilitating the analysis.

With the objective of illustrating some of the detailed steps required in a life cycle analysis, several individual case studies are introduced in this chapter. In each case study, only enough detail is included to provide an understanding of the requirements involved in such an analysis. A complete step-by-step procedure covering each element of the system in question would be too comprehensive within the confines of this book; however, the highlights and critical areas are addressed.

The case studies are varied and presented in different levels of detail. As every LCC analysis is unique, the case

Building Applications	Structural	Architectural	Mechanical	Electrical	Site/Civil
Computer Center					
Case Study 1 Daylighting		•	•	•	
Case Study 2 Cooling Medium (cooling tower)	•	•	•		
Case Study 3 Emergency Power (generators)				•	
Branch Bank					
Case Study 4 Building Layout	•	•	•	•	•
Exhibit Center					
Case Study 5 Roof/Roofing System	•	•			•
Office Facility					
Case Study 6 Solar Collector System			•	•	
Industrial Facility Applications					
Wastewater Treatment Plant					
Case Study 7 Primary Sedimation Tank		•		•	
Waterfront Facility					
Case Study 8 Pier	•		•	•	•
Ammunition Plant					
Case Study 9 Conveyors	•		•	•	•
Rehabilitation and Modernization Applications					
Engineering Training Facility Modernization					
Case Study 10 Floor/Flooring System	•	•			
Case Study 11 HVAC System			•		

FIGURE 7-1
Listing of case studies.

studies will not in all instances completely respond to the designer's specific problem; however, by reviewing these cases, one should acquire enough insight to help resolve the many unique problems that arise on a day-to-day basis. It is hoped that the reader will review each case study in detail; that a self-analysis will take place, stimulating additional interest in the approach suggested; and that the knowledge gained will enhance the reader's understanding of the LCC process.

The following case studies, numbered 7-1 through 7-11, are taken from actual projects that date back to the early nineteen seventies, when the formal application of the methodology was first implemented.

With each case study is a brief narrative of its back-

ground. Selected case studies have complete LCC forms to further illustrate the methodology discussed in Chapter 6.

Figure 7-1 presents a summary of the case studies contained in this chapter. These are organized first by type of application: building, industrial facility, and rehabilitation and modernization. They are further categorized by the type of facility.

CASE STUDY 7-1: DAYLIGHTING

Life Cycle Costing Summary

Page 1 of 2

Computer Center
_____
Project

Daylighting
_____
Item

_____
Team Members

_____
Team

_____
Team Members

_____
Date

Summary of Change (Study Area, Original & Proposed)

Study Area

The location and exposure of office areas (north & east) and the goal of energy conservation by the client strongly suggested that an analysis of various combinations of daylighting schemes and supplemental lighting systems be made.

Several issues were to be examined indepth during the course of a week. These included: a) fenestration, b) artificial lighting, c) energy conservation d) mechanical requirements, e) direct versus indirect lighting, f) coffered versus flat ceiling, g) lighting reflective devices, h) fixed versus operable sash, i) window washing, j) emergency ventilation, k) venetian blinds, 1) initial & life cycle costs.

Original Design

The original daylighting scheme consisted of two 4'-0'' high windows in a curtain wall. The ceiling was coffered to allow natural lighting to penetrate into the space to a greater degree. A reflective louver located along the exterior wall served to decrease glare and focus the natural light.

Three daylighting scheme alternatives were compared to the original in terms of both life cycle costs and other important criteria. The first alternative consisted of a coffered ceiling and one 6'-0'' high window. The second alternative was similar to the original design, i.e. two 4'-0'' windows and a coffered ceiling, but without the reflective louvers and surfaces. The final daylighting alternative consisted of a recessed single 6'-0'' high window, slightly sloped, a reflective ceiling panel and an 9'-0'' ceiling height. (See Figure 3, Case Study 1.)

FIGURE 7-1-1
Life cycle costing summary.

Life Cycle Costing Summary

Four means of providing supplemental lighting to the office space to attain an ambient level of 50 footcandles were selected for comparison with the schemes. These included: a fluorescent, parabolic 3-tube, direct, 2' x 4' fixture; a fluorescent, 2-tube, indirect 6'' x 4' fixture; high pressure sodium, 250 watt fixture capable of being dimmed; and a HPS 250 watt fixture with switching capability.

Because of the interaction of the daylighting schemes with the various supplemental lighting means, 16 (4 x 4) possible solutions were evaluated. Criteria and their corresponding weight of importance were next established by the team. The following criteria was felt to be significant in the evaluation of the various alternatives: glare control, spatial brightness, initial cost, life cycle cost, aesthetics—appearance of device, energy conservation, aesthetics—color rendition/temperature, fixture response time, and maintainability.

Life cycle cost estimates were next prepared for the various daylighting and lighting fixture alternates. Supplement lighting energy requirements were estimated from daylighting data provided by a computer analysis program, LUMEN 2. A computer analysis was also made to determine the cooling energy requirements based on the alternate configurations.

Proposal Design

Once the life cycle costs were established for each of the 16 combinations, these schemes were evaluated in "points" by the techniques of weighted evaluation. From the analysis, the high pressure sodium fixture appeared most appropriate. Daylighting alternative no. 1 using a single 6' -0'' high window satisfies the required functions at the least life cycle cost. The added value of the coffered ceiling convinced the team to recommend this daylighting scheme.

Estimated Savings Cost Summary:

	Arch.	Struct.	Mech.	Elec.	Site	Total
Initial Cost Savings						384,918
Life Cycle Cost Savings (PW)						421,321
Annual Energy Savings (EU)						243,900 kWh

Percent Savings Initial	23.9%
Percent Savings Life Cycle	19.1%
Percent Savings Energy	3.6%

Function Analysis

Quantity	Component	Function Verb	Noun	Kind	Original Cost	TARGET
	DAYLIGHTING _Item_	**PROVIDE ILLUMINATION** _Basic Function_				_Date_
	ALUMINUM CURTAIN WALL	CONTROL	ELEMENTS	S	774,570	503,974
	GLAZING SYSTEM	ADMIT	LIGHT	B	208,430	156,322
	PARABOLIC REFLECTIVE LOUVERS	CONTROL	GLARE	S	60,000	10,000
		DISTRIB.	LIGHT	S		
	REFLECTIVE SURFACES & SUPPORTS	REFLECT	LIGHT	S	18,000	2,000
	VENETIAN BLINDS	CONTROL	LIGHT	S	16,000	12,000
		REFLECT	HEAT	S		
	ACOUSTICAL TILE ON FURRING	FINISH	SPACE	S	67,746	40,000
	CEILING FURRING	FINISH	SPACE	S	36,000	30,000
	LIGHTING FIXTURES	PROVIDE	ILLUM.	B	60,500	38,000

B = BASIC ; S = SECONDARY

Graphical Function Analysis

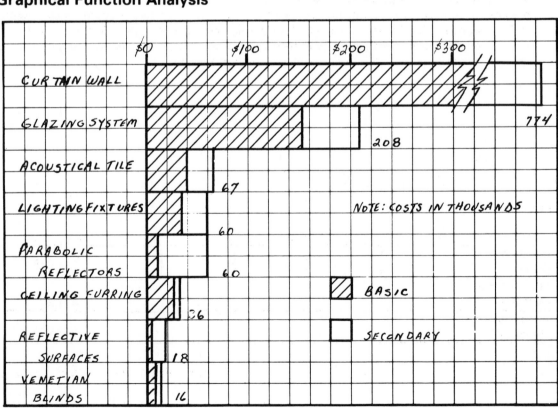

FIGURE 7-1-2
Function analysis.

112

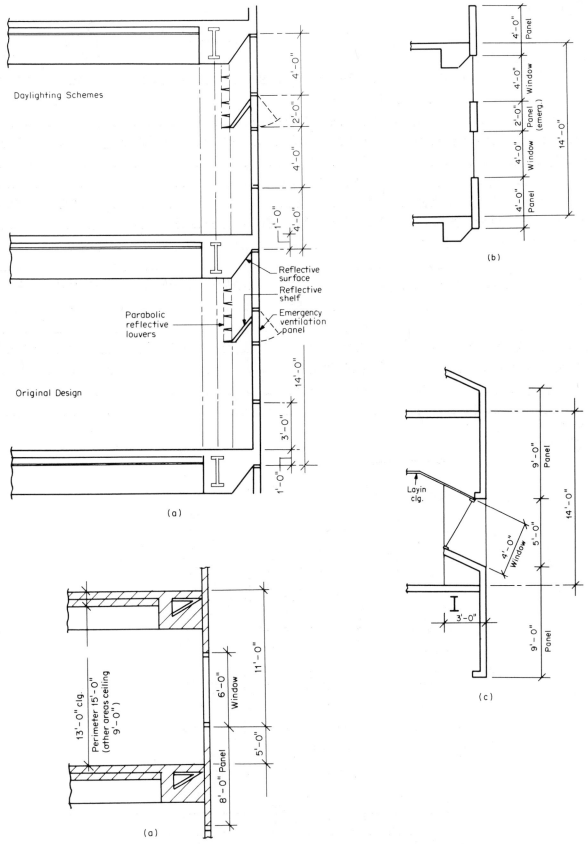

FIGURE 7-1-3
Daylighting sketches. (*a*) Alternative 1; (*b*) alternative 2; (*c*) alternative 3.

Idea Comparison

Idea	Advantages	Disadvantages	Estimated Potential Savings Inital	Life Cycle
ELIMINATE PARABOLIC REFLECTORS	REDUCES MAINTENANCE / LOWER INITIAL COST / SIMPLIFIES CONSTRUCTION	LOSS OF GLARE CONTROL	IMPROVED	IMPROVED
USE STANDARD WINDOW WALL WITH FIXED SASH	LESS MAINTENANCE / IMPROVES HVAC / LOWER INITIAL COST	EMERGENCY VENTILATION	IMPROVED	IMPROVED
USE ARTIFICIAL LIGHT SWITCHING PROGRESSIVE INTO SPACE FROM WINDOWS FOR USE OF "DAYLIGHT"	SAVES ENERGY / INCREASED LAMP LIFE / IMPROVED LCC	INITIAL COST / SYSTEM INTEGRATION	INCREASE	IMPROVED
USE VENETIAN BLINDS TO CONTROL GLARE	SIMPLICITY / STANDARD ITEM / LESS MAINTENANCE	MANUAL OPERATION	IMPROVED	IMPROVED
USE HIGH PRESSURE SODIUM (HPS) ARTIFICIAL LIGHTING	SAVES ENERGY / FEWER FIXTURES / LESS MAINTENANCE	SPACE FLEXIBILITY	INCREASE	IMPROVED

FIGURE 7-1-4
Idea comparison.

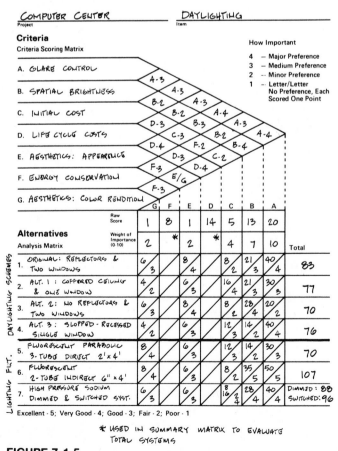

FIGURE 7-1-5
Weighted evaluation.

114

Life Cycle Costing Estimate
General Purpose Work Sheet

Study Title: DAY LIGHTING SCHEMES
HIGH PRESSURE SODIUM *FIXTURES- SWITCHED ½ BAY
Discount Rate: 10% Economic Life: 40 YEARS
* NEW (W)LAMP 250W H S 7500 HRS/LIFE

	Original Describe: TWO 4'-0" WINDOWS, REFLECTIVE LOUVERS AND COFFERED CEILING FIXED SASH		Alternative 1 Describe: COFFERED CEILING W/ONE 4'-0" WINDOW FIXED SASH		Alternative 2 Describe: HIGH WINDOWS NO REFLECTIVE LOUVERS FIXED SASH		Alternative 3 Describe: RECESSED SINGLE SLOPED 4'-0" WINDOWS FIXED SASH	
	Estimated Costs	Present Worth	Estimated Costs	Present Worth	Estimated Costs	Present Worth	Estimated Costs	Present Worth
Initial Costs								
A. ALUM. & GLASS CURTIN WALL - N&E ELEV.	22.00/WSF	800,800	19.00/WSF	691,580	22.00/WSF	800,800	22.00/WSF	800,800
B. VENETIAN BLINDS VERTICAL REFLECTIVE BACKING	10.00/WSF	16,000	10.00/WSF	12,000	10.00/WSF	16,000	10.00/INSF	8,000
C. PARABOLIC REFLECTIVE LOUVERS 4"HIGH E.ELEV.	50.00/LF	60,000		—		—		—
D. BASEBOARD CONVECTOR HVAC SYST. (DIFFERENTIALS)	25.00/LF	63,000		0	25.00/LF	63,000		0
E. REFLECTIVE SURFACE - ALZAK 24 GA &FURRING	3.00/SF	18,000		—		—		—
F. LAYIN CEILING SYSTEM (224½ LF)		—		—		—	1.04/SF	44,550
G. ACOUSTICAL TILE ON FURRING	1.31/SF	67,746	1.31/SF	59,000	1.31/SF	67,746		—
H. CEILING FURRING - 5/8"GYP & PAINT (30,000 SF)	1.20/SF	36,000		—	1.70/SF	36,000	1.20/SF	15,120
I. H.P.SODIUM FIXTURES-SWITCHED DISTRIBUTION, CONTROLS		354040		354,040		354040		354040
J. Contingencies 5%	1,415586	70,779	1,116,620	55,831	1,337,586	66,879	1,222,510	66,126
K. Escalation 5%		70,779		55,831		66,879		66,126
Total Initial Cost		1,557,144		1,228,282		1,476,344		1,344,762
Operations (Annual) ENERGY		Diff. Escal. Rate / PWA W/Escal.						
A. HIGH PRESSURE SODIUM	0% / 9.779	7032 / 68,766	7.695 / 75,249		6.833 / 66,820		8.889 / 86,926	
B. HVAC SPACE COOLING	0% / 9.779	13.589 / 132,887	11.000 / 107,569		13.589 / 132,887		11.000 / 107,569	
C. HIGH PRESSURE SODIUM (REMAINING AREA)	0% / 9.779	14.742 / 144,162	14.742 / 144,162		14.742 / 144,162		14.742 / 144,162	
D.								
E.								
F.								
Total Annual Operations Costs		345,815		326,980		343,869		338,657
Maintenance (Annual)		Diff. Escal. Rate / PWA W/Escal.						
A. ALUM. PANEL-CLEAN ($0.09/SF/YR)	0% / 9.779	1,400 / 13,692	1,750 / 17,115		1,400 / 13,692		2,800 / 27,384	
B. WINDOW-WASHING ($.17/SF/YR)	0% / 9.779	3,543 / 34,650	2,657 / 25,958		3,543 / 38,650		1,772 / 17,324	
C. PARABOLIC LOUVER ($.25/SF/YR)	0% / 9.779	1,200 / 11,735		—		—		—
D. BASEBOARD HVAC ($.32/LF/YR)	0% / 9.779	806 / 7,885		—	806 / 7,885			—
E. REFLECTIVE SURFACE ($.25/SF/YR)	0% / 9.779	1500 / 14,669		—		—		—
F. VENETIAN BLINDS ($.20/SF/YR)	0% / 9.779	3,200 / 31,293	2,400 / 23,470		3,200 / 31,293		1,600 / 15,646	
G. H.P. SODIUM FIXT. (6.00/FIXT./YR)	0% / 9.779	12,822 / 125,386	12,822 / 125,386		12,822 / 125,386		12,822 / 125,386	
Total Annual Maintenance Costs		139,310		191,956		212,906		185,740
Replacement/Alterations (Single Expenditure)	Year / PW Factor							
A. PARABOLIC REFLECTIVE LOUVERS	10 / .386	60,000 / 23,160		—		—		—
B. PARABOLIC REFLECTIVE LOUVERS	20 / .149	60,000 / 8,940		—		—		—
C. PARABOLIC REFLECTIVE LOUVERS	30 / .057	60,000 / 3,520		—		—		—
D. VENETIAN BLINDS	10 / .386	16,000 / 6,176	12,000 / 4,632		16,000 / 6,176		8,000 / 3,088	
E. VENETIAN BLINDS	20 / .149	16,000 / 2,384	12,000 / 1,788		16,000 / 2,384		8,000 / 1,192	
F. VENETIAN BLINDS	30 / .057	16,000 / 912	18,000 / 684		16,000 / 912		8,000 / 456	
G. BASEBOARD CONVECTOR HVAC	20 / .149	20,000 / 2,980		—	20,000 / 2,980			—
H. HIGH PRESSURE SODIUM FIXTURE	20 / .149	354040 / 52,752	354,040 / 52,752		354,040 / 52,752		354,040 / 52,752	
I.								
J.								
Total Replacement/Alteration Costs		100,724		59,856		65,204		57,488
Tax Elements	Diff. Escal. Rate / PWA W/Escal.							
A. PARABOLIC REFLECTIVE LOUVERS	1 / .909	(6,000) / (5,454)		—		—		—
B. REFLECTIVE SURFACE	1 / .909	(1,800) / (1,636)		—		—		—
C. HIGH PRESSURE SODIUM -								
D. DEPRECIATION OVER 7 YEARS		(22,457)		(22,457)		(22,457)		(22,457)
E.								
F.								
G.								
Total Tax Elements		(29,547)		(22,457)		(22,457)		(22,457)
Associated (Annual)	Diff. Escal. Rate / PWA W/Escal.							
A. DENIAL OF USE (SPACE) LOSS	0% / 9.779		—		—		—	75,600 / 739,300
B. ($10.00/SF/YR/ x 7560 SF)								
C.								
Total Annual Associated Costs		—		—		—		739,300
Total Owning Present Worth Costs								
Salvage At End Of Economic Life	Year / PW Factor							
Building (Struc., Arch., Mech., Elec., Equip.)	40 / .022	(141,559) / (3,114)	(111,643) / (2,456)		(133,759) / (2,502)		(122,251) / (2,689)	
Other 10% OF INITIAL COST								
Sitework								
Total Salvage		(3,114)		(2,456)		(2,502)		(2,689)
Total Present Worth Life Cycle Costs		2,210,332		1,782,161		2,068,364		2,640,801
Life-Cycle Present Worth Dollar Savings		—		428,171		141,968		(430,469)

PW — Present Worth   PWA — Present Worth Of Annuity

FIGURE 7-1-6
Life cycle costing estimate.

115

Lighting Fixture Description:	Criteria:	Original: Two 4'-0" High Windows Refl. Louvers & Coffered Ceiling	Alt. 1: Coffered Ceiling w/one 6'-0" Window	Alt. 2: Two 4'-0" High Windows, No Reflectors, Coffer Ceiling	Alt. 3: Recessed Single 4'-0" Window, 9'-0" Ceiling
		Daylighting Schemes			
Fluorescent Parabolic 3-tube, Direct	Energy	40	45	45	40
	Life Cycle Cost	50	70	55	30
	Other*	153	147	140	146
	Total	243	262 (4)	240	216
	Initial Cost	$1,613,200	$1,284,338	$1,527,400	$1,400,816
	Life Cycle Cost	2,203,482	1,778,704	2,046,933	2,644,575
	Energy Cost	339,175	323,783	323,088	341,923
Fluorescent 2-tube, Indirect 6" x 4' Fixture	Energy	15	15	20	10
	Life Cycle Cost	35	55	45	15
	Other*	190	184	177	183
	Total	240	254	242	208
	Initial Cost	$1,723,677	$1,394,815	$1,637,877	$1,511,293
	Life Cycle Cost	2,484,842	2,064,873	2,319,894	2,938,525
	Energy Cost	456,131	445,498	431,645	472,189
High Pressure Sodium Fixture, Dimmed	Energy	40	50	50	45
	Life Cycle Cost	45	65	50	20
	Other*	171	165	158	164
	Total	256 (7)	280 (2)	258 (6)	229
	Initial Cost	$1,720,384	$1,391,522	$1,634,584	$1,508,002
	Life Cycle Cost	2,381,953	1,936,710	2,206,244	2,800,842
	Energy Cost	332,410	296,499	297,164	313,681
High Pressure Sodium Fixture, Switched	Energy	35	40	40	40
	Life Cycle Cost	50	70	55	30
	Other*	179	173	166	172
	Total	264 (3)	283 (1)	261 (5)	242
	Initial Cost	$1,557,144	$1,228,282	$1,471,344	$1,344,762
	Life Cycle Cost	2,210,332	1,782,161	2,068,364	2,640,801
	Energy Cost	345,815	326,980	343,869	338,657

*Criteria: Glare control, spatial brightless, initial costs,
   Appearance of device, color rendition/temp., maintainability.

FIGURE 7-1-7
Summary matrix.

Life Cycle Costing Summary

Computer Center	Cooling Medium (Cooling Tower)
Project	Item

Team Members	Team

Team Members	Date

Summary of Change (Study Area, Original & Proposed)

Study Area

    Team study included the review of various water cooling tower systems for the proposed Computer Center.

Original

    The current design indicated the use of a closed circuit evaporative cooling tower.

Proposed

    A life cycle costing estimate was prepared for both ceramic high horsepower (HP) and low horsepower towers, as well as the original design. The low H. P. ceramic cooling tower was recommended as the most cost effective.

Estimated Savings Cost Summary:

	Arch.	Struct.	Mech.	Elec.	Site	Total
Initial Cost Savings			169,873			169,873
Life Cycle Cost Savings (PW)						999,381
Annual Energy Savings (EU)						$100,000 \times 10^6$ Btu

Percent Savings Initial   41%

Percent Savings Life Cycle   71%

Percent Savings Energy   80%

FIGURE 7-2-1

Life cycle costing summary.

Water Cooling Tower System
Life-Cycle Cost Estimate

	Original Describe: CLOSED CIRCUIT EVAP. COOLERS		Alternative 1 Describe: CERAMIC TOWER HIGH HP		Alternative 2 Describe: CERAMIC TOWER LOW HP		Alternative 3 Describe:	
	Estimated Costs	Present Worth	Estimated Costs	Present Worth	Estimated Costs	Present Worth	Estimated Costs	Present Worth
Element								
Water Cooling Tower System								
A. Site Preparation:								
Concrete Foundations								
Concrete Basin __INCLUDING STRUCTURAL__		41,400		32,400		35,224		
Masonry Housing (Ceramic Fill Tower)								
Structural Steelwork								
Enclosure __ASSUMING TEXTURED PRE-CAST $13.23/SF__		71,971		43,394		50,274		
B. On-Site Utilities:								
Water Service								
Fire Line								
Power								
Steam								
C. Cooling Tower a) Package Complete __INSTALLED__		278,000						
b) Components (Ceramic Tile, Etc.)				135,000		155,000		
c) Accessories (Pan Heater, Etc.)								
D. Connections a) Mechanical __WATER PIPING (DIFF.)__		4,000		–		–		
b) Plumbing								
c) Electrical		18,000		5,000		3,000		
E. Interface a) Water Treatment System __TRADE-OFF__		–		–		–		
b) Sprinkler System								
c) Pumps __TRADE-OFF__		–		–		–		
d) Piping								
e) Controls								
F. Guideline Cost (Fig. 10)								
Initial Costs — Total Initial Cost		413,371		215,794		243,498		
Operation Costs Annual Costs @ _10_ % Discount Rate Escal. Rate _0_ % PWA (With Escal.) Factor _9.779_								
A. Salaries (Operation, Etc.) __TRADE-OFF__		–		–		–		
B. Make-up Water __TRADE-OFF__		–		–		–		
C. Water Treatment __TRADE-OFF__		–		–		–		
D. Equipment (Fans, Pumps, Heaters, Etc.)	72,500	708,978	18,060	176,608	10,536	103,032		
E. Fire Protection								
F. Insurance								
G. Sewer								
H. THERMAL PERFORMANCE LOSS	12,732	124,506		–		–		
I.								
J.								
K. Guideline Costs (Fig. 11 X Fig. 12)								
Total Annual Operation Costs		833,484		176,608		103,032		
Maintenance Costs Annual Costs @ _10_ % Discount Rate Escal. Rate _0_ % PWA (With Escal.) Factor _9.779_ Water Cooling Tower System								
A. Cooling Tower Structure	1200	11,735	250	2,445	250	2,445		
B. Cooling Tower Fill								
C. Cooling Tower Basin	150	1,467	100	978	100	978		
D. Mechanical Equipment (Fans, Motors, Gears)	6,000	58,614	3,000	29,357	3,000	29,357		
E. Accessories (Pan Heaters, Dampers, Etc.) __LOUVERS/GRATINGS__	1,000	9,779	250	2,445	250	2,445		
F. Controls	750	7,334	200	1,956	200	1,956		
G. Water Treatment System								
H. Pumps (Circulating)								
I. Piping, Fittings, Valves, Etc.								
J. Fire Protection								
K. Salaries (If not included in costs)								
L. Inspection	1500	14,670	750	7,334	750	7,334		
M. Painting	200	1,956						
N. Plumbing (Drains, Sewer, Etc.)								
O.								
P.								
Q.								
R. Guideline Costs (Fig. 13)								
Total Annual Maintenance Costs		105,615		44,495		44,495		
Replacement Costs Single Expenditures @ ___ % Discount Rate	Year:	PW Factor:						
A. Structure								
B. Fill } 20 MAJOR REHAB, STRUCT., FILL & BASIN PW= 0.148	278,000	41,144	15,000	2,220	15,000	2,220		
C. Basin								
D. Fan/Fan Ring								
E. Motor 15 .24	3,000	720	1,000	240	1,000	240		
F. Drive/Gear 15 .24	1,000	240	4,000	960	4,000	960		
G. Discharge Cone 30 .06	3,000	180	1,000	60	1,000	60		
H. Accessories 30 .06	1,000	60	4,000	240	4,000	240		
I. Spray Nozzles 20 .148	2,000	296	–					
J. Shafts 15 .24	2,000	480	1,000	240	1,000	240		
K. Bearings 30 .06	5,000	300	3,000	180	5,000	300		
L. Controls 20 .148	6,000	888	4,000	592	4,000	592		
M. Water Treatment __TRADE-OFF__								
N. Fire Protection								
O. ELIMINATORS 20 .148			5,000	740	5,000	740		
P. ELIMINATORS 30 .06	2,000	120	15,000	900	15,000	900		
Q. Guideline Cost (Fig. 13) x PWA								
Total Replacement Costs		44,428		6,372		6,492		
Associated Costs Annual Costs @ ___ % Discount Rate Escal. Rate ___ % PWA (With Escal.) Factor ___								
A.								
B.								
Total Annual Associated Costs		N/A		N/A		N/A		
Salvage Value Final Value @ ___ Year ___ PW Factor Cooling Tower System __INSIGNIFICANT__								
Total Salvage Value		N/A		N/A		N/A		
LCC — Total Present Worth Costs		1,396,898		443,269		397,517		

PW - Present Worth   PWA - Present Worth Of Annuity   PW SAVINGS   953,629   999,381

FIGURE 7-2-2
Life cycle costing estimate, water cooling tower system.

118

Life Cycle Costing Summary

Computer Center	Emergency Power (Generators)
Project	Item
Team Members	Team
Team Members	Date

Summary of Change (Study Area, Original & Proposed)

Study Area

   The team concentrated its efforts in reviewing various alternatives to the function of providing emergency power for computers.

Original

   The original concept of using eight 1000 kW reciprocating diesel engines was challenged. Concern was expressed that the diesels were less reliable and required more space than similiar gas turbine engines. Also, use of larger diesels was studied.

Proposed

   The Weighted Evaluation presents a summary of the criteria & the analysis matrix used to evaluate two sizes of diesel and turbine engines. The general purpose LCC sheet illustrates the life cycle costing estimate for the alternatives. The results of this study reinforce the earlier decision to utilize eight 1000 kW diesel engines.

Estimated Savings Cost Summary:

	Arch.	Struct.	Mech.	Elec.	Site	Total
Initial Cost Savings						No Change
Life Cycle Cost Savings (PW)						
Annual Energy Savings (EU)						

Percent Savings Initial   No Change

Percent Savings Life Cycle _____

Percent Savings Energy   _____

FIGURE 7-3-1

Life cycle costing summary.

Function Analysis

Item	Basic Function	Date
EMERGENCY POWER (GENERATORS)	PROVIDE POWER	

Quantity	Component	Function Verb	Noun	Kind *	Original Cost	TARGET
6	2000 KVA SUBSTATION TRANSFORM.	CHANGE	VOLTAGE	B	260,800	251,100
3	3000 A SECONDARY SUBSTATION	SWITCH	POWER	B	401,400	300,000
VARIES	SWITCHBOARDS	SWITCH	POWER	B	768,100	550,000
18	75 KVA FREQUENCY CONVERSION	CHANGE	FREQ.	B	540,000	369,000
VARIES	POWER DISTRIBUTION	TRANSP.	POWER	B	472,600	460,000
VARIES	POWER PANELS	SWITCH	POWER	B	127,000	120,000
VARIES	BRANCH CIRCUIT DISTRIBUTION	TRANS.	POWER	B	263,000	240,000
10	1000 KW GENERATORS (STANDBY)	GENER.	POWER	B	1,350,000	950,000
9	500 KW UPS (SOLID STATE)	MAINTAIN	POWER	B	1,950,000	1,300,000
VARIES	UPS BATTERIES	RETAIN	POWER	B	650,000	650,000

* B = BASIC

Graphical Function Analysis

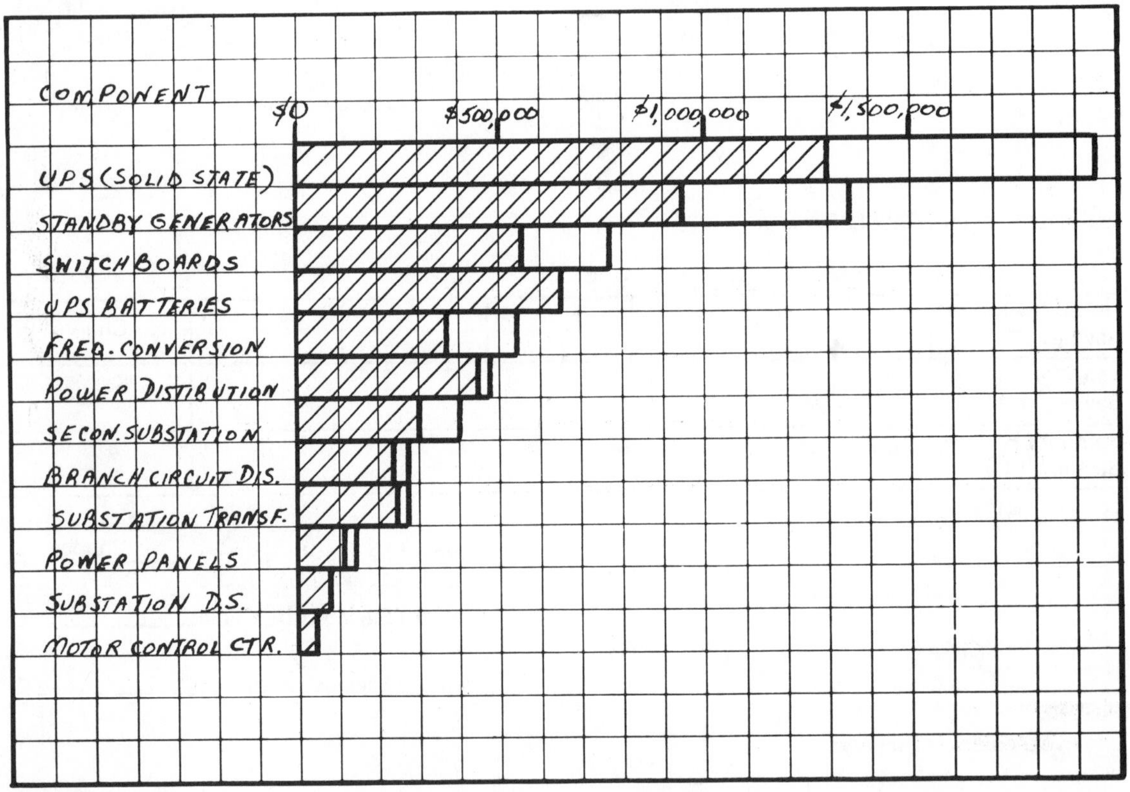

FIGURE 7-3-2
Function analysis.

Idea Comparison

Idea	Advantages	Disadvantages	Estimated Potential Savings Inital	Life Cycle
USE SMALL DIESELS	LOW COST	MAINTENANCE	IMPROVED	POOR
	HIGH RELIABILITY			
USE LARGE DIESELS	LOW COST	SIZE & WEIGHT	IMPROVED	FAIR
USE SMALL TURBINES	LONG LIFE	COST	POOR	FAIR
	LESS MAINTENANCE	STARTING TIME		
LARGE TURBINES	LONG LIFE	COST	POOR	FAIR
	LESS MAINTENANCE	STARTING TIME		
NO BATTERY CHARGE OFF GENERATOR	REDUCES GEN. LOAD	RELIABILITY	IMPROVED	POOR
PEAK LOAD SHAVE W/ STANDBY GEN.	SAVE ENERGY COST		INCREASE	IMPROVE
SEQUENCE LOAD TRANSF. CO-EMERG.	REDUCES INRUSH		INCREASE	IMPROVE

FIGURE 7-3-3
Idea comparison.

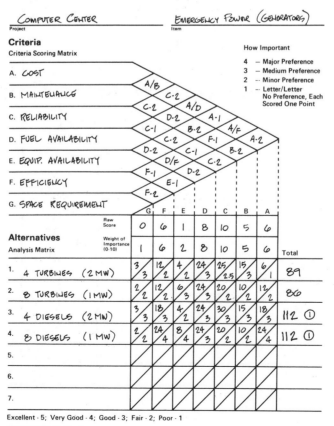

Weighted Evaluation

Excellent - 5; Very Good - 4; Good - 3; Fair - 2; Poor - 1

FIGURE 7-3-4
Weighted evaluation.

121

Life Cycle Costing Estimate
General Purpose Work Sheet

Study Title: _STANDBY GENERATORS_

Discount Rate: _10%_ Economic Life: _40 YEARS_

	Original Describe: _8-1000 KW RECIP. DIESEL ENGINES_		Alternative 1 Describe: _4-2000 KW RECIP. DIESEL ENGINES_		Alternative 2 Describe: _8-1000 KW GAS TURBINES_		Alternative 3 Describe: _4-2000 KW GAS TURBINES_	
	Estimated Costs	Present Worth	Estimated Costs	Present Worth	Estimated Costs	Present Worth	Estimated Costs	Present Worth

Initial Costs

	Estimated Costs	Present Worth	Estimated Costs	Present Worth	Estimated Costs	Present Worth	Estimated Costs	Present Worth
A. GENERATORS	1,400,000		1,800,000		2,000,000		2,000,000	
B. SWITCHGEAR	128,000		126,000		128,000		126,000	
C. MECHANICAL	157,000		175,000		157,000		173,000	
D.								
E.								
F.								
G.								
H.								
I.								
J. Contingencies ___%								
K. Escalation ___%								
Total Initial Cost		1,685,000		2,101,000		2,285,000		2,301,000

Operations (Annual)

	Diff. Escal. Rate	PWA W/Escal.	Est. Costs	Present Worth	Est. Costs	Present Worth	Est. Costs	Present Worth	Est. Costs	Present Worth
A.										
B. 1 MW RECIP 70 GAL/HR x 8 UNITS	0%	9.779	89,600	876,200						
C. 2 MW RECIP 140 GAL/HR x 4 UNITS	0%	9.779			89,600	876,700				
D. 1 MW TURB 161 GAL/HR x 8 UNITS	0%	9.779					155,080	1,516,500		
E. 2 MW TURB 268 GAL/HR x 4 UNITS	0%	9.779							128,600	1,258,000
F.										
Total Annual Operations Costs				876,700		876,200		1,516,600		1,258,000

Maintenance (Annual)

	Diff. Escal. Rate	PWA W/Escal.	Est. Costs	Present Worth	Est. Costs	Present Worth	Est. Costs	Present Worth	Est. Costs	Present Worth
A. LUBRICATE, CHANGE FILTERS,	0%	9.779	10,200	99,700	9,000	88,000	10,200	99,700	9,000	88,000
B. CHECK & ADJUST IGNITION										
C. INSPECT WIRING RINGS										
D. BELTS, ETC. CHECK FUEL										
E. COOLANT, ELECTROLYTS, ETC.										
F. REPLACE FAILED COMPONENTS	0%	9.779	800	7,800	400	3,900	2,000	19,600	1,000	9,800
G. AS REQUIRED										
Total Annual Maintenance Costs				107,500		91,900		119,300		97,800

Replacement/Alterations (Single Expenditure)

	Year	PW Factor	Est. Costs	Present Worth	Est. Costs	Present Worth	Est. Costs	Present Worth	Est. Costs	Present Worth
A. FAILURE (ONE IN FOUR):										
B. 1 MW TURBINE	25	.0923					500,000	46,700		
C. 2 MW TURBINE	25	.0923							500,000	46,700
D. 1 MW DIESEL	25	.0923	350,000	32,300						
E. 2 MW DIESEL					450,000	41,500				
F.										
G.										
H.										
I.										
J.										
Total Replacement/Alteration Costs				32,300		41,500		46,700		46,700

Tax Elements

	Diff. Escal. Rate	PWA W/Escal.	Est. Costs	Present Worth	Est. Costs	Present Worth	Est. Costs	Present Worth	Est. Costs	Present Worth
A.										
B.										
C.										
D.										
E.										
F.										
G.										
Total Tax Elements										

Associated (Annual)

	Diff. Escal. Rate	PWA W/Escal.	Est. Costs	Present Worth	Est. Costs	Present Worth	Est. Costs	Present Worth	Est. Costs	Present Worth
A. SPACE COST @ $45.00/SF			6000 SF		3500 SF		1,000 SF			
B.										
C.										
Total Annual Associated Costs				270,000		157,500		45,000		N/A
Total Owning Present Worth Costs				1,286,000		1,167,100		1,727,000		1,402,000

Salvage

	Year	PW Factor	Est. Costs	Present Worth	Est. Costs	Present Worth	Est. Costs	Present Worth	Est. Costs	Present Worth
Salvage At End Of Economic Life Building (Struc., Arch., Mech., Elec., Equip.) @ 10%		.022	(140,000)	(3,100)	(180,000)	(4,000)	(224,000)	(4,900)	(200,000)	(4,400)
Other										
Sitework										
Total Salvage				(3,100)		(4,000)		(4,900)		(4,400)

LCC

	Est. Costs	Present Worth	Est. Costs	Present Worth	Est. Costs	Present Worth	Est. Costs	Present Worth
Total Present Worth Life Cycle Costs		2,967,900		3,264,100		4,007,100		3,698,600
Life-Cycle Present Worth Dollar Savings				MORE 296,200		MORE 1,039,200		MORE 730,700

PW — Present Worth   PWA — Present Worth Of Annuity

FIGURE 7-3-5

Life cycle costing estimate.

122

Life Cycle Costing Summary

Branch Bank		Building Layout	
Project		**Item**	
Team Members		**Team**	
Team Members		**Date**	

Summary of Change (Study Area, Original & Proposed)

Study Area

   This team was tasked to develop a prototype branch bank layout which would reflect the initial, energy, and total life cycle cost targets established by the owner from historical data collected from similar projects

Original

   Several branch banks had been designed & built for the owner over the past several years. To better understand the functional relationships between spaces a comparison matrix and a diagram was prepared to illustrate their implications. A "typical" existing bank was selected for a life cycle computer analysis.

Proposed

   Numerous design alternative layouts were prepared by the team. The most promising schemes were selected for computer analysis. The layout selected by the team based on the functional requirements and the life cycle cost analysis results is illustrated. The alternative layout was recommended for future branch banks.

Estimated Savings Cost Summary:

	Arch.	Struct.	Mech.	Elec.	Site	Total
Initial Cost Savings	55,000	19,000	17,000	12,000	15,000	$117,768
Life Cycle Cost Savings (PW)						$173,225
Annual Energy Savings (EU)						453×10^6 Btu

Note: Only selected worksheets from LCC Study presented for this example.

Percent Savings Initial ___45%___

Percent Savings Life Cycle ___44%___

Percent Savings Energy ___55%___

FIGURE 7-4-1
Life cycle costing summary.

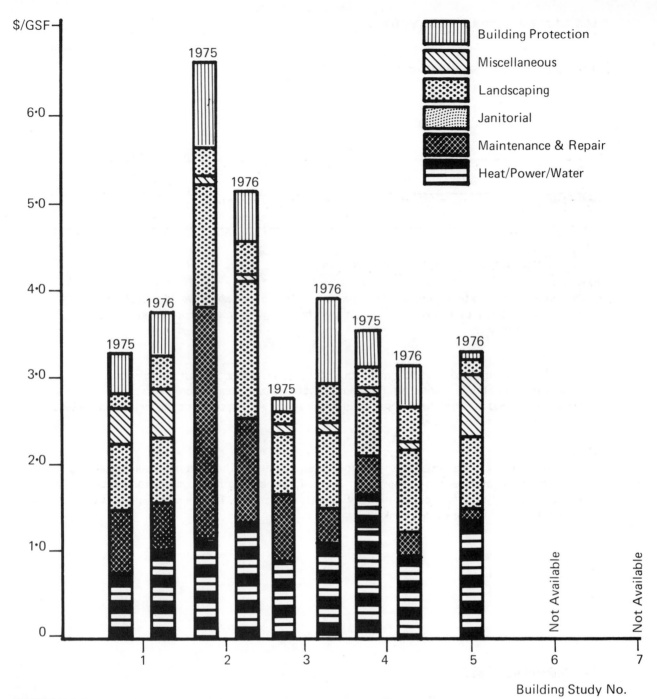

FIGURE 7-4-2
Branch banks, historical occupancy cost/GSF.

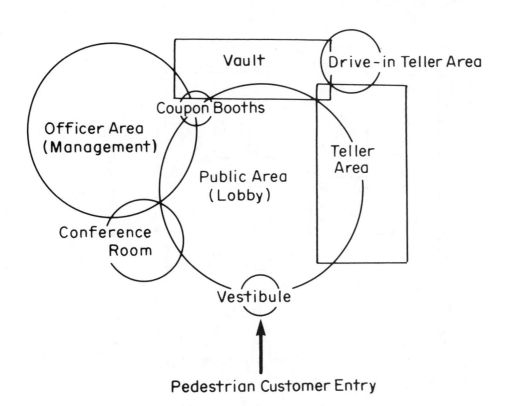

Vehicular Customer

Vault

Drive-in Teller Area

Officer Area
(Management)

Coupon Booths

Public Area
(Lobby)

Teller
Area

Conference
Room

Vestibule

Pedestrian Customer Entry

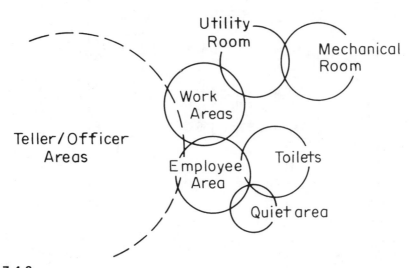

Utility
Room

Mechanical
Room

Teller/Officer
Areas

Work
Areas

Toilets

Employee
Area

Quiet area

FIGURE 7-4-3
Space affinity diagrams. (*a*) Public service spaces. (*b*) Bank support spaces.

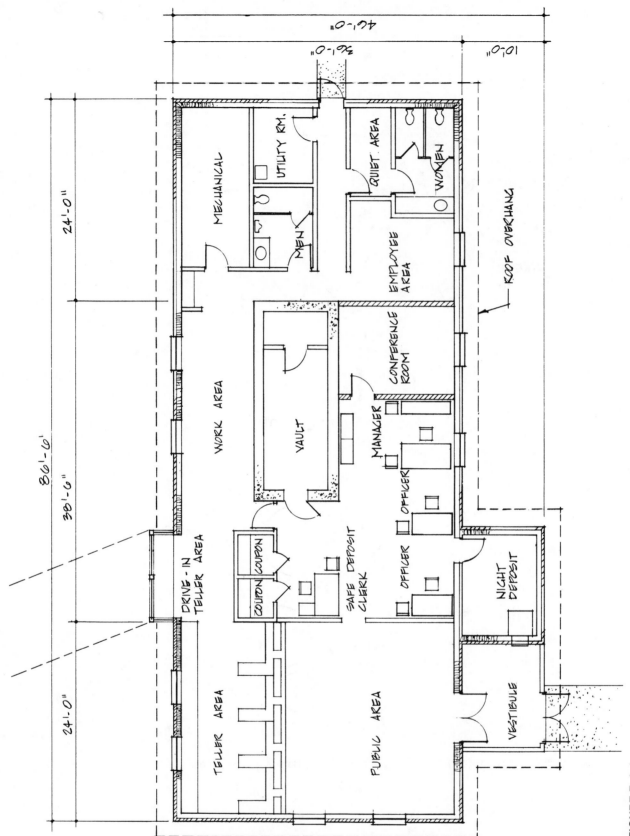

FIGURE 7-4-4
Typical existing bank layout.

```
                            SMITH HINCHMAN & GRYLLS ASSOCIATES INC

                            ECONOMIC BUILDING PERFORMANCE MODEL
                                   DESIGN ALTERNATIVE  1
                                     DATE  1 MAR 78

                        ******  LIFE CYCLE BUILDING COST SUMMARY  ******


A.  THE INITAL COST FOR THE PROPOSED PROJECT IS   259066.42 DOLLARS

B.  THE AVERAGE ANNUAL OWNING AND OPERATING COSTS ARE  19074.59 DOLLARS

              PROJECT DISCOUNT RATE (I) = 10.0 PER CENT
              PROJECT DESIGN TIME TO CONSTRUCTION = 0.25 YEARS
              PROJECT CONSTRUCTION TIME = 1.00 YEARS

C.  SUMMARY OF YEAR BY YEAR ECONOMIC BUILDING PERFORMANCE:
```

END OF YEAR	HEATING	COOLING	LIGHTING	EQUIP.	ALTERATION COSTS	MAINTENANCE COSTS	REPLACEMENT COSTS	FIRE PROTECTION COSTS	ANNUAL EXPENDITURE	PRESENT WORTH
0									9383.15	9383.15
1	1743.21	461.77	1667.03	649.35	132.42	3894.08	0.00	411.28	8826.70	8024.28
2	1830.37	484.86	1750.38	681.81	141.08	3933.02	0.00	415.39	9095.83	7517.21
3	1921.88	509.10	1837.90	715.91	149.74	3972.35	0.00	419.55	9376.68	7044.84
4	2017.98	534.55	1929.79	751.70	158.41	4012.07	0.00	423.74	9669.84	6604.63
5	2118.88	561.28	2026.28	789.29	167.07	4052.19	0.00	427.98	9975.90	6194.25
6	2224.82	589.35	2127.59	828.75	175.73	4092.71	0.00	432.26	10295.49	5811.53
7	2336.06	618.81	2233.97	870.19	184.40	4133.64	610.15	436.58	11239.42	5767.60
8	2452.87	649.75	2345.67	913.70	193.06	4174.98	114.71	440.95	11092.62	5174.79
9	2575.51	682.24	2462.96	959.38	201.72	4216.73	0.00	445.36	11342.17	4810.19
10	2704.28	716.35	2586.10	1007.35	210.38	4258.89	1901.69	449.81	13624.49	5252.83
11	2839.50	752.17	2715.41	1057.72	219.05	4301.48	0.00	454.31	12120.59	4248.19
12	2981.47	789.78	2851.18	1110.60	227.71	4344.50	12481.07	458.85	25017.46	7971.33
13	3130.55	829.27	2993.74	1166.13	236.37	4387.94	0.00	463.44	12971.07	3757.26
14	3287.07	870.73	3143.43	1224.44	245.04	4431.82	810.81	468.07	14236.38	3748.88
15	3451.43	914.27	3300.60	1285.66	253.70	4476.14	25242.95	472.76	39143.81	9370.72
16	3624.00	959.98	3465.63	1349.95	262.36	4520.90	155.88	477.48	14553.83	3167.34
17	3805.20	1007.98	3638.91	1417.44	271.02	4566.11	1274.11	482.26	16192.01	3203.50
18	3995.46	1058.38	3820.85	1488.32	279.69	4611.77	0.00	487.08	15461.86	2780.95
19	4195.23	1111.30	4011.90	1562.73	288.35	4657.89	0.00	491.95	16031.00	2621.20
20	4404.99	1166.87	4212.49	1640.87	297.01	4704.47	44069.04	496.87	60695.60	9022.01
21	4625.24	1225.21	4423.12	1722.91	305.68	4751.51	1011.47	501.84	18261.30	2467.66
22	4856.51	1286.47	4644.27	1809.06	314.34	4799.03	0.00	506.86	17902.19	2199.21
23	5099.33	1350.79	4876.49	1899.51	323.00	4847.02	0.00	511.93	18585.07	2075.55
24	5354.30	1418.33	5120.31	1994.49	331.66	4895.49	18376.01	517.05	37675.97	3825.08
25	5622.01	1489.25	5376.33	2094.21	340.33	4944.44	33429.03	522.22	53477.49	4935.76
TOTALS	83198.	22039.	79562.	30991.	5909.32	109981.	139477.	11616.	486247.93	136979.94

```
D.  THE TOTAL COST OF THE PROPOSED PROJECT OVER ITS LIFE OF  25 YEARS IN PRESENT WORTH DOLLARS IS    396046.36

E.  THE ENERGY CONSUMED BY THIS DESIGN ON A YEARLY BASIS IS     841. MILLION BTU

              HEATING ENERGY    =      593. MILLION BTU
              COOLING ENERGY    =       41. MILLION BTU
              LIGHTING ENERGY   =      146. MILLION BTU
              EQUIPMENT ENERGY  =       61. MILLION BTU

              HEAT RECOVERY DOLLAR SAVINGS PER YEAR =    0.
```

FIGURE 7-4-5

Life cycle costing estimate (automated), typical existing bank layout.

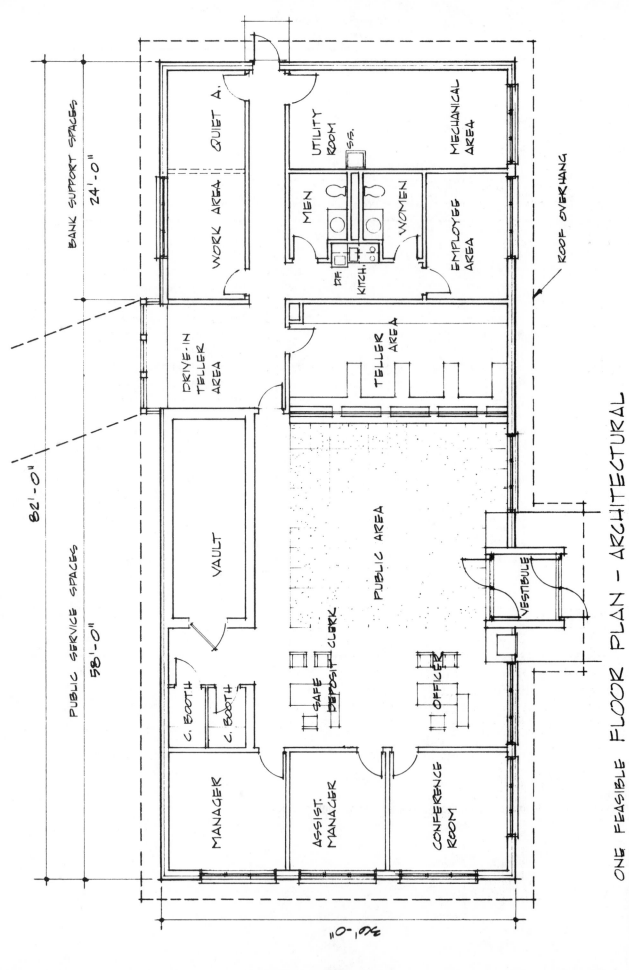

ONE FEASIBLE FLOOR PLAN – ARCHITECTURAL

FIGURE 7-4-6
Proposed bank layout, floor plan.

128

****** LIFE CYCLE BUILDING COST SUMMARY ******

A. THE INITAL COST FOR THE PROPOSED PROJECT IS 141298.43 DOLLARS

B. THE AVERAGE ANNUAL OWNING AND OPERATING COSTS ARE 11802.41 DOLLARS

       PROJECT DISCOUNT RATE (I) = 10.0 PER CENT
       PROJECT DESIGN TIME TO CONSTRUCTION = 0. YEARS
       PROJECT CONSTRUCTION TIME = 0. YEARS

C. SUMMARY OF YEAR BY YEAR ECONOMIC BUILDING PERFORMANCE:

	ENERGY CONSUMPTION COSTS				ALTERATION	MAINTENANCE	REPLACEMENT	FIRE PROTECTION	COST SUMMARY	
END OF YEAR	HEATING	COOLING	LIGHTING	EQUIP.	COSTS	COSTS	COSTS	COSTS	ANNUAL EXPENDITURE	PRESENT WORTH
0									0.	0.
1	627.88	195.92	773.89	997.30	177.81	2838.67	0.00	277.67	5711.33	5192.11
2	671.84	205.71	812.59	1047.17	189.45	2867.05	0.00	280.44	5884.80	4863.47
3	718.87	216.00	853.22	1099.53	201.08	2895.72	0.00	283.25	6066.57	4557.91
4	769.19	226.80	895.88	1154.50	212.71	2924.68	0.00	286.08	6257.12	4273.70
5	823.03	238.14	940.67	1212.23	224.35	2953.93	165.51	288.94	6622.44	4112.01
6	880.64	250.04	987.70	1272.84	235.98	2983.47	0.00	291.83	6666.52	3763.08
7	942.29	262.55	1037.09	1336.48	247.61	3013.30	0.00	294.75	6886.45	3533.84
8	1008.25	275.67	1088.94	1403.30	259.24	3043.43	0.00	297.69	7117.30	3320.27
9	1078.82	289.46	1143.39	1473.47	270.88	3073.87	0.00	300.67	7359.68	3121.22
10	1154.34	303.93	1200.56	1547.14	282.51	3104.61	2909.72	303.68	10523.98	4057.45
11	1235.14	319.13	1260.59	1624.50	294.14	3135.65	0.00	306.72	7881.73	2762.50
12	1321.60	335.08	1323.62	1705.73	305.77	3167.01	6127.20	309.78	14290.02	4553.24
13	1414.12	351.84	1389.80	1791.01	317.41	3198.68	0.00	312.88	8458.32	2450.08
14	1513.10	369.43	1459.29	1880.56	329.04	3230.67	0.00	316.01	8769.06	2309.17
15	1619.02	387.90	1532.25	1974.59	340.67	3262.97	21319.13	319.17	30415.04	7281.12
16	1732.35	407.30	1608.87	2073.32	352.30	3295.60	4164.95	322.36	13604.75	2960.79
17	1853.62	427.66	1689.31	2176.99	363.94	3328.56	1274.11	325.58	11075.82	2191.29
18	1983.37	449.04	1773.77	2285.84	375.57	3361.84	0.00	328.84	10182.71	1831.45
19	2122.21	471.50	1862.46	2400.13	387.20	3395.46	0.00	332.13	10583.88	1730.55
20	2270.76	495.07	1955.59	2520.13	398.84	3429.42	9274.66	335.45	20281.08	3014.65
21	2429.72	519.82	2053.37	2646.14	410.47	3463.71	0.00	338.80	11451.56	1547.46
22	2599.80	545.82	2156.03	2778.45	422.10	3498.35	0.00	342.19	11920.63	1464.40
23	2781.78	573.11	2263.84	2917.37	433.73	3533.33	0.00	345.61	12415.04	1386.49
24	2976.51	601.76	2377.03	3063.24	445.37	3568.67	8924.40	349.07	21860.67	2219.42
25	3184.86	631.85	2495.88	3216.40	457.00	3604.35	19287.95	352.56	32773.86	3024.90
TOTALS	39713.	9351.	36936.	47598.	7935.17	80173.	73448.	7842.	295060.36	81522.56

D. THE TOTAL COST OF THE PROPOSED PROJECT OVER ITS LIFE OF 25 YEARS IN PRESENT WORTH DOLLARS IS 222821.00

E. THE ENERGY CONSUMED BY THIS DESIGN ON A YEARLY BASIS IS 388. MILLION BTU

       HEATING ENERGY = 210. MILLION BTU
       COOLING ENERGY = 17. MILLION BTU
       LIGHTING ENERGY = 68. MILLION BTU
       EQUIPMENT ENERGY = 93. MILLION BTU

       HEAT RECOVERY DOLLAR SAVINGS PER YEAR = 0.

FIGURE 7-4-7
Life cycle costing estimate (automated), proposed bank layout.

Life Cycle Costing Summary

Exhibit Center	Roof/Roofing System
Project	**Item**

Team Members	**Team**

Team Members	**Date**

Summary of Change (Study Area, Original & Proposed)

Study Area
   The team concentrated their efforts on the functional aspects of the roof and roofing system. Due to the subterranean nature of the design, particular attention was directed toward architectural concepts which would have a beneficial impact on site and structural costs.

Original
   The original roof system consisted of 18 in. of soil, a fiberglass separation, 4 in. of gravel, 4 in. of Styrofoam insulation, a 6 mil polymembrane and a bentonite waterproofing.

Proposed
   A series of alternatives were considered, ranging from increased soil depth to lower depth and elimination of soil altogether. From the weighted evaluation and the life cycle cost analysis, a 6 in. soil covered roof structure is recommended. This alternative reduces the weight on the roof structure while maintaining the planting area on the roof.

Estimated Savings Cost Summary:

	Arch.	Struct.	Mech.	Elec.	Site	Total
Initial Cost Savings	9,960	18,000			18,900	46,860
Life Cycle Cost Savings (PW)						46,795
Annual Energy Savings (EU)						minor increase

Percent Savings Initial	64.7%
Percent Savings Life Cycle	53%
Percent Savings Energy	minor increase

FIGURE 7-5-1
Life cycle costing summary.

Idea Comparison

Idea	Advantages	Disadvantages	Estimated Potential Savings Inital	Life Cycle
1. 36-in. soil covering without insulation on concrete roof.	maintain aesthetics functional usage	cost	increase	savings
2. Inverted roof covering on concrete roof.	cost savings	aesthetics	savings	increase
3. 18-in. soil covering with insulation on concrete roof.	maintain aesthetics functional usage	cost	savings	savings
4. Use conventional 5 ply built-up roof on concrete roof	cost savings	aesthetics	savings	savings
5. 6-in. soil covering with insulation on concrete roof	lower cost/weight maintain aesthetics	less soil depth for plants	savings	same

FIGURE 7-5-2
Idea comparison.

Weighted Evaluation

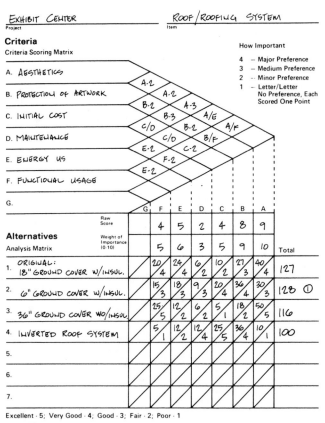

FIGURE 7-5-3
Weighted evaluation.

131

Life Cycle Costing Estimate
General Purpose Work Sheet

Study Title: _ROOF/ROOFING SYSTEM_

Discount Rate: _10%_   Economic Life: _40 YEARS_

	Original — Describe: 18" DIRT COVER W/INSUL.		Alternative 1 — Describe: 6" DIRT COVER W/INSUL		Alternative 2 — Describe: 36" DIRT COVER WO/INSUL		Alternative 3 — Describe: INVERTED ROOF	
	Estimated Costs	Present Worth	Estimated Costs	Present Worth	Estimated Costs	Present Worth	Estimated Costs	Present Worth
Initial Costs								
A. _DIRT/FIBERGLASS/GRAVEL_	23,580		13,670		33,430			
B. _INSUL/POLY/WATERPROOFING_	48,960		48,960		32,670			
C. _STRUCTURAL REVISIONS_	–		(18,000)		9,000		(18,000)	
D. _EXCAVATION COSTS (TOTAL SITE)_	–		(18,900)		28,350		(34,650)	
E. _INVERTED ROOF (2" STYRO; 1500# PER SQ OF ROCK)_	–						37,800	
F.								
G.								
H.								
I.								
J. Contingencies ___%								
K. Escalation ___%								
Total Initial Cost		72,540		25,680		108,450		(14,850)

	Diff. Escal. Rate	PWA W/Escal.	Estimated Costs	Present Worth	Estimated Costs	Present Worth	Estimated Costs	Present Worth	Estimated Costs	Present Worth
Operations (Annual)										
A. _HEATING_	3%	13.654	438	5980	580	7920	1011	13,805	823	11,240
B. _COOLING_	3%	13.654	0		0		0		86	1175
C.										
D.										
E.										
F.										
Total Annual Operations Costs				5,980		7,920		13,805		12,415
Maintenance (Annual)										
A. _CUT GRASS - MAINTAIN COVER_	2%	12.128	135	1635	135	1635	135	1635	0	0
B. _REPAIR MEMBRANE_	2%	12.128	380	4610	250	3030	450	5460	55	670
C. _MAINTAIN ROCK SURFACE_	2%	12.128							100	1215
D.										
E.										
F.										
G.										
Total Annual Maintenance Costs				6245		4665		7095		1885

	Year	PW Factor	Estimated Costs	Present Worth	Estimated Costs	Present Worth	Estimated Costs	Present Worth	Estimated Costs	Present Worth
Replacement/Alterations (Single Expenditure)										
A. _INVERTED ROOF_	20	0.1486							37,800	5615
B. _SUBGRADE MEMBRANE (20%)_	20	0.1486	14,510	7,155	12,515	1,860	14,220	2,115		
C.										
D.										
E.										
F.										
G.										
H.										
I.										
J.										
Total Replacement/Alteration Costs				7,155		1860		2115		5615

	Diff. Escal. Rate	PWA W/Escal.	Estimated Costs	Present Worth	Estimated Costs	Present Worth	Estimated Costs	Present Worth	Estimated Costs	Present Worth
Tax Elements										
A.										
B.										
C.										
D.										
E.										
F.										
G.										
Total Tax Elements										
Associated (Annual)										
A.										
B.										
C.										
Total Annual Associated Costs										
Total Owning Present Worth Costs				14,380		14,445		23,015		19,915

	Year	PW Factor								
Salvage At End Of Economic Life										
Building (Struc., Arch., Mech., Elec., Equip.)										
Other										
Sitework										
Total Salvage										

	Estimated Costs	Present Worth	Estimated Costs	Present Worth	Estimated Costs	Present Worth	Estimated Costs	Present Worth
Total Present Worth Life Cycle Costs		86,920		40,125		131,465		5,065
Life-Cycle Present Worth Dollar Savings				46,795		(44,545)		81,855

PW — Present Worth   PWA — Present Worth Of Annuity

FIGURE 7-5-4
Life cycle costing estimate.

132

Life Cycle Costing Summary

Office Facility	Solar Collector System
Project	Item

Team Members	Team

Team Members	Date

Summary of Change (Study Area, Original & Proposed)

Study Area

> The task of this team was to select for life cycle cost analysis various solar collector schemes for a Cleveland, Ohio facility. To provide a fair comparison, each collector was sized to collect an equal amount of energy.

Original

> The solar collector types which were studied in detail include:

- A flat-plate collector with two glass covers and black chrome coated absorber plate.

- An evacuated-tubular collector with a V-trough reflector.

- A vertical tracking collector with a parabolic reflecting concentrator.

- An east-west tracking collector with a fresnel lens concentrator.

- An evacuated-tubular collector with a flat diffuse reflector.

Proposed

> The Solar Energy Collector Assembly (Short Form) presents the life cycle cost comparison between the various collector types. The flat plate system has the lowest LCC. After considering other "non-economic" criteria, however, the evacuated tube with diffuse reflector was recommended. This performance evaluation is shown on the collector performance summary.

Estimated Savings Cost Summary:

	Arch.	Struct.	Mech.	Elec.	Site	Total
Initial Cost Savings						(3136)*
Life Cycle Cost Savings (PW)						(11628)*
Annual Energy Savings (EU)						

Percent Savings Initial _____

Note: Only selected worksheets used for this example

Percent Savings Life Cycle _____

* Compared with Flat Plate Collector

Percent Savings Energy _____

FIGURE 7-6-1
Life cycle costing summary.

Solar Energy Collector Assembly
Short Form
Life Cycle Costing Estimate

CLEVELAND, OHIO 160°F W.F.T. 15 YEARS

	Original Describe: FLAT PLATE 1000 S.F. Est. Costs	Present Worth	Alternative 1 Describe: EVAC. TUBE W/TROUGH REFL. 1392 SF Est. Costs	Present Worth	Alternative 2 Describe: VERT. TRACK 996 SF Est. Costs	Present Worth	Alternative 3 Describe: E-W TRACK 835 SF Est. Costs	Present Worth	Alternative 4 Describe: EVAC. TUBE W/DIFF. REF. 913 SF Est. Costs	Present Worth	Alternative 5 Describe: Est. Costs	Present Worth
Element Solar Energy Collector Assembly												
A. Site Preparation __NO DIFF__												
B. Structural Supports		4800		6682		2988		2922		4382		
Enclosure __NO DIFF__		–		–		–		–		–		
B. Utilities & CONTIN.		2000		2284		2490		2087		1826		
C. Solar Collector INCL. INSTALLATION		18400		41,760		29880		29,225		26,020		
*D. Installation Complete PIPING & INSULATION		8000		9,744		3984		4175		4,108		
*(Including Supply & Return Fluid Mains 5'-0'' From Collector Field) **Total Initial Cost (For Equivalent Btu/YR**		33,200		60,970		39,342		38,409		36,336		
Annual Costs @ 10% Discount Rate Escal. Rate 0 % PWA (With Escal.) Factor 7.606												
A. Salaries (Operation, Etc.) __NO DIFF__												
B. Make-up Water " "												
C. Water Treatment " "												
D. Equipment (Tracking Motors, Etc.)					50	380	75	570				
E. Insurance												
F.												
Total Annual Operation Costs		–		–		380		570		–		
Annual Costs @ 10 % Discount Rate Escal. Rate 0 % PWA (With Escal.) Factor 7.606 Solar Energy Collector System												
A. Inspection	1500	11,409	2,000	15,212	2,500	19,015	3,000	22,818	2,000	15,212		
B. Solar Collectors												
C. Structural												
D. Cleaning												
E. Mechanical Equipment (Drives, Motors)					100	760	125	951				
F. Accessories												
G. Controls												
H. Water Treatment System												
I. Repairs (Insulation, Valves, Etc.)	500	3803	1,000	7606	1500	11,409	2,000	15,212	750	5704		
J. Painting	250	1902	250	1902	200	1521	400	3042	250	1902		
K.												
Total Annual Maintenance Costs		17,114		24,720		32,705		42,023		22,818		
Single Expenditures @ 10% Discount Rate Item Replaced: Year: PW Factor: AS NOTED.												
A. Solar Collectors 4 .683					5512	3765						
B. 5 .621	3320	2062	6,000	3726			7682	4770	3500	2173		
C. 8 .466					11,800	5499						
D. Structure 10 .385	6640	2556	12,000	4620			13,443	5175	7000	2695		
E. Accessories 12 .319					23,495	7495						
F.												
G.												
H. Controls __NO DIFF__												
I.												
Total Replacement Costs		4,618		8346		16,759		9945		4868		
Annual Costs @ % Discount Rate Escal. Rate % PWA (With Escal.) Factor												
A.												
B.												
Total Annual Associated Costs												
Final Value @ 15 Year PW Factor .239 Solar Energy Collector Field	4980	(1190)	9000	(2151)	4000	(956)	4000	(956)	3600	(860)		
Total Salvage Value												
Total Present Worth Costs		53742		91,885		88,230		89,991		63,162		

PW- Present Worth   PWA- Present Worth of Annuity

FIGURE 7-6-2

Life cycle costing estimate, solar energy collector assembly.

160° F Inlet Temperature

	Possible Points	Flat Plate	Evacuated Tube with V-trough Reflector	Vertical Tracking	East-West Tracking	Evacuated Tube with Diffuse Reflector
Life-Cycle Cost $/10^6 Btu		$54	$92	$88	$90	$63
Collector Response Rating – Variable Cloudiness	23	4.3	7.8	5.9	5.2	9.4
Seasonal Output Ratio Rating	50	12.0	10.2	18.8	14.6	18.6
Peak/Average Day Ratio Rating	15	6.9	6.9	6.3	5.8	7.8
Totals from Subjective Analysis	12	10.5	9.7	9.2	7.7	10.4
Grand Total Subjective Rating	100	33.7	34.6	40.2	33.3	46.2

190° F Inlet Temperature

	Possible Points	Flat Plate	Evacuated Tube with V-trough Reflector	Vertical Tracking	East-West Tracking	Evacuated Tube with Diffuse Reflector
Life-Cycle Cost $/10^6 Btu		$63	$108	$95	$101	$70
Collector Response Rating Variable Cloudiness	23	4.3	7.8	5.9	5.2	9.4
Seasonal Output Ratio Rating	50	8.9	6.3	18.3	11.0	16.8
Peak/Average Day Ratio Rating	15	6.6	6.7	6.3	5.3	7.5
Totals from Subjective Analysis	12	10.5	9.7	9.2	7.9	10.4
Grand Total Subjective Rating	100	30.3	30.5	39.7	29.2	44.1

220° F Inlet Temperature

	Possible Points	Flat Plate	Evacuated Tube with V-trough Reflector	Vertical Tracking	East-West Tracking	Evacuated Tube with Diffuse Reflector
Life-Cycle Cost $/10^6 Btu		$77	$131	$110	$117	$80
Collector Response Rating– Variable Cloudiness	23	4.3	7.8	5.9	5.2	9.4
Seasonal Output Ratio Rating	50	5.5	4.8	17.5	6.9	15.4
Peak/Average Day Ratio Rating	15	6.5	6.7	6.0	5.0	7.3
Totals from Subjective Analysis	12	10.5	9.7	9.2	7.7	10.4
Grand Total Subjective Rating	100	26.8	29.0	38.6	24.8	42.5

FIGURE 7-6-3
Collector performance summary.

Life Cycle Costing Summary

Waste Water Treatment Plant	Primary Sedimentation Tank
Project	Item

Team Members	Team

Team Members	Date

Summary of Change (Study Area, Original & Proposed)

Study Area

A three (3) mgd modified activated sludge treatment plant was reviewed. One team was assigned to evaluate structures. The cost model helped identify the primary sedimentation basin for possible cost savings.

Original

The original design called for two (2) basins 20'-0'' x 100'-0'' long with traveling bridge sludge collection mechanisms and a pumping station.

The function analysis indicated that savings could be realized by changing shape of basins and changing collector mechanism.

Proposed

Use two of (2) 40'-0'' diameter circular basins with rotating mechanisms was life cycle cost evaluated. (See Figure 2).

The annualized method of LCC estimated an annual savings of $17,000 by using this system over the rectangular basins and traveling bridge.

Estimated Savings Cost Summary:

	Arch.	Struct.	Mech.	Elec.	Site	Total
Initial Cost Savings						187,500
Life Cycle Cost Savings (PW)						180,030
Annual Energy Savings (EU)						4,000 kWh

NOTE· Only selected worksheets used for this example.

Percent Savings Initial ___37%___

Percent Savings Life Cycle ___36%___

Percent Savings Energy ___9%___

FIGURE 7-7-1
Life cycle costing summary.

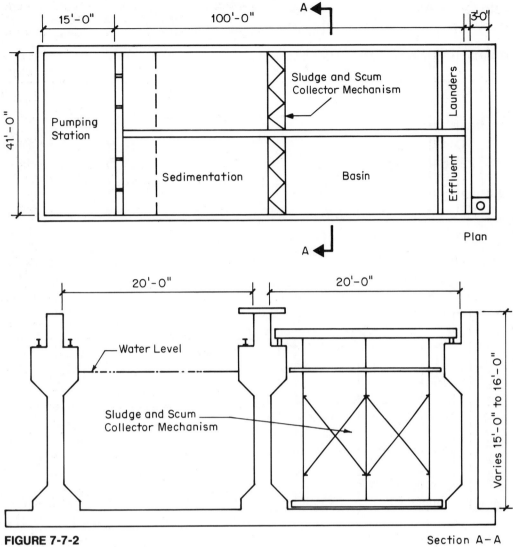

FIGURE 7-7-2
Original layout, plan and section.

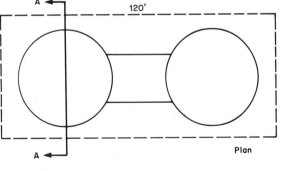

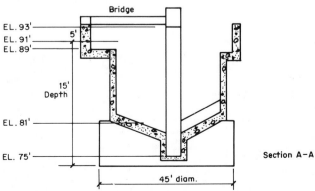

FIGURE 7-7-3
Proposed layout, plan and section.

Life Cycle Cost Analysis
Using Annual Owning & Operating Costs

ORIGINAL - RECT. BASINS w/ TRAVELING BRIDGE
ALT #1 - CIRCULAR CLARIFIERS
ALT #2 - RECT. BASINS w/ CHAIN & FLIGHT

Item __PRIMARY SEDIMENTATION BASINS__   Date __1-18-1977__

			Original	Alt. No. 1	Alt. No. 2
Collateral & Instant Contract Costs	**Initial Costs**				
	Base Cost				
	Interface Costs				
	a. STRUCTURES		160,500	75,300	132,500
	b. MECHANISMS		240,300	165,300	146,300
	c. PUMPS		26,000	26,000	26,000
	Other Initial Costs				
	a. 17% GC OH&P ON TANKS & EQUIPMENT		72,600	45,300	51,800
	b. _____				
	c. _____				
	Total Initial Cost Impact (IC)		499,400	311,900	356,600
	Initial Cost Savings			187,500	142,800
Salvage & Replacement Costs	Single Expenditures @ __7%__ Interest				
	Present Worth				
	1. Year __10__ 30,400 Amount				
	PW = Amount x (PW Factor 0.508349) =		15,500	15,500	15,500
	2. Year _____ Amount				
	Amount x (PW Factor _____) =				
	3. Year _____ Amount				
	Amount x (PW Factor _____) =				
	4. Year _____ Amount				
	Amount x (PW Factor _____) =				
	5. Year __20__ Amount				
	✱ Amount x (PW Factor _____) =				
	Salvage Amount x (PW Factor 0.258419) =		(24,900)	(11,400)	(20,000)

ORIGINAL - 96,500
#1 - 44,000   ] 1/2 STRUCTURE COST INCL. OH&P
#2 - 77,500

✱

			Original	Alt. No. 1	Alt. No. 2
Life Cycle Costs (Annualized)	**Annual Owning & Operating Costs**				
	1. Capital IC x (PP __0.094393__) =		47,100	29,400	33,00
	Recovery __20__ Years @ __7__ %				
	Replacement Cost: PP x PW				
	a. Year __10, PUMPS @ 15,500__		1,500	1,500	1,500
	b. Year _____				
	c. Year _____				
	d. Year _____				
	e. Year _____				
	Salvage: 24,900; 11,400; 20,000		(2,400)	(1,100)	(1,900)
	2. Annual Costs				
	a. Maintenance		3,100	2,900	3,100
	b. Operations		2,200	2,000	2,000
	c. _____				
	d. _____				
	e. _____				
	3. Total Annual Costs		51,500	34,700	38,400
	Annual Difference (AD)		—	16,800	13,100
	4. Present Worth of Annual Difference				
	(PWA Factor __10.59__) x AD		—	177,912	138,729

PP· Periodic Payment to pay off loan of $1.
PWA· Present Worth of Annuity (What $1 payable periodically is worth today).
PW· Present Worth (What $1 due in future is worth today).

▨ Future Costs
☐ Present Costs

FIGURE 7-7-4
Life cycle costing estimate (annualized).

138

Life Cycle Costing Summary

Waterfront Facility	Pier
Project	Item

Team Members	Team

Team Members	Date

Summary of Change (Study Area, Original & Proposed)

Study Area

The project consisted of construction of a new waterfront pier 702' long and 90' wide at Adak, Alaska. Several areas of potential life cycle cost savings were identified by brainstorming techniques.

Original

The original pier design consisted of precast concrete piles, a concrete utility trench, cast in place pilecaps, and precast deck panels with concrete topping slab. Two single force pumps for ship sewage removal were provided. Steel fender piles were used to protect both the ships and the pier while moored.

Proposal

Relocation of batter piles no longer requires concrete haunches on the pile cap beams and one row of vertical piles. Use of asphaltic concrete with portland cement topping improves the deck. By suspending utilities below the pier deck the utility trench can be omitted. Use wood fender piles for protection of ships and the pier rather than the steel fender system. All recommendations are illustrated on the Summary Matrix.

Estimated Savings Cost Summary:

	Arch.	Struct.	Mech.	Elec.	Site	Total
Initial Cost Savings						1,285,000
Life Cycle Cost Savings (PW)						1,811,000
Annual Energy Savings (EU)						293×10^6 Btu

Note: Only selected worksheets used for this example.

Percent Savings Initial _____ 9%

Percent Savings Life Cycle _____ 15%

Percent Savings Energy _____ 12%

FIGURE 7-8-1
Life cycle costing summary.

Value Items Considered:	Mole Pier Alternative No.1	Stl. Piles Alternative No.2	Wood Fender Piles Alternative No. 3	Utilities Under Pier Alternative No. 4	A.C. Deck Topping Alternative No. 5	Curb & Pole Lighting Alternative No. 6	Precast Pile Caps Alternative No. 7	Batter Pile Location Alternative No. 8	Base Run (As Design) Alternative No. 9	Revised Analysis Alternative No. 10
Sheet Piling	●									
Fill	●									
Asphaltic Conc Topping	●				●					
Utility Tunnel	●									
Cathodic Protection	●	●		●●	●●	●●	●●	●●	●●	●
Pulling Piles			●							
Wood Fender Piles	●		●	●	●	●		●	●	●
Steel Fender Piles		●	●							
Steel Piles		●	●	●●	●	●	●●	●●	●	●●
Precast Conc Piles							●●			●●
Metal Catwalk (Utilities)										
Conc Utility Trench		●	●		●	●		●	●	●
Precast Pilecaps		●	●●	●	●	●	●	●●	●●	
CIP Pilecaps				●	●	●				
2 Single Force Pumps	●	●								
1 Duplex Force Pump										●
Stadium Lighting	●	●	●	●	●	●	●	●	●	●
Local Lighting						●				
Conc Topping Slab		●	●●●	●●●●	●	●	●●●	●●●	●●●	●●
Precast Deck Panels		●				●				
Precast Conc Batter										●●
Prediction Summary:										
Initial Cost Savings	892,000	936,000	215,000	-322,000	97,000	-4,000	536,000	435,000		1,285,000
Life Cycle Cost Savings	33,000	66,000	451,000	-437,000	442,000	64,000	435,000	446,000		1,811,000
Energy Savings (Million Btu)	-4,188	-896	299	-6	0	313	0	0		293

FIGURE 7-8-2
Summary matrix.

140

ECONOMIC BUILDING PERFORMANCE MODEL

DESIGN ALTERNATIVE 10
DATE 7 FEB 77

****** LIFE CYCLE BUILDING COST SUMMARY ******

A. THE INITAL COST FOR THE PROPOSED PROJECT IS 3887861.00 DOLLARS

B. THE AVERAGE ANNUAL OWNING AND OPERATING COSTS ARE 110149.31 DOLLARS

        PROJECT DISCOUNT RATE (I) = 10.0 PER CENT
        PROJECT DESIGN TIME TO CONSTRUCTION = 1.15 YEARS
        PROJECT CONSTRUCTION TIME = 0.49 YEARS

C. SUMMARY OF YEAR BY YEAR ECONOMIC BUILDING PERFORMANCE:

| END OF YEAR | ENERGY CONSUMPTION COSTS | | | | | MAINTENANCE COSTS | REPLACEMENT COSTS | FIRE PROTECTION COSTS | COST SUMMARY | |
	HEATING	COOLING	LIGHTING	EQUIP.	TOTAL				ANNUAL EXPENDITURE	PRESENT WORTH
0									95865.06	95865.06
1	0.0	0.00	5038.50	297.22	5335.71	2655.74	0.00	0.0	7991.45	7264.96
2	0.0	0.00	5391.19	318.02	5709.21	2841.64	0.00	0.0	8550.85	7066.82
3	0.0	0.00	5768.57	340.28	6108.85	3040.56	0.00	0.0	9149.41	6874.09
4	0.0	0.00	6172.37	364.10	6536.47	3253.40	0.00	0.0	9789.86	6686.62
5	0.0	0.00	6604.43	389.59	6994.02	3481.13	0.00	0.0	10475.14	6504.25
6	0.0	0.00	7066.74	416.86	7483.60	3724.81	0.00	0.0	11208.41	6326.87
7	0.0	0.00	7561.41	446.04	8007.45	3985.55	135752.37	0.0	147745.31	75816.94
8	0.0	0.00	8090.70	477.26	8567.96	4264.54	0.00	0.0	12832.50	5986.48
9	0.0	0.00	8657.05	510.67	9167.72	4563.05	0.00	0.0	13730.77	5823.21
10	0.0	0.00	9263.04	546.42	9809.46	4882.46	0.00	0.0	14691.92	5664.40
11	0.0	0.00	9911.45	584.67	10496.12	5224.23	0.00	0.0	15720.35	5509.92
12	0.0	0.00	10605.25	625.59	11230.84	5589.93	0.00	0.0	16820.77	5359.65
13	0.0	0.00	11347.62	669.38	12017.00	5981.22	0.00	0.0	17998.22	5213.48
14	0.0	0.00	12141.95	716.24	12858.19	6399.90	180395.75	0.0	199653.81	52575.46
15	0.0	0.00	12991.89	766.38	13758.26	6847.89	27165.35	0.0	47771.50	11436.21
16	0.0	0.00	13901.52	820.02	14721.34	7327.25	0.00	0.0	22048.59	4798.45
17	0.0	0.00	14874.41	877.43	15751.83	7840.15	0.00	0.0	23591.98	4667.59
18	0.0	0.00	15915.61	938.84	16854.46	8388.96	0.00	0.0	25243.42	4540.29
19	0.0	0.00	17029.70	1004.56	18034.27	8976.19	0.00	0.0	27010.45	4416.46
20	0.0	0.00	18221.78	1074.88	19296.66	9604.52	0.00	0.0	28901.18	4296.02
21	0.0	0.00	19497.30	1150.12	20647.43	10276.83	225039.19	0.0	255963.44	34588.85
22	0.0	0.00	20862.11	1230.63	22092.75	10996.21	0.00	0.0	33088.95	4064.89
23	0.0	0.00	22322.46	1316.78	23639.24	11765.94	0.00	0.0	35405.18	3954.03
24	0.0	0.00	23885.03	1408.95	25293.98	12589.55	0.00	0.0	37883.54	3846.20
25	0.0	0.00	25556.98	1507.58	27064.56	13470.82	1679933.00	0.0	1720468.00	158794.31
TOTALS	0.0	0.00	518678.37	18798.50	537476.87	167972.19	2248285.00	0.0	2849599.00	537941.00

D. THE TOTAL COST OF THE PROPOSED PROJECT OVER ITS LIFE OF 25 YEARS IN PRESENT WORTH DOLLARS IS   4425802.00

E. THE ENERGY CONSUMED BY THIS DESIGN ON A YEARLY BASIS IS   397. MILLION BTU

        HEATING ENERGY   =   0. MILLION BTU
        COOLING ENERGY   =   0. MILLION BTU
        LIGHTING ENERGY =   373. MILLION BTU
        EQUIPMENT ENERGY =   24. MILLION BTU

FIGURE 7-8-3
Life cycle costing estimate (automated).

Life Cycle Costing Summary

Process Plant (Ammunition)		Conveyors
Project		Item

Team Members		Team

Team Members		Date

Summary of Change (Study Area, Original & Proposed)

Study Area

Processed material is transported from the processing complex to the traying building. The team reviewed the functions of the conveying system.

Original

The original design for the conveying system consisted of specially designed belt conveyors.

Proposed

Based on the functional requirements of the process, a safer, more reliable conveying system was sought. Both "off the shelf" standard belt conveyors (unitized) and power & free conveyors, among others, were suggested. The life cycle analysis clearly documents the savings potential, including functional use (staffing) costs, using the power & free conveyors and is recommended.

Estimated Savings Cost Summary:

	Arch.	Struct.	Mech.	Elec.	Site	Total
Initial Cost Savings					$621,000	$621,000
Life Cycle Cost Savings (PW)						$8,975.000
Annual Energy Savings (EU)						900,000 kWh

Note: Only selected worksheets used for this example

Percent Savings Initial ___55%___

Percent Savings Life Cycle ___51%___

Percent Savings Energy ___50%___

FIGURE 7-9-1
Life cycle costing summary.

Life Cycle Costing Estimate
General Purpose Work Sheet

Study Title: _CONVEYORS : GLC TO TRAYING BLDGS._

Discount Rate: _10%_ Economic Life: _25 YEARS_

		Original Describe: BELT CONVEYOR (SPECIAL DESIGN)		Alternative 1 Describe: "OFF THE SHELF" STANDARD BELT CONVEYOR (UNITIZED)		Alternative 2 Describe: POWER & FREE CONVEYOR (SPARK PROOF)		Alternative 3 Describe:	
		Estimated Costs	Present Worth	Estimated Costs	Present Worth	Estimated Costs	Present Worth	Estimated Costs	Present Worth
Initial Costs									
A. STRUCTURAL SUPPORTS, ETC.			60,000		60,000		60,000		
B. BELT CONVEYOR (SPECIAL DESIGN)			1,200,000						
C. BELT CONVEYOR (UNITIZED STANDARD DESIGN)					700,000				
D. POWER & FREE CONVEYOR & COVERED WALKWAY							700,000		
E.									
F. OWNER SUPPLIED EQUIPM'T:									
G. SHAKER TABLE, SCALES, SIDEBOARDS			121,000		121,000		0		
H.									
I.									
J. Contingencies ___%									
K. Escalation ___%									
Total Initial Cost			1,381,000		881,000		760,000		

	Diff. Escal. Rate	PWA W/Escal.	Est.	PW	Est.	PW	Est.	PW		
Operations (Annual)										
A. ENERGY FOR CONVEYORS	7%	17.80	5,000	89,000	5,000	89,000	2500	44,000		
B. (UP TO AMOUNT SHOWN)										
C.										
D.										
E.										
F.										
Total Annual Operations Costs				89,000		89,000		44,000		

	Diff. Escal. Rate	PWA W/Escal.	Est.	PW	Est.	PW	Est.	PW		
Maintenance (Annual)										
A. BELT CONVEYOR (2 MEN/YR)	4%	13.069	75,000	980,000	75,000	980,000				
B. POWER & FREE CONVEYOR (1 MAN/YR)	4%	13.069					25,000	327,000		
C.										
D.										
E.										
F.										
G.										
Total Annual Maintenance Costs				980,000		980,000		327,000		

	Year	PW Factor	Est.	PW	Est.	PW	Est.	PW		
Replacement/Alterations (Single Expenditure)										
A.										
B. BELT REPLACEMENT @ 20% I.C.	10	.386	240,000	93,000	240,000	93,000	—			
C.										
D. BELT REPLACEMENT @ 20% I.C.	20	.149	240,000	36,000	240,000	36,000	—			
E.										
F.										
G.										
H. I.C. = INITIAL COST										
I.										
J.										
Total Replacement/Alteration Costs				129,000		129,000		0		

	Diff. Escal. Rate	PWA W/Escal.	Est.	PW	Est.	PW	Est.	PW		
Tax Elements										
A. (NOT APPLICABLE)										
B.										
C.										
D.										
E.										
F.										
G.										
Total Tax Elements										

	Diff. Escal. Rate	PWA W/Escal.	Est.	PW	Est.	PW	Est.	PW		
Associated (Annual)										
A. FUNCTIONAL USE - PROCESS STAFFING	4%	13.069	1,152,000	15,055,000	1,152,000	15,055,000	576,000	7,528,000		
B. (4.8 PEOPLE X $30,000/YR X 4 BLDG.										
C. STAFF REDUCTION)										
Total Annual Associated Costs				15,055,000		15,055,000		7,528,000		
Total Owning Present Worth Costs				16,253,000		16,253,000		7,899,000		

	Year	PW Factor	Est.	PW	Est.	PW	Est.	PW		
Salvage At End Of Economic Life										
Building (Struc., Arch., Mech., Elec., Equip.)				0		0		0		
Other ASSUME 0% SALVAGE										
Sitework										
Total Salvage				0		0		0		

		Est.	PW	Est.	PW	Est.	PW		
Total Present Worth Life Cycle Costs			17,634,000		17,134,000		8,659,000		
Life-Cycle Present Worth Dollar Savings			—		500,000		8,975,000		

PW – Present Worth   PWA – Present Worth Of Annuity

FIGURE 7-9-2

Life cycle costing estimate.

Life Cycle Costing Summary

Engineering Training Facility Modernization
_____
Project

Floor & Flooring System
_____
Item

_____
Team Members

_____
Team

_____
Team Members

_____
Date

Summary of Change (Study Area, Original & Proposed)

Study Area

The team reviewed the high cost items identified from the cost model. The floor structure and the floor finish appeared to have savings potential.

Original

The original design concept included the complete removal of all maple wood flooring. It was to be replaced with a new concrete slab and finished with V.A. tile.

Proposed

The life cycle cost analysis indicated a substantial savings could be achieved with a combination of carpet glued directly to the existing wood floor and restoring of the maple floor in selected areas. Other favorable benefits included acoustical absorption and interior aesthetics (color, etc.).

Estimated Savings Cost Summary:

	Arch.	Struct.	Mech.	Elec.	Site	Total
Initial Cost Savings						24,967
Life Cycle Cost Savings (PW)						22,617
Annual Energy Savings (EU)						N/A

Note: Only selected worksheets used for this example.

Percent Savings Initial _____41%_____

Percent Savings Life Cycle ___16%___

Percent Savings Energy _____N/A_____

FIGURE 7-10-1
Life cycle costing summary.

Weighted Evaluation

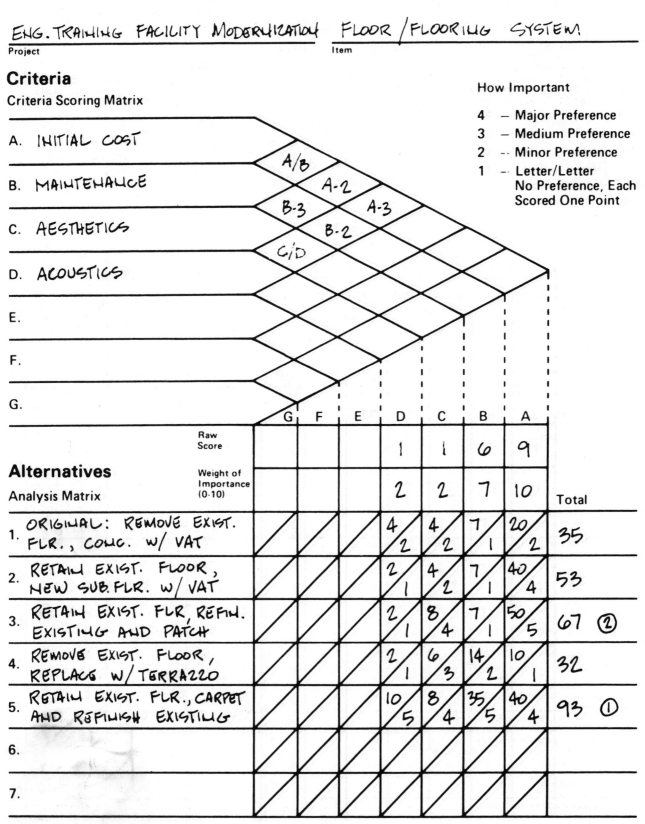

Project: ENG. TRAINING FACILITY MODERNIZATION   **Item:** FLOOR/FLOORING SYSTEM

Criteria

Criteria Scoring Matrix

A. INITIAL COST

B. MAINTENANCE

C. AESTHETICS

D. ACOUSTICS

E.

F.

G.

How Important

4 — Major Preference
3 — Medium Preference
2 — Minor Preference
1 — Letter/Letter
No Preference, Each Scored One Point

A/B
A-2
B-3 A-3
B-2
C/D

Alternatives

Analysis Matrix

	Raw Score	G	F	E	D	C	B	A	Total
					1	1	6	9	
Weight of Importance (0-10)					2	2	7	10	
1. ORIGINAL: REMOVE EXIST. FLR., CONC. w/ VAT					4 / 2	4 / 2	7 / 1	20 / 2	35
2. RETAIN EXIST. FLOOR, NEW SUB. FLR. w/ VAT					2 / 1	4 / 2	7 / 1	40 / 4	53
3. RETAIN EXIST. FLR, REFIN. EXISTING AND PATCH					2 / 1	8 / 4	7 / 1	50 / 5	67 ②
4. REMOVE EXIST. FLOOR, REPLACE w/ TERRAZZO					2 / 1	6 / 3	14 / 2	10 / 1	32
5. RETAIN EXIST. FLR., CARPET AND REFINISH EXISTING					10 / 5	8 / 4	35 / 5	40 / 4	93 ①
6.									
7.									

Excellent - 5; Very Good - 4; Good - 3; Fair - 2; Poor - 1

FIGURE 7-10-2
Weighted evaluation.

145

Life Cycle Costing Estimate
General Purpose Work Sheet

Study Title: FLOOR & FLOORING SYSTEM
ENGINEERING BUILDING REMODEL
Discount Rate: 10%   Economic Life: 25 YEARS

		Original Describe: REMOVE ALL FLOORS & FIXING & REPLACE W/ CONC. TOPPING & V.A. TILE		Alternative 1 Describe: MAPLE FLR. RETAINED - ADD PARTICLE BOARD FLOOR & V.A. TILE		Alternative 2 Describe: MAPLE FLOOR RETAINED - REPAIR DAMAGED AREAS & RE-FINISH MAPLE FLOOR		Alternative 3 Describe: MAPLE FLOOR RETAINED - COMBINATION CARPET & RE-FINISH MAPLE	
		Estimated Costs	Present Worth	Estimated Costs	Present Worth	Estimated Costs	Present Worth	Estimated Costs	Present Worth
Initial Costs	Initial Costs								
	A. REMOVE EXISTING FLOOR (@ $1.60/SF)	22,160							
	B. CONC. TOPPING & V.A.T. (@ $2.21/SF)	30,608							
	C. NEW PARTICLE BOARD & V.A.T.			22,853					
	D. PATCH & REPAIR EXIST. MAPLE FLOOR (@ $1.29/SF)			2,000		17,866		8,933	
	E. CARPET (@ $16.00/SY)							12,311	
	F. STRUCTURAL REPAIR - FLOOR			10,000		10,000		10,000	
	G.								
	H. SUBTOTAL	52,768		34,853		27,866		31,244	
	I.								
	J. Contingencies 5 %	2,638		1,743		1,393		1,562	
	K. Escalation 11 %	5,804		3,834		3,065		3,437	
	Total Initial Cost	61,210		40,430		32,324		36,243	
Owning Costs	**Operations (Annual)** Diff. Escal. Rate PWA W/Escal.								
	A. N/A								
	B.								
	C.								
	D.								
	E.								
	F.								
	Total Annual Operations Costs		N/A		N/A		N/A		N/A
	Maintenance (Annual) Diff. Escal. Rate PWA W/Escal.								
	A. FLR CLEANING DAILY ($.41/SF/YR) 4% 13.069	5,678	74,212	5,678	74,212	5,678	74,212	2,839	37,106
	B. CARPET CLEANING ($.25/SF/YR) 4% 13.069							1,731	22,622
	C. RE-FINISH MAPLE ONCE 4% 13.069					2,077	27,150	1,039	13,575
	D. PER YEAR ($.15/SF/YR)								
	E.								
	F.								
	G.								
	Total Annual Maintenance Costs		74,212		74,212		101,362		73,303
	Replacement/Alterations (Single Expenditure) Year / PW Factor								
	A. CARPET 10 .3855							12,311	4,746
	B. V.A.T. 15 .2394	13,850	3,316	13,850	3,316				
	C. CARPET 20 .1486							12,311	1,829
	D.								
	E.								
	F.								
	G.								
	H.								
	I.								
	J.								
	Total Replacement/Alteration Costs		3,316		3,316		0		6,575
	Tax Elements Diff. Escal. Rate PWA W/Escal.								
	A. GOVERNMENT FACILITY								
	B.								
	C.								
	D.								
	E.								
	F.								
	G.								
	Total Tax Elements		N/A		N/A		N/A		N/A
	Associated (Annual) Diff. Escal. Rate PWA W/Escal.								
	A.								
	B.								
	C.								
	Total Annual Associated Costs		N/A		N/A		N/A		N/A
	Total Owning Present Worth Costs		77,528		77,528		101,362		79,878
Salvage	**Salvage At End Of Economic Life** Year / PW Factor								
	Building (Struc., Arch., Mech., Elec., Equip.)								
	Other								
	Sitework								
	Total Salvage		N/A		N/A		N/A		N/A
LCC	**Total Present Worth Life Cycle Costs**		138,738		117,958		133,686		116,121
	Life-Cycle Present Worth Dollar Savings		—		20,780		5,052		22,617

PW — Present Worth   PWA — Present Worth Of Annuity

FIGURE 7-10-3
Life cycle costing estimate.

Life Cycle Costing Summary

Engineering Training Facility Modernization	HVAC System
Project	Item

Team Members	Team

Team Members	Date

Summary of Change (Study Area, Original & Proposed)

Study Area
   Review mechanical design of the renovation of an engineering laboratory building with existing constant volume discharge air-handling and steam radiation.

Original
   The original design consisted of a variable air volume (VAV) system with fan coil units on the building perimeter.

Proposed
   From the life cycle cost analysis, a variable air volume system with hot water fin-tube heat radiation on the perimeter is recommended.

Estimated Savings Cost Summary:

	Arch.	Struct.	Mech.	Elec.	Site	Total
Initial Cost Savings			30,000			30,000
Life Cycle Cost Savings (PW)						76,653
Annual Energy Savings (EU)						$3,000 \times 10^6$ Btu

Note: Only selected worksheets used in this example

Percent Savings Initial ___4%___

Percent Savings Life Cycle ___5%___

Percent Savings Energy ___3%___

FIGURE 7-11-1
Life cycle costing summary.

Idea Comparison

Idea	Advantages	Disadvantages	Estimated Potential Savings Initial	Life Cycle
USE VARIABLE AIR VOLUME SYSTEM W/ TWO PIPE FAN COIL AT PERIMETER	ACCESSABILITY TO UNITS MAINTENANCE	INITIAL COST		
BLOCK UP NORTH WINDOWS AND REDUCE THE WEST WINDOW SIZES	SAVES ENERGY	EXTERIOR APPEARANCE	INCREASED	IMPROVED
DELETE DOMESTIC HOT WATER REQM'T. AND CONSIDER USING ONE SOURCE TEMPERED WATER USING HEAT RECOVERY FROM STORES, ETC.	SAVES ENERGY IMPROVED INITIAL COST	AVAILABILITY AND DEMAND DIFFICULT TO MATCH	IMPROVED	IMPROVED
USE VARIABLE AIR VOLUME SYSTEM W/ HOT WATER FIN TUBE PERIMETER	INITIAL COST OPERATING COST	CONTROLS ABOVE CEILING	IMPROVED	IMPROVED
USE PACKAGED AIR HANDLING UNITS FOR EACH FLOOR W/ FAN COIL AT PERIMETER — ELIMINATE PENTHOUSE	OMITS PENTHOUSE AESTHETICS	NET SPACE REDUCED		

FIGURE 7-11-2
Idea comparison.

Data Required for Life Cycle Cost Estimating

Type	Variable Symbol	Nomenclature	Units Of Measure	Reference	Original	Alternative 1	Alternative 2	Alternative 3
						SAME		
Economic	AA	Building Economic Life	Years	R-2	25			
	AB	Project Discount Rate	% Of Cost	R-2	9%			
	AC	Escalation Rate/Yr.—Labor & Materials	% Of Cost	R-2	10%			
	AD	Escalation Rate/Yr.—Heating Fuel	% Of Cost	R-2	10%			
	AE	Escalation Rate/Yr.—Cooling Fuel	% Of Cost	R-2	10%			
	AF	Escalation Rate/Yr.—Lighting Fuel	% Of Cost	R-2	0			
	AG	Escalation Rate/Yr.—Domestic Hot Water Fuel	% Of Cost	R-2	8%			
	AH	Escalation Rate/Yr.— Maintenance	% Of Cost	R-2	1%			
	AI	Escalation Rate/Yr — Associated Costs	% Of Cost	R-2	0%			
Facility	BA	Gross Area Of Building	Sq. Ft.	Sketch	60,000			
	BB	Normal Building Population	Each	Project	375			
	BC	Required Lighting/Year	Hours	Project	3,000			
	BD	Average Amount Of Lighting Power Required Over Floor Area	Watt/Sq. Ft.	R-5	1.6			
	BE	Domestic Hot Water Boiler Energy Required/Gallon Heated	Btu/Gal.	Manuf.	833			
	BF	Domestic Hot Water Usage/Year	Days	Project	220			
	BG	Daily Hot Water Gallons/Person	Gallon	R-6	2			
	BH	Estimated Hourly Heating Load	Btu/HR	ASHRAE	2×10^6			
	BI	Estimated Hourly Cooling Load	Btu/HR	ASHRAE	5.07×10^6			
	BJ	Air Conditioning Power Per Design Ton	KW	R-7	.98			
		AVERAGE AMOUNT OF EQUIP. POWER REQ'D. OVER FLOOR AREA	WATT/SF		7.5			
		FAN	KW/HP		1.2			
Site & Climatic	CA	Area Design Cost Factor	N/A	R 8				
	CB	Fuel Costs -- Heating	$/Million Btu	R 8	4.5			
	CC	Fuel Costs — Cooling	S/KWh	R 8	5.86			
	CD	Fuel Costs — Domestic Hot Water	$/Million Btu	R 8	4.45			
	CE	Fuel Costs — Lighting	S/KWh	R 8	5.86			
	CF	Equiv. Full Load Hrs. A.C. Equip. Per Year	Hr.	R 8	800			
	CG	Heating Degree Days	Day °F	R 8	6270			
	CH	Summer Inside Design Temperature	°F	R 8	75°			
	CI	Winter Inside Design Temperature	°F	R 8	70°			
	CJ	Summer Outside Design Temperature	°F	R 8	96/76°			
	CK	Winter Outside Design Temperature	°F	R 8	-15%			

FIGURE 7-11-3

Data required for LCC estimating.

Life Cycle Costing Estimate
General Purpose Work Sheet

Study Title: _ENGINEERING TRAINING FACILITY_
MODERNIZATION HVAC SYSTEM
Discount Rate: _9 %_ Economic Life: _25 YRS._

		Original Describe: VAV CORE w/ FAN COILS ON PERIMETER		Alternative 1 Describe: VAV w/ HOT WATER PERIM. FIN.TUBE		Alternative 2 Describe:		Alternative 3 Describe:	
		Estimated Costs	Present Worth	Estimated Costs	Present Worth	Estimated Costs	Present Worth	Estimated Costs	Present Worth
Initial Costs									
A. _PLUMBING_			174905		174905				
B. _HEATING, COOLING, & VENTILATION_			453,083		423,083				
C. _SPECIAL MECHANICAL SYSTEMS_			71,184		71,184				
D. ___									
E. ___									
F. ___									
G. ___									
H. ___									
I. ___									
J. Contingencies ___% ___									
K. Escalation ___% ___									
Total Initial Cost			699,172		669,172				

	Diff. Escal. Rate	PWA W/Escal.							
Operations (Annual)									
A. _HEATING ENERGY_	10%	28.5	10,093	287,651	9,799	279,272			
B. _COOLING ENERGY_	10%	28.5	15,410	439,185	14,960	426,360			
C. _PUMPS, MOTORS, ETC. ENERGY_	10%	28.5	5,094	145,179	4,940	140,790			
D. ___									
E. ___									
F. ___									
Total Annual Operations Costs				872,015		846,422			

	Diff. Escal. Rate	PWA W/Escal.							
Maintenance (Annual)									
A. _REPAIR A.C. SYSTEM_	1%	10.8	8,025	86,670	6,075	65,610			
B. ___									
C. _OTHER_				SAME		SAME			
D. ___									
E. ___									
F. ___									
G. ___									
Total Annual Maintenance Costs				86,670		65,610			

	Year	PW Factor							
Replacement/Alterations (Single Expenditure)									
A. _N/A_									
B. ___									
C. ___									
D. ___									
E. ___									
F. ___									
G. ___									
H. ___									
I. ___									
J. ___									
Total Replacement/Alteration Costs				N/A		N/A			

	Diff. Escal. Rate	PWA W/Escal.							
Tax Elements									
A. ___									
B. ___									
C. ___									
D. ___									
E. ___									
F. ___									
G. ___									
Total Tax Elements									

	Diff. Escal. Rate	PWA W/Escal.							
Associated (Annual)									
A. _N/A_									
B. ___									
C. ___									
Total Annual Associated Costs				N/A		N/A			
Total Owning Present Worth Costs									

	Year	PW Factor							
Salvage At End Of Economic Life									
Building (Struc., Arch., Mech., Elec., Equip.) ___									
Other ___									
Sitework ___									
Total Salvage				N/A		N/A			

Total Present Worth Life Cycle Costs				1,657,857		1,581,204			
Life-Cycle Present Worth Dollar Savings						76,653			

PW — Present Worth   PWA — Present Worth Of Annuity

FIGURE 7-11-4
Life cycle costing estimate.

CHAPTER EIGHT
OTHER USES

"If, in a business enterprise or in government, many important decisions that in the aggregate can have a major influence on the success (and sometimes on the survival) of the enterprise are badly made by persons of modest incompetence; these bad decisions are not primarily the fault of those persons; they are the fault of management."

Grant and Ireson
Principles of Engineering Economy
1970.

INTRODUCTION

Life cycle costing techniques can be used for other purposes than selecting among competing design alternatives. It can be used in financial planning, equipment selection, construction contract change orders, and during the facility maintenance and operating phase.

PLANNING AND BUDGETING

LCC is an essential tool in the conceptual phase of a project. This technique is especially important to an owner or developer who must make a profit to warrant an investment in a facility. Figure 8-1 charts the key input factors and computations required for an in-depth investment program. This program, developed by a consultant in real estate investments, indicates the complexity and the mix of the various types of costs involved.

Example: Real Estate Investment Computer Program

The Real Estate Investment Analysis Program developed by Terra Development, part of the Smith Group, Detroit, Michigan, allows the developer, investor, and owner to analyze their investments beyond the traditional first year of operation. The program produces a set of investment indices that not only analyze the individual project but also enable the project to be compared with other real estate investment opportunities to determine which possess the best potential for successful development. The program produces these indices in terms of annual cash flow and rate of return on investment at three different levels of analysis: before income taxes, after income taxes, and with assumed sale of the project at year-end after capital gains taxes.

This analysis is done for a period of 1 to 10 years. The program allows for escalation of costs, giving the developer a clear picture of the project's financial status throughout this period. Figure 8-2 is a sample analysis for 5 years.

Example: Feasibility Study—Office Facility

The following is an example of the LCC technique applied to the facility-planning phase of a project. The example is a developer's feasibility study of a hypothetical office building. The developer can borrow up to 75 percent of the initial costs of an interest rate of 10 percent. The market study indicated that the area will support approximately 600,000 square feet of rentable space and 1500 parking spaces. Land held on option (112,000 square feet) costs $40 per square foot. Space rentals in the area are going for $20 per square foot for the prime ground floor and $13 per square foot for upper floors. Garage rentals are anticipated at $65 per space, with transient parking space income available at approximately $5 per day for some 250 days.

Using building costs of $40 per square foot and annual operating costs of $3.50 per square foot, with taxes of $1.20 per square foot and the garage space prorated, how would LCC be used to determine the before–income tax stabilized cash flow? The following is a discussion of how this problem may be analyzed.

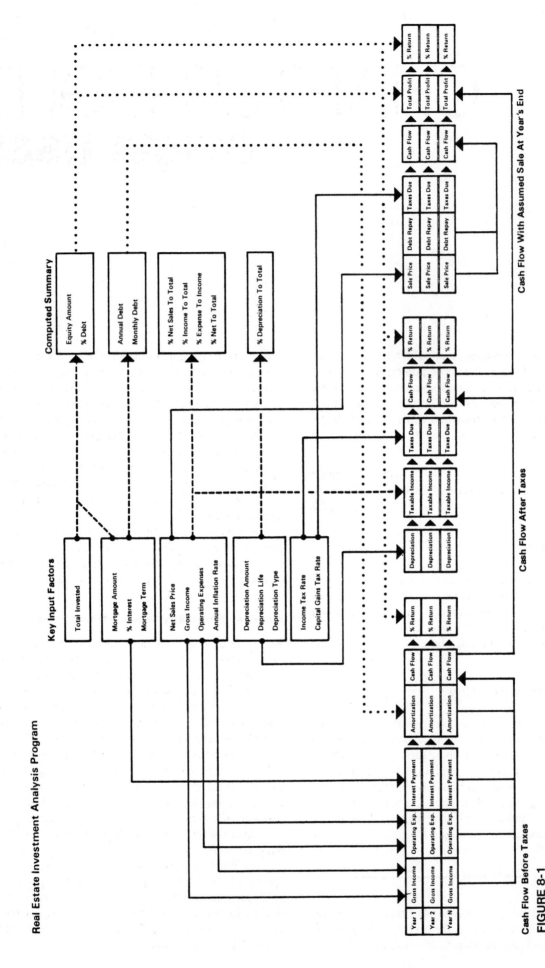

Real Estate Investment Analysis Program

FIGURE 8-1

Real estate investment analysis program. *(Source: Terra Development Corporation, Detroit, Mich.)*

TERRA DEVELOPMENT CORPORATION

220 WCB COMPANY   07/17/79

KEY FACTORS ARE ---

TOTAL	----MORTGAGE TERMS----			----OPERATING & INFLATION ASSUMPTIONS----				----DEPRECIATION----			----TAX RATES----	
				NET SALE	GROSS	OPERATING	% ANNUAL					
INVESTED	AMOUNT	% INTR	LIFE	PRICE	INCOME	EXPENSE	INFLATION	AMOUNT	LIFE	TYPE	INCOME	CAP GAIN
1200000	900000	9.50	28	1200000	265000	124000	5.0	1050000	15	100%	50%	28%

COMPUTED SUMMARY ---

EQUITY	----MORTGAGE TERMS----		% NET SALE	% INCOME	% EXPENSE	% NET	% DEPREC
AMOUNT	% DEBT	MONTHLY YEARLY	TO TOTAL	TO TOTAL	TO INCOME	TO TOTAL	TO TOTAL
300000	75.0	7666.94 92003	100.0	22.1	46.8	11.8	87.5

COMPUTED RESULTS ---

	----HOLDING RESULTS BEFORE INCOME TAXES----						----HOLDING RESULTS AFTER TAXES---					---OVERALL RESULTS WITH SALE AT YEAR END---					
	GROSS	OPERATE	--MORTGAGE--		CASH	% RE	DEPREC	TAXABLE	TAXES	CASH	% RE	SALE	DEBT	TAXES	CASH	TOTAL	% RE
YR	INCOME	EXPENSE	INTR	AMORT	FLOW	TURN	IATION	INCOME	DUE	FLOW	TURN	PRICE	REPAY	DUE	FLOW	PROFIT	TURN
1	265000	124000	85209	6794	48997	16.3	70000	-14209	-7105	56101	18.7	1260000	893206	36400	330394	86495	28.8
2	278250	130200	84535	7468	56047	18.7	70000	-6485	-3242	59289	19.8	1323000	885738	73640	363622	179013	28.4
3	292163	136710	83794	8210	63449	21.1	70000	1659	829	62620	20.9	1389150	877528	111762	399860	277870	28.1
4	306771	143545	82979	9024	71222	23.7	70000	10246	5123	66099	22.0	1458607	868504	150810	439294	383403	27.8
5	322109	150723	82083	9920	79383	26.5	70000	19303	9652	69732	23.2	1531538	858584	190831	482124	495964	27.4
6	338215	158259	81099	10905	87952	29.3	70000	28857	14428	73524	24.5	1608115	847679	231872	528563	615928	27.2
7	355125	166172	80017	11987	96950	32.3	70000	38937	19468	77482	25.8	1688520	835692	273986	578842	743689	26.9
8	372882	174480	78827	13176	106398	35.5	70000	49574	24787	81611	27.2	1772947	822516	317225	633206	879663	26.6
9	391526	183204	77519	14484	116318	38.8	70000	60802	30401	85917	28.6	1861594	808032	361646	691916	1024290	26.4
10	411102	192365	76082	15922	126734	42.2	70000	72656	36328	90406	30.1	1954674	792110	407309	755255	1178035	26.2

FIGURE 8-2
Example of real estate investment analysis (automated). *(Source: Terra Development Corporation, Detroit, Mich.)*

Table 8-1 provides an economic summary of the hypothetical office building development. The total cost is projected to be $48,486,000. The 30-year mortgage loan based on a 10 percent interest rate is $40,583,000. This leaves an equity investment to the developer of $7,903,000. The net anticipated operating income from the project is $5,740,000. This is 11.8 percent of the total project cost. With this net income, the developer must do two things: pay off a mortgage and keep the remainder of the income (the cash flow) as payment on equity. The most commonly used ratio is 1.25:1; meaning that for each $1.25 of gross income, $1.00 is allotted to debt service and $.25 is the cash flow to the developer. In this example, therefore, the developer would divide the net income of $5,740,000 by 1.25 to determine the debt service on this project ($4,592,000). The before-tax stabilized cash flow becomes $1,148,000, or 14.5 percent of the equity investment.

Table 8-2 presents the area analysis performed for the project. The facility has 32 upper floors, each with 93 percent rentable floor area.

A cost projection is made of the office building development presented as Table 8-3. The total construction cost

TABLE 8-1
HYPOTHETICAL OFFICE BUILDING DEVELOPMENT: ECONOMIC SUMMARY

Total construction cost	$34,757,000
Indirect costs	9,249,000
Total cost of improvements	44,006,000
Land cost	4,480,000
Total project cost	48,486,000
Less mortgage loan*	40,583,000
Equity investment	7,903,000
Net operating income (11.8% of cost)	$5,740,000
Less debt service	$\dfrac{5,740,000}{1.25} = 4,592,000$
Before-tax stabilized cash flow (14.5% of equity investment)	1,148,000

*Loan amount

	$5,740,000
Net operating income Capitalized @ 9.25%	$54,111,000
Loan percent	× 0.75
Loan amount	$40,583,000

TABLE 8-2
HYPOTHETICAL OFFICE BUILDING DEVELOPMENT: AREA ANALYSIS

	Gross area, ft²	BOMA full-floor rentable area, ft²	BOMA divided-floor net rentable area, ft²
Building			
Ground floor	22,000	17,000	17,000
32 upper floors*	704,000	654,720	577,280
Mechanical penthouse	11,000		
Total office building	737,000	671,720	594,280

Parking garage

1 parking space per 500 ft² gross area = 1,474 spaces

6 levels above grade @ 80,000 ft² = 480,000 ft² (325 ft²/space)

Site			
Building site	32,000 ft²		
Garage site	80,000 ft²		
Total site	112,000 ft²		

*For a typical floor, gross area = 22,000 ft², full-floor rentable area = 20,460 ft² (93%), and divided-floor net rentable area = 18,040 ft² (82%).

is estimated at $34,757,000. Indirect costs, which include architectural and engineering fees, taxes, insurance, etc.,

amount to $9,249,000. Land costs, at $40 per square foot, total $4,480,000. The total project cost, which includes all these costs, thus becomes $48,486,000.

Table 8-4 summarizes the stabilized income projection. The effective gross income for the offices per year is estimated at $7,452,000. Total parking income per year is $1,398,000. Considering operating costs and property taxes, this income becomes a net $5,740,000 per year.

Table 8-5, is a cash-flow analysis of the first 18 months of the development. It shows the office and parking income versus the cash expenditures. The final column lists the cash losses (and income) for each of the 18 months. Leasing concessions were estimated to be $1 per square foot on the competitive rental space.

As the figures in the illustrations show, there are many costs of development that must be balanced against each other. Typically, actual bricks and mortar account for 50 percent of the total project—a portion that can be manipulated, especially by the architect, to make the difference between a plausible project and a failure.

The process just outlined takes only a few hours, but it is the safe way to test the project's potential for success. Working together, the designer and the developer have a variety of options for making the project a success. But discovering the discrepancies in the package at its inception—though a good financial analysis—costs little at the start.

TABLE 8-3

HYPOTHETICAL OFFICE BUILDING DEVELOPMENT: COST PROJECTION

Building, including tenant finish	737,000 ft² @ $40.00	$29,480,000
Walkways and plaza	10,000 ft² @ 10.00	100,000
Garage	480,000 ft² @ 8.00	3,840,000
Subtotal		$33,420,000
Contingency @ 4%		1,337,000
Total construction		$34,757,000
Indirect costs:		
Architecture and engineering @ 4.75% + 0.5%	$1,825,000	
Taxes during construction	450,000	
Insurance during construction	40,000	
Interim financing: $39,076,000 @ 11% over 2 years as used	$4,298,000	
Permanent loan fees: 1 point to lender, 0.5 point to broker	586,000	
Legal costs	60,000	
Closing costs	18,000	
Title insurance	60,000	
Completion bond	150,000	
Leasing commissions	500,000	
Tenant space layouts	50,000	
Construction supervision	174,000	
Development fees and overhead	700,000	
Initial losses and leasing concessions	338,000	
Total indirect costs		$ 9,249,000
Total cost of improvements		44,006,000
Land	112,000 ft² @ $40.00	4,480,000
Total project cost		$48,486,000

TABLE 8-4

HYPOTHETICAL OFFICE BUILDING DEVELOPMENT: STABILIZED INCOME PROJECTION

Offices			
Owner occupied (initially)			
Ground floor	17,000 ft² @ $20,00		$ 340,000
16 upper floors	288,640 ft² @ 13.00		3,752,000
Subtotal			
Competitive rental space (including leasing)	288,640 ft² @ 13.00		3,752,000
Gross potential income: Offices			7,844,000
Less vacancy on competitive space @ 5%			392,000
Effective gross income: Offices			7,452,000
Parking			
1,032 monthly spaces @ $65 + 5% oversell		845,000	
442 Transient spaces @ $2.00 × 2½ turns × 250 days		553,000	
Total parking income			1,398,000
Total effective gross income			8,850,000
Operating and fixed charges			
Building			
Operating costs	594,280 ft² @ $3.50	2,080,000	
Property taxes	594,280 ft² @ 1.20	713,000	
Parking garage			
Operating costs	1,474 spaces @ $145	214,000	
Property taxes	1,474 spaces @ 70	103,000	
Total operating and fixed charges			3,110,000
Net operating income (12.0% of cost)			$5,740,000

Note: All areas are divided-floor basis.

EQUIPMENT PROCUREMENT

LCC can be used to optimize equipment selection and minimize costs by measuring and combining all expenditures and translating them to equivalent dollars. LCC, by putting all costs on a common basis, allows engineers to select the optimum solution. One method is to monitor cash flows during the projected equipment life. Figure 8-3

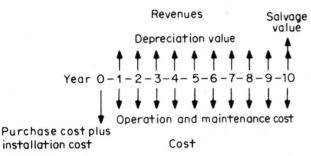

Revenues

Salvage value

Depreciation value

Year 0 - 1 - 2 - 3 - 4 - 5 - 6 - 7 - 8 - 9 - 10

Operation and maintenance cost

Purchase cost plus installation cost

Cost

FIGURE 8-3

Typical cash-flow chart, equipment. *(Credit: Jim Conway and Jeff Jacenty, "Saving Money on Your Baghouse," Plant Engineering, Apr. 19, 1979, Barrington, Ill.)*

illustrates a typical cash-flow chart. These charts assist in visually portraying all expenditures in a simple format. These expenditures can then be formalized using a present-worth format.

Example—Baghouse: The application of LCC for selection of housing for industrial filters in a baghouse is illustrated by the following case.

A compressed-air–type cleaning baghouse must be installed to remove dust from a 40,000 cubic foot per minute air stream. The plant has several existing baghouses, all made by the same manufacturer.

The plant engineer calls the manufacturer's local representative and asks for a quotation for four units that can handle the new application. The representative suggests the baghouses described in Table 8-6, part I. Total installed cost includes freight and taxes.

If only installed cost is considered, the 4200-square-foot baghouse appears to be the best choice. But this information is not sufficient to justify a final decision. Other data must be considered: The equipment is expected to have a 10-year useful life, the cost of electricity if $.04 per kilowatthour and is expected to increase 8 percent per year,

TABLE 8-5

HYPOTHETICAL OFFICE BUILDING DEVELOPMENT: CALCULATION OF INITIAL LOSSES AND LEASING CONCESSIONS (IN DOLLARS × 1000)

Month of operation	Office income	Parking income	Total cash inflows	Office, operating and fixed charges	Parking, operating and fixed charges	Debt service	Total cash outflows	(Cash losses)
1	445	86	531	206	26	326	558	(27)
2	455	88	543	208	26	326	560	(17)
3	466	90	556	209	26	326	561	(5)
4	477	91	568	211	26	326	563	5
5	488	93	581	212	26	326	564	17
6	498	95	593	214	26	326	566	27
7	508	97	605	216	26	326	568	37
8	519	98	617	217	26	326	569	48
9	529	100	629	219	26	326	571	58
10	539	101	640	220	26	326	572	68
11	549	103	652	222	26	326	574	78
12	559	105	664	223	26	326	575	89
13	569	106	675	225	26	326	577	98
14	580	108	688	226	26	326	578	110
15	590	110	700	228	26	326	580	120
16	600	112	712	229	26	326	581	131
17	610	114	724	231	26	326	583	141
18	621	116	737	233	26	326	585	152
Total initial losses								49
Add leasing concessions, est. @ $1.00 ft² on competitive rental space of 288,640 ft²								289
Total initial losses and leasing concessions								338

Assumptions: Owner-occupied space and 33 percent of competitive rental space is leased upon opening; 18 months to reach stabilized occupancy. Parking income increases pro rata with building income. Operating and fixed charges on vacant office space are projected at $3.00/ft² during fill-up; parking garage operating and fixed charges are assumed to begin at the stabilized level. Interest-only payments to mortgage loan in first 18 months.

and the total efficiency of the equipment's exhaust fan is 65 percent. All other factors—such as additional maintenance and bag-cleaning costs—will be approximately the same for each baghouse.

For this example, the only maintenance cost that differs with the different sizes of baghouses is the cost of installing the bags. The only significantly differing operating expense is the cost of overcoming the baghouse's resistance to air flow. Depreciation can be allocated equally over the expected 10-year life; therefore, yearly depreciation will be the installed cost less salvage value times 10 percent.

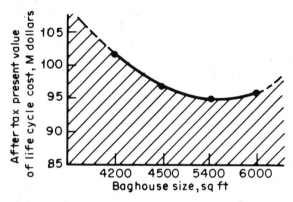

FIGURE 8-4
Summary of LCC, baghouse. *(Credit: Jim Conway and Jeff Jacenty, "Saving Money on your Baghouse," Plant Engineering, Apr. 19, 1979, Barrington, Ill.)*

TABLE 8-6
COMPARISONS OF PROPOSED BAGHOUSES

Part I Economic comparisons of proposed baghouses				
Baghouse size, sq ft filter area	4,200	4,800	5,400	6,000
Purchase cost, dollars	21,000	23,200	25,400	27,600
Replacement filter cost, dollars	1,680	1,920	2,160	2,400
Air-to-cloth ratio	9.5:1	8.3	7.4:1	6.7:1
Total anticipated resistance to air flow, inches w.g.	6.5	5.8	5.4	5.2
Total installed cost, dollars	33,600	36,600	39,600	42,600

Part II LCC comparisons of proposed baghouses				
Baghouse size, sq ft	4,200	4,800	5,400	6,000
Installed cost, dollars	33,600	36,600	39,600	42,600
Maintenance cost, dollars	5,162	5,899	6,636	7,374
Operating cost, dollars	73,800	65,853	61,311	59,040
Depreciation, dollars	−9,291	−10,120	−10,950	−11,779
Salvage value, dollars	−1,295	−1,430	−1,565	−1,700
Total after-tax present value, dollars	101,976	96,802	95,032	95,535

SOURCE: Jim Conway and Jeff Jacenty, "Saving Money on Your Baghouse," *Plant Engineering*, April 19, 1979, Barrington, Ill.

The cost capital is determined by expressing all cash flows in present-value (present-worth) terms. Since the primary concern is with the after-tax effect, cash flows must be corrected to an after-tax basis. With an effective tax rate of 50 percent, the after-tax result of maintenance costs, operating costs, and depreciation is half of the before-tax effect. The after-tax present values of each of the four possible selections are shown in Table 8-6, part II.

The baghouse with the smallest after-tax present-value cost is the best selection. Surprisingly, it is not the 4200-square-foot unit. The 5400-square-foot unit, which has an initial installed cost of $6,000 more than the smaller baghouse and an after-tax present-value cost 7 percent less than the smaller unit, is best. Figure 8-4 graphically illustrates the results.

Example—Freezer: This example outlines a formal procedure for equipment procurement (freezer) using LCC techniques.* For this procurement bidder D was awarded the contract even though his initial unit cost was $309.50 versus $231.53 for bidder B. (See Figure 8-5 for a summary of bidder LCC costs.) The difference in recurring costs ($357.42 for D versus $464.91 for B) more than offset (on the basis of present-worth analysis) the difference in initial costs. This procurement, based on anticipated demand quantities, provided a projected cost savings over the useful life (15 years) of some $260,000.

Summary of Life Cycle Costs – Top-Mounted Freezer

Zone	Type Cost	A	B	C	D	E	F
1	A	242.21	231.53	263.45	309.50	252.90	248.36
	R	518.01	464.91	431.24	357.42	486.96	493.40
	LCC	760.22	696.44	694.69	666.92	739.86	741.76
2	A	243.33	230.37	263.45	309.50	244.95	248.36
	R	518.01	464.91	431.24	357.42	486.96	493.40
	LCC	761.34	695.28	694.69	666.92	731.91	741.76
3	A	250.84	232.98	263.45	309.50	251.69	248.36
	R	518.01	464.91	431.24	357.42	486.96	493.40
	LCC	768.85	697.89	694.69	666.92	738.65	741.76
4	A	272.09	245.04	257.45	309.50	267.25	248.36
	R	518.01	464.91	431.24	357.42	486.96	493.40
	LCC	790.10	709.95	688.69	666.92	754.21	741.76

Type Cost:

A Acquisition
R Recurring
LCC Life Cycle Costs-Present Worth

FIGURE 8-5
Summary of life cycle costs, top-mounted freezer.

*NBS-GCR-ETIP 76-10, *Life Cycle Costing in the Procurement of Refrigerator-Freezers*, National Technical Information Service, Springfield, Va.

The LCC formula used in this procurement is as follows:

$$LCC = A + R$$

where LCC = life cycle cost in present-value dollars
A = the acquisition cost (bid price)
R = present-value sum of cost of electrical energy required by refrigerator-freezer during its useful life

and

$$R = P \times C \times T \times d$$

where P = computed electrical energy, kilowatthours, required during 24 hours of operation
C = cost of 1 kilowatthour of electrical energy
T = annual operating time in days
d = total discount factor, which will convert the stream of operating costs over life of equipment to present-value form

The discounted cash-flow or present-value methodology is used as a decision-making tool to allow direct comparison between different expenditure patterns of alternative investment opportunities. The present-value sum represents the amount of money that would be invested today, at a given rate of interest, to pay the expected future costs associated with a particular investment alternative. For purposes of this procurement, the Federal Supply Service used a discount rate of 8 percent and a product life of 15 years.

The value of P in the energy cost equation is a function of the net refrigerated volume V of the product being offered and the energy factor EF, which relates refrigerated volume and the electrical energy consumed to maintain the refrigerated volume. Stated in mathematical notation, the value of P is determined as follows:

$$P = \frac{V}{EF}$$

where

$$EF = \frac{\begin{array}{c}\text{Volume of frozen food compartment} \\ \times \text{ correction factor} + \text{food compartment}\end{array}}{\begin{array}{c}\text{Kilowatthours of electrical energy} \\ \text{consumed in 24 hours of operation}\end{array}}$$

and the correction factor is a constant of 1.63. Thus the LCC evaluation formula:

$$LCC = A + R = A + (P \times C \times T \times d)$$

can be rewritten as follows:

$$LCC = A + \frac{V}{EF} \times \$.04 \times 365 \times 8.559$$
$$= A + \frac{V}{EF} \times \$124.961$$

AUDITS AND RETROFITS

There are many existing facilities in which LCC concepts can be used to economic advantage. Return on investments can be much greater than those available from new facilities.

Example—Audit

The President has issued a directive to all federal agencies (See Appendix B, "Government Regulations") to reduce energy consumption on all old facilities by 20 percent by 1985 over a 1975 base. As a result, energy audits of existing facilities have been undertaken to establish the 1975 base from which to calculate reductions.

As an example of the results, the General Services Administration (GSA) used LCC to justify facility retrofits. Their energy bills have been reduced by some $20 million in 1 year.

Example—Retrofit

The following study illustrates how to evaluate a lighting system retrofit using LCC. The example is based on a 10,000-square-foot manufacturing area illuminated to 100 footcandles by an existing 400-watt mercury system. Figure 8-6 presents characteristics of common industrial light sources. Costs for replacing a 400-watt mercury lighting system with relatively low-wattage (250 and 400 watt) metal halide and high-pressure sodium (HPS) lighting are analyzed in Figure 8-7. The analysis is based on operating the facility 4000 hours per year, with an electrical energy rate of $.04 per kilowatthour. The table shows that an investment of less than $10,000 to replace the existing lighting with a 400-watt HPS system can be recovered in 2 years. Amortized over a period of 20 years at 10 percent interest, the replacement project will return more than $84,000 in savings to the owner.

CONTRACTOR INCENTIVES

Saving owner's money is just as important during the construction and the owning and operating phases of a building as in the design phase. During construction, however, an additional party is involved—the contractor. Making changes to the building during construction is much more expensive. Because of this, a larger cost savings incentive must usually be present before any change will be made. To further compound the situation, the cost incentive must be jointly shared with the two parties involved.

Construction Phase

The GSA value incentive clause (VIC) for construction is outlined in Figure 8-8. It describes how cost savings can be implemented during the construction phase.

CHARACTERISTICS OF COMMON INDUSTRIAL LIGHT SOURCES

Type of Lamp	Lamp Size Range, Watts	Average Efficacy, Lumens per Watt		Lumen Maintenance, Percent	Average Rated Life, Hours	Warmup/Restrike Time, Minutes
		Initial	Mean			
Low-pressure sodium	35 to 180	137 to 183	122 to 164	100 to 108	18,000	8-10/0-2
High-pressure sodium	70 to 1000	83 to 140	75 to 127	90 to 91	20,000 to 24,000	3-4/0.5-1
Metal halide	175 to 1500	80 to 125	62 to 92	77 to 80	10,000 to 15,000	2-5/10-20
Mercury vapor	50 to 1000	32 to 63	25 to 48	75 to 89	16,000 to 24,000[+]	5-7/3-6
Fluorescent	40 to 215	74 to 100	49 to 88	66 to 88	12,000 to 20,000[+]	Immediate
Incandescent	100 to 1500	17 to 24	15 to 23	90 to 95	750 to 2500	Immediate

FIGURE 8-6
Characteristics of common industrial light sources. (*Credit: Lewis Tagliaferre, "Scrap Your Mercury Lighting System," Plant Engineering, Apr. 19, 1979, Barrington, Ill.*)

COST ANALYSIS—REPLACEMENT OF EXISTING MERCURY SYSTEM WITH FOUR ALTERNATIVE SYSTEMS*

	Existing 400 W Mercury System	250 W Metal-Halide System	400 W Metal-Halide System	250 W HPS System	400 W HPS System
Number of luminaires required	108	97	68	70	42
Luminaire spacing (square grid), ft	9.62	10.15	12.13	11.95	15.43
Initial lamp lumens per lamp	22,500	20,500	34,000	30,000	50,000
Lamp lumen depreciation factor	0.78	0.83	0.75	0.90	0.90
Estimated lamp life, hr	24,000	10,000	15,000	24,000	24,000
Average lamp replacements per year	18	38.8	18.13	11.67	7
Lamp net cost, dollars per lamp	10.23	23.55	22.35	38.40	36.00
Luminaire input watts	450	285	460	300	475
Average watts per sq ft	4.9	2.8	3.1	2.1	2.0
Total connected load, kw	48.6	27.65	31.28	21	19.95
Luminaire per unit cost, dollars	-0-	68	85	145	150
Installation labor per unit, dollars	-0-	36	36	36	36
Installation cost summary					
Luminaire cost, dollars	-0-	6,596.00	5,780.00	10,150.00	6,300.00
Initial lamp cost, dollars	-0-	2,284.35	1,519.80	2,688.00	1,512.00
Installation labor cost, dollars	-0-	3,492.00	2,448.00	2,520.00	1,512.00
Total installation costs, dollars	-0-	12,372.35	9,747.80	15,358.00	9,324.00
Annual operating cost summary					
Lamp cost, dollars	184.18	913.74	405.28	448.00	252.00
Maintenance labor, dollars	180.00	388.00	181.33	116.67	70.00
Energy cost, dollars	7,776.00	4,423.20	5,004.80	3,360.00	3,192.00
Total annual operating cost, dollars	8,140.14	5,724.94	5,591.41	3,924.67	3,514.00
Relative operating cost, percent	100.00	70.33	68.69	48.21	43.17
Total annual cost summary					
Annual owning cost, dollars	-0-	1,513.20	1,234.20	1,900.50	1,171.80
Owning and operating cost, dollars	8,140.14	7,238.14	6,825.61	5,825.17	4,685.80
Relative owning and operating cost, percent	100.00	88.92	83.85	71.56	57.56
Annual cost per fc per sq ft, dollars	0.8107	0.7216	0.6832	0.5819	0.4681
Lighting investment payback summary					
Annual operating cost, dollars	8,140.14	5,724.94	5,591.41	3,924.67	3,514.00
Operating cost savings, dollars	-0-	2,415.20	2,548.73	4,215.47	4,626.14
Total new investment, dollars	-0-	12,372.35	9,747.80	15,358.00	9,324.00
Simple investment payback interval, years	-0-	5.12	3.82	3.64	2.02
Simple return on investment, percent	-0-	19.52	26.15	27.45	49.62
Adjusted discounted investment payback interval, months	-0-	90.4	60.7	57.0	28.3
Summary of costs over next 20 years					
Net lamp costs, dollars	3,682.80	17,132.62	7,345.70	7,616.00	4,284.00
Lamp replacement labor costs (at $10 per lamp), dollars	3,600.00	7,760.00	3,626.67	2,333.33	1,400.00
Energy consumption, kwh	3,888,000	2,211,600	2,502,400	1,680,000	1,596,000
Total energy costs, dollars	155,520.00	88,464.00	100,096.00	67,200.00	63,840.00
Total initial costs, dollars	-0-	12,372.35	9,747.80	15,358.00	9,324.00
Total 20 year life-cycle costs, dollars	162,802.80	125,728.97	120,816.17	92,507.33	78,848.00

*Basis: 10,000 sq ft manufacturing area illuminated to 100 fc, 4000 burning hours per year, effective electrical energy rate (including demand and other charges) 4¢/kwh, average dirt conditions, 20 year amortization at interest rate of 10 percent.

FIGURE 8-7
Cost analysis, replacement of existing mercury system with four alternative systems. (*Credit: Lewis Tagliaferre, "Scrap Your Mercury Lighting System," Plant Engineering, Apr. 19, 1979, Barrington, Ill.*)

VALUE INCENTIVE CLAUSE

(CONSTRUCTION CONTRACT)

1. OBJECTIVES—This clause applies to any cost reduction proposal (hereinafter referred to as a Value Change Proposal or VCP) initiated and developed by the Contractor for the purpose of changing any requirement of this contract. This clause does not, however, apply to any such proposal unless it is identified by the Contractor, at the time of its submission to the Government, as a proposal submitted pursuant to this clause.

1.1 VCP's contemplated are those that would result in net savings to the Government by providing either: (1) a decrease in the cost of performance of this contract, or; (2) a reduction in the cost of ownership (hereinafter referred to as collateral costs) of the work provided by this contract, regardless of acquisition costs. VCP's must result in savings without impairing any required functions and characteristics such as service life, reliability, economy of operation, ease of maintenance, standardized features, esthetics, fire protection features and safety features presently required by this contract. However, nothing herein precludes the submittal of VCPs where the Contractor considers that the required functions and characteristics could be combined, reduced or eliminated as being nonessential or excessive to the satisfactory function served by the work involved.

1.2 A VCP identical to one submitted under any other contract with the Contractor or another Contractor may also be submitted under this contract.

1.3 A proposal to decrease the cost of performing the contract solely or principally by substituting another Subcontractor for one listed by the Contractor in his bid is not a VCP. In considering a VCP which, as an incident thereof, would entail substitution for a listed Subcontractor, maintaining the objective of the Subcontractor listing will be taken into account along with factors cited in paragraph 1.1 above.

2. SUBCONTRACTOR INCLUSION—The Contractor shall include the provisions of this clause, with a provision for sharing arrangements that meet or exceed the minimum percentage contained herein, in all first-tier subcontracts in excess of $25,000, and in any other subcontract which, in the judgment of the Contractor, is of such nature as to offer reasonable likelihood of value change proposals. At the option of the first-tier Subcontractor, this clause may be included in lower tier subcontracts. The Contractor shall encourage submission of VCPs from Subcontractors; however, it is not mandatory that the Contractor accept and/or transmit to the Government VCPs proposed by his Subcontractors.

3. DATA REQUIREMENTS—As a minimum, the following information shall be submitted by the Contractor with each VCP:

3.1 A description of the difference between the existing contract requirement and the proposed change, and the comparative advantages and disadvantages of each; including justification where function or characteristic of a work item is being reduced;

3.2 Separate detailed cost estimates for both the existing contract requirement and the proposed change, and an estimate of the change in contract price including consideration of the costs of development and implementation of the VCP and the sharing arrangement set forth in this clause;

3.3 An estimate of the effects the VCP would have on collateral costs to the Government, including an estimate of the sharing that

the Contractor requests be paid by the Government upon approval of the VCP;

3.4 Architectural, engineering or other analysis, in sufficient detail to identify and describe each requirement of the contract which must be changed if the VCP is accepted, with recommendation as to how to accomplish each such change and its effect on unchanged work;

3.5 A statement of the time by which approval of the VCP must be issued by the Government to obtain the maximum cost reduction during the remainder of this contract, noting any effect on the contract completion time or delivery schedule; and,

3.6 Identification of any previous submission of the VCP including the dates submitted, the agencies involved, the numbers of the Government contracts involved, and the previous actions by the Government, if known.

4. PROCESSING PROCEDURES—Six copies of each VCP shall be submitted to the Contracting Officer, or his duly authorized representative. VCPs will be processed expeditiously; however, the Government will not be liable for any delay in acting upon a VCP submitted pursuant to this clause. The Contractor may withdraw, in whole or in part, a VCP not accepted by the Government within the period specified in the VCP. The Government shall not be liable for VCP development cost in the case where a VCP is rejected or withdrawn. The decision of the Contracting Officer as to the acceptance of a VCP under this contract shall be final and shall not be subject to the "Disputes" clause of this contract.

4.1 The Contracting Officer may modify a VCP, with the concurrence of the Contractor, to make it acceptable, and the Contractor's fair share will be based on the VCP as modified.

4.2 Pending written acceptance of a VCP in whole or in part, the Contractor shall remain obligated to perform in accordance with the terms of the existing contract.

4.3 An approved VCP shall be finalized through an equitable adjustment in the contract price and time of performance by the execution of a contract modification pursuant to the provisions of this clause bearing a notation so stating.

4.4 When the necessity to proceed with a VCP (in whole or in part) does not allow sufficient time for execution of a contract modification, the Government may issue a letter accepting the VCP (in whole or in part), authorizing the Contractor to proceed with the work, as changed, on the basis of contract price adjustment to be determined at the earliest practicable date but not to be less than the decrease nor more than the increase, as the case may be, than the decrease or increase set forth in the VCP submitted and accepted.

5. COMPUTATIONS FOR CHANGE IN CONTRACT COST OF PERFORMANCE—Separate estimates shall be prepared for both the existing (instant) contract requirement and the proposed change. Each estimate shall consist of an itemized breakdown of all costs of the Contractor and all Subcontractors' work in sufficient detail to show unit quantities and costs of labor, material, and equipment.

FIGURE 8-8

Value incentive clause (construction contract). (*Source: General Services Administration, November 1977.*)

5.1 Contractor development and implementation costs for the VCP shall be included in the estimate for the proposed change. However, these costs will not be allowable if they are otherwise reimbursable as a direct charge under this contract.

5.2 Government costs of processing or implementation of a VCP shall not be included in the estimate.

5.3 If the difference in the estimates indicate a net reduction in contract price, no allowance will be made for overhead, profit and bond. The resultant net reduction in contract cost of performance shall be shared as provided hereinafter.

5.4 If the difference in the estimates indicate a net increase in contract price, the price shall be adjusted pursuant to an equitable adjustment that will include Contractor's overhead and profit on his additional work or the additional work of one of his subcontractors.

6. COMPUTATIONS FOR COLLATERAL COSTS—Separate estimates shall be prepared for collateral costs of both the existing contract requirement and the proposed change. Each estimate shall consist of an itemized breakdown of all costs and the basis for the data used in the estimate. Cost benefits to the Government include, but are not limited to: reduced costs of operation, maintenance or repair, extended useful service life, increases in usable floor space, and reduction in the requirements for Government furnished property. Increased collateral costs include the converse of such factors. Computation shall be as follows:

6.1 Costs shall be calculated over a 20-year period on a uniform basis for each estimate and shall include Government costs of processing or implementing the VCP.

6.2 If the difference in the estimates as approved by the Government indicate a savings, the Contractor shall divide the resultant amount by 20 to arrive at the average annual net collateral savings. The resultant savings shall be shared as provided hereinafter.

6.3 In the event that agreement cannot be reached on the amount of estimated collateral costs, the Contracting Officer shall determine the amount. His decision is final and is not subject to the provisions of the "Disputes" clause of this contract.

7. SHARING ARRANGEMENTS—If a VCP is accepted by the Government, the Contractor is entitled to share in instant contract savings and collateral savings not as alternatives, but rather to the full extent provided for in this clause. For the purposes of sharing under this clause, the term "instant contract" will include any changes to or other modifications of this contract, executed subsequent to acceptance of the particular VCP, by which the Government increases the quantity of any item of work or adds any item of work. It will also include any extension of the instant contract through exercise of an option (if any) provided under this contract after acceptance of the VCP. The Contractor shall be entitled to a contract modification for instant or collateral savings shares on changes or options only at such time as a change order has been issued or an option has been exercised.

7.1 When only the prime Contractor is involved, he shall receive 50% and the Government 50% of the net reduction in the cost of performance of this contract.

7.2 When a first-tier Subcontractor is involved, he shall receive a minimum of 30%, the prime Contractor a maximum of 30%, and the Government a fixed 40% of the net reduction in the cost of performance of this contract. Other Subcontractors shall receive a portion of the first-tier Subcontractor savings in accordance with the terms of their contracts with the first-tier Subcontractor.

7.3 When collateral savings occur the Contractor shall receive 20% of the average one years net collateral savings.

8. ADJUSTMENTS TO CONTRACT PRICE—

8.1 The method for payment of instant savings shares shall be accomplished by reducing the contract price by an amount equal to the Government's share of the savings.

8.2 Collateral savings shares and costs of increased work shall be paid by increasing the contract price.

9. DATA RESTRICTION RIGHTS—The contractor may restrict the Government's right to use any sheet of a VCP or the supporting data, submitted pursuant to this clause, in accordance with the terms of the following legend if it is marked on each such sheet:

The data furnished pursuant to the Value Incentive Clause of contract No. _____ shall not be disclosed outside the Government for any purpose other than to evaluate a VCP submitted under said clause. This restriction does not limit the Government's right to use information otherwise available, from the contractor or from another source without limitations, or if release of the data is required under the Freedom of Information Act.

In the event of acceptance of a VCP, the Government shall have the right fully to utilize such proposal on this and any other Government contract.

FIGURE 8-8 (Continued)

The VIC invites the contractor to challenge unrealistic or unessential owner contract requirements and to profit by doing so. The procurement phase is the last opportunity to save on work before it is actually delivered and is very often the last opportunity to have significant impact on ownership costs. These types of clauses are useful when owners desire to benefit from the experience and knowledge of contractors in the areas of cost, new materials, techniques, and industry standards.

The VIC rewards contractors who propose changes in contract documents that will result in reducing cost without sacrificing required quality or function. The sharing incentive arrangement is established to encourage contractor initiative and ingenuity in identifying and successfully challenging high-cost areas in contracts. The following types of incentives can be provided in the VIC:

1. *Instant sharing:* Contractors may share in savings realized by modifying or eliminating work required under the terms of the instant contract. All VICs provide for instant sharing.

2. *Collateral sharing:* In addition to instant sharing, all VICs provide that *a contractor may share in any savings caused as a result of a proposal to change contract requirements, in future government costs of ownership* of the work provided under the instant contract. Note that although there need not be a savings in the instant contract, there must be a life cycle savings for the contractor to qualify for collateral sharing.

Contractor proposals, both approved and disapproved, are discussed in the following examples.*

Example—Chillers: The contractor for the St. Louis, Missouri, Federal Office Building 103F proposed substituting two 380-kilowatt 600-ton air-conditioning chillers for the specified two 450-kilowatt 600-ton chillers at an increased cost of $39,970. Region 6 indicated that the chillers with 140 kilowatts of reduced energy use were desirable but told the contractor that the proposal was disapproved because funding limitations prevented accepting it.

Actually, the region thought that it had used all of the prospectus limitation authority on the project under construction, even though $1.5 million was reserved for a solar system.

Appeals to buildings management to do something about this resulted in a decision too late to do the contractor any good. Much debate ensued over whether the payback period for the change was less than 3 or 6 years. Such an issue is moot when the primary goal should be to save energy at any reasonable expense. GSA did not retrofit the chillers in Building 103F. They will be used—one for 24

hours a day year-round—and the damage is done.

Should a similar situation occur again, GSA has prepared a legislative proposal to give latitude on the prospectus limitation. However, the problems of compartmentalization of funds on a project basis, the lack of energy plans and priorities within given buildings, and the lack of decisiveness displayed by this example remain.

Example—Reduced Air Volume: The original mechanical design in this example was based on accepted parameters for supply air quantities, GSA's *Energy Conservation Guidelines for Existing Office Buildings,* and previous regional design experience with Building 101 (the region's first in-house retrofit design based on GSA's energy conservation guidelines).

Both Buildings 101 and 103 were designed with a single-zone, cooling-only, variable air volume (VAV) air handling system and with a constant-volume perimeter heating system. Cooling-only VAV terminals were specified to vary air flow from full open (0.7 cfm per square foot) to about 20 percent open (0.14 cfm per square foot). Minimum air flow settings of approximately 50 percent full air flow were not specified because it was believed the building's interior heat generation would require year-round cooling. During the first winter's operation of Building 101, the interior heat gain was not sufficient to maintain the building's temperature above 68°F. As the building's temperature fell below 78°F, all VAV terminals closed to 0.14 cfm per square foot supply air volume, and poor air motion was experienced in the building.

As GSA was studying the winter air motion characteristics of Building 101, the contractor for Building 103 presented a VIC proposal for the mechanical system. His proposal included lowering the supply air volume delivered to the occupied space from 0.7 cfm per square foot to 0.4 cfm per square foot. This initial proposal was rejected by regional engineers because of the winter air motion characteristics of Building 101. It was the opinion of the regional engineers that the contractor proposal of 0.4 cfm per square foot in summer was marginal and that its winter air flow characteristics of less than that of Building 101 were unacceptable.

A supply air volume of 0.55 cfm per square foot was accepted after much discussion with the contractor and his consultant. GSA's concern for adequate winter air motion was described in detail. The agreed-on revised system would still retain the VAV approach of the original design, but minimum settings would be provided in each VAV terminal to prevent stagnant room air motion. A heating coil was added to the VAV air handling units to prevent subcooling of the space below 68°F when the terminals are at their minimum settings. The winter heating supply air temperature will be reset upward as the outside air temperature drops. GSA instructed the contractor to set the minimum winter supply air flow setting at 0.3 cfm per square foot. It can be adjusted upward if poor winter air motion is encountered.

---

*Provided by Donald Parker, director, Value Management, GSA, Washington.

```
Situation:  Guard service contract where below described change will be implemented in the last
            six months of a one year contract.  Contract contains a one year renewal option.

Description of change:

            Revise the contractors approved manpower plan to delete all guard service from
            door #2 of building 21 and install a video camera and buzzer lock system to be
            controlled at door #1 of the building.
```

INSTANT CONTRACT COMPUTATIONS

	Contract Cost		Proposal Cost	Difference
Prime contractor:				
direct labor 1/2 year		VCP processing	$ 100	
normal hours	$ 2,000			
overtime	750			
holidays, weekends	1,200			
fringe benefits	800			
	$ 4,750		$ 100	($ 4,650)
Subcontractor A:				
	N.A.	monitoring sys.	$3,000	
		overhead & prof.	300	$ 3,300
			$3,300	
Prime contractor:				
			net saving 1st year	($ 1,350)
optional year				
normal hours	$ 4,000			
overtime	1,500			
holidays, weekends	2,400			
fringe benefits	1,600		0	($ 9,500)
	$ 9,500		0	
			net saving 2nd year	($10,850)

COLLATERAL COMPUTATIONS

	Costs Before		Costs After	Difference
10 years labor	$91,000	instant contract increase	0	
		10 yrs system maintenance	$5,000	
		10 yrs electricity	1,000	
totals	$91,000		$6,000	($85,000)
		average one years savings		($ 8,500)

ADJUSTMENT TO CONTRACT PRICE

Method 1:

    <u>Under Option 1</u> reduce contract price by 50% of $1,350 or, $675 and,
    <u>Under Option 2</u> increase contract price by 20% of $8,500 or, $1,700.

Method 2:

    <u>Under Option 2</u> increase contract price by $3,300 for monitoring system plus
    $1,700 for contractor collateral share and,
    <u>Under Option 5</u> reduce the full quantities of labor from the manpower plan to
    reflect an annual savings of $9,500 and make a lump sum payment of $675.

FIGURE 8-9
Service contract example. (*Source: General Services Administration Handbook, Contract Value Incentive Clauses, PBS P 8020.2, Aug. 1, 1978, p. 24.*)

GSA expects the change to improve the operation of the building. Fan horsepower will be reduced significantly. The reduction of air quantities reduces room air conditions from 78°F, 60 percent relative humidity, to 78°F, 50 percent relative humidity, improving occupant comfort. The winter air motion characteristics of Building 101 will not occur. At present, GSA engineers have limited experience in dealing with air quantities at these low levels; however, the air quantities provide satisfactory air motion in summer and winter.

GSA is now applying the concepts learned through the Building 103 change to future renovations throughout the region. An in-house change has been performed on Building 105, similar to that accomplished for Building 103. The net result of the VIC was to reduce the number of air handling units from 8 to 6 and reduce the quantity of air delivered to the building's interior from 0.7 cfm per square foot to 0.55 cfm per square foot.

Ownership Phase

Clauses similar to those illustrated in Figure 8-8 have been developed by GSA for use during the facility owning and operating phase. The maintenance and operating (M&O) contractor (or in-house staff) can provide proposals to reduce M&O costs as well as provide feedback necessary to design personnel so that future projects will benefit.

Example—Service Contract: Figure 8-9 provides an example computation for a change in a facility and workforce plan (of a service contract) under the "service and term" contract clause of GSA. The facility, in an as-is condition, is considered a constructive part of the contract, hence is subject to a value change proposal (VCP). Similarly, the workforce plan developed by the contractor—not the government in this example—is also part of the contract conditions by the very nature of its use and acceptance. Subcontractor A is a new party to the contract and receives overhead and profit on its new work. In adjusting the contract price there are two possible methods subject to mutual agreement. Method 1 requires the contractor to pay for the new work from the savings accumulated over the contract period but does not change the unit prices. Method 2 advances the contractor money for the new work, while the government accumulates the full savings over the contract period through reduced unit prices.

In either method, however, the example illustrates the savings potential still present for the owner using the concept of LCC during building operations. In this case, the guard service was omitted from the second door, with a video camera and buzzer lock system taking its place.

SUMMARY

The LCC technique has many uses. The concept of conducting an economic analysis using equivalent costs is an investor's and owner's tool to optimize expenditures or profit or both. Once the concepts are understood, the applications of LCC are limited only by the imagination of the user.

CHAPTER NINE
SUMMARY AND CONCLUSIONS

"GAO says again that A-E selection should be based on design competition, estimated project costs and technical competence to better assure optimal designs with available funding. **The agency also wants life-cycle cost estimates by A-Es,** government reimbursement of A-Es for certain work associated with precontract proposals and repeal of the 6% design fee limitation."

Engineering News Record
June 21, 1979.

INTRODUCTION

The decision-making process in building is traditionally fragmented, with major disciplines making decisions in relative isolation. As a result, each discipline's decision casts costs to other disciplines. The total cost of ownership is not adequately considered. To date, one of the principal reasons for unnecessary costs has been the unidisciplinary approach used by designers. In too many cases, the design has been dictated by the designer, and the other disciplines have merely responded to those dictates. On the other hand, a multidisciplinary approach to optimizing the building as a system has produced significant results.

Of the input data required to perform LCC, the specific project information and site data are usually available, but it is a different story for the facility components data. Where does a designer go to get data regarding useful life, maintenance, and operations? This input is needed to calculate roughly one-third of total costs. Few designers have had access to comprehensive data in these areas in a format facilitating LCC analysis. One reason for this is that there has not been a retrieval format readily available for these data. This, combined with the fact that in order to do LCC (and eventually develop automated programs),

the initial-cost data banks must be compatible with the follow-on-cost data banks. There is an abundance of references for initial costs, for instance, Dodge, Means, and Cost Data File, but few references for follow-on costs for maintenance, operations, replacements, etc. A recognized format for LCC is also lacking. Each owner using LCC sets up an individual procedure. As a result, any cross-feed of data or results is difficult.

Owners talk about increasing their initial costs for the project in return for future fuel savings. With that, they want payoff periods of less than 4 years, which is equivalent to an approximate 25 percent return on investment. To gain that return, how much are they willing to spend? They immediately will negotiate front-end design fees to the bone or, more commonly, expect these additional services within the fee structure.

Designers talk about their interest in LCC. Yet where have they made this a qualification for the design professional and what positive efforts have they made to meet owner demands? For example, the American Institute of Architects and American Consulting Engineers Council has sponsored a 2½-day seminar on LCC for the past 2 years; response from architects and engineers has been so lacking that over half the seminars had to be cancelled.

Recommended Fees

It is strongly recommended that the LCC requirements be separately analyzed in terms of scope, and separate fees negotiated. This will assure owners that attention will be focused properly.

Figure 9-1 is a recommended fee structure in work hours for a range of project costs. This fee structure should allow use of the methodology indicated in Chapter 6. The low range is for a single application—say, at the early design development. The higher range allows two applications—one at the concept and another during early design

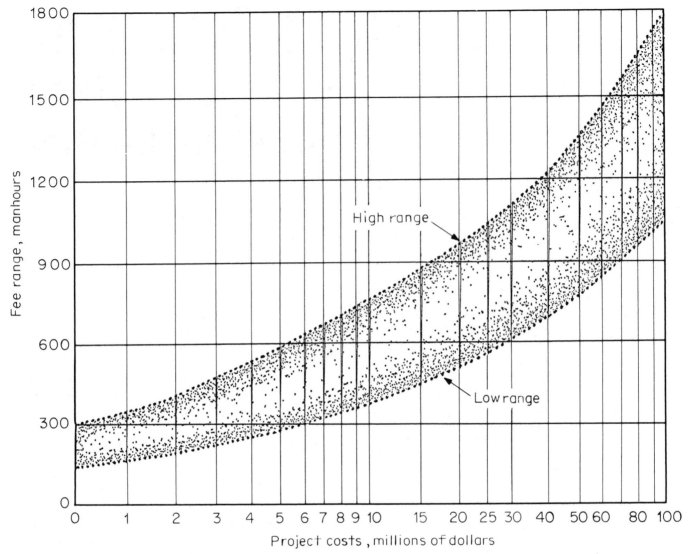

FIGURE 9-1
Life cycle analysis services, proposed fee schedule.

development. Appendix A contains a sample designer proposal for performing LCC analysis services. A sample request for proposal from the state of Illinois is also presented.

FUTURE TRENDS

Owners are becoming more concerned about the cost of ownership. A recent survey indicated that they ranked "greater initial costs to reduce fuel costs later" as the second most important industry trend. "Life cycle costing" ranked ninth, and "value engineering" thirteenth.

Coupled with these owner trends is the time period sought for payoff of these higher initial costs. Figure 9-2

is a graph of the payoff period expected by owners, taken from the same survey. Actual experience by the authors confirms that an even earlier payoff period is expected by industrial, profit-oriented owners and a longer period for governmental, nonprofit-oriented owners.

Combined with this list of owner trends is the increasing number of government agencies considering (or having passed) mandatory LCC requirements. Foremost of these is the Environmental Protection Agency (EPA), which requires a cost-effectiveness analysis of alternative processes for the early planning and design of wastewater treatment plants (see Appendix B). The Air Force was one of the first government agencies to use LCC for their housing procurements. Since then, the Naval Facilities Engineering Command has published a guide *(Economic Analysis Handbook, P-442),* and the Corps of Engineers is planning

FIGURE 9-2
What payback will owners expect for life cycle cost savings? (*Credit: Building Design and Construction, February 1979, p. 49.*)

to issue a manual. In addition, the National Aeronautics and Space Administration (NASA) has recently published a draft of an LCC guide for its centers.

Several years ago, Florida became the first state to have mandatory LCC for all the procurements passed by its legislature. It was followed closely by Alaska. In 1979 Colorado, Idaho, Maryland, Massachusetts, Nebraska, North Carolina, Texas, Washington, Wisconsin, and Wyoming had passed mandatory provisions.

Today all the states are seriously thinking about LCC; but so far only a few states, such as Florida, have issued LCC guide manuals. Wyoming issued an LCC guide for its procurements in 1979.

CONCLUSIONS

With increased client pressures on initial costs, maintenance, operating costs, energy conservation, and profit, designers are going to have to reassess their role. The reas-

sessment will be for improved cost control—using a "design-to-cost" philosophy with more input from the maintenance and operating areas regarding follow-on costs and energy conservation.

This will require expanded services from designers, which owners will feel are part of the basic fee structure. Although inflation has raised construction costs so that the designers' fees have increased, designer costs are more labor-intensive than construction costs, and so their costs have risen even faster. It is now time for designers to improve internal management of time and costs to offset the squeeze on profits. That is, improved management of the design process will itself reduce time and costs. To do this will require increasing use of automation to relieve designers of time-consuming procedures that detract from their basic role. LCC is a challenging area, which designers must formalize.

Nothing of any consequence will occur in the use of LCC until owners make it a mandatory part of the planning, programming, and design of their facilities. The requirement should be based on a scope of services that will be a separate fee package—not included in an overall fee. The mandatory requirement should include use of the value engineering methodology to ensure a multidisciplinary approach, the generation of viable alternatives, and a positive approach to modifying habits and attitudes that contribute to unnecessary costs. The mandatory services can be performed by the owners, designer, or separate consultants, depending on qualifications and availability of personnel.

Designers have been promising total cost evaluation for their clients for a long time (see Figure 9-3). Oliver Smith, the first Smith in the chain of architects that became Smith, Hinchman & Grylls, Associates, recognized this when he stated in 1842: "It is important to expend all money in building to the best possible advantage."

It is hoped this book will set in motion a standard, formal approach to LCC. This approach should be supported by new cost data banks to include cost elements in all categories: initial, maintenance, operating, energy, etc. The system must be organized so that it can either be used manually or be automated. The best solutions are going to be developed when all the participants cooperate in developing optimum solutions to the total problem, using life cycle costing toward the goal of making better design decisions.

O. P. SMITH,

Architect, and Teacher of Architectural Drawing. Plans and specifications for buildings drawn with special reference to convenience, economy, taste, and durability. Gentlemen who are concerned in erecting either public or private buildings, will find it to their advantage to consult an architect, as it is important to expend all money in building to the best possible advantage.

He will also teach builders the principles of architecture, and the rules of architectural drawing, and shading.

Jamestown, Chaut. County, N. Y.

FIGURE 9-3
Advertisement from the *Jamestown Liberty Star* (1842). *(Credit: Thomas J. Holleman and James P. Gallagher, Smith, Hinchman & Grylls, 125 Years of Architecture and Engineering, 1853–1978, p. 16.)*

APPENDIX A
SAMPLE LCC SCOPE OF SERVICES

This appendix provides the design professional with appropriate material to be used in negotiating with an owner the scope of services to be provided. Phases of work to be accomplished as well as work hours to complete the work are illustrated by assuming a typical building and size.

Information is also provided for the owner to use when requesting life cycle costing services from design professionals. An actual example request for proposal (RFP) illustrates what another owner considered important in controlling the initial, energy, and follow-on costs of ownership.

CONSULTANT PROPOSAL TO PERFORM LCC SERVICES

INTRODUCTION

The consultant proposes to furnish comprehensive, life cycle costing (LCC) analysis consulting services to the designer-owner. The consultant will act in assisting the designer-owner in meeting the LCC requirements of the owner.

The goal of this effort will be to "minimize life cycle costs without sacrificing essential functions" by using multidisciplinary teams at various stages of design, and following up with a post-occupancy evaluation. Each team will analyze the project's systems using a formal methodology outlined in the book by Alphonse Dell'Isola and Stephen Kirk, *Life Cycle Costing for Design Professionals.* LCC input should occur early in concept/design development. The LCC application will be devoted to actions feasible at this phase, focusing on alternative design selections encompassing the areas of greatest savings potential.

PERSONNEL

All work will be conducted under the direction of personnel trained in LCC methodology. The LCC tasks will be performed using a multidisciplined approach to optimize total costs.

SCOPE OF WORK
Phase I: Data Collection and Analysis

The consultant will collect all information relative to the project from the designer and owner. The consultant team members will then review the project documents and familiarize themselves with the program and design parameters to identify required functions. A life cycle cost model will be prepared using information supplied by the designer and owner.

If desired, the consultant will conduct a one-day LCC executive seminar in a location selected by the client. Attendance is expected from designer personnel involved with this project and interested client representatives, particularly those to be assigned to maintain and operate the proposed facility. The seminar will consist of a half day of formal presentation and a half day of project familiarization and information collection. Each participant will be presented with a printed copy of the briefing. The seminar objectives include a summary of LCC concepts and a discussion of procedures during the concept and design development process.

Phase II: Concept and Design Development Review and Interim Report

The LCC team will again be assembled for a 3- to 5-day study to prepare in-depth LCC studies. Areas for LCC will be isolated. Related ratios, e.g. net/gross, dollar/ton of air conditioning, Btu per square foot per year, etc., will also be evaluated. An idea listing of potential LCC savings will be generated using brainstorming techniques. The owner's and designer's input will be solicited to assist in selecting areas for in-depth study. The in-depth study format will follow the methodology outlined in the text *Life Cycle Costing for Design Professionals.* Each LCC idea listing will have life cycle costs estimated.

The emphasis in this phase will be on component and systems decisions. The team will focus on areas where implementation is feasible and where it can be accomplished quickly to realize optimum LCC cost potential. Subsequently, preliminary findings of the study will be presented to designer-owner for timely consideration. An interim typed report will be prepared by the consultant upon completion of the workshop for review with the designer and owner.

It should be noted that as the size or complexity of the project increases, additional reviews should be performed; i.e., predesign, concept, schematic, and design development stages of the design process. Personnel requirements would increase proportionately.

Phase III: Postoccupancy Evaluation and Final Report

After the project has been bid and occupied, the owner will be asked to collect energy, maintenance, and other LCC data. The consultant will review the results of his input and compare with the actual building data. The consultant will attempt to reconcile the data with the design team and make recommendations for future studies and corrective (if any) actions. The consultant will assemble the results of each of the phases of the study into a final report. Six copies of the final report will be presented to designer-owner for review and comment. The contract will be considered complete at the conclusion of this phase.

Phase IV: Computer Simulation Energy Profile Systems (Optional)

The consultant will develop a computerized energy program for the facility, using one of the nationally recognized systems, e.g., TRACE, ESP-1, AXCESS, NECAP, ECUBE, CAL/CON I. This input will be used by the consultant to augment data used in decision making and for postoccupancy evaluation.

PERSONNEL REQUIREMENTS: TYPICAL PROJECT, $4 to $6 MILLION RANGE

Phase I: Data Collection and Analysis

LCC Team Coordinator	2 days
LCC Team	4 days
Typist	1 day
	7 days

Phase II: Concept and Design Development Review and Interim Report

LCC Team Coordinator	8 days
LCC Team:	

Architectural	
Structural	
Mechanical, Energy	12 days
Electrical	
Estimator-Programmer	
Typist	2 days

Interim Report

LCC Coordinator	2 days
LCC Team	2 days
	26 days

Phase III: Postoccupancy Evaluation and Final Report

LCC Team Coordinator	5 days
LCC Team	6 days
Technical Typist	2 days
	13 days

Phase IV: Computer Simulation Energy Profile Systems (Optional)

Lump Sum Approx. ($.05–.10/ft²)	as required
Grand Total	46 days

OWNER REQUEST FOR PROPOSAL TO PERFORM LCC SERVICES

INTRODUCTION

The Capital Development Board of the State of Illinois, in their continuing effort to provide cost effective capital improvements for the State, has prepared this Request for Proposal for a Value Analysis for the proposed Department of Revenue Building.

The results of this study will be a cost plan for the project. This cost plan and the supporting value analysis will allow the Capital Development Board to make decisions that have cost-saving impact during the pre-design phase of the project.

The professional firms involved in the construction industry have long advocated establishment of detailed budgets and associated building performance levels before any design work is started on a project. The Capital Development Board agrees and this document implements that concept.

CAPITAL DEVELOPMENT BOARD

Donald S. Glickman
Executive Director
November 30, 1977

1. Invitation

The Capital Development Board of the State of Illinois

invites qualified firms to submit proposals for the preparation of a value analysis for the proposed Department of Revenue Building in Springfield, Illinois.

2. Purpose Of The Request

This value analysis is to be an accurate conceptual cost plan for the project. The analysis is to include the initial costs and the ownership costs associated with various conceptual building configurations and their component systems. These total life cycle costs of various conceptual design alternatives will be utilized as cost criteria for the subsequent phases of the project.

3. Project Description

The project, "New Illinois Department of Revenue Building in Springfield" is a proposed state facility to functionally support the operations of that Department. The facility will house over 1850 employees of that Department. Over four hundred thousand gross square feet of space is required in the building. The project is further defined in the "Program Statement for Administration and Processing Building, Department of Revenue", dated January, 1977, as prepared by the Capital Development Board. This program statement is to be the basis for the Value Analysis requested herein.

4. Scope Of Work

1. The Consultant is to determine three conceptual design alternatives based on the spatial layout to functionally support the activities of the Department of Revenue.

2. The Consultant also is to determine the two most efficiently designed energy systems for the facility.

3. For the six conceptual design alternatives outlined above, complete the design only *as necessary* to facilitate the required value analysis.

4. Perform a value analysis of the facility and its component parts, using energy use analysis and life cycle cost analysis as selection criteria.

5. Prepare a Cost Plan for control of subsequent phases of the project.

5. Conceptual Design Alternatives

The conceptual design alternatives are to be based on the possible configurations of the facility required to functionally support the activities of the Department of Revenue. The ability of the Revenue Department to efficiently meet their responsibilities is partially dependent upon the spatiality of the configuration of the facility. Stated differently, the efficiency of the activities may be correlated to a minimum floor size. That conclusion will define the minimum footprint of the building configuration. The footprint of the building is defined as the gross square footage enclosed at grade level.

Therefore, the Consultant is to analyze and, through consultation with the management of the Department of Revenue, determine the functional use requirements to be satisfied by the facility. These requirements include primary and secondary functional relationships among the Department's sections, work patterns, traffic flows, materials and supply handling, adjacency requirements, security, and other special requirements.

Based upon the analysis specified above, the Consultant is to prepare three spatial layouts to satisfy the required use of the facility as determined from that analysis. The three spatial layouts will include the minimum floor size feasible (and the number of floors required) and the maximum reasonable floor size. The third conceptual design alternative would be based on a floor size falling between the minimum size feasible and the reasonable maximum floor size.

The results should be three conceptual design alternatives based on three sizes of primary floor levels or footprints. The conceptual design alternatives then are to be developed as required for the energy analysis and qualification of components for the value analysis. No design effort is to be performed that will unduly restrain the professional firms during the design phase of the project.

6. Energy Systems

It is imperative to view any facility as a total energy consuming system of integrated subsystems related by performance. The conceptual design alternatives are further defined by conceptual energy systems designs. The energy systems are defined as the building systems that either convert, transmit, or utilize energy.

The Consultant is to determine the two (2) most feasible conceptual energy systems designs for the facility. The analysis required to determine these designs should take into consideration such factors as:

1. Raw energy availability

2. Energy conversion equipment

3. Energy distribution systems

4. Thermal properties of the enclosure

5. Compatibility with all other building systems

These conceptual energy system designs are to be submitted to CDB for approval prior to their inclusion in value analysis and the energy use analysis. The descriptions of the mechanical and related systems are to be of sufficient detail to permit incorporation of these systems in the final design of the building. The Consultant is to present all rationale supporting his recommendations when requesting approval of these designs for inclusion in the conceptual design alternatives.

7. Subsystem Alternatives

The Consultant is to evaluate subsystem alternatives (where required) and determine the best subsystem alternative to be incorporated in the building and included in the total Value Analysis and Cost Plan. These subsystem alternatives are generally specified at the UNIFORMAT Level 4.

For example, perform a preliminary value analysis on electrical distribution subsystems, select the best that satisfies the value analysis criteria, and include that selected system in the design alternatives of the building. Ensure that the selected subsystem is compatible with all other subsystems and also determine any cost effects on other subsystems.

8. Energy Use Analysis

The Energy Analysis is to be performed with a computer software program which will simulate the energy performance of the building. This program must embody the current ASHRAE state-of-the-art techniques for calculating thermal loads and energy usage predictions. This program should be capable of calculating transient heat flow through the building envelope systems via the Response Factor Method. It also must be capable of examining various thermal zones within the building. Acceptable programs are NECAP, SCOUT, or Meriwether. Any other program must be submitted to and approved by the CDB.

Based on the above energy utilization analysis, calculate annual energy cost for each design alternative. Predicted costs per energy unit must be approved by the CDB prior to application within the overall value analysis.

Copies of all input/output files associated with this energy analysis are to be included with the final report.

9. Value Analysis

Value analysis is defined as a detailed and comprehensive analysis and recommendation of specific building systems with respect to:

1. Construction feasibility
2. Quality and aesthetic integrity
3. Minimum life cycle cost
4. Optimum energy conservation performance
5. Flexibility for space changes
6. Subsystem compatibility
7. Potential cost savings

The value analysis shall be performed and presented at a "UNIFORMAT Level 4" cost detail data base. First costs and life cycle costs shall be determined for each Level 4 element. In addition, for each first cost, state the total element cost, the parameter (unit of measure), quantity of that parameter, parameter unit cost, and the cost per gross square foot of each Level 4 element.

The cost data files utilized by the Consultant must be of sufficient quality and detail to permit accurate costing of Level 4 elements. An elemental parameter estimating technique requires that the cost per element parameter be linked to the selected *performance* and *quality* of the subsystem. This unit cost for the subsystem must not be the average of samples reflecting wide ranges of performance and quality criteria. The consultant must be able to demonstrate this cost sensitivity compliance to the satisfaction of the CDB.

10. Life Cycle Cost Analysis

Life cycle cost analysis is a financial model that examines both the initial costs and the future costs associated with the proposed capital investment with respect to the cost of capital to the owner. The alternate conceptual designs and subsystems are to be subjected to life cycle cost analysis as a selection criterion. The initial costs and annual ownership costs of the facility or subsystems are to be forecasted and the associated cash-flow stream determined. The present value of that cash-flow stream is to be calculated using the cost of capital to the State of Illinois over a 40-year economic life.

Escalation rates are to be forecasted and applied at the subsystem level. Only those costs associated with and influenced by the facility or its component parts are to be considered.

A sensitivity analysis of the input parameters to the life cycle cost analysis is also required.

11. Cost Plan

A detailed cost plan shall be included in the final report. This plan should state at the "UNIFORMAT Level 4" detail level the optimum cost budget for the project. The subsystem's quality and/or density levels that define these budget levels must also be stated. This cost plan shall be the basis for cost control during subsequent phases of this project.

12. Site Consideration

This study is to exclude any analysis of specific sites; it is not site specific. For purposes of the study, assume a site of sufficient size to support the building and other uses that the State might desire. Also, assume the configurations as defined herein comply with all zoning requirements of the City of Springfield. The study must include an analysis and plan for CDB to evaluate the effect that land and site development costs might have on each conceptual design alternative.

APPENDIX B
SELECTED GOVERNMENT REQUIREMENTS FOR LCC

"Life Cycle Costing should be legislated for all state-financed construction inasmuch as it is capable of producing large savings in tax dollars and energy resources."

Judith C. Toth, Member of House of Delegates
  Maryland Legislature, paper delivered to AIE/AACE Joint Conference, Washington, D.C., October 5–6, 1977.

This appendix first lists those public and private agencies or industries currently requiring that some form of life cycle cost analysis be performed. Excerpts from selected federal, state, and local governments requirements provide the reader with some indication of the broad terminology and scope of services necessary to satisfy agency requirements.

DIRECTIVES AND REGULATIONS PERTAINING TO LIFE CYCLE COSTING

The following table provides a brief list of the status of LCC directives and regulations. Additional information may be obtained by contacting the appropriate agency or organization.

Directives and Regulations Pertaining to LCC

Presidential Order 12003, Energy Policy and Conservation, 1977
Department of Defense, *Construction Criteria Manual, Economic Studies*, 1972.
Office of Management and Budget, Circular No. A-94, *Evaluation of Costs and/or Benefits of Programs or Projects*.
Environmental Protection Agency, *Cost Effectiveness Analysis Guidelines*.
Alaska, Life Cycle Cost Law, 1975.

Agency or organization	Status and comments
National	
Enviromental Protective Agency (EPA)	*Cost Effectiveness Analysis Guidelines, 1978*
U.S. Congress	*National Energy Conservation Policy Act, 1978*
GAO	*Report on LCC,* 1973
Presidential directive	Executive Order 12003, 1977
Department of Defense	*Construction Criteria Manual,* 1972
General Services Administration	*Procedures for LCC Analysis,* 1977
Federal Supply Service	*LCC Equipment Procurement,* 1977
Department of Energy	Final rule to establish a methodology and procedures to conduct LCC analyses, 1980

Agency or organization	Status and comments
Regional	
Alaska	Procurement of public facilities analyzed based on LCC passed 1975.
Arkansas	LCC not used in construction of facilities; used in equipment procurements.
Colorado	Passed 1977. LCC is permissive not mandatory in supplies and equipment. LCC is part of construction/renovation of public facilities.
Florida	Passed 1974; primarily facility energy analysis; LCC used in equipment procurement.
Georgia	LCC not used in construction.
Hawaii	Statute for energy conservation in building design and construction; LCC used in procurement of autos.
Idaho	Executive Order LCC requirement for facilities.
Illinois	No statute; LCC not used in procurement or building design.
Iowa	New statute; procedures for implementation are not completed.
Kansas	Legislation for value engineering and LCC.
Louisana	Beginning to use LCC in procurements.
Maine	No statute. They use "good judgment" in procurements.
Maryland	Passed 1978, for facilities LCC. Also, equipment procurement using LCC.
Massachusetts	Passed 1976, for facilities LCC.
Nebraska	Passed 1978, for facilities LCC.
Nevada	State law requires the Public Works Board to provide the Legislature with LCC data on projects; Board does LCC on mechanical/electrical projects.
New Hampshire	Not using LCC except for procurement of autos, developing LCC program.
New Jersey	Proposed statute for facilities; currently use LCC on equipment procurement.
New Mexico	No requirement for LCC; not using it.
New York	No statute for LCC; use LCC in equipment procurement.
North Carolina	Statute for LCC for buildings.
North Dakota	Executive Order on Energy Conservation Plans; applies to equipment but not buildings.
Oklahoma	Executive Order for Energy Conservation; applies to equipment not buildings.
Oregon	No legislative requirement; LCC is permitted in equipment procurement.
Pennsylvania	LCC manual in print; will be implemented by Executive Directive.
Rhode Island	No state requirement; no procedures.
Tennessee	Statute for LCC applied to equipment procurement.
Texas	Statute for LCC.
Virginia	No statute. LCC sometimes used in equipment procurement.
Washington	Statute on LCC; one paragraph addressing LCC in facility design.
Wisconsin	Procedures for LCC in facilities.
Wyoming	Passed 1977, for facilities LCC; implementation booklet by the energy office.
Organizational	
City of Atlanta	Implemented
City of Phoenix	Implemented
City of Chicago	Implemented
Illinois Capital Development Board	Typical request for proposal includes LCC
American Telephone &Telegraph	*Engineering Economics*, 2d ed., 1975

PRESIDENTIAL DOCUMENTS

TITLE 3—THE PRESIDENT
Executive Order 12003—July 20, 1977, Relating to Energy Policy and Conservation

By virtue of the authority vested in me by the Constitution and the statutes of the United States of America, including the Energy Policy and Conservation Act (89 Stat. 871, 42 U.S.C. 6201 *et seq.*), the Motor Vehicle Information and Cost Savings Act, as amended (15 U.S.C. 1901 *et seq.*), Section 205(a) of the Federal Property and Administrative Services Act of 1949, as amended (40 U.S.C. 486(a)), and Section 301 of Title 3 of the United States Code, and as President of the United States of America, it is hereby ordered as follows:

SEC. 2. Executive Order No. 11912 of April 13, 1976, is further amended by adding the following new Section:

"Sec. 10.(a)(1) The Administrator of the Federal Energy Administration, hereinafter referred to as the Administrator, shall develop, with the concurrence of the Director of the Office of Management and Budget, and in consultation with the Secretary of Defense, the Secretary of Housing and Urban Development, the Administrator of Veterans' Affairs, the Administrator of the Energy Research and Development Administration, the Administrator of General Services, and the heads of such other Executive agencies as he deems appropriate, the ten-year plan for energy conservation with respect to Government buildings, as provided by section 381(a)(2) of the Energy Policy and Conservation Act (42 U.S.C. 6361(a)(2)).

(2) The goals established in subsection (b) shall apply to the following categories of Federally-owned buildings: (i) office buildings, (ii) hospitals, (iii) schools, (iv) prison facilities, (v) multi-family dwellings, (vi) storage facilities, and (vii) such other categories of buildings for which the Administrator determines the establishment of energy-efficiency performance goals is feasible.

"(b) The Administrator shall establish requirements and procedures, which shall be observed by each agency unless a waiver is granted by the Administrator, designed to ensure that each agency to the maximum extent practicable aims to achieve the following goals:

(1) For the total of all *Federally-owned existing buildings the goal shall be a reduction of 20 percent in the average annual energy use per gross square foot of floor area in 1985 from the average energy use per gross square foot of floor area in 1975.* [Italics added.]This goal shall apply to all buildings for which construction was or design specifications were completed prior to the date of promulgation of the guidelines pursuant to subsection (d) of this Section.

(2) For the total of all *Federally-owned new buildings the goal shall be a reduction of 45 percent in the average annual energy requirement per gross square foot of floor area in 1985 from the average annual energy use per gross square foot of floor area in 1975.* [Italics added.] This goal

shall apply to all new buildings for which design specifications are completed after the date of promulgation of the guidelines pursuant to subsection (d) of this Section.

"(c) The Administrator with the concurrence of the Director of the Office of Management and Budget, in consultation with the heads of the Executive agencies specified in subsection (a) and the Director of the National Bureau of Standards, shall establish, *for purposes of developing the ten-year plan, a practical and effective method for estimating and comparing life cycle capital and operating costs* for Federal buildings, including residential, commercial, and industrial type categories. [Italics added.] Such method shall be consistent with the Office of Management and Budget Circular No. A-94, and shall be adopted and used by all agencies in developing their plans pursuant to subsection (e), annual reports pursuant to subsection (g), and budget estimates pursuant to subsection (h). For purposes of this paragraph, *the term "life cycle cost" means the total costs of owning, operating, and maintaining a building over its economic life, including its fuel and energy costs, determined on the basis of a systematic evaluation and comparison of alternative building systems.* [Italics added.]

Jimmy Carter [signed]
THE WHITE HOUSE, *July 20, 1977.*

DOD CONSTRUCTION CRITERIA MANUAL, 1972, ECONOMIC STUDIES

Listed below are excerpts from the Department of Defense (DOD) *Construction Criteria Manual* 1972. These portions of the manual are directly related to the life cycle costing responsibilities in facility design and construction.

1-3 Organization Of Manual

A. The following chapters of this Manual set forth DOD technical criteria for construction of military facilities, including Reserve Forces facilities and family housing.

1-4 Design Considerations

1-4.1 Economic Studies: The architectural and engineering design of military facilites shall be determined by engineering, economical, and environmental studies. In order to provide the optimum combination of an efficient and effective facility at the most economical cost and least adverse environmental impact, these studies should include, but not be limited to, those design features of the facility which contribute most to the construction cost and environmental impact, such as (a) siting and orientation; (b) architectural features, including building configuration, column spacing, and story heights; (c) structural systems; (d) exterior and interior finishes; (e) plumbing systems;

(f) electrical systems; (g) heating and air conditioning systems; and (h) exterior supporting utilities and roads.

A. Such studies *should consider the life cycle cost of the facility* so as to arrive at an economical cost which takes into consideration not only the initial construction cost, but also operation and maintenance costs reflecting the best information available on the behavior of materials in the environment to which they will be subjected and on the projected operation, maintenance and repair costs of utility systems. [Italics added.]

B. For projects having an estimated cost over $300,000 the project file shall provide suitable documentation to (a) verify that the necessary studies have been made; (b) identify the alternatives considered; (c) state the decisions made; and (d) indicate the basis for the decisions.

1-4.2 Design Requirements: Design of facilities shall:

(a) Be based on the actual requirements of the project.

(b) Meet the operating requirements of the using activity and provide reasonable flexibility to accommodate foreseeable changes in requirements by the using activity.

(c) *Provide highly functional facilities at the lowest practicable construction costs, with due regard for economy in maintenance and operation of the facility.* [Italics added.]

OMB (OFFICE OF MANAGEMENT AND BUDGET) CIRCULAR NO. A-94 (REVISED; MARCH 27, 1972) EVALUATION OF COSTS AND/OR BENEFITS OF PROGRAMS OR PROJECTS

To the Heads of Executive Departments and Establishments

Subject: Discount rates to be used in evaluating time-distributed costs and benefits

1. *Purpose* This Circular prescribes a standard discount rate to be used in evaluating the measurable costs and/or benefits of programs or projects when they are distributed over time.

2. *Rescission* This Circular replaces and rescinds Office of Management and Budget (OMB) Circular No. A-94 dated June 26, 1969.

3. *Scope*
   (a) This Circular applies to all agencies of the executive branch of the Federal Government except the U.S. Postal Service. The discount rate prescribed in this Circular applies to the evaluation of Government decisions concerning the initiation, renewal or expansion of all programs or projects, other than those specifically exempted below, for which the adoption is expected to commit the Government to a series of measurable costs ex-

tending over three years or more or which result in a series of benefits that extend three or more years beyond the inception date.

(b) Specifically exempted from the scope of this Circular are decisions concerning water resource projects (guidance for which is the approved Water Resources Principles and Standards), the Government of the District of Columbia, and non-Federal recipients of Federal loans or grants.

(c) The remaining exemptions derive from the secondary nature of the decisions involved; that is, how to acquire assets or proceed with a program after an affirmative decision to initiate, renew, or expand such a program using this Circular. Thus:

(1) This Circular would not apply to the evaluation of decisions concerning how to obtain use of real property, such as by lease or purchase.

(2) This Circular would not apply to the evaluation of decisions concerning the acquisition of commercial-type services by Government or contractor operation, guidance for which is OMB Circular No. A-76.

(3) This Circular would not apply to the evaluation of decisions concerning how to select automatic data processing equipment, guidance for which is OMB Circular No. 60-6.

(d) The discount rates prescribed in this Circular are:

(1) Suggested for use in the internal planning documents of the agencies in the executive branch:

(2) Required for use in program analyses submitted to the Office of Management and Budget in support of legislative and budget programs.

This Circular does not supersede agency practices which are prescribed by or pursuant to law, Executive order, or other relevant Circulars. Agencies should evaluate their programs and projects in accordance with existing requirements and, in addition, summarize the present value costs and/or benefits using the discount rate prescribed in this Circular.

4. *Definitions* Analytic documents submitted to the Office of Management and Budget should be based on the following concepts where relevant:

(a) **Expected annual cost** means the expected annual dollar value (in constant dollars) of resources, goods and services required to establish and carry out a program or project. Estimates of expected yearly costs will be based on established definitions and practices for program and project evaluation. However, all economic costs, including acquisition, possession, and operation costs, must be included whether or not actually paid by the Federal Government. Such costs not generally involving a direct Federal payment include imputed market values of public property and State and local property taxes foregone.

(b) **Expected annual benefit** means the dollar value (in constant dollars) of goods and services expected to result from a program or project for each of the years it is in operation. Estimates of expected yearly benefits will be based on established definitions and practices developed by agencies for program and project evaluation.

(c) **Expected annual effects** means an objective, non-monetary measure of program effects expected for each of the years a program or project is in operation. When dollar value cannot be placed on the effects of comparable programs or projects, an objective measure of effects may be available and useful to enable the comparison of alternative means of achieving specified objectives on the basis of their estimated cost for each year of the planning period and are not to be discounted.

(d) **Discount rate** means the interest rate used in calculating the present value of expected yearly costs and benefits.

(e) **Discount factor** means the factor for any specific discount rate which translates expected cost or benefit in any specific future year into its present value. The discount factor is equal to $1/(1 + r)t$, where r is the discount rate and t is the number of years since the date of initiation, renewal, or expansion of a program or project.

(f) **Present value cost** means each year's expected yearly cost multiplied by its discount factor and then summed over all years of the planning period.

(g) **Present value benefit** means each year's expected yearly benefit multiplied by its discount factor and then summed over all years of the planning period.

(h) **Present value net benefit** means the difference between present value benefit (item g) and present value cost (item f).

(i) **Benefit-cost ratio** means present value benefit (item g) divided by present value cost (item f).

Attachment A contains an example that illustrates calculation of the present value information.

5. *Treatment of Inflation* All estimates of the costs and benefits for each year of the planning period should be made in constant dollars; i.e., in terms of the general purchasing power of the dollar at the time of decision. Estimates may reflect changes in the relative prices of cost and/or benefit components, where there is a reasonable basis for estimating such changes, but should not include any forecasted change in the general price level during the planning period.

6. *Treatment of Uncertainty* Actual costs and benefits in future years are likely to differ from those expected at the time of decision. For those cases for which there is a reasonable basis to estimate the variability of future costs and benefits, the sensitivity of proposed programs and projects to this variability should be evaluated.

The expected annual costs and benefits (or effects) should be supplemented with estimates of minimum and maximum values. Present value cost and benefits should be calculated for each of these estimates. The probability that each of the possible cost and benefits estimates may be realized should also be discussed, even when there is not basis for a precise quantitative estimate. Uncertainty of the cost and benefit (or effects) estimates should be treated explicitly, as described above. The prescribed discount rate should be used to evaluate all alternatives. Specifically, the evaluations should not use different discount rates to reflect the relative uncertainty of the alternatives.

7. *Discount Rate Policy* The discount rates to be used for evaluations of programs and projects subject to the guidance of this Circular are as follows:

(a) A rate of 10 percent, and, where relevant,

(b) Any other rates prescribed by or pursuant to law, Executive order, or other relevant Circulars.

The prescribed discount rate of 10 percent represents an estimate of the average rate of return on private investment, before taxes and after inflation.

To assist in calculation, Attachment B contains discount factors for the discount rate of 10 percent for each of the years from one to fifty.

8. *Interpretation* Questions concerning interpretation of this Circular should be addressed to the Assistant Director for Evaluation, Office of Management and Budget (395-3614).

George P. Schultz
Director

TITLE 40, CHAPTER 1, PART 35, APPENDIX; PUBLISHED: FEDERAL REGISTER, ENVIRONMENTAL PROTECTION AGENCY (EPA) COST-EFFECTIVENESS ANALYSIS GUIDELINES

APPENDIX A
Cost-Effectiveness Analysis Guidelines

1. *Purpose.* These guidelines represent Agency policies and procedures for determining the most cost-effective waste treatment management system or component part.

2. *Authority.* These guidelines are provided under sections 212(2)(C) and 217 of the Clean Water Act.

3. *Applicability.* These guidelines, except as otherwise noted, apply to all facilities planning under step 1 grant assistance awarded after September 30, 1978. The guidelines also apply to State or locally financed facilities planning on which subsequent step 2 or step 3 Federal grant assistance is based.

4. *Definitions.* Terms used in these guidelines are defined as follows:

a. *Waste treatment management system.* Used synonymously with "complete waste treatment system" as defined in § 35.905 of this subpart.

b. *Cost-effectiveness analysis.* An analysis performed to determine which waste treatment management system or component part will result in the minimum total resources costs over time to meet Federal, State, or local requirements.

c. *Planning period.* The period over which a waste treatment management system is evaluated for cost-effectiveness. The planning period begins with the system's initial operation.

d. *Useful life.* The estimated period of time during which a treatment works or a component of a waste treatment management system will be operated.

e. *Disaggregation.* The process or result of breaking down a sum total of population or economic activity for a State or other jurisdiction (i.e., designated 208 area or SMSA) into smaller areas or jurisdictions.

5. *Identification, selection, and screening of alternatives.* a. *Identification of alternatives.* All feasible alternative waste management systems shall be initially identified. These alternatives should include systems discharging to receiving waters, land application systems, on-site and other noncentralized systems, including revenue generating applications, and systems employing the reuse of wastewater and recycling of pollutants. In identifying alternatives, the applicant shall consider the possibility of no action and staged development of the system.

b. *Screening of alternatives.* The identified alternatives shall be systematically screened to determine those capable of meeting the applicable Federal, State and local criteria.

c. *Selection of alternatives.* The identified alternatives shall be initially analyzed to determine which systems have cost-effective potential and which should be fully evaluated according to the cost-effectiveness analysis procedures established in the guidelines.

d. *Extent of effort.* The extent of effort and the level of sophistication used in the cost-effectiveness analysis should reflect the project's size and importance. Where processes or techniques are claimed to be innovative technology on the basis of the cost reduction criterion contained in paragraph 6e(1) of appendix E to this subpart, a sufficiently detailed cost analysis shall be included to substantiate the claim to the satisfaction of the Regional Administrator.

6. *Cost-effectiveness analysis procedures.*

a. *Method of analysis.* The resources costs shall be determined by evaluating opportunity costs. For resources that can be expressed in monetary terms, the analysis will use the interest (discount) rate established in paragraph 6e. Monetary costs shall be calculated in terms of present worth values or equivalent annual values over the planning period defined in section 6b. The analysis shall descriptively present nonmonetary factors (e.g., social and environmental) in order to determine their significance and impact. Nonmonetary factors include primary and secondary environmental effects, implementation capability, operability, performance reliability and flexibility. Although such factors as use and recovery of energy and scarce resources and recycling of nutrients are to be included in the monetary cost analysis, the nonmonetary evaluation shall also include them. The most cost-effective alternative shall be the waste treatment management system which the analysis determines to have the lowest present worth or equivalent annual value unless nonmonetary costs are overriding. The most cost-effective alternative must also meet the minimum requirements of applicable effluent limitations, groundwater protection, or other applicable standards established under the Act.

b. *Planning period.* The planning period for the cost-effectiveness analysis shall be 20 years.

c. *Elements of monetary costs.* The monetary costs to be considered shall include the total value of the resources which are attributable to the waste treatment management system or to one of its component parts. To determine these values, all monies necessary for capital construction costs and operation and maintenance costs shall be identified.

(1) Capital construction costs used in a cost-effective analysis shall include all contractors' costs of construction including overhead and profit, costs of land, relocation, and right-of-way and easement acquisition; costs of design engineering, field exploration and engineering services during construction; costs of administrative and legal services including costs of bond sales; startup costs such as operator training; and interest during construction. Capital construction costs shall also include contingency allowances consistent with the cost estimate's level of precision and detail.

(2) The cost-effectiveness analysis shall include annual costs for operation and maintenance (including routine replacement of equipment and equipment parts). These costs shall be adequate to ensure effective and dependable operation during the system's planning period. Annual costs shall be divided between fixed annual costs and costs which would depend on the annual quantity of waste water collected and treated. Annual revenues generated by the waste treatment management system through energy recovery, crop production, or other outputs shall be deducted from the annual costs for operation and maintenance in accordance with guidance issued by the Administrator.

d. *Prices.* The applicant shall calculate the various

components of costs on the basis of market prices prevailing at the time of the cost-effectiveness analysis. The analysis shall not allow for inflation of wages and prices, except those for land, as described in paragraph 6h(1) and for natural gas. This stipulation is based on the implied assumption that prices, other than the exceptions, for resources involved in treatment works construction and operation, will tend to change over time by approximately the same percentage. Changes in the general level of prices will not affect the results of the cost-effectiveness analysis. Natural gas prices shall be escalated at a compound rate of 4 percent annually over the planning period, unless the Regional Administrator determines that the grantee has justified use of a greater or lesser percentage based upon regional differentials between historical natural gas price escalation and construction cost escalation. Land prices shall be appreciated as provided in paragraph 6h(1). Both historical data and future projections support the gas and land price escalations relative to those for other goods and services related to waste water treatment. Price escalation rates may be updated periodically in accordance with Agency guidelines.

e. *Interest (discount) rate.* The rate which the Water Resources Council establishes annually for evaluation of water resource projects shall be used.

f. *Interest during construction.* (1) Where capital expenditures can be expected to be fairly uniform during the construction period, interest during construction may be calculated at $I = \frac{1}{2}PCi$ where:

I = the interest accrued during the construction period,
P = the construction period in years,
C = the total capital expenditures,
i = the interest rate (discount rate in section 6e).

(2) Where expenditures will not be uniform, or when the construction period will be greater than 4 years, interest during construction shall be calculated on a year-by-year basis.

g. *Useful life.* (1) The treatment works' useful life for a cost-effectiveness analysis shall be as follows:

Land—permanent.
Waste water conveyance structures (includes collection systems, outfall pipes, interceptors, force mains, tunnels, etc.)—50 years.
Other structures (includes plant building, concrete process tankage, basins, lift stations structures, etc.)—30–50 years.
Process equipment—15–20 years.
Auxiliary equipment—10–15 years.

(2) Other useful life periods will be acceptable when sufficient justification can be provided. Where a system or a component is for interim service, the anticipated useful life shall be reduced to the period for interim service.

h. *Salvage value.* (1) Land purchased for treatment works, including land used as part of the treatment process or for ultimate disposal of residues, may be assumed to have a salvage value at the end of the planning period at least equal to its prevailing market value at the time of the analysis. In calculating the salvage value of land, the land value shall be appreciated at a compound rate of 3 percent annually over the planning period, unless the Regional Administrator determines that the grantee has justified the use of a greater or lesser percentage based upon historical differences between local land cost escalation and construction cost escalation. The land cost escalation rate may be updated periodically in accordance with Agency guidelines. Right-of-way easements shall be considered to have a salvage value not greater than the prevailing market value at the time of the analysis.

(2) Structures will be assumed to have a salvage value if there is a use for them at the end of the planning period. In this case, salvage value shall be estimated using straight line depreciation during the useful life of the treatment works.

(3) The method used in paragraph 6h(2) may be used to estimate salvage value at the end of the planning period for phased additions of process equipment and auxiliary equipment.

(4) When the anticipated useful life of a facility is less than 20 years (for analysis of interim facilities), salvage value can be claimed for equipment if it can be clearly demonstrated that a specific market or reuse opportunity will exist.

7. *Innovative and alternative wastewater treatment processes and techniques.*

a. Beginning October 1, 1978, the capital costs of publicly owned treatment works which use processes and techniques meeting the criteria of appendix E to this subpart and which have only a water pollution control function, may be eligible if the present worth cost of the treatment works is not more than 115 percent of the present worth cost of the most cost-effective pollution control system, exclusive of collection sewers and interceptors common to the two systems being compared, by 115 percent, except for the following situation.

b. Where innovative or alternative unit processes would serve in lieu of conventional unit processes in a conventional waste water treatment plant, and the present worth costs of the nonconventional unit processes are less than 50 percent of the present worth costs of the treatment plant, multiply the present worth costs of the replaced conventional processes by 115 percent, and add the cost of nonreplaced unit processes.

c. The eligibility of multipurpose projects which combine a water pollution control function with another function, and which use processes and techniques meeting the criteria of appendix E to this subpart, shall be determined in accordance with guidance issued by the Administrator.

d. The above provisions exclude individual systems under § 35.918. The regional Administrator may allow a grantee to apply the 15-percent preference authorized by this section to facility plans prepared under step 1 grant assistance awarded before October 1, 1978.

ALASKA ENACTS LIFE CYCLE COST LAW, 1975

The state of Alaska has permitted to come into law, effective July 3, 1975, a new law that requires procurement of public facilities to be analyzed based on life cycle costs. Chapter 216 of the laws of Alaska were amended as follows:

Section 1. As 35.10 is amended by adding new sections to read:
Article 5. Public Facility Procurement Policy
Section 35.10.160 Findings and Purpose
The legislature finds that, since the needs of the state for physical facilities of all kinds are diverse, the planning, design and construction of public facilities should be executed in accordance with facility procurement policies development by the Department of Public Works and reviewed annually by the legislature.
Section 35.10.170 Duties of Department
In addition to other duties prescribed by statute, the department shall

(1) develop facility procurement policies for the planning, design, construction, maintenance and operation of public facilities of the state;

(2) develop and maintain an inventory of physical facilities currently owned or occupied by the state;

(3) make projections of future public facility needs of the state, analyze facilities needed, and establish methodology for program planning and facilities project planning, design and construction;

(4) engage in experimental projects as necessary relating to any available or future method of facility procurement, design or construction and any method of improving existing design, planning and construction techniques;

(5) develop life cycle costs of public facilities of the state;

(6) develop life cycle costing methodologies for the following special purposes:

(A) budget forecasting to support facility program planning and analysis,
(B) systematic cost estimating to forecast planning, design and construction,
(C) budget forecasting to support development of annual maintenance and operating strategies and life cycle cost plans,
(D) alternative methods of space acquisition and space equalization which will maximize the effectiveness of public funds;

(7) apply for and accept, on behalf of the state, grants from the federal government or an agency of it or from another state foundation, corporation, association or individual for any of the functions or purposes of the department and may expend any of the money received under this section for any of the functions or purposes of the department.

Section 35.10.180 Physical Facility Procurement and Planning Policies
(a) The department shall develop and keep current by periodic revision physical procurement and planning policies for rural schools, public buildings, and other state facilities, and shall develop regulations and guidelines for the implementation of these policies.

(b) In developing and revising these policies the department shall seek public review and evaluation by any reasonable means and shall

(1) consult and cooperate with officials of the federal government, local governments, other political subdivisions of the state, and other interested persons regarding physical facility procurement planning;

(2) request and receive from an agency or other unit of the state government the assistance and data needed to carry out the requirements of this section.

(c) The commissioner shall submit copies of proposed policies and plans annually, within ten days after the legislature convenes, to the legislature. The legislature may approve, reject or modify the policies and plans before they are approved.

Section 35.10.190 Coordination By Department
(a) The department shall coordinate the procurement of physical facilities for the state to insure the greatest cost savings of planning, design and contractual techniques.

(b) When the state or an agency of the state determines that a public facility is to be constructed or renovated, it shall, unless exempted by regulations of the department, submit to the department an application for a certificate that the proposed facility complies with adopted facility procurement policies. The department may reject the application, but if it does so it shall state in writing the reasons for the rejection. If a written statement that the application is rejected does not issue within 30 days after receipt of the application by the department, unless the department and the applicant have agreed upon an extension of time for consideration, the certificate of compliance shall not be required. Except as provided otherwise by regulation or by this section, no public facility of the state may be constructed or renovated by the state unless a certificate that the facility complies with adopted facility procurement has been issued.

Section 35.10.200 Definitions (in Sections 160–200 of this chapter),

(1) "life cycle costs" means analytic techniques which provide data to describe the first cost of procurement of public facilities and the maintenance cost, operation cost, and occupancy cost of the facilities;

(2) "policies" includes but is not limited to budget accounting, and cost planning techniques, and contractual techniques for the procurement of labor, materials and contractual services;

(3) "public facilities" does not include highways or vessels of the marine highway system.

Section 2 There is within the Department of Public Works a public facility procurement planning fund. The fund is a working capital reserve fund and consists of money appropriated by the legislature for the purpose of providing procurement planning working capital and is available on a reimbursable basis for procurement planning. The fund shall be used by the commissioner to develop facility procurement planning methodologies for submission for review by the legislature by January 1, 1976. The commissioner shall prepare a report delineating the various procurement policies which shall govern the expenditures of capital funds necessary for the implementation of these policies.

Section 3 AS 35.05.040 is amended by adding a new paragraph to read:

(10) procure directly materials, labor and contractual services for planning, designing and constructing public facilities of the state

Section 4 This act takes effect immediately in accordance with AS 01.10.070(c).

APPENDIX C
ECONOMIC TABLES

This appendix provides the reader with quick reference tables to deal with the time value of money. Several chapters in the text (expecially the economics chapter) refer to these tables for conversion factors. This appendix provides material for use in present worth and the annualized analysis for LCC. Of special significance are the present worth of annuity tables which incorporate various escalation rates. For a discussion in the use of these tables, refer to Chapter 3, "Economics."

TABLE C-1
PRESENT WORTH (PW)

Compound Interest Factors

Present Worth (PW)
What $1 Due in the Future is Worth Today

(Present Worth) Single Payment

Yrs.	6% Present Worth	7% Present Worth	8% Present worth	9% Present worth	10% Present worth	12% Present worth	14% Present worth	16% Present worth	18% Present worth	20% Present worth	Yrs.
1	0.943396	0.934579	0.925926	0.917431	0.909091	0.892857	0.877193	0.862069	0.847458	0.833333	1
2	0.889996	0.873439	0.857339	0.841680	0.826446	0.797194	0.769468	0.743163	0.718184	0.694444	2
3	0.839169	0.816298	0.793832	0.772183	0.751315	0.711780	0.674972	0.640658	0.608631	0.578704	3
4	0.792094	0.762895	0.735030	0.708425	0.683013	0.635518	0.592080	0.552291	0.515789	0.482253	4
5	0.747258	0.712986	0.680583	0.649931	0.620921	0.567427	0.519369	0.476113	0.437109	0.401878	5
6	0.704961	0.666342	0.630170	0.596267	0.564474	0.506631	0.455587	0.410442	0.370432	0.334898	6
7	0.665057	0.622750	0.583490	0.547034	0.513158	0.452349	0.399637	0.353830	0.313925	0.279082	7
8	0.627412	0.582009	0.540269	0.501866	0.466507	0.403883	0.350559	0.305025	0.266038	0.232568	8
9	0.591898	0.543934	0.500249	0.460428	0.424098	0.360610	0.307508	0.262953	0.225456	0.193807	9
10	0.558395	0.508349	0.463193	0.422411	0.385543	0.321973	0.269744	0.226684	0.191064	0.161506	10
11	0.526788	0.475093	0.428883	0.387533	0.350494	0.287476	0.236617	0.195417	0.161919	0.134588	11
12	0.496969	0.444012	0.397114	0.355535	0.318631	0.256675	0.207559	0.168463	0.137220	0.112157	12
13	0.468839	0.414964	0.367698	0.326170	0.289664	0.229174	0.182069	0.145227	0.116288	0.093464	13
14	0.442301	0.387817	0.340461	0.299246	0.263331	0.204620	0.159710	0.125195	0.098549	0.077887	14
15	0.417265	0.362446	0.315242	0.274538	0.239392	0.182696	0.140096	0.107927	0.083516	0.064905	15
16	0.393646	0.338735	0.291890	0.251870	0.217629	0.163122	0.122892				16
17	0.371364	0.316574	0.270269	0.231073	0.197845	0.145644	0.107800				17
18	0.350344	0.295864	0.250249	0.211994	0.179859	0.130040	0.094561				18
19	0.330513	0.276508	0.231712	0.194490	0.163508	0.116107	0.082948				19
20	0.311805	0.258419	0.214548	0.178431	0.148644	0.103667	0.072762	0.051385	0.036506	0.026084	20
21	0.294155	0.241513	0.198656	0.163698	0.135131	0.092560	0.063826				21
22	0.277505	0.225713	0.183941	0.150182	0.122846	0.082643	0.055988				22
23	0.261797	0.210947	0.170315	0.137781	0.111678	0.073788	0.049112				23
24	0.246979	0.197147	0.157699	0.126405	0.101526	0.065882	0.043081				24
25	0.232999	0.184249	0.146018	0.115968	0.092296	0.058823	0.037790	0.024465	0.015957	0.010482	25
26	0.210810	0.172195	0.135202	0.106393	0.083905	0.052521	0.033149				26
27	0.207368	0.160930	0.125187	0.097608	0.076278	0.046894	0.029078				27
28	0.195630	0.150102	0.115914	0.089548	0.069343	0.041869	0.025507				28
29	0.184557	0.140563	0.107328	0.082155	0.063039	0.037383	0.022375				29
30	0.174110	0.131367	0.099377	0.075371	0.057309	0.033378	0.019627	0.011648	0.006975	0.004212	30
31	0.164255	0.122773	0.092016	0.069148	0.052090	0.029802	0.017217				31
32	0.154957	0.114741	0.085200	0.063438	0.017362	0.026609	0.015102				32
33	0.146186	0.107235	0.078889	0.058200	0.043057	0.023758	0.013248				33
34	0.137912	0.100219	0.073045	0.053395	0.039143	0.021212	0.011621				34
35	0.130105	0.093663	0.067635	0.048986	0.035584	0.018940	0.010194	0.005546	0.0030488	0.001693	35
36	0.122741	0.087535	0.062625	0.044941	0.032349	0.016910	0.008942				36
37	0.115793	0.081809	0.057986	0.041231	0.029408	0.015098	0.007844				37
38	0.109239	0.076457	0.053690	0.037826	0.026735	0.013481	0.006880				38
39	0.103056	0.071455	0.049713	0.034703	0.024304	0.012036	0.006035				39
40	0.097222	0.066780	0.046031	0.031838	0.022095	0.010747	0.005294	0.002640	0.001333	0.000680	40

Formula

$$P = F \left[\frac{1}{(1+i)^n} \right]$$

i   Represents an interest rate per interest period.
n   Represents a number of interest periods.
P   Represents a present sum of money.
F   Represents a sum of money at the end of n periods from the present date that is equivalent to P with interest i.

TABLE C-2
PRESENT WORTH OF ANNUITY (PWA)

Compound Interest Factors

Present Worth of Annuity (PWA)
What $1 Payable Periodically is Worth Today

Yrs.	6% Present worth	7% Present worth	8% Present worth	9% Present worth	10% Present worth	12% Present worth	14% Present worth	16% Present worth	18% Present worth	20% Present worth	Yrs.
1	0.943396	0.934570	0.925926	0.917431	0.909001	0.89286	0.877193	0.862089	0.847458	0.833333	1
2	1.833393	1.808018	1.783265	1.759111	1.735537	1.69005	1.646661	1.605232	1.565642	1.527778	2
3	2.673012	2.624316	2.577097	2.531295	2.486852	2.40183	2.321632	2.245890	2.174273	2.106481	3
4	3.465106	3.387211	3.312127	3.329720	3.169865	3.03735	2.913712	2.798181	2.690062	2.588735	4
5	4.212364	4.100197	3.992710	3.889651	3.790787	3.60477	3.433081	3.274294	3.127171	2.990612	5
6	4.917324	4.766540	4.622880	4.485919	4.355261	4.11140	3.888668	3.684736	3.497603	3.325510	6
7	5.582381	5.389289	5.206370	5.032953	4.868419	4.56375	4.288305	4.038565	3.811528	3.604592	7
8	6.209794	5.971299	5.746639	5.534819	5.334926	4.96764	4.638864	4.343591	4.077566	3.837160	8
9	6.801602	6.515232	6.246888	5.995247	5.759024	5.32825	4.946372	4.606544	4.303022	4.030967	9
10	7.360087	7.023582	6.710081	6.417658	6.144567	5.65023	5.216116	4.833227	4.494086	4.192472	10
11	7.886875	7.498674	7.138964	6.805191	6.495061	5.93771	5.452733	5.028644	4.656005	4.327060	11
12	8.383844	7.942686	7.536078	7.160725	6.813692	6.19437	5.660292	5.197107	4.793225	4.439217	12
13	8.852683	8.357651	7.903776	7.486904	7.103356	6.42356	5.842362	5.342334	4.909513	4.532681	13
14	9.294984	8.745468	8.244237	7.786150	7.366687	6.62818	6.002072	5.467529	5.008062	4.610567	14
15	10.712249	9.107914	8 559479	8.060688	7.606080	6.81088	6.142168	5.575456	5.091578	4.675473	15
16	10.105895	9.446649	8.851369	8.312558	7.823709	6.97399	6.265060				16
17	10.477260	9.763223	9.121638	8.543631	8.021553	7.11962	6.372859				17
18	10.827603	10.059087	9.371887	8.755625	8.201412	7.24969	6.467420				18
19	11.158116	10.335595	9.603599	8.950115	8.364920	7.36578	6.550369				19
20	11.409921	10.594014	9.818147	9.128546	8.513564	7.46943	6.623131	5.928844	5.352744	4.869580	20
21	11.764077	10.835527	10.016803	9.292244	8.648694	7.56201	6.686957				21
22	12.041582	11.061240	10.200744	9.442425	8.771540	7.64462	6.742944				22
23	12.303379	11.272187	10.371059	9.580207	8.883218	7.71843	6.792056				23
24	12.550358	11.469334	10.528758	9.706612	8.984744	7.78434	6.835137				24
25	12.783356	11.653583	10.674776	9.822580	9.077040	7.84314	6.872927	6.097094	5.466905	4.947590	25
26	13.003186	11.825779	10.809978	9.928972	9.160945	7.89565	6.906077				26
27	13.210536	11.986709	10.935165	10.026580	9.237223	7.94256	6.935155				27
28	13.406166	12.137111	11.051078	10.116128	9.306567	7.98441	6.960662				28
29	13.590721	12.277674	11.158406	10.198283	9.369606	8.02182	6.983037				29
30	13.764831	12.409041	11.257783	10.273654	9.426914	8.05516	7.002664	6.177200	5.516805	4.978940	30
31	13.929086	12.531814	11.349799	10.342802	9.479013	8.08499	7.019881				31
32	14.084013	12.646555	11.434999	10.406240	9.526376	8.11162	7.034983				32
33	14.230230	12.753790	11.513888	10.464441	9.569432	8.13537	7.048231				33
34	14.368141	12.854009	11.586934	10.517835	9.608575	8.15654	7.059852				34
35	14.498246	12.947672	11.654568	10.566821	9.644159	8.17548	7.070045	6.215337	5.538618	4.991535	35
36	14.620987	13.035208	11.717193	10.611763	9.676508	8.19242	7.078987				36
37	14.736780	13.117017	11.775179	10.652993	9.705917	8.20749	7.086831				37
38	14.846019	13.193473	11.828869	10.690820	9.732651	8.22098	7.093711				38
39	14.949073	13.264928	11.878582	10.722523	9.756956	8.23303	7.099747				39
40	15.046297	13.331700	11.924613	10.757360	9.779051	8.24375	7.105041	6.233500	5.548150	4.996600	40

Formula

$$P = A \left[\frac{(1+i)^n - 1}{i(1+i)^n} \right]$$

A Represents the end-of-period payment or receipt in a uniform series continuing for the coming n periods, the entire series equivalent to P at interest rate i.

TABLE C-3
PERIODIC PAYMENT (PP). CAPITAL RECOVERY

Compound Interest Factors

Periodic Payment (PP)
Periodic Payment Necessary to Pay Off a Loan of $1
(Capital Recovery) Annuities (Uniform Series Payments)

Yrs	6% Capital recovery	7% Capital recovery	8% Capital recovery	9% Capital recovery	10% Capital recovery	12% Capital recovery	14% Capital recovery	16% Capital recovery	18% Capital recovery	20% Capital recovery	Yrs.
1	1.060000	1.070000	1.080000	1.090000	1.100000	1.120000	1.14000000	1.16000000	1.18000000	1.20000000	1
2	0.545437	0.553092	0.560769	0.568469	0.576190	0.591698	0.60728972	0.62296296	0.63871560	0.65454545	2
3	0.374110	0.381052	0.388034	0.395055	0.402115	0.416349	0.43073148	0.44525787	0.45992386	0.47472527	3
4	0.288591	0.295228	0.301921	0.308669	0.315471	0.329234	0.34320478	0.35737507	0.37173867	0.38628912	4
5	0.237396	0.243891	0.250156	0.257092	0.263797	0.277410	0.29128355	0.30540938	0.31977784	0.33437970	5
6	0.203363	0.209796	0.216315	0.222920	0.229607	0.243226	0.25715750	0.27138987	0.28591013	0.30070575	6
7	0.179135	0.185553	0.192072	0.198691	0.205405	0.219118	0.23319238	0.24761268	0.26236200	0.27742393	7
8	0.161036	0.167468	0.174015	0.180674	0.187444	0.201303	0.21557002	0.23022426	0.24524436	0.26060942	8
9	0.147022	0.153486	0.160080	0.166799	0.173641	0.187679	0.20216838	0.21708249	0.23239482	0.24807946	9
10	0.135868	0.142378	0.149029	0.155820	0.162745	0.176984	0.19171354	0.20690108	0.22251464	0.23852276	10
11	0.126793	0.133357	0.140076	0.146947	0.153963	0.168415	0.18339427	0.19886075	0.21477639	0.23110379	11
12	0.119277	0.125902	0.132695	0.139651	0.146763	0.161437	0.17666933	0.19241473	0.20862781	0.22526496	12
13	0.112960	0.119651	0.126522	0.133567	0.140779	0.155677	0.17116366	0.18718411	0.20368621	0.22062000	13
14	0.107585	0.114345	0.211297	0.128433	0.135746	0.150871	0.16660914	0.18289797	0.19967806	0.21689306	14
15	0.102963	0.109795	0.116830	0.124059	0.131474	0.146824	0.16280896	0.17935752	0.19640278	0.21388212	15
16	0.098952	0.105858	0.112977	0.120300	0.127817	0.143390	0.15961540				16
17	0.095445	0.102425	0.109629	0.117046	0.124664	0.140457	0.15691544				17
18	0.092357	0.099413	0.106702	0.114212	0.121930	0.137937	0.15462115				18
19	0.089621	0.096753	0.104128	0.111730	0.119547	0.135763	0.15266316				19
20	0.087185	0.094393	0.101852	0.109546	0.117460	0.133879	0.15098600	0.168667	0.186820	0.205356	20
21	0.085005	0.092289	0.099832	0.107617	0.115624	0.132240	0.14954486				21
22	0.083016	0.090106	0.098032	0.105905	0.114005	0.130811	0.14830317				22
23	0.081278	0.088714	0.096422	0.104382	0.112572	0.129560	0.14723081				23
24	0.079679	0.087189	0.094978	0.103023	0.111300	0.128463	0.14630284				24
25	0.078227	0.085811	0.093679	0.101806	0.110168	0.127500	0.14549841	0.164012	0.182919	0.202119	25
26	0.076904	0.081561	0.092507	0.100715	0.109159	0.126652	0.14480001				26
27	0.075697	0.083426	0.091448	0.099735	0.108258	0.125904	0.14419288				27
28	0.074593	0.082392	0.090489	0.098852	0.107451	0.125244	0.14366449				28
29	0.073580	0.081449	0.089619	0.098056	0.106728	0.124660	0.14320417				29
30	0.072649	0.089586	0.088827	0.097336	0.106079	0.124144	0.14280279	0.161886	0.181264	0.200846	30
31	0.071792	0.079797	0.088107	0.096686	0.105496	0.123686	0.14245256				31
32	0.071002	0.079073	0.087451	0.096090	0.104972	0.123280	0.14214675				32
33	0.070273	0.078408	0.086852	0.095562	0.101499	0.122920	0.14187958				33
34	0.069598	0.077797	0.086304	0.095077	0.104074	0.122601	0.14164604				34
35	0.068974	0.077234	0.085803	0.094636	0.103690	0.122317	0.14144181	0.160892	0.180550	0.200339	35
36	0.068395	0.076715	0.085345	0.094235	0.103343	0.122064	0.14126315				36
37	0.067857	0.076237	0.084924	0.093870	0.103030	0.121840	0.14110680				37
38	0.067358	0.075795	0.084539	0.093538	0.102747	0.121640	0.14096993				38
39	0.066894	0.075387	0.084185	0.093236	0.102491	0.121462	0.14085010				39
40	0.066462	0.075009	0.083860	0.092960	0.102259	0.121304	0.14074514	0.160423	0.180240	0.200136	40

Formula

$$A = P \left[\frac{i(1+i)^n}{(1+i)^n - 1} \right]$$

TABLE C-4
PRESENT WORTH OF AN ESCALATING ANNUAL AMOUNT, 6%

PRESENT WORTH OF AN ESCALATING ANNUAL AMOUNT

6 PERCENT DISCOUNT RATE

$$P = A \frac{\left[\dfrac{1+e}{1+i}\right]\cdot\left[\left(\dfrac{1+e}{1+i}\right)^n - 1\right]}{\dfrac{1+e}{1+i} - 1}$$

where e represents the escalation rate
Note: when e=i, P=A·n

ESCALATION RATE

YEAR	0%	1%	2%	3%	4%	5%	6%	7%	8%	9%	10%	11%	12%	13%	14%	YEAR
1	0.943	0.953	0.962	0.972	0.981	0.991	1.000	1.009	1.019	1.028	1.038	1.047	1.057	1.066	1.075	1
2	1.833	1.861	1.888	1.916	1.944	1.972	2.000	2.028	2.057	2.086	2.115	2.144	2.173	2.202	2.232	2
3	2.673	2.726	2.779	2.833	2.888	2.944	3.000	3.057	3.115	3.173	3.232	3.292	3.353	3.414	3.476	3
4	3.465	3.550	3.637	3.725	3.815	3.907	4.000	4.095	4.192	4.291	4.392	4.494	4.599	4.705	4.814	4
5	4.212	4.335	4.462	4.591	4.724	4.860	5.000	5.143	5.290	5.441	5.595	5.754	5.916	6.082	6.253	5
6	4.917	5.084	5.256	5.433	5.616	5.805	6.000	6.201	6.409	6.623	6.844	7.072	7.307	7.550	7.800	6
7	5.582	5.797	6.019	6.251	6.491	6.741	7.000	7.269	7.549	7.839	8.140	8.453	8.778	9.115	9.464	7
8	6.210	6.476	6.755	7.046	7.350	7.668	8.000	8.347	8.710	9.089	9.485	9.899	10.331	10.782	11.254	8
9	6.802	7.124	7.462	7.818	8.192	8.586	9.000	9.435	9.893	10.375	10.881	11.413	11.972	12.561	13.179	9
10	7.360	7.740	8.143	8.568	9.019	9.496	10.000	10.534	11.099	11.697	12.329	12.998	13.707	14.456	15.249	10
11	7.887	8.328	8.798	9.298	9.830	10.397	11.000	11.643	12.327	13.056	13.832	14.659	15.539	16.477	17.475	11
12	8.384	8.888	9.428	10.006	10.625	11.289	12.000	12.762	13.578	14.454	15.392	16.397	17.475	18.631	19.870	12
13	8.853	9.422	10.034	10.695	11.406	12.173	13.000	13.892	14.854	15.891	17.010	18.218	19.521	20.927	22.445	13
14	9.295	9.930	10.618	11.364	12.172	13.049	14.000	15.032	16.153	17.369	18.690	20.125	21.683	23.375	25.214	14
15	9.712	10.414	11.180	12.014	12.924	13.916	15.000	16.183	17.476	18.889	20.433	22.121	23.967	25.985	28.192	15
16	10.106	10.876	11.720	12.645	13.661	14.776	16.000	17.346	18.825	20.452	22.242	24.212	26.380	28.767	31.396	16
17	10.477	11.316	12.240	13.259	14.384	15.627	17.000	18.519	20.199	22.059	24.116	26.401	28.930	31.733	34.841	17
18	10.828	11.735	12.740	13.856	15.094	16.470	18.000	19.703	21.599	23.712	26.067	28.693	31.624	34.894	38.545	18
19	11.158	12.134	13.222	14.435	15.790	17.305	19.000	20.898	23.025	25.411	28.088	31.094	34.470	38.265	42.530	19
20	11.470	12.515	13.685	14.998	16.473	18.132	20.000	22.105	24.479	27.159	30.186	33.608	37.478	41.858	46.815	20
21	11.764	12.877	14.131	15.546	17.144	18.952	21.000	23.323	25.959	28.955	32.363	36.240	40.656	45.688	51.424	21
22	12.042	13.223	14.560	16.077	17.801	19.764	22.000	24.552	27.468	30.803	34.622	38.997	44.014	49.771	56.381	22
23	12.303	13.552	14.973	16.594	18.447	20.568	23.000	25.793	29.005	32.703	36.966	41.884	47.562	54.124	61.711	23
24	12.550	13.865	15.370	17.096	19.080	21.364	24.000	27.046	30.571	34.657	39.398	44.906	51.311	58.764	67.444	24
25	12.783	14.164	15.752	17.584	19.701	22.153	25.000	28.311	32.167	36.666	41.923	48.072	55.272	63.711	73.610	25
26	13.003	14.449	16.120	18.058	20.310	22.935	26.000	29.587	33.793	38.732	44.543	51.386	59.457	68.984	80.241	26
27	13.211	14.720	16.474	18.519	20.908	23.709	27.000	30.876	35.449	40.857	47.261	54.858	63.879	74.606	87.372	27
28	13.406	14.979	16.815	18.966	21.495	24.476	28.000	32.176	37.137	43.042	50.082	58.492	68.552	80.599	95.042	28
29	13.591	15.225	17.143	19.401	22.070	25.236	29.000	33.489	38.857	45.288	53.010	62.299	73.488	86.987	103.290	29
30	13.765	15.460	17.458	19.824	22.635	25.988	30.000	34.815	40.609	47.598	56.040	66.284	78.705	93.798	112.161	30
31	13.929	15.683	17.761	20.234	23.189	26.734	31.000	36.153	42.394	49.973	59.201	70.458	84.216	101.058	121.701	31
32	14.084	15.896	18.053	20.633	23.733	27.472	32.000	37.503	44.212	52.416	62.473	74.829	90.040	108.798	131.962	32
33	14.230	16.099	18.334	21.021	24.266	28.203	33.000	38.866	46.065	54.928	65.868	79.406	96.193	117.048	142.997	33
34	14.368	16.293	18.605	21.398	24.789	28.928	34.000	40.242	47.953	57.511	69.391	84.198	102.695	125.844	154.864	34
35	14.498	16.477	18.865	21.764	25.303	29.645	35.000	41.631	49.877	60.167	73.047	89.217	109.564	135.220	167.628	35
36	14.621	16.653	19.115	22.120	25.807	30.356	36.000	43.034	51.837	62.898	76.842	94.473	116.822	145.216	181.354	36
37	14.737	16.820	19.356	22.465	26.301	31.061	37.000	44.449	53.834	65.706	80.779	99.976	124.492	155.872	196.117	37
38	14.846	16.979	19.588	22.801	26.786	31.758	38.000	45.878	55.869	68.594	84.865	105.739	132.595	167.231	211.994	38
39	14.949	17.131	19.811	23.128	27.261	32.449	39.000	47.320	57.942	71.564	89.105	111.774	141.157	179.341	229.069	39
40	15.046	17.276	20.026	23.445	27.728	33.133	40.000	48.776	60.054	74.618	93.506	118.093	150.204	192.250	247.432	40

TABLE C-5
PRESENT WORTH OF AN ESCALATING ANNUAL AMOUNT, 8%

PRESENT WORTH OF AN ESCALATING ANNUAL AMOUNT

8 PERCENT DISCOUNT RATE

ESCALATION RATE

YEAR	0%	1%	2%	3%	4%	5%	6%	7%	8%	9%	10%	11%	12%	13%	14%
1	0.926	0.935	0.944	0.954	0.963	0.972	0.981	0.991	1.000	1.009	1.019	1.028	1.037	1.046	1.056
2	1.783	1.810	1.836	1.863	1.890	1.917	1.945	1.972	2.000	2.028	2.056	2.084	2.112	2.141	2.170
3	2.577	2.628	2.679	2.731	2.783	2.836	2.890	2.945	3.000	3.056	3.112	3.170	3.228	3.286	3.346
4	3.312	3.393	3.474	3.558	3.643	3.730	3.818	3.908	4.000	4.093	4.189	4.286	4.384	4.485	4.587
5	3.993	4.108	4.226	4.347	4.471	4.598	4.729	4.863	5.000	5.141	5.285	5.432	5.584	5.739	5.898
6	4.623	4.777	4.936	5.099	5.268	5.443	5.623	5.809	6.000	6.197	6.401	6.611	6.828	7.051	7.281
7	5.206	5.402	5.605	5.817	6.035	6.264	6.500	6.745	7.000	7.264	7.538	7.823	8.118	8.424	8.741
8	5.747	5.987	6.239	6.501	6.776	7.062	7.361	7.674	8.000	8.341	8.696	9.068	9.455	9.860	10.282
9	6.247	6.534	6.837	7.154	7.488	7.838	8.207	8.593	9.000	9.427	9.876	10.347	10.842	11.363	11.909
10	6.710	7.046	7.401	7.777	8.173	8.593	9.036	9.505	10.000	10.524	11.077	11.662	12.281	12.935	13.626
11	7.139	7.525	7.935	8.370	8.834	9.326	9.850	10.407	11.000	11.630	12.301	13.014	13.773	14.580	15.439
12	7.536	7.972	8.438	8.937	9.469	10.039	10.649	11.302	12.000	12.747	13.547	14.403	15.320	16.301	17.352
13	7.904	8.391	8.914	9.476	10.082	10.733	11.434	12.188	13.000	13.875	14.817	15.831	16.925	18.102	19.371
14	8.244	8.782	9.353	9.991	10.671	11.407	12.203	13.066	14.000	15.012	16.110	17.299	18.588	19.987	21.503
15	8.559	9.148	9.787	10.483	11.239	12.062	12.959	13.935	15.000	16.161	17.426	18.807	20.314	21.958	23.753
16	8.851	9.490	10.188	10.951	11.786	12.699	13.700	14.797	16.000	17.319	18.768	20.357	22.103	24.021	26.129
17	9.122	9.810	10.556	11.398	12.312	13.319	14.428	15.651	17.000	18.489	20.134	21.951	23.959	26.180	28.636
18	9.372	10.110	10.924	11.824	12.819	13.921	15.142	16.497	18.000	19.670	21.525	23.588	25.883	28.438	31.282
19	9.604	10.390	11.251	12.230	13.307	14.507	15.843	17.335	19.000	20.861	22.942	25.271	27.879	30.801	34.075
20	9.818	10.651	11.580	12.618	13.777	15.076	16.531	18.165	20.000	22.063	24.386	27.001	29.949	33.273	37.024
21	10.017	10.896	11.881	12.987	14.230	15.629	17.207	18.988	21.000	23.277	25.856	28.779	32.095	35.860	40.137
22	10.201	11.125	12.156	13.340	14.666	16.167	17.870	19.802	22.000	24.502	27.353	30.506	34.321	38.566	43.422
23	10.371	11.339	12.434	13.676	15.086	16.691	18.520	20.610	23.000	25.738	28.878	32.484	36.629	41.398	46.890
24	10.529	11.539	12.688	13.996	15.490	17.199	19.155	21.410	24.000	26.985	30.431	34.414	39.022	44.361	50.550
25	10.675	11.727	12.928	14.302	15.879	17.694	19.785	22.202	25.000	28.245	32.013	36.398	41.505	47.461	54.414
26	10.810	11.902	13.154	14.594	16.254	18.174	20.401	22.987	26.000	29.515	33.625	38.436	44.079	50.704	58.493
27	10.935	12.066	13.357	14.872	16.615	18.642	21.004	23.765	27.000	30.798	35.266	40.532	46.749	54.098	62.798
28	11.051	12.219	13.569	15.137	16.963	19.096	21.597	24.536	28.000	32.092	36.938	42.686	49.517	57.649	67.342
29	11.158	12.362	13.760	15.390	17.297	19.538	22.178	25.300	29.000	33.399	38.640	44.899	52.338	61.364	72.139
30	11.258	12.496	13.940	15.631	17.620	19.967	22.749	26.056	30.000	34.717	40.374	47.174	55.365	65.251	77.202
31	11.350	12.621	14.110	15.861	17.930	20.385	23.309	26.806	31.000	36.048	42.140	49.512	58.453	69.319	82.547
32	11.435	12.738	14.270	16.080	18.229	20.791	23.859	27.548	32.000	37.391	43.939	51.915	61.655	73.574	88.189
33	11.514	12.848	14.422	16.290	18.517	21.186	24.399	28.284	33.000	38.746	45.771	54.385	64.976	78.027	94.143
34	11.587	12.950	14.555	16.489	18.794	21.569	24.928	29.013	34.000	40.114	47.638	56.924	68.419	82.685	100.429
35	11.655	13.046	14.701	16.680	19.061	21.942	25.448	29.735	35.000	41.495	49.538	59.533	71.993	87.560	107.064
36	11.717	13.136	14.828	16.861	19.318	22.305	25.958	30.450	36.000	42.889	51.474	62.214	75.694	92.660	114.068
37	11.775	13.220	14.949	17.034	19.565	22.658	26.459	31.159	37.000	44.295	53.446	64.970	79.534	97.996	121.460
38	11.829	13.298	15.063	17.199	19.804	23.001	26.951	31.861	38.000	45.714	55.454	67.803	83.517	103.579	129.264
39	11.879	13.371	15.171	17.357	20.033	23.334	27.431	32.556	39.000	47.147	57.500	70.714	87.647	109.420	137.501
40	11.925	13.440	15.272	17.507	20.254	23.658	27.907	33.246	40.000	48.593	59.583	73.706	91.930	115.533	146.195

TABLE C-6
PRESENT WORTH OF AN ESCALATING ANNUAL AMOUNT, 10%

PRESENT WORTH OF AN ESCALATING ANNUAL AMOUNT

10 PERCENT DISCOUNT RATE

ESCALATION RATE

YEAR	0%	1%	2%	3%	4%	5%	6%	7%	8%	9%	10%	11%	12%	13%	14%	YEAR
1	0.909	0.918	0.927	0.936	0.945	0.955	0.964	0.973	0.982	0.991	1.000	1.009	1.018	1.027	1.036	1
2	1.736	1.761	1.787	1.813	1.839	1.866	1.892	1.919	1.946	1.973	2.000	2.027	2.055	2.083	2.110	2
3	2.487	2.535	2.584	2.634	2.684	2.735	2.787	2.839	2.892	2.946	3.000	3.055	3.110	3.167	3.224	3
4	3.170	3.246	3.324	3.403	3.483	3.566	3.649	3.735	3.821	3.910	4.000	4.092	4.185	4.280	4.377	4
5	3.791	3.899	4.009	4.123	4.239	4.358	4.480	4.605	4.734	4.865	5.000	5.138	5.279	5.424	5.573	5
6	4.355	4.498	4.645	4.797	4.953	5.115	5.281	5.453	5.630	5.812	6.000	6.194	6.394	6.599	6.812	6
7	4.868	5.048	5.234	5.428	5.629	5.837	6.053	6.278	6.509	6.750	7.000	7.259	7.528	7.807	8.096	7
8	5.335	5.553	5.781	6.019	6.267	6.526	6.796	7.078	7.372	7.680	8.000	8.334	8.683	9.047	9.426	8
9	5.759	6.017	6.288	6.572	6.871	7.184	7.513	7.858	8.220	8.601	9.000	9.419	9.859	10.321	10.806	9
10	6.145	6.443	6.758	7.090	7.441	7.812	8.203	8.616	9.053	9.513	10.000	10.514	11.057	11.630	12.235	10
11	6.495	6.834	7.194	7.575	7.981	8.411	8.866	9.354	9.870	10.416	11.000	11.617	12.276	12.974	13.716	11
12	6.814	7.193	7.598	8.030	8.491	8.983	9.510	10.072	10.672	11.314	12.000	12.733	13.517	14.355	15.251	12
13	7.103	7.523	7.972	8.455	8.973	9.530	10.127	10.770	11.460	12.202	13.000	13.858	14.781	15.774	16.842	13
14	7.367	7.825	8.320	8.853	9.429	10.051	10.723	11.449	12.233	13.082	14.000	14.995	16.068	17.231	18.491	14
15	7.606	8.103	8.642	9.226	9.860	10.549	11.296	12.109	12.993	13.954	15.000	16.139	17.378	18.729	20.200	15
16	7.824	8.358	8.941	9.576	10.268	11.024	11.849	12.752	13.738	14.818	16.000	17.294	18.713	20.267	21.971	16
17	8.022	8.593	9.218	9.903	10.653	11.477	12.382	13.377	14.470	15.674	17.000	18.461	20.071	21.847	23.806	17
18	8.201	8.808	9.475	10.209	11.018	11.910	12.895	13.985	15.189	16.525	18.000	19.638	21.454	23.470	25.708	18
19	8.365	9.005	9.713	10.496	11.362	12.323	13.390	14.576	15.895	17.363	19.000	20.825	22.862	25.137	27.679	19
20	8.514	9.187	9.934	10.764	11.688	12.718	13.867	15.151	16.586	18.196	20.000	22.024	24.296	26.850	29.722	20
21	8.649	9.353	10.139	11.015	11.996	13.094	14.326	15.711	17.260	19.022	21.000	23.233	25.756	28.610	31.839	21
22	8.772	9.506	10.329	11.251	12.287	13.454	14.769	16.255	17.930	19.840	22.000	24.453	27.243	30.417	34.033	22
23	8.883	9.647	10.505	11.471	12.562	13.797	15.196	16.784	18.591	20.650	23.000	25.685	28.756	32.274	36.307	23
24	8.985	9.776	10.668	11.678	12.822	14.124	15.607	17.299	19.235	21.454	24.000	26.927	30.297	34.181	38.664	24
25	9.077	9.894	10.819	11.871	13.069	14.437	16.003	17.800	19.867	22.250	25.000	28.181	31.866	36.141	41.106	25
26	9.161	10.003	10.960	12.052	13.301	14.735	16.384	18.287	20.468	23.038	26.000	29.446	33.464	38.154	43.638	26
27	9.237	10.102	11.090	12.221	13.521	15.020	16.752	18.761	21.097	23.820	27.000	30.723	35.090	40.222	46.261	27
28	9.307	10.194	11.211	12.380	13.729	15.291	17.107	19.222	21.695	24.594	28.000	32.012	36.746	42.346	48.979	28
29	9.370	10.278	11.323	12.528	13.926	15.551	17.448	19.671	22.283	25.361	29.000	33.312	38.433	44.528	51.797	29
30	9.427	10.355	11.426	12.667	14.112	15.799	17.777	20.107	22.859	26.122	30.000	34.624	40.150	46.770	54.717	30
31	9.479	10.426	11.523	12.798	14.287	16.035	18.095	20.532	23.426	26.875	31.000	35.947	41.898	49.073	57.743	31
32	9.526	10.491	11.612	12.920	14.453	16.261	18.400	20.944	23.982	27.622	32.000	37.283	43.678	51.438	60.879	32
33	9.569	10.551	11.695	13.034	14.610	16.476	18.695	21.346	24.527	28.362	33.000	38.631	45.490	53.868	64.129	33
34	9.606	10.606	11.771	13.141	14.759	16.682	18.979	21.736	25.063	29.095	34.000	39.992	47.335	56.365	67.497	34
35	9.644	10.657	11.843	13.241	14.899	16.878	19.252	22.116	25.589	29.821	35.000	41.364	49.214	58.929	70.988	35
36	9.677	10.703	11.909	13.335	15.032	17.065	19.516	22.486	26.106	30.541	36.000	42.749	51.127	61.564	74.606	36
37	9.706	10.745	11.970	13.423	15.158	17.244	19.770	22.845	26.613	31.254	37.000	44.147	53.075	64.270	78.355	37
38	9.733	10.784	12.027	13.505	15.276	17.415	20.014	23.195	27.111	31.961	38.000	45.553	55.058	67.050	82.241	38
39	9.757	10.820	12.079	13.582	15.389	17.578	20.250	23.535	27.600	32.661	39.000	46.981	57.077	69.906	86.268	39
40	9.779	10.853	12.128	13.654	15.495	17.733	20.478	23.866	28.080	33.355	40.000	48.417	59.133	72.840	90.441	40

TABLE C-7
PRESENT WORTH OF AN ESCALATING ANNUAL AMOUNT, 12%

PRESENT WORTH OF AN ESCALATING ANNUAL AMOUNT

12 PERCENT DISCOUNT RATE

ESCALATION RATE

YEAR	0%	1%	2%	3%	4%	5%	6%	7%	8%	9%	10%	11%	12%	13%	14%	YEAR
1	0.893	0.902	0.911	0.920	0.929	0.937	0.946	0.955	0.964	0.973	0.982	0.991	1.000	1.009	1.018	1
2	1.690	1.715	1.740	1.765	1.791	1.816	1.842	1.868	1.894	1.920	1.947	1.973	2.000	2.027	2.054	2
3	2.402	2.448	2.495	2.543	2.591	2.640	2.690	2.740	2.791	2.842	2.894	2.947	3.000	3.054	3.108	3
4	3.037	3.110	3.185	3.258	3.335	3.415	3.492	3.575	3.657	3.737	3.825	3.912	4.000	4.090	4.182	4
5	3.605	3.706	3.810	3.916	4.025	4.137	4.252	4.369	4.489	4.612	4.736	4.866	5.000	5.136	5.274	5
6	4.111	4.244	4.380	4.521	4.660	4.816	4.970	5.129	5.293	5.462	5.636	5.815	6.000	6.190	6.386	6
7	4.564	4.729	4.900	5.078	5.262	5.452	5.650	5.850	6.060	6.267	6.517	6.754	7.000	7.255	7.518	7
8	4.968	5.166	5.375	5.589	5.814	6.049	6.294	6.550	6.819	7.094	7.363	7.685	8.000	8.328	8.670	8
9	5.328	5.561	5.804	6.060	6.328	6.609	6.903	7.213	7.537	7.877	8.234	8.606	9.000	9.412	9.843	9
10	5.650	5.916	6.197	6.492	6.804	7.133	7.480	7.846	8.232	8.637	9.069	9.522	10.000	10.504	11.037	10
11	5.938	6.237	6.554	6.890	7.247	7.625	8.026	8.451	8.902	9.381	9.889	10.428	11.000	11.607	12.252	11
12	6.194	6.526	6.880	7.256	7.658	8.086	8.542	9.027	9.549	10.103	10.694	11.326	12.000	12.720	13.488	12
13	6.424	6.787	7.176	7.593	8.039	8.518	9.031	9.581	10.172	10.805	11.486	12.210	13.000	13.842	14.747	13
14	6.628	7.022	7.446	7.902	8.394	8.923	9.494	10.109	10.775	11.487	12.263	13.098	14.000	14.975	16.028	14
15	6.811	7.234	7.692	8.187	8.723	9.303	9.931	10.613	11.352	12.155	13.026	13.972	15.000	16.117	17.332	15
16	6.974	7.426	7.916	8.449	9.028	9.659	10.340	11.095	11.911	12.802	13.775	14.838	16.000	17.270	18.660	16
17	7.120	7.598	8.126	8.689	9.312	9.993	10.738	11.555	12.450	13.433	14.511	15.697	17.000	18.433	20.011	17
18	7.250	7.754	8.306	8.911	9.575	10.306	11.109	11.994	12.970	14.040	15.234	16.548	18.000	19.607	21.386	18
19	7.366	7.894	8.475	9.114	9.820	10.599	11.460	12.414	13.471	14.643	15.945	17.391	19.000	20.791	22.786	19
20	7.469	8.020	8.629	9.302	10.047	10.874	11.793	12.815	13.954	15.224	16.642	18.227	20.000	21.985	24.210	20
21	7.562	8.134	8.769	9.474	10.258	11.132	12.108	13.198	14.420	15.789	17.327	19.055	21.000	23.191	25.661	21
22	7.645	8.237	8.897	9.632	10.454	11.374	12.405	13.565	14.867	16.340	18.000	19.870	22.000	24.407	27.137	22
23	7.718	8.330	9.013	9.778	10.636	11.600	12.687	13.914	15.302	16.875	18.660	20.690	23.000	25.633	28.639	23
24	7.784	8.414	9.119	9.912	10.805	11.813	12.954	14.249	15.720	17.396	19.309	21.496	24.000	26.870	30.168	24
25	7.843	8.489	9.216	10.035	10.961	12.012	13.207	14.568	16.123	17.904	19.947	22.295	25.000	28.120	31.725	25
26	7.896	8.557	9.304	10.148	11.107	12.199	13.445	14.873	16.512	18.397	20.573	23.087	26.000	29.380	33.309	26
27	7.943	8.619	9.384	10.252	11.242	12.374	13.672	15.164	16.886	18.877	21.187	23.872	27.000	30.651	34.922	27
28	7.984	8.674	9.456	10.348	11.368	12.538	13.886	15.443	17.247	19.345	21.791	24.650	28.000	31.934	36.563	28
29	8.022	8.724	9.523	10.436	11.484	12.692	14.088	15.709	17.596	19.800	22.384	25.421	29.000	33.228	38.234	29
30	8.055	8.769	9.583	10.517	11.593	12.836	14.280	15.963	17.931	20.243	22.967	26.185	30.000	34.534	39.935	30
31	8.085	8.809	9.636	10.592	11.693	12.971	14.461	16.205	18.255	20.674	23.539	26.942	31.000	35.851	41.666	31
32	8.112	8.846	9.689	10.660	11.787	13.098	14.633	16.437	18.568	21.094	24.100	27.693	32.000	37.180	43.428	32
33	8.135	8.879	9.734	10.723	11.873	13.217	14.796	16.659	18.869	21.502	24.652	28.437	33.000	38.521	45.221	33
34	8.157	8.909	9.776	10.781	11.954	13.328	14.949	16.871	19.159	21.899	25.194	29.174	34.000	39.874	47.046	34
35	8.176	8.935	9.814	10.835	12.028	13.433	15.095	17.073	19.439	22.285	25.726	29.905	35.000	41.239	48.904	35
36	8.192	8.960	9.848	10.884	12.098	13.531	15.233	17.266	19.709	22.662	26.249	30.629	36.000	42.616	50.795	36
37	8.208	8.981	9.880	10.929	12.162	13.623	15.363	17.450	19.970	23.026	26.763	31.346	37.000	44.005	52.720	37
38	8.221	9.001	9.908	10.970	12.222	13.709	15.486	17.627	20.221	23.385	27.267	32.057	38.000	45.407	54.680	38
39	8.233	9.019	9.934	11.008	12.278	13.789	15.603	17.795	20.463	23.731	27.762	32.762	39.000	46.821	56.674	39
40	8.244	9.035	9.958	11.043	12.329	13.865	15.714	17.956	20.696	24.069	28.248	33.461	40.000	48.248	58.704	40

TABLE C-8
PRESENT WORTH OF AN ESCALATING ANNUAL AMOUNT, 15%

PRESENT WORTH OF AN ESCALATING ANNUAL AMOUNT

15 PERCENT DISCOUNT RATE

ESCALATION RATE

YEAR	0%	1%	2%	3%	4%	5%	6%	7%	8%	9%	10%	11%	12%	13%	14%	YEAR
1	0.870	0.878	0.887	0.896	0.904	0.913	0.922	0.930	0.939	0.948	0.957	0.965	0.974	0.983	0.991	1
2	1.626	1.650	1.674	1.698	1.722	1.747	1.771	1.796	1.821	1.846	1.871	1.897	1.922	1.948	1.974	2
3	2.283	2.327	2.371	2.416	2.462	2.508	2.554	2.602	2.649	2.698	2.747	2.796	2.846	2.897	2.948	3
4	2.855	2.922	2.990	3.060	3.131	3.203	3.276	3.351	3.427	3.505	3.584	3.664	3.746	3.829	3.914	4
5	3.352	3.445	3.539	3.636	3.736	3.837	3.942	4.048	4.158	4.270	4.384	4.502	4.622	4.745	4.871	5
6	3.784	3.903	4.026	4.152	4.283	4.417	4.555	4.697	4.844	4.995	5.150	5.310	5.475	5.645	5.820	6
7	4.160	4.307	4.458	4.615	4.777	4.946	5.120	5.301	5.488	5.682	5.883	6.091	6.306	6.530	6.761	7
8	4.487	4.661	4.841	5.029	5.225	5.429	5.641	5.863	6.093	6.333	6.584	6.844	7.116	7.399	7.693	8
9	4.772	4.971	5.181	5.400	5.629	5.870	6.121	6.385	6.661	6.951	7.254	7.571	7.904	8.253	8.618	9
10	5.019	5.244	5.482	5.732	5.995	6.272	6.564	6.871	7.195	7.536	7.895	8.273	8.672	9.092	9.534	10
11	5.234	5.484	5.749	6.029	6.326	6.640	6.972	7.324	7.696	8.091	8.508	8.951	9.419	9.916	10.442	11
12	5.421	5.695	5.986	6.296	6.625	6.976	7.348	7.745	8.167	8.616	9.095	9.605	10.148	10.726	11.343	12
13	5.583	5.880	6.197	6.535	6.896	7.282	7.695	8.136	8.609	9.115	9.656	10.236	10.857	11.522	12.236	13
14	5.724	6.042	6.383	6.748	7.141	7.562	8.014	8.501	9.024	9.587	10.193	10.845	11.548	12.305	13.120	14
15	5.847	6.185	6.548	6.940	7.362	7.817	8.309	8.840	9.414	10.035	10.706	11.433	12.220	13.073	13.998	15
16	5.954	6.310	6.695	7.111	7.562	8.051	8.580	9.155	9.780	10.459	11.197	12.001	12.875	13.828	14.867	16
17	6.047	6.420	6.825	7.265	7.743	8.264	8.831	9.449	10.124	10.861	11.667	12.548	13.513	14.571	15.729	17
18	6.128	6.517	6.941	7.403	7.907	8.458	9.061	9.722	10.447	11.242	12.116	13.077	14.135	15.300	16.584	18
19	6.198	6.602	7.043	7.526	8.055	8.636	9.274	9.976	10.750	11.603	12.546	13.587	14.740	16.016	17.431	19
20	6.259	6.676	7.134	7.635	8.189	8.798	9.470	10.213	11.035	11.946	12.957	14.080	15.329	16.720	18.271	20
21	6.312	6.742	7.214	7.735	8.310	8.946	9.650	10.433	11.302	12.270	13.350	14.556	15.903	17.412	19.103	21
22	6.359	6.799	7.286	7.823	8.419	9.081	9.817	10.637	11.553	12.578	13.726	15.014	16.462	18.092	19.928	22
23	6.399	6.850	7.349	7.903	8.518	9.204	9.970	10.828	11.789	12.870	14.086	15.457	17.007	18.760	20.746	23
24	6.434	6.894	7.405	7.974	8.608	9.317	10.112	11.005	12.011	13.146	14.430	15.885	17.537	19.416	21.557	24
25	6.464	6.933	7.455	8.037	8.689	9.420	10.242	11.170	12.217	13.408	14.759	16.298	18.054	20.061	22.361	25
26	6.491	6.967	7.499	8.094	8.762	9.514	10.362	11.323	12.414	13.656	15.074	16.696	18.557	20.695	23.158	26
27	6.514	6.998	7.539	8.145	8.828	9.600	10.473	11.466	12.598	13.892	15.375	17.081	19.046	21.318	23.948	27
28	6.534	7.024	7.573	8.191	8.888	9.678	10.575	11.599	12.770	14.115	15.663	17.452	19.523	21.930	24.731	28
29	6.551	7.047	7.604	8.232	8.942	9.749	10.669	11.722	12.932	14.326	15.939	17.810	19.988	22.531	25.507	29
30	6.566	7.067	7.632	8.269	8.991	9.815	10.756	11.837	13.084	14.526	16.202	18.156	20.441	23.122	26.277	30
31	6.579	7.085	7.656	8.302	9.036	9.874	10.836	11.944	13.227	14.716	16.454	18.489	20.881	23.702	27.039	31
32	6.591	7.101	7.677	8.331	9.076	9.929	10.910	12.044	13.361	14.896	16.695	18.811	21.310	24.272	27.796	32
33	6.600	7.115	7.696	8.357	9.112	9.978	10.978	12.136	13.485	15.067	16.926	19.122	21.728	24.833	28.545	33
34	6.609	7.127	7.713	8.381	9.145	10.024	11.040	12.223	13.605	15.229	17.147	19.422	22.135	25.384	29.288	34
35	6.617	7.138	7.728	8.402	9.174	10.065	11.098	12.303	13.716	15.382	17.356	19.712	22.532	25.925	30.025	35
36	6.623	7.147	7.742	8.421	9.201	10.103	11.151	12.377	13.820	15.527	17.559	19.992	22.918	26.457	30.755	36
37	6.629	7.155	7.753	8.438	9.225	10.137	11.200	12.447	13.918	15.665	17.753	20.261	23.294	26.979	31.479	37
38	6.634	7.162	7.764	8.453	9.247	10.169	11.245	12.511	14.010	15.795	17.937	20.522	23.660	27.492	32.197	38
39	6.638	7.169	7.773	8.467	9.267	10.198	11.287	12.571	14.096	15.919	18.114	20.775	24.017	27.997	32.908	39
40	6.642	7.174	7.781	8.479	9.285	10.224	11.326	12.627	14.177	16.036	18.283	21.016	24.364	28.493	33.613	40

TABLE C-9
PRESENT WORTH OF AN ESCALATING ANNUAL AMOUNT, 20%

PRESENT WORTH OF AN ESCALATING ANNUAL AMOUNT

20 PERCENT DISCOUNT RATE

ESCALATION RATE

YEAR	0%	1%	2%	3%	4%	5%	6%	7%	8%	9%	10%	11%	12%	13%	14%	YEAR
1	0.833	0.842	0.850	0.858	0.867	0.875	0.883	0.892	0.900	0.908	0.917	0.925	0.933	0.942	0.950	1
2	1.528	1.550	1.572	1.595	1.618	1.641	1.664	1.687	1.710	1.733	1.757	1.781	1.804	1.828	1.853	2
3	2.106	2.146	2.187	2.227	2.269	2.311	2.353	2.396	2.439	2.485	2.527	2.572	2.617	2.663	2.710	3
4	2.589	2.648	2.709	2.770	2.833	2.897	2.962	3.028	3.095	3.164	3.235	3.304	3.376	3.450	3.524	4
5	2.991	3.071	3.152	3.236	3.322	3.410	3.499	3.591	3.686	3.782	3.880	3.981	4.085	4.190	4.298	5
6	3.326	3.426	3.529	3.636	3.746	3.858	3.975	4.074	4.217	4.344	4.474	4.608	4.745	4.887	5.033	6
7	3.605	3.725	3.850	3.979	4.113	4.251	4.394	4.542	4.695	4.854	5.018	5.187	5.363	5.544	5.732	7
8	3.837	3.977	4.123	4.274	4.431	4.595	4.765	4.942	5.126	5.317	5.516	5.723	5.935	6.162	6.395	8
9	4.031	4.189	4.354	4.527	4.707	4.895	5.092	5.296	5.513	5.738	5.973	6.219	6.476	6.744	7.025	9
10	4.192	4.367	4.551	4.744	4.946	5.158	5.382	5.616	5.862	6.120	6.392	6.677	6.977	7.295	7.624	10
11	4.327	4.516	4.718	4.930	5.153	5.388	5.637	5.899	6.176	6.467	6.776	7.102	7.446	7.809	8.193	11
12	4.439	4.644	4.861	5.090	5.333	5.590	5.862	6.152	6.458	6.783	7.128	7.494	7.883	8.295	8.733	12
13	4.533	4.750	4.982	5.227	5.488	5.766	6.062	6.377	6.712	7.070	7.451	7.857	8.290	8.753	9.247	13
14	4.611	4.840	5.084	5.345	5.623	5.921	6.238	6.576	6.941	7.330	7.746	8.193	8.671	9.184	9.734	14
15	4.675	4.915	5.172	5.446	5.740	6.055	6.394	6.757	7.147	7.566	8.018	8.503	9.026	9.590	10.197	15
16	4.730	4.979	5.246	5.533	5.842	6.174	6.531	6.917	7.332	7.781	8.266	8.791	9.358	9.972	10.638	16
17	4.775	5.032	5.309	5.607	5.929	6.277	6.652	7.059	7.499	7.976	8.494	9.056	9.667	10.332	11.056	17
18	4.812	5.077	5.363	5.671	6.005	6.367	6.760	7.186	7.649	8.153	8.703	9.302	9.956	10.671	11.453	18
19	4.843	5.115	5.408	5.726	6.071	6.446	6.854	7.299	7.784	8.314	8.894	9.529	10.226	10.990	11.830	19
20	4.870	5.147	5.447	5.773	6.129	6.516	6.938	7.400	7.906	8.461	9.070	9.740	10.477	11.291	12.189	20
21	4.891	5.173	5.480	5.814	6.178	6.576	7.012	7.490	8.015	8.593	9.231	9.934	10.712	11.574	12.529	21
22	4.909	5.196	5.508	5.849	6.221	6.629	7.077	7.570	8.114	8.714	9.378	10.114	10.931	11.840	12.853	22
23	4.925	5.215	5.532	5.878	6.258	6.675	7.135	7.642	8.202	8.825	9.513	10.281	11.136	12.091	13.160	23
24	4.937	5.231	5.552	5.904	6.290	6.716	7.186	7.706	8.282	8.923	9.637	10.435	11.327	12.328	13.452	24
25	4.948	5.244	5.569	5.926	6.318	6.752	7.231	7.762	8.354	9.015	9.751	10.577	11.505	12.550	13.730	25
26	4.956	5.256	5.584	5.945	6.343	6.783	7.271	7.813	8.419	9.095	9.855	10.709	11.671	12.760	13.993	26
27	4.964	5.265	5.596	5.961	6.364	6.810	7.306	7.858	8.477	9.170	9.950	10.831	11.827	12.957	14.243	27
28	4.970	5.273	5.607	5.975	6.382	6.834	7.337	7.899	8.529	9.238	10.038	10.945	11.972	13.143	14.481	28
29	4.975	5.280	5.616	5.987	6.398	6.854	7.364	7.935	8.576	9.299	10.118	11.047	12.107	13.318	14.707	29
30	4.979	5.286	5.623	5.997	6.411	6.873	7.388	7.967	8.618	9.355	10.191	11.144	12.233	13.483	14.922	30
31	4.982	5.290	5.630	6.006	6.423	6.888	7.410	7.995	8.657	9.406	10.259	11.233	12.351	13.638	15.126	31
32	4.985	5.294	5.635	6.013	6.433	6.902	7.429	8.021	8.691	9.452	10.321	11.316	12.461	13.784	15.319	32
33	4.988	5.298	5.640	6.020	6.442	6.915	7.445	8.044	8.722	9.494	10.377	11.392	12.563	13.922	15.504	33
34	4.990	5.301	5.644	6.025	6.450	6.925	7.460	8.064	8.750	9.532	10.429	11.463	12.659	14.051	15.678	34
35	4.992	5.303	5.647	6.030	6.457	6.935	7.473	8.082	8.775	9.567	10.477	11.528	12.743	14.173	15.844	35
36	4.993	5.305	5.650	6.034	6.462	6.943	7.484	8.098	8.797	9.598	10.520	11.588	12.832	14.288	16.002	36
37	4.994	5.307	5.653	6.038	6.467	6.950	7.495	8.112	8.818	9.627	10.560	11.644	12.910	14.396	16.152	37
38	4.995	5.308	5.655	6.041	6.472	6.956	7.504	8.125	8.836	9.652	10.597	11.696	12.983	14.498	16.294	38
39	4.996	5.309	5.657	6.043	6.476	6.962	7.511	8.137	8.852	9.676	10.630	11.744	13.050	14.594	16.430	39
40	4.997	5.310	5.658	6.045	6.479	6.966	7.518	8.147	8.867	9.697	10.661	11.788	13.114	14.684	16.558	40

APPENDIX D
ENERGY-ESTIMATING DATA

This appendix assists the reader in budgeting and developing preliminary energy estimates for various types of facilities. These tables, when coupled with engineering judgment, allow the design professional to estimate the energy consumption of various design alternatives. Chapter 4, "Life Cycle Estimating Procedures," provides a discussion in the use of the tables.

Numerous energy consumption methods are available to the reader for similar but much more detailed analysis. A brief discussion of these methods is contained in Chapter 4. The bibliography also contains sources for more detailed information.

TABLE D-1a

FACTORS FOR DETERMINING HEAT LOSS FOR VARIOUS TYPES OF BUILDINGS

Building Type	Conditions	Qualifications	Loss Factor
Factories & Industrial Plants at 70°F Inside	One Story	Skylight in Roof No Skylight in Roof	6.2 5.7
	Multiple Story	Two Story Three Story Four Story Five Story Six Story	4.6 4.3 4.1 3.9 3.6
Warehouses, etc. at 60°F Inside	All Walls Exposed	Skylights in Roof No Skylights in Roof Heated Space Above	5.5 5.1 4.0
	One Long Warm Common Wall	Skylight in Roof No Skylight in Roof Heated Space Above	5.0 4.9 3.4
	Warm Common Walls on Both Long Sides	Skylight in Roof No Skylight in Roof Heated Space Above	4.7 4.4 3.0
General Office Areas at 70°F Inside	All Walls Exposed	Flat Roof Heated Space Above	6.9 5.2
	One Long Warm Common Wall	Flat Roof Heated Space Above	6.3 4.7
	Warm Common Walls on Both Long Sides	Flat Roof Heated Space Above	5.8 4.1

Outside Design Temperature	50	40	30	20	10	0	-10	-20	-30
Correction Factor	0.29	0.43	0.57	0.72	0.86	1.00	1.14	1.28	1.43

Design Heat Loss = Building Volume (CF) X Loss Factor X Correction Factor

SOURCE: *1979 Mechanical and Electrical Cost Data*, Robert Snow Means Company, Inc. Copyright 1979. Reproduced by permission.

$$E = \left(\frac{H_L \times D \times 24}{\Delta t \times \eta \times V}\right) (C_D)(C_F) \qquad\qquad (1)$$

where

E = Fuel or energy consumption for the estimate period.

H_L = Design heat loss, including infiltration, Btu per hour.

D = Number of 65 F degree days for the estimate period.

Δt = Design temperature difference, Fahrenheit.

η = Rated full load efficiency, decimal.

V = Heating value of fuel, consistent with H_L and E.

C_D = Interim correction factor for heating effect vs. degree days.

C_F = Interim part-load correction factor for fueled systems only; equals 1.0 for electric resistance heating.

Heat Loss vs. Degree Days Interim Factor C_D

Outdoor Design Temp, F	-20	-10	0	+10	+20
Factor C_D	0.57	0.64	0.71	0.79	0.89

The multipliers in the above Table are high for mild climates and low for cold regions, are not in error as might appear. For equivalent buildings, those in warm climates have a greater portion of their heating requirements on days when the mean temperature is close to 65°F, and thus the actual heat loss is not reflected.

Part-Load Correction Factor for Fuel-Fired Equipment

Percent oversizing	0	20	40	60	80
Factor C_F	1.36	1.56	1.79	2.04	2.32

Because equipment performance at extremely low loads is highly variable, it is strongly recommended that the values in the above Table not be extrapolated.

TABLE D-2
ANNUAL HEATING DEGREE DAYS

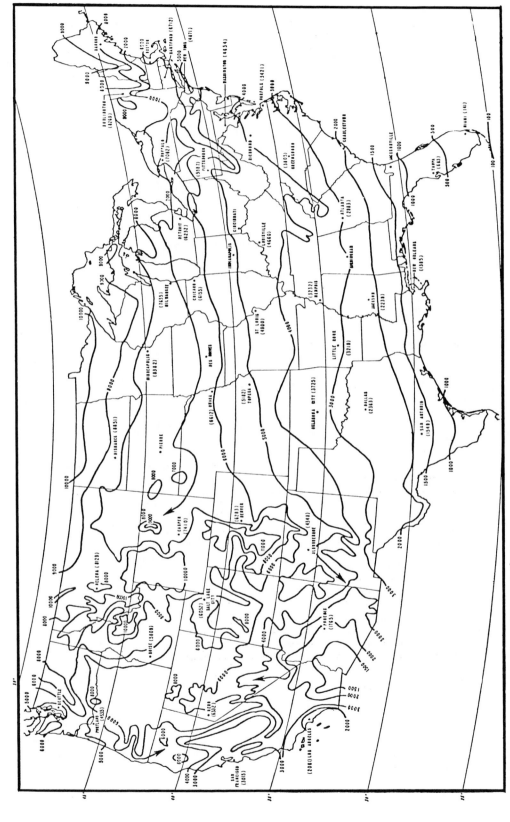

annual heating degree days (base 65° F)

Source: FEA Conservation Paper No. 20

TABLE D-3
APPROXIMATE AIR CONDITION REQUIREMENTS

Btu's per hour per S.F. of floor area and S.F. per ton of air conditioning. (Source: R.S. Means Mech. Elect. Data)

Type Building	Btu per S.F.	S.F. per ton	Type Building	Btu per S.F.	S.F. per ton
Apartments, individual	26	450	Hotel, Guest Room	44	275
Corridors	22	550	Public Spaces	55	220
Auditoriums & Theaters	666	18*	Corridors	30	400
Banks	50	240	Indus. Plants, Offices	38	320
Barber Shops	48	250	General Offices	34	350
Bars & Taverns	133	90	Plant Areas	40	300
Beauty Parlors	66	180	Libraries	50	240
Bowling Alley	68	175	Lo Rise Office, Exterior	38	320
Churches	600	20*	Interior	33	360
Cocktail Lounge	68	175	Medical Centers	28	425
Computer Rooms	141	85	Motels	28	425
Dental Offices	52	230	Office (small suite)	43	280
Dept. Stores, Basement	34	350	Post Office, Ind. Office	42	285
Main Floor	40	300	Central Area	46	260
Upper Floor	30	400	Residences	20	600
Dormitory, Rooms	40	300	Restaurants	60	200
Corridors	30	400	Schools & Colleges	46	260
Dress Shops	43	280	Shoe Stores	55	220
Drug Stores	80	150	Shop'g Ctrs., Super Markets	34	350
Factories	40	300	Retail Stores	48	250
High Rise Office — Ext. Rms.	46	263	Specialty Shops	60	200
Interior Rooms	37	325			
Hospitals, Core	43	280			
Perimeter	46	260			

Cooling, Energy Calculation
Equivalent Full Load Hours

$$E = T \times EH \times PI$$

Where

E	= Energy Consumption KWH	EH	= Equivalent full load hours
T	= Design tonnage	PI	= Power input per design ton

*PERSONS PER TON

Approximate Power Inputs

System	Compressor Kw/Design Ton	Auxiliaries Kw/Design Ton
Window Units	1.46	0.32
Through-Wall Units	1.64	0.30
Dwelling Unit, Central Air-Cooled	1.49	0.14
Central, Group, or Bldg. Cooling Plants		
(3 to 25 tons) Air-Cooled	1.20	0.20
(25 to 100 tons) Air-Cooled	1.18	0.21
(25 to 100 tons) Water-Cooled	0.94	0.17
(Over 100 tons) Water-Cooled	0.79	0.20

SOURCE: *1979 Mechanical and Electrical Cost Data*, Robert Snow Means Company, Inc. Copyright 1979. Reproduced by permission.

TABLE D-4
EQUIVALENT FULL-LOAD HOURS OF OPERATION PER YEAR

	Atlanta	Baltimore	Boston	Chicago	Dallas	Denver	Detroit	Los Angeles	Miami	Milwaukee	Minneapolis	New Orleans	Okla. City	Philadelphia	Phoenix	Portland Ore.	San Fran.	Saint Louis	Wash., D.C.	New York
Restaurants	1750	1620	1050	1250	2240	1050	1250	1150	2020	1050	1050	2020	2240	1480	2240	1050	450	2020	1820	1430
Drug Stores	1700	1580	1030	1220	2170	1030	1220	1120	1850	1030	1030	1950	2170	1440	2170	1030	400	1950	1580	1400
Cafeterias	1370	1270	825	990	1750	825	990	910	1580	825	825	1580	1750	1160	1750	825	350	1580	1270	1120
Jewelry Stores	1020	950	620	750	1300	620	750	700	1170	620	620	1170	1300	875	1300	620	250	1170	950	850
Barber Shops	1020	950	620	750	1300	620	750	700	1170	620	620	1170	1300	875	1300	620	250	1170	950	850
Night Clubs	1010	940	610	730	1280	610	730	675	1150	610	610	1150	1280	860	1280	610	240	1150	940	840
Theaters	650-1000	600-1000	400-650	500-800	850-1400	400-650	500-800	475-750	800-1300	400-650	400-650	800-1300	850-1400	550-920	850-1400	400-650	200-400	800-1300	600-1000	550-900
Dress Shops	940	870	565	675	1200	565	675	630	1080	565	565	1080	1200	800	1200	565	225	1080	870	780
Large Offices	915	850	550	660	1180	550	660	610	1060	550	550	1060	1180	775	1180	550	200	1060	850	750
Department Stores	850	790	515	650	1100	515	650	600	1000	515	515	1000	1100	725	1100	515	175	1000	790	700
Specialty Shops (5 & 10)	840	780	510	640	1080	510	640	590	975	510	510	975	1080	710	1080	510	175	975	780	700
Residences	810	750	490	600	1050	490	600	550	950	490	490	950	1050	690	1050	490	170	950	750	670
Shoe Stores	650	600	400	500	850	400	500	475	775	400	400	775	850	575	850	400	150	775	600	550
Beauty Shops	625	580	380	450	800	380	450	425	750	380	380	750	800	540	800	380	150	750	580	525
Small Offices	540	500	425	450	700	425	450	410	650	425	425	650	700	490	700	425	125	650	500	475
Recreation Spaces	520	480	450	400	675	450	400	380	650	450	450	650	675	470	675	450	125	650	480	450
Funeral Parlors	460	425	350	375	600	350	375	350	575	350	350	575	600	410	600	350	100	575	425	400

SOURCE: Trane Air Conditioning Manual.

195

TABLE D-5
VENTILATION ENERGY

Ventilation Volume

$$V = \frac{CS \times SF}{PO}$$

Where
V = CFM air supplied
CS = Average CFM/SF of outside air (0.1 to 0.3)
SF = Total square footage
PO = Percent outside air (0.1 to 0.25)

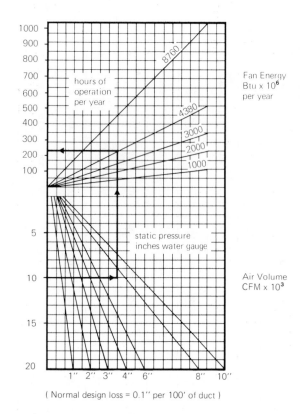

(Normal design loss = 0.1'' per 100' of duct)

SOURCE: Federal Energy Administration, *Conservation Paper No. 20.*

TABLE D-6
IES RECOMMENDED ILLUMINATION LEVELS IN FOOTCANDLES
(Source: R.S. Means)

Commercial Buildings		
Type	Description	Foot-Candles
Bank	Lobby	50
	Customer Areas	70
	Teller Stations	150
	Accounting Areas	150
Offices	Routine Work	100
	Accounting	150
	Drafting	200
	Corridors, Halls, Washrooms	30
Schools	Reading or Writing	70
	Drafting, Labs, Shops	100
	Libraries	70
	Auditoriums, Assembly	15
	Auditoriums, Exhibition	30
Stores	Circulation Areas	30
	Stock Rooms	30
	Merchandise Areas, Service	100
	Self-Service Areas	200

Industrial Buildings		
Type	Description	Foot-Candles
Assembly Areas	Rough bench & machine work	50
	Medium bench & machine work	100
	Fine bench & machine work	500
Inspection Areas	Ordinary	50
	Difficult	100
	Highly Difficult	200
Material Handling	Loading	20
	Stock Picking	30
	Packing, Wrapping	50
Stairways	Service Areas	20
Washrooms	Service Areas	20
Storage Areas	Inactive	5
	Active, Rough, Bulky	10
	Active, Medium	20
	Active, Fine	50
Garages	Active Traffic Areas	20
	Service & Repair	100

Lighting Energy Calculations

$$E = \frac{W \times SF \times Hr}{1000}$$

E = Annual Lighting Energy (KWH)
W = Approximate Watts/SF for area considered
SF = Square Footage of area served
Hr = Annual Use Hours

TABLE D-7
APPROXIMATE INITIAL LUMENS PER WATT
(Source: NEMA)

Lamp Type	Smaller Sizes	Middle Sizes	Larger Sizes
Low Pressure Sodium	90	120	150
High Pressure Sodium	84	105	126
Metal Halide	67	75	93
Fluorescent	66	74	70
Mercury	44	51	57
Incandescent	17	22	24

SOURCE: NEMA.

TABLE D-8
APPROXIMATE WATTS PER SQUARE FOOT FOR POPULAR FIXTURE TYPES

Calculation Of Approximate Footcandles (Initial)

$$FC = \left(\frac{TW \times L \times CU}{SF} \right) \times MF$$

Where
FC = Initial footcandles
TW = Total wattage
 L   = Initial lumens per watt (Table D-7)
CU = Coefficient of utilization (.3 to .6)
SF = Square footage served
MF = Maintenance factor (.8 - clean to .5 - dirty)

TABLE D—8
Approximate Watts Per Square Foot For Popular Fixture Types (Source R.S. Means)

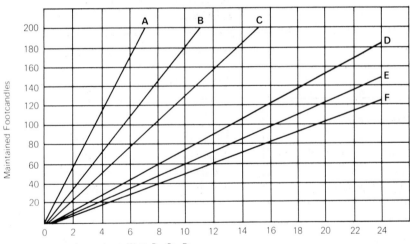

A. Fluorescent — industrial
B. Fluorescent — recessed
C. Fluorescent — louvered unit
D. Incandescent — open reflector
E. Incandescent — recessed
F. Incandescent — down light

SOURCE: *1979 Mechanical and Electrical Cost Data*, Robert Snow Means Company, Inc. Copyright 1979. Reproduced by permission.

Energy Calculation

$$E = \frac{GPD \times 8.3 \times t \times DAYS}{EFF.}$$

Where

E	=	Energy consumption (Btu)
GPD	=	Average gallons per day for facility
t	=	Temperature diff. (70 - 120)
DAYS	=	Average days of operation per year
EFF.	=	Efficiency of unit (Electric = 0.95, Gas = 0.75 & Oil = 0.70)

Type of Building	Maximum Hour	Maximum Day	Average Day
Men's Dormitories	3.8 gal/student	22.0 gal/student	13.1 gal/student
Women's Dormitories	5.0 gal/student	26.5 gal/student	12.3 gal/student
Motels: No. of Units**			
20 or less	6.0 gal/unit	35.0 gal/unit	20.0 gal/unit
60	5.0 gal/unit	25.0 gal/unit	14.0 gal/unit
100 or More	4.0 gal/unit	15.0 gal/unit	10.0 gal/unit
Nursing Homes	4.5 gal/bed	30.0 gal/bed	18.4 gal/bed
Office Buildings	0.4 gal/person	2.0 gal/person	1.0 gal/person
Food Service Establishments:			
Type A — Full Meal Restaurants and Cafeterias	1.5 gal/max meals/hr	11.0 gal/max meals/hr	2.4 gal/avg meals/day*
Type B — Drive-Ins, Grilles, Luncheonettes, Sandwich and Snack Shops	0.7 gal/max meals/hr	6.0 gal/max meals/hr	0.7 gal/avg meals/day*
Apartment Houses: No. of Apartments			
20 or less	12.0 gal/apt.	80.0 gal/apt.	42.0 gal/apt.
50	10.0 gal/apt.	73.0 gal/apt.	40.0 gal/apt.
75	8.5 gal/apt.	66.0 gal/apt.	38.0 gal/apt.
100	7.0 gal/apt.	60.0 gal/apt.	37.0 gal/apt.
200 or More	5.0 gal/apt.	50.0 gal/apt.	35.0 gal/apt.
Elementary Schools	0.6 gal/student	1.5 gal/student	0.6 gal/student*
Junior and Senior High Schools	1.0 gal/student	3.6 gal/student	1.8 gal/student*

* PER DAY OPERATION

** INTERPOLATE FOR INTERMEDIATE VALUES

SOURCE: ASPE Data Book, 1974.

TABLE D-10
PUMP ENERGY

Pump Horsepower (Closed System)

$$Hp = \frac{GPM \times HD}{EFF. \times 3960}$$

Where

Hp = Pump operating horsepower
GPM = Gallon per minute flow
HD = Total head (Ft.)
(Average loss = 1 to 5 Ft./100' of pipe)
(For open system, add static loss)
EFF. = Efficiency (0.6 to 0.75)

Pump Energy

$$E = Hp \times OH \times .746 \, KW/Hp$$

Where

E = Pump energy (KWH)
Hp = Pump horsepower
(Assumes average motor efficiency = 75%)
OH = Operating Hours per Year

TABLE D-11
HEATING VALUES FOR VARIOUS FUELS

Fuel	Average Heating Value
Fuel Oil	
Kerosene	134,000 Btu/gal.
No. 2 Burner Fuel Oil	140,000 Btu/gal.
No. 4 Heavy Fuel Oil	144,000 Btu/gal.
No. 5 Heavy Fuel Oil	150,000 Btu/gal.
No. 6 Heavy Fuel Oil 2.7% sulfur	152,000 Btu/gal.
No. 6 Heavy Fuel Oil 0.3% sulfur	143,800 Btu/gal.
Coal	
Anthracite	13,900 Btu/lb.
Bituminous	14,000 Btu/lb.
Sub-bituminous	12,600 Btu/lb.
Lignite	11,000 Btu/lb.
Gas	
Natural	1,000 Btu/cu. ft
Liquefied butane	103,300 Btu/gal.
Liquefied propane	91,600 Btu/gal.

TABLE D-12
LIST OF ENERGY CONVERSION FACTORS

1 U.S. barrel	= 42 U.S. gallons
1 atmosphere	= 14.7 pounds per square inch absolute (psia)
1 atmosphere	= 760 mm (29.92 in) mercury with density of 13.6 grams per cubic centimeter
1 pound per square inch	= 2.04 inches head of mercury
	= 2.31 feet head of water
1 inch head of water	= 5.20 pounds per square foot
1 foot head of water	= 0.433 pound per square inch
1 British thermal unit (Btu)	= heat required to raise the temperature of 1 pound of water by 1°F
1 therm	= 100,000 Btu
1 kilowatt (Kw)	= 1.341 horsepower (hp)
1 kilowatt-hour (Kwh)	= 1.34 horsepower-hour
1 horsepower (hp)	= 0.746 kilowatt (Kw)
1 horsepower-hour	= 0.746 kilowatt hour (Kwh)
1 horsepower-hour	= 2545 Btu
To generate 1 kilowatt-hour (Kwh) requires 10,000 Btu of fuel burned by average utility	
1 ton of refrigeration	= 12,000 Btu per hr
1 ton of refrigeration requires about 1 Kw (or 1.341 hp) in commercial air conditioning	
1 standard cubic foot is at standard conditions of 60°F and 14.7 psia.	
1 degree day	= 65°F minus mean temperature of the day, °F

Note: In these conversions, inches and feet of water are measured at 62°F (16.7°C), and inches and millimeters of mercury at 32°F (0°C).

PREFIXES:

Multiplying Factor	Prefix	Symbol
$1\,000\,000\,000\,000 = 10^{12}$	tera	T
$1\,000\,000\,000 = 10^{9}$	giga	G
$1\,000\,000 = 10^{6}$	mega	M
$1\,000 = 10^{3}$	kilo	k
$100 = 10^{2}$	hecto^a	h
$10 = 10^{1}$	deka^a	da
$0.1 = 10^{-1}$	deci^a	d
$0.01 = 10^{-2}$	centi^a	c
$0.001 = 10^{-3}$	milli	m
$0.000\,001 = 10^{-6}$	micro	μ
$0.000\,000\,001 = 10^{-9}$	nano	n
$0.000\,000\,000\,001 = 10^{-12}$	pico	p

UNITS:

	Units	
Dimensions	**English Engineering System**	**International System**
Mass	pound mass (lbm)	kilogram (kg)
Length	foot (ft)	meter (m)
Time	second (sec)	second (s)
Temperature	degree Fahrenheit (F)	degree Kelvin (K)

DERIVED UNITS:

Dimension	Unit	Special Name and Symbol
Energy	N-m	joule (J)
Force	$(kg\text{-}m)/s^2$	newton (N)
Frequency	$1/s$	hertz (Hz)
Power	J/s	watt (W)
Pressure - Stress	N/m^2	pascal (Pa)

CONVERSION FACTORS:

Length
1 m = 3.281 ft
1 m = 3.937 × 10 in.

Area
$1\ m^2 = 1.550 \times 10^3\ in.^2$
$1\ m^2 = 1.076 \times 10\ ft^2$

Volume
$1\ m^3 = 6.102 \times 10^4\ in.^3$
$1\ m^3 = 3.532 \times 10\ ft^3$
$1\ m^3 = 2.642 \times 10^2$ U.S. gallons

Mass
1 kg = 2.205 lbm

Force
$1\ N = 2.248 \times 10^{-1}\ lbf$

Energy
$1\ J = 9.478 \times 10^{-4}\ Btu = 7.376 \times 10^{-1}$ ft-lbf
$1\ kW\text{-}hr = 3.412 \times 10^3\ Btu = 2.655 \times 10^6$ ft-lbf

Power
1 W = 3.412 Btu/hr
$1\ W = 1.341 \times 10^{-3}$ hp
$1\ W = 2.844 \times 10^{-4}$ tons of refrigeration

Pressure
$1\ Pa = 1.450 \times 10^{-4}\ lbf/in.^2$
$1\ Pa = 2.088 \times 10^{-2}\ lbf/ft^2$
$1\ Pa = 9.869 \times 10^{-6}$ std atm
$1\ Pa = 2.961 \times 10^{-4}$ in. mercury
$1\ Pa = 4.019 \times 10^{-3}$ in. water

Temperature
1 deg R difference = 1 deg F difference = 5/9 deg C difference = 5/9 deg K difference
deg F = 9/5 (deg C) + 32

Velocity
$1\ m/s = 1.969 \times 10^2$ ft/min
1 m/s = 3.281 ft/sec

Acceleration
$1\ m/s^2 = 3.281\ ft/sec^2$

Mass Density
$1\ kg/m^3 = 6.243 \times 10^{-2}\ lbm/ft^3$

Mass Flow Rate
1 kg/s = 2.205 lbm/sec
$1\ kg/s = 7.937 \times 10^3$ lbm/hr

Volume Flow Rate
$1\ m^3/s = 2.119 \times 10^3\ ft^3/min$
$1\ m^3/s = 1.585 \times 10^4$ gal/min

Thermal Conductivity
$1\ \dfrac{W}{m\text{-}K} = 5.778 \times 10^{-1}\ \dfrac{Btu}{hr\text{-}ft\text{-}F}$

$1\ \dfrac{W}{m\text{-}K} = 6.934\ \dfrac{Btu\text{-}in}{hr\text{-}ft^2\text{-}F}$

Heat Transfer Coefficient
$1\ \dfrac{W}{m^2\text{-}K} = 1.761 \times 10^{-1}\ \dfrac{Btu}{hr\text{-}ft^2\text{-}F}$

Specific Heat
$1\ \dfrac{J}{kg\text{-}K} = 2.389 \times 10^{-4}\ \dfrac{Btu}{lbm\text{-}F}$

APPENDIX E
SELECT LIFE CYCLE COSTING DATA

This appendix provides the reader with example life cycle costing data for the areas of architectural, mechanical, electrical, and site. It is suggested that the readers organize their data in a similar fashion using the UNIFORMAT cost accounting structure. Chapter 4, "Life Cycle Estimating Procedures," provides a discussion in the use of such data.

All maintenance costs have been based on the assumption that the building owner will exercise a preventative maintenance program to meet or exceed the minimal standards of maintenance as recommended by the manufacturers of the installed equipment or materials. Failure to do this will result in escalated replacement and maintenance costs.

Equipment replacement costs are based on the assumption that the building owner will maintain a spare parts inventory on a repair and restore program rather than on a redundant equipment standby basis.

The design professional must use extreme care in the use of this information. Factors that influence these costs include: labor rates, in-house versus contracted maintenance, preventative maintenance program strategy, climatic conditions, functional-use of the facility, and management emphasis on maintenance. The authors assume no responsibility nor liability in connection with the use of this data.

ABBREVIATIONS USED FOR LIFE CYCLE COSTING DATA

Btu	British thermal units
ea.	Each item described
EU	Energy units
Flight	Per flight of item described
HW	Hot water
I.C.	Initial cost
kW	Kilowatt (power)
LF	Lineal foot of item described
LS	Lump sum total of item described
MH	Manhours of labor for maintenance
N/A	Not applicable to item described
RSF	Roof square foot of item described
SF	Square foot of item described
Stop	Per stop of elevator described
V	Volt
WSF	Wall square foot of item described

TABLE E-1

LIFE CYCLE DATA

ITEM DESCRIPTION		UNIT OF MEASURE	MAINTENANCE DESCRIPTION	MAINTENANCE ANNUAL COST			ENERGY DEMAND (EU)	REPLACE MENT LIFE (YRS)	PERCENT REPLACED
				LABOR	MATERIAL	EQUIPMENT			
04	EXTERIOR CLOSURE								
041	EXTERIOR WALLS								
0411	EXTERIOR WALL CONSTRUCTION								
	Masonry Veneer; 4" brick & 4" block, insulation & vapor barrier	WSF	Repointing joints (4.0min. every 15 years)	.06	.02	.001	N/A	75	100
	Aluminum Panel: insulation & vapor barrier	WSF	Minor repair, cleaning (2.0 min. every 6 years)	.08	.01	.001	N/A	50	100
	Metal Panel; insulation & vapor barrier	WSF	Minor repair, cleaning (2.0 min. every 6 years)	.08	.01	.001	N/A	40	100
04	EXTERIOR CLOSURE								
042	EXTERIOR DOORS & WINDOWS								
0421	WINDOWS								
	Fixed glazing frame, hardware	WSF	Lobby, storefront,: Wash and Squeegee dry both sides of glass. (.18 min/ week)	1,87	2,0	.04	N/A	40	100
		WSF	Office, other areas: (.18 min./quarter)	.14	.02	.01			
		WSF	Repair glazing, frame & hardware	.01	.01	.001			

ITEM DESCRIPTION		UNIT OF MEASURE	MAINTENANCE DESCRIPTION	MAINTENANCE ANNUAL COST			ENERGY DEMAND (EU)	REPLACE MENT LIFE (YRS)	PERCENT REPLACED
				LABOR	MATERIAL	EQUIPMENT			
04	EXTERIOR CLOSURE								
042	EXTERIOR DOORS & WINDOWS								
0423	EXTERIOR DOORS								
	Hollow metal door, frame, hardware	WSF	Damp clean both sides (.12 min/quarter)	.08	.01	.01	N/A	40	100
		WSF	Repair door, frame, hardware	.10	.05	.02			
	Solid Core Wood Door	WSF	Damp clean both sides (.12 min/quarter)	.08	.01	.01	N/A	40	100
		WSF	Repair door, frame, hardware	.12	.06	.02			
		WSF	Paint, 2 coats every 4 years	.07	.02	.02			
05	ROOFING								
0501	ROOF COVERINGS								
	Tar and gravel built-up Membrane roofing, 5 ply - 15# felt	RSF	Preventative inspection (.01 min. per year)	.001	N/A	N/A	N/A	20	100
		RSF	Minor repair (.02 min. per year)	.002	.001	N/A			
	Prepared roll Roofing, 15# felt	RSF	Preventative inspection (.01 min. per year)	.001	N/A	N/A	N/A	12	100
		RSF	Minor repair (.03 min. per year)	.003	.002	N/A			

TABLE E-1

(*continued*)

ITEM DESCRIPTION		UNIT OF MEASURE	MAINTENANCE DESCRIPTION	MAINTENANCE ANNUAL COST			ENERGY DEMAND (EU)	REPLACE MENT LIFE (YRS)	PERCENT REPLACED
				LABOR	MATERIAL	EQUIPMENT			
06	INTERIOR CONSTRUCTION								
061	PARTITIONS								
0611	FIXED PARTITIONS								
	Drywall Partitions, Metal or Wood Studs	WSF	Minor repair (1.0 min. every 10 years)	.03	.01	.001	N/A	35	100
06	INTERIOR CONSTRUCTION								
061	PARTITIONS								
0612	DEMOUNTABLE PARTITIONS								
	Baked Enamel Steel Partitions, Demountable, Full or Bank Height	WSF	Damp clean both sides (.12 min. per quarter)	.08	.01	N/A	N/A	25	100
		WSF	Minor repair (1.0 min. every 10 years)	.02	.01	.001			
06	INTERIOR CONSTRUCTION								
061	PARTITIONS								
0616	INTERIOR DOORS AND FRAMES								
	Hollow Metal Door and Frame, Hardware	WSF	Damp clean both sides (.12 min/quarter)	.08	.01	N/A	N/A	30	100
		WSF	Repair Door, Frame, Hardware	.08	.04	.01			
	Hollow Core Wood Door with Metal Frame, Hardware	WSF	Damp clean both sides (.12 min./quarter)	.08	.01	N/A	N/A	20	100
		WSF	Repair Door, Frame, Hardware	.10	.05	.02			
		WSF	Painting – 2 coats (1.0 every 6 years)	.03	.01	.001			

ITEM DESCRIPTION		UNIT OF MEASURE	MAINTENANCE DESCRIPTION	MAINTENANCE ANNUAL COST			ENERGY DEMAND (EU)	REPLACE MENT LIFE (YRS)	PERCENT REPLACED
				LABOR	MATERIAL	EQUIPMENT			
06	INTERIOR CONSTRUCTION								
062	INTERIOR FINISHES								
0621	WALL FINISHES								
	Interior Paint on Masonry	WSF	High Use Areas: Paint – 2 Coats (1.0 min. every 2 years)	.13	.03	.02	N/A	(See Maint)	N/A
		WSF	Low Use Areas Paint – 2 coats (1.0 min. every 7 years)	.04	.01	.01	N/A	(See Maint)	N/A
	Interior Paint on Drywall	WSF	Change of Color: Paint – 2 coats (1.0 min. every 2 years)	.13	.03	.02	N/A	(See Maint)	N/A
		WSF	Otherwise: Paint – 2 coats (1.0 min. every 7 years)	.04	.01	.01	N/A	(See Maint)	N/A
	Ceramic Tile, Glazed with Organic Adhesive	WSF	High Use Areas: Damp Cleaning Daily (.06 min. per day)	2.6	.10	.02	N/A	25	100
		WSF	Minor Repair Yearly	.01	.01	.001			
		WSF	Low Use Areas: Minor Cleaning	.10	.02	N/A			
		WSF	Minor Repairs, yearly	.01	.01	N/A			

ITEM DESCRIPTION		UNIT OF MEASURE	MAINTENANCE DESCRIPTION	MAINTENANCE ANNUAL COST			ENERGY DEMAND (EU)	REPLACE MENT LIFE (YRS)	PERCENT REPLACED
				LABOR	MATERIAL	EQUIPMENT			
06	INTERIOR CONSTRUCTION								
062	INTERIOR FINISHES								
0622	FLOOR FINISHES								
	Resilient Vinyl Tile, 1/8" Thick	SF	Cleaning, waxing (.2 min every month)	.40	.11	.02	N/A	20	100
	Carpeting, Standard Acrylic or Nylon	SF	Vacuuming, shampoo (.02 min. every week)	.17	.02	.01	N/A	12	100
	Terrazzo, 2½-3" Thick	SF	Cleaning, waxing (.2 min. every month)	.40	.11	.02	N/A	50	100
06	INTERIOR CONSTRUCTION								
062	INTERIOR FINISHES								
0623	CEILING FINISHES								
	Acoustical Tile, Exposed 2' x 4' Grid w/Hangers	SF	Cleaning & Repair (.05 min. per year)	.005	.005	N/A	N/A	10	100
	Acoustical Tile, Mineral Fiber, 12" x 12"	SF	Cleaning & Repair (.01 min per year)	.001	.001	N/A	N/A	12	100
	Gypsum Board, Painted	SF	Change of Color: Painting - 2 coats (1.0 min. every 2 years)	.13	.03	.02	N/A	(See Maint)	N/A
		SF	Useful Life: Painting - 2 coats (1.0 min every 7 years)	.04	.01	.01			

ITEM DESCRIPTION		UNIT OF MEASURE	MAINTENANCE DESCRIPTION	MAINTENANCE ANNUAL COST			ENERGY DEMAND (EU)	REPLACE MENT LIFE (YRS)	PERCENT REPLACED
				LABOR	MATERIAL	EQUIPMENT			
07	CONVEYING SYSTEM								
0701	ELEVATORS								
	Passenger Elevators - high Speed, automatic (25 HP; 75% efficiency)	Ea.	Remove gum, sweep and damp mop or vacuum carpet. Damp wipe walls trim and doors. Wax or shampoo as necessary (20.0 min. twice weekly)	346.6	15.0	3.0		20	100
		Stop	Inspection & Repair (35.0 hours per year)	525	500	50.0			
08	MECHANICAL								
081	PLUMBING								
0811	DOMESTIC WATER SUPPLY SYSTEM								
	o Domestic Hot Water Generators								
	Electric Heated Hot Water Generator Residential, Glass Lined, 100% Eff., 8 Gal.-120 Gal./Hr. Recovery Rate	ea.	Preventative maintenance & repair (.5 MH/year)	7.5	1.0	.1	.22 KW per Gal. (50°F. incoming water)	20	100
08	MECHANICAL								
081	PLUMBING								
0814	PLUMBING FIXTURES								
	o Water Closets								
	Floor Mounted Water Closets washdown & siphon jet types	ea.	Clean interior & exterior surfaces (5.0 min./day)	83.0	5.0	1.0	N/A	25	100
		ea.	Maintenance & repair as required (1.0 MH/year)	15.0	2.0	.5			

ITEM DESCRIPTION	UNIT OF MEASURE	MAINTENANCE DESCRIPTION	MAINTENANCE ANNUAL COST			ENERGY DEMAND (EU)	REPLACEMENT LIFE (YRS)	PERCENT REPLACED
			LABOR	MATERIAL	EQUIPMENT			
08 MECHANICAL 081 PLUMBING 0814 PLUMBING FIXTURES (cont'd.)								
Wall Mounted Water Closets washdown & siphon jet types	ea.	Clean interior & exterior surfaces (4.5 min./day)	76.0	5.0	1.0	N/A	25	100
	ea.	Maintenance & repair as required (1.0 MH/year)	15.0	2.0	.5			
o Lavatories								
Vitreous China, Wall Hung Lavatory, 20" x 18" Size	ea.	Clean interior & exterior surfaces (4.5 min./day)	76.0	5.0	1.0	N/A	20	100
	ea.	Maintenance & repair as required (1.0 MH/year)	15.0	2.0	.5			
	ea.	Maintenance & repair as required (1.0 MH/year)	15.0	2.0	.5			
Enameled Steel, Wall Hung Lavatory 20" x 18" Size	ea.	Clean interior & exterior surfaces (4.5 min./day)	76.0	5.0	1.0	N/A	25	100
	ea.	Maintenance & repair as required (1.0 MH/year)	15.0	2.0	.5			
08 MECHANICAL 082 HVAC 0821 ENERGY SUPPLY								
o Pumps; up to 3" -Oil	ea.	Preventative inspection & general maintenance - repack. glands, seals, etc. (1.0 MH/year)	15.0	5.0	1.0	3.7 KW	15	50

ITEM DESCRIPTION	UNIT OF MEASURE	MAINTENANCE DESCRIPTION	MAINTENANCE ANNUAL COST			ENERGY DEMAND (EU)	REPLACEMENT LIFE (YRS)	PERCENT REPLACED
			LABOR	MATERIAL	EQUIPMENT			
08 MECHANICAL 082 HVAC 0822 HEAT GENERATING SYSTEM								
o Boilers - Steam -Packaged Marine Type (NO. 2 Oil)								
40 HP	ea.	Preventative & insurance inspection and general maintenance (350 MH/year)	5,000	350	100	1.25 KW	25	100
50 HP	ea.	Preventative & insurance inspection and general maintenance (350 MH/year)	5,000	400	120	1.6 KW	25	100
150 HP	ea,	Preventative & insurance inspection and general maintenance (400 MH/year)	6,000	500	150	6.4 KW	25	100
o Furnaces								
-Up Flow - Gas Fired								
80,0000 BTU	ea,	Preventative and insurance inspection and general maintenance (20 MH/year)	308	10	4	0.25 KW	20	100
105,000 BTU	ea.	Preventative & insurance inspection and general maintenance (20 MH/year)	300	10	4	.35 KW	20	100

ITEM DESCRIPTION	UNIT OF MEASURE	MAINTENANCE DESCRIPTION	MAINTENANCE ANNUAL COST			ENERGY DEMAND (EU)	REPLACEMENT LIFE (YRS)	PERCENT REPLACED
			LABOR	MATERIAL	EQUIPMENT			
08 MECHANICAL 082 HVAC 0823 COOLING GENERATING SYSTEM								
ᵒWater Chillers								
-Reciprocating Compressor Electric								
81 Ton Capacity	ea.	Preventative & insurance inspection and general maintenance (160 MH/year)	2,400	1,000	350	as req'd	20	100
-Centrifugal Compressor Electric								
120 Ton Capacity	ea.	Preventative & insurance inspection and general maintenance (100 MH/year)	1,500	1,150	300	as req'd	20	100
ᵒ Cooling Towers								
.Packaged Centrifugal Blow Thru								
200 Ton Capacity	ea.	Preventative & insurance inspection and general maintenance (140 MH/year)	2,100	880	280	as req'd	15	100

ITEM DESCRIPTION	UNIT OF MEASURE	MAINTENANCE DESCRIPTION	MAINTENANCE ANNUAL COST			ENERGY DEMAND (EU)	REPLACEMENT LIFE (YRS)	PERCENT REPLACED
			LABOR	MATERIAL	EQUIPMENT			
08 MECHANICAL 082 HVAC 0824 DISTRIBUTION SYSTEMS								
ᵒAir Handling Equipment								
.Single zone with mixing box HW coil, CW coil, flat filter								
1750 - 2750 CFM	ea.	Preventative & insurance inspection and general maintenance (20 MY/year)	300	90	30	0.75 KW	20	100
.Single zone with mixing box HW coil, CW coil, manual roll filter								
1750 - 2750	ea.	Preventative & insurance inspection and general maintenance (25 MH/year)	375	165	40	0.75 KW	20	100
08 MECHANICAL 083 FIRE PROTECTION 0832 SPRINKLERS								
Automatic Sprinkler System, Wet Type, Concealed Piping	HEAD	Preventative maintenance & repair (.05 MH/year)	.75	.10	.05	N/A	25	100
09 ELECTRICAL 091 SERVICE & DISTRIBUTION 0911 HIGH TENSION SERVICE & DIST.								
Circuit Breakers, metalclad drawout, 0-599 volts, all sizes	EA.	Preventative inspection & general maintenance (1.0 M.H./yr.)	14.6	1.0	.1	N/A	(See maint	N/A
(Cont.)	EA.	Repair failed component (.0027 failures/yr. x 47.2 M. H./Failure)	1.86	.0027 times' I.C.	N/A			

ITEM DESCRIPTION	UNIT OF MEASURE	MAINTENANCE DESCRIPTION	MAINTENANCE ANNUAL COST			ENERGY DEMAND (EU)	REPLACEMENT LIFE (YRS)	PERCENT REPLACED
			LABOR	MATERIAL	EQUIPMENT			
09 ELECTRICAL 091 SERVICE & DISTRIBUTION 0911 HIGH TENSION SERVICE & DIST.								
Circuit Breakers, metalclad drawout, 0-599 volts, all sizes	EA.	Replacement of component with spare (.0027 failure/yr. x 2.9 M. H. Failure)	.01	.0027 times I.C.	N/A			
Transformers, dry tape 0-750 KVA, below 15,000 volts	ea.	Preventative inspection & general maintenance (20.0 M.H./yr.)	292.4	30.0	2.0	1½-3%	30	100
	ea.	Repair failed component (.0036 failures/yr. x 67.0 M.H. failures)	3.53	.0036 times I.C.	N/A			
	ea.	Replacement of component with spare (.0036 failure/yr. x 39.9 M.H. failure)	2.10	.0036 times I.C.	N/A			
	ea.	Preventative inspection & general maintenance (30 M.H. /yr.)	438.6	50.0	4.0	1½-3% KW loss	30	100
09 ELECTRICAL 092 LIGHTING & POWER 0922 LIGHTING EQUIPMENT								
Fluorescent interior lighting fixtures - 2/40 watt tubes (20,000 burning hours)	EA.	Dusting - feather duster (.25 min. per quarter)	.19	.01	N/A	1 KW	20	100
(Cont.)								

ITEM DESCRIPTION	UNIT OF MEASURE	MAINTENANCE DESCRIPTION	MAINTENANCE ANNUAL COST			ENERGY DEMAND (EU)	REPLACEMENT LIFE (YRS)	PERCENT REPLACED
			LABOR	MATERIAL	EQUIPMENT			
09 ELECTRICAL 092 LIGHTING & POWER 0922 LIGHTING EQUIPMENT								
Fluorescent interior lighting fixtures - 2/40 watt tubes (20,000 burning hours)	EA.	Washing fixture lense, etc. High use areas(10.0 min/quarter)	7.69	.40	.10			
	EA.	Washing fixture lense, etc. - low use areas (10.0 min./year)	1.92	.10	.03			
	EA.	Re-Lamp fixture (5.0 min. every 2.5 years)	.38	.64	N/A			
	EA.	Repair fixture	.10	.10	N/A			
Hi-pressure sodium vapor lighting fixtures, 250 watt (20,000 burning hours)	Ea.	Cleaning (5.0 min/yr.)	.96	.10	N/A			
	Ea.	Re-lamp fixture (20.0 min. every 2.5 years)	1.55	18.0	N/A			
	Ea.	Re-pair fixture	.10	.10	N/A			
09 ELECTRICAL 093 SPEC. ELECTRICAL SYSTEM 0933 EMERGENCY LIGHT & POWER								
Generators, steam turbine driven, 1000 KW	EA.	Preventative inspection & general maintenance (50 MH/yr.)	765	300	75		25	100
	EA.	Repair failed component (.350 failures/yr. x 234.0 MH/failure)	1253	600	75			
(Cont.)								

ITEM DESCRIPTION		UNIT OF MEASURE	MAINTENANCE DESCRIPTION	MAINTENANCE ANNUAL COST			ENERGY DEMAND (EU)	REPLACE-MENT LIFE (YRS)	PERCENT REPLACED
				LABOR	MATERIAL	EQUIPMENT			
09	ELECTRICAL								
093	SPEC. ELECTRICAL SYSTEM								
0933	EMERGENCY LIGHT & POWER								
	Generators, steam turbine driven, 1000 KW (600 PSI @ 750° F w/4" mercury back pressure)	EA.	Preventative inspection & general maintenance (50 MH/yr.)	765	300	75	14,000 lb/hr.	25	100
		EA.	Repair failed component (.350 failures/yr. x 234.0 MH/failure)	1253	600	75			
		EA.	Replacement of component with spare (.350 failures/yr. x 201.0 MH/failure)	1076	800	75			
	Generators, gas turbine driven, 1000 KW	EA.	Preventative inspection & general maintenance (72 MH/yr.)	1100	400	100	106 gal per hr. (JP fuel)	25	100
		EA.	Repair failed component (.550 failures/yr. x 190.0 MH/failure	1599	800	100			
		EA.	Replacement of component with spare (.550 failures/yr. x 400 MH/failure)	3366	1200	100			
	Generators, Recip. Diesel, 1000 KW	EA.	Preventative inspection & general maintenance (72 MH/yr.)	1100	400	100	74 gal per hr. (Diesel fuel)	25	100
		EA.	Repair failed component (133 MH/yr.)	2035	1000	125			
		EA.	Replacement of component with spare.	4284	1200	125			

APPENDIX F
LIFE CYCLE COSTING FORMS

This appendix provides the design professional with recommended formats to perform a life cycle cost analysis. The forms are designed to be used in conjunction with the methodology discussed in Chapter 6, "Design Methodology." Both Chapter 5, "Formats," and Chapter 6 provide a discussion in the use of these forms. Chapter 7, "Case Studies," illustrates by examples how these sheets can be utilized.

Life Cycle Costing Summary

Project _____   Item _____

Team Members _____   Team _____

Team Members _____   Date _____

Summary of Change (Study Area, Original & Proposed)

Estimated Savings Cost Summary:

	Arch.	Struct.	Mech.	Elec.	Site	Total
Initial Cost Savings						
Life Cycle Cost Savings (PW)						
Annual Energy Savings (EU)						

Percent Savings Initial _____

Percent Savings Life Cycle _____

Percent Savings Energy _____

FIGURE F-1 Life cycle costing summary.

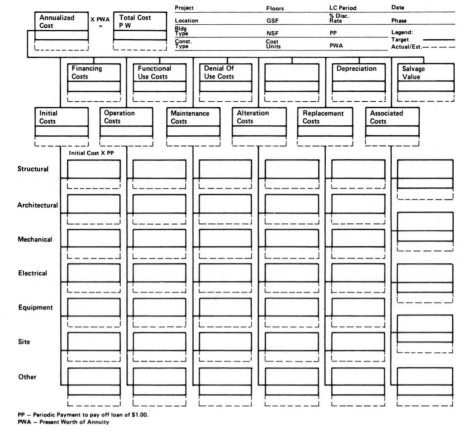

PP — Periodic Payment to pay off loan of $1.00.
PWA — Present Worth of Annuity

FIGURE F-2 Life cycle cost model.

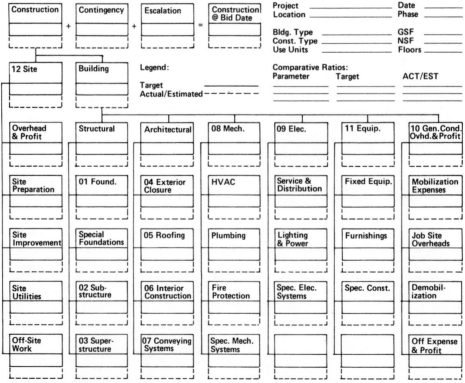

FIGURE F-3 Initial-cost model.

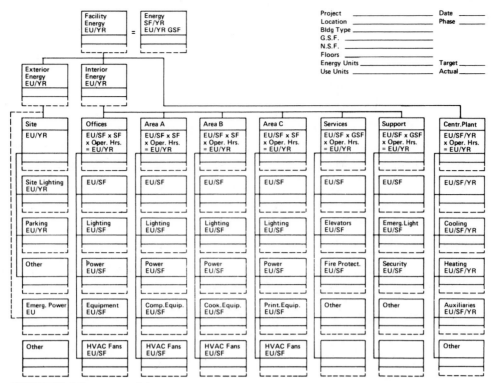

FIGURE F-4 Energy model.

Function Analysis

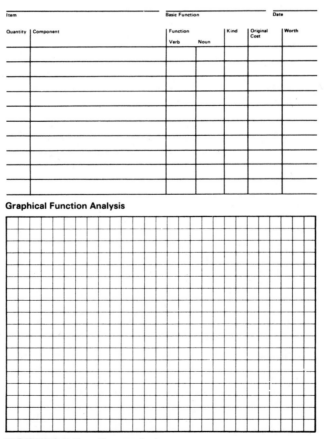

Quantity	Component	Function		Kind	Original Cost	Worth
		Verb	Noun			

Graphical Function Analysis

FIGURE F-5 Function analysis.

Idea Comparison

Idea	Advantages	Disadvantages	Estimated Potential Savings	
			Inital	Life Cycle

FIGURE F-6 Idea comparison (advantages and disadvantages).

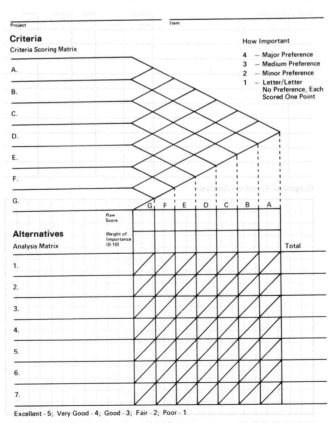

Weighted Evaluation

FIGURE F-7 Weighted evaluation

Life Cycle Cost Analysis
Using Annualized Costs

Item _____ Date _____

		Original	Alt. No. 1	Alt. No. 2

Input Data

Collateral & Instant Contract Costs

Initial Costs	Original	Alt. No. 1	Alt. No. 2
Base Cost			
Interface Costs			
a. _____			
b. _____			
c. _____			
Other Initial Costs			
a. _____			
b. _____			
c. _____			
Total Initial Cost Impact (IC)			
Initial Cost Savings			

Salvage & Replacement Costs

Single Expenditures @ _____ Interest	Original	Alt. No. 1	Alt. No. 2
Present Worth			
1. Year _____ Amount			
PW = Amount x (PW Factor _____) =			
2. Year _____ Amount			
Amount x (PW Factor _____) =			
3. Year _____ Amount			
Amount x (PW Factor _____) =			
4. Year _____ Amount			
Amount x (PW Factor _____) =			
5. Year _____ Amount			
Amount x (PW Factor _____) =			
Salvage Amount x (PW Factor _____) =			

Output

Life Cycle Costs (Annualized)

Annual Owning & Operating Costs	Original	Alt. No. 1	Alt. No. 2
1. Capital IC x (PP_____) =			
Recovery _____ Years @ _____ %			
Replacement Cost: PP x PW			
a. Year _____			
b. Year _____			
c. Year _____			
d. Year _____			
e. Year _____			
Salvage:			
2. Annual Costs			
a. Maintenance			
b. Operations			
c. _____			
d. _____			
e. _____			
3. Total Annual Costs			
Annual Difference (AD)			
4. Present Worth of Annual Difference			
(PWA Factor_____) x AD			

PP· Periodic Payment to pay off loan of $1.
PWA· Present Worth of Annuity (What $1 payable periodically is worth today).
PW· Present Worth (What $1 due in future is worth today).

▨ Future Costs
▢ Present Costs

FIGURE F-8 Life cycle cost analysis—annualized method.

Item:		Original		Alternate No. 1		Alternate No. 2		Alternate No 3.	
Life Cycle Period: Date:		Estimated Costs	Present Worth	Estimated Costs	Present Worth	Estimated Costs	Present Worth	Estimated Costs	Present Worth
Collateral/Initial Costs	Base Cost _____								
	Interface Costs								
	a. _____								
	b. _____								
	c. _____								
	Other Initial Costs								
	a. _____								
	b. _____								
	Total Initial Cost Impact (IC)								
Salvage & Replacement Costs	Single Expenditures @ _____ Interest								
	1. Year_____PW Factor _____								
	2. Year_____PW Factor _____								
	3. Year_____PW Factor _____								
	4. Year_____PW Factor _____								
	5. Year_____PW Factor _____								
	Salvage Yr._____PW Factor _____								
	Total Present Worth								
Annual Costs	Annual Costs @ _____ Interest								
	a. Maintenance								
	Escal.Rate _____ PWA Factor _____								
	b. Operations								
	Escal.Rate _____ PWA Factor _____								
	c. Others								
	Escal.Rate _____ PWA Factor _____								
	d. Others								
	Escal.Rate _____ PWA Factor _____								
	e. Others								
	Escal.Rate _____ PWA Factor _____								
	Total Annual Costs								
	Total Present Worth Costs								
	Life Cycle (PW) Savings								

PW — Present Worth   PWA — Present Worth Of Annuity

FIGURE F-9 Life cycle cost analysis—present-worth method.

Life Cycle Costing Estimate
General Purpose Work Sheet

Study Title: _____

Discount Rate: _____ Economic Life: _____

		Original Describe:		Alternative 1 Describe:		Alternative 2 Describe:		Alternative 3 Describe:	
		Estimated Costs	Present Worth	Estimated Costs	Present Worth	Estimated Costs	Present Worth	Estimated Costs	Present Worth
Initial Costs	**Initial Costs** A. _____ B. _____ C. _____ D. _____ E. _____ F. _____ G. _____ H. _____ I. _____ J. Contingencies ___%_____ K. Escalation ___%_____ **Total Initial Cost**								
Owning Costs	**Operations (Annual)** Diff. Escal. Rate PWA W/Escal. A. _____ B. _____ C. _____ D. _____ E. _____ F. _____ **Total Annual Operations Costs**								
	Maintenance (Annual) Diff. Escal. Rate PWA W/Escal. A. _____ B. _____ C. _____ D. _____ E. _____ F. _____ G. _____ **Total Annual Maintenance Costs**								
	Replacement/Alterations (Single Expenditure) Year PW Factor A. _____ B. _____ C. _____ D. _____ E. _____ F. _____ G. _____ H. _____ I. _____ J. _____ **Total Replacement/Alteration Costs**								
	Tax Elements Diff. Escal. Rate PWA W/Escal. A. _____ B. _____ C. _____ D. _____ E. _____ F. _____ G. _____ **Total Tax Elements**								
	Associated (Annual) Diff. Escal. Rate PWA W/Escal. A. _____ B. _____ C. _____ **Total Annual Associated Costs**								
	Total Owning Present Worth Costs								
Salvage	**Salvage At End Of Economic Life** Year PW Factor Building (Struc., Arch., Mech., Elec., Equip.) Other _____ Sitework _____ **Total Salvage**								
LCC	**Total Present Worth Life Cycle Costs**								
	Life-Cycle Present Worth Dollar Savings								

PW — Present Worth   PWA — Present Worth Of Annuity

FIGURE F-10 Life cycle costing estimate—general purpose.

GLOSSARY

TERM	DEFINITION
Alteration costs	Those costs for anticipated modernization or changing of a facility or space to provide a new function.
Alternatives	The different choices or methods by which functions may be attained.
Annualized method	Economic method that requires conversion of all present and future expenditures to a uniform annual cost.
Annuity	A series of equal payments or receipts to be paid or received at the ends of successive periods of equal time.
Associated costs	These costs may include: functional use, denial of use, security and insurance, utilities (other than energy), waste disposal, start-up, etc.
Baseline	The point in time against which investment opportunities are measured.
Benefit/cost analysis	Technique intended to relate the economic benefits of a solution to the costs incurred in providing the solution.
Brainstorming	A widely used creativity technique for generating a large quantity and wide variety of ideas for alternative ways of solving a problem or making a decision. All judgment and evaluation are suspended during the free-wheeling generation of ideas.
Constant dollars	Dollars that have not been adjusted for the effects of expected future inflation or deflation; sometimes referred to as dollars as of a specific date (for example, "1980 dollars").
Constraint	A condition, specification, requirement, code, standard, guide, or program item that limits the ways in which a function can be achieved; a type of criterion.
Cost/energy model	A diagram, graph, tabulation, or equation whose elements and subelements provide a breakdown of the actual, estimated, or target costs and energy units, or both, of an item and its subitems.
Depreciation	An accounting device that distributes the monetary value (less salvage value) of a tangible asset over the estimated years of productive or useful life. It is a process of allocation, not valuation.
Discount factor	The factor for any specific discount rate that translates expected cost or benefit in any specific future year into its present value. The discount factor is equal to $1/(1 + r)^t$, where r is the discount rate and t is the number of years since the date of initiation, renewal or expansion of a program or project.
Discount or interest rate	The minimum acceptable rate of return for the client for investment purposes, or the current prime or borrowing rate of interest.

TERM	DEFINITION
Economic life	That period over which an investment is considered for satisfying a particular need. Normally, the owner must establish this time frame.
Engineering economics	Technique that allows the assessment of proposed engineering alternatives on the basis of considering their economic consequences over time.
Equivalent dollars	Dollars, both present and future, expressed in a common baseline reflecting the time value of money and inflation. (See Present Worth and Annualized Method.)
Equivalent full-load hours	Total energy consumption divided by the full-load energy input. This gives the number of hours a piece of equipment would need to operate at its full capacity to consume as much energy as it did operating at various part-loads.
Escalation (differential) rate	That rate of inflation above the general devaluation of the purchasing power of the dollar.
Financing costs	The costs of any debt associated with the facility's capital costs.
Function analysis	A technique using a verb-noun relationship for identifying and describing the functions of an item in a general way so that some functions can be eliminated and other functions combined.
Inflation	A continuing rise in the general price levels, caused usually by an increase in the volume of money and credit relative to available goods.
Initial costs	Costs associated with initial development of a facility, including project costs (fees, real estate, site, etc.) as well as construction cost.
Interest rate	See Discount Rate.
Life cycle costing	An economic assessment of an item, area, system, or facility and competing design alternatives considering all significant costs of ownership over the economic life, expressed in terms of equivalent dollars.
Maintenance costs	The regular custodial care and repair, annual maintenance contracts, and salaries of facility staff performing maintenance tasks. Usually replacement items less than $5,000 in value or having a life of less than 5 years are also included.
Nonrecurring cost	Cost that occurs, or is expected to occur, only once.
Operation (energy) costs	The category of items such as fuel, salaries, etc., required to operate the facility or installation.
Payback period	The time it takes the savings resulting from a modification to pay back the costs involved. A simple payback period does not consider the time value of money. A discounted payback period does.
Present-worth method	Economic method that requires conversion of all present and future expenditures to a baseline of today's cost.
Rate of return	The interest rate that, over a period of time, equates the benefits derived from an opportunity to the investment cost of the project.
Recurring costs	Costs that recur on a periodic basis throughout the life of a project.
Replacement costs	Those one-time costs to be incurred in the future to maintain the original function of the facility or item.
Roadblock	An objection or a delaying tactic from a person or a group of people attempting to resist changes.
Salvage value	The value (positive if it has residual economic value and negative if requiring demolition) of competing alternatives at the end of the life cycle period.

TERM	DEFINITION
Sensitivity analysis	A technique to assess the relative effect a change in the input variable(s) has on the resulting output.
Sunk cost	Cost which has already been incurred and should not be considered in future economic decision making.
Target (cost or energy)	A goal, expectation, budget, or estimate of the minimum an item should cost (or consume energy) during one or more phases of its life cycle. There is often very poor correlation of the value of a cost (energy) target for an item relative to the needs and wants contained in the requirements, specifications, and conditions for the item. The value of the target is frequently based on how much a similar item has cost in the past, how much money is or can be made available for the item, or how much the item is worth to the buyer and user of the item. The worth of an item, as used in value engineering, is the lowest possible target for the item.
Tax elements	Those assignable costs pertaining to taxes, credits, and depreciation.
Time horizon	The ending point of the life cycle cost analysis, the cutoff, or last year, of the analysis.
Time value of money	A name given to the notion that the use of money costs money. Commitment of dollars to a project requires that it either be borrowed (thus incurring an interest charge) or that it be taken from owner resources (thus foregoing potential interest income). Because of these interest costs, the time at which money is required (today, next year, 10 years from now) becomes very important in economic decision making.
UNIFORMAT	A framework of construction cost categories suggested by the AIA and developed by the General Services Administration to be used by designers and others working in the various phases of a project.
Useful life	The period of time over which a building element may be expected to give service. It may represent physical, technological, or economic life.
Value Engineering (VE)	"A creative, organized approach whose objective is to optimize the life cycle costs and performance of a facility"—A. J. Dell'Isola.

BIBLIOGRAPHY

LIFE CYCLE COSTING

Apartment Building Income/Expense Analysis, The Institute of Real Estate Management, 430 N. Michigan Avenue, Chicago, IL 60611. This report compiles both annual operating expenses and rental income information by building location, age, and type of ownership.

Discount Rates to Be Used in Evaluating Time Distributed Costs and Benefits, Office of Management and Budget Circular A-94, Washington, Mar. 27, 1972.

Evaluation of the Health Facilities Building Process, vol. IV, *Evaluation of LCC,* U.S. Department of Health, Education, and Welfare, Washington, Mar. 31, 1973.

Feldman, Edwin B., *Building Design for Maintainability,* McGraw-Hill Book Company, New York, 1975.

Griffith, J. W., *Life Cycle Cost-Benefit Analysis: A Basic Course in Economic Decision Making,* 1975. Document PB-251 848/LK, National Technical Information Center, Springfield, VA 22151.

Harper, G. Neil (ed.), *Computer Applications in Architecture and Engineering,* McGraw-Hill Book Company, New York, 1968.

HAS Six-Month National Data, Hospital Administration Services, Division of the American Hospital Association, 840 Lake Shore Drive, Chicago, IL 60611. Includes institutional and departmental-level expenses for both general and teaching hospitals gathered from some 2000 hospitals participating in the system.

Haviland, David S., *Life Cycle Cost Analysis 2: Using It in Practice,* The American Institute of Architects, Washington, 1978.

Kirk, Stephen J., "Economic Building Performance Model," unpublished thesis, School of Architecture and Urban Design, University of Kansas, 1974.

Kirk, Stephen J., "Life Cycle Costing Can Be a Problem Solving Methodology," *Specifying Engineer,* June 1979.

Kirk, Stephen J., "Life Cycle Costing: Increasingly Popular Route to Design Value," *Architectural Record,* December 1979 and January 1980 (2-part article).

Laventhol and Horwath, *Lodging Industry.* This accounting firm specializing in operations of the hotel industry produces reports each year detailing operating ratios for selected major hotels and motels.

LCC-1, Life Cycle Costing Procurement Guide, U.S. Department of Defense, Washington, July 1970.

LCC-2, Casebook—Life Cycle Costing in Equipment Procurement, U.S. Department of Defense, Washington, July 1970.

LCC-3, Life Cycle Costing Guide For System Acquisition, U.S. Department of Defense, Washington, January 1973.

Life Cycle Budgeting as an Aid to Decision Making, Building Information Circular, U.S. Department of Health, Education, and Welfare, Office of Facilities Engineering and Property Management, Washington, 1973 (draft).

Life Cycle Cost Analysis, A Guide for Architects, The American Institute of Architects, Washington, 1977.

Life Cycle Costing Guide, Facilities Group, National Aeronautics and Space Administration, Washington, April 24, 1978.

Life Cycle Costing in the Public Buildings Service, General Services Administration, Public Building Service, Washington, 1976.

Life Cycle Costing—The Concept—Application in Conventional Design, Air Force Civil Engineering.

Life Cycle Costing Workbook: A Guide for the Implementation of Life Cycle Costing in the Federal Supply Service, General Services Administration, Washington, 1977.

Life Cycle Management Model for Project Management of Buildings, General Services Administration, Public Building Service, July 1972.

Major Systems Acquisitions, Office of Management and Budget Circular A-109, Washington, April 5, 1976.

National Energy Conservation Policy Act, Public Law 95-619, Nov. 9, 1978.

Nielsen, Kris R., "Tax Consideration in Building Design," *AIA Journal,* September 1973.

Office Building Experience Exchange Report, The Building Owners and Managers Association International, 1221 Massachusetts Avenue, N.W., Washington, DC 20005. Report includes data and analyses of office building costs. Over 1000 buildings and data are also broken down by age, height, size, and location of buildings.

"Operating Percentages, Income and Net Profit Data for Motels of Different Sizes," *Motel/Motor Inn Journal,* Temple, Texas, each year in July.

Ruegg, Rosalie T., *Solar Heating and Cooling in Buildings: Methods of Economic Evaluation,* NBSIR 75-712, National Bureau of Standards, Washington, July 1975.

Sizemore, M. M., H. O. Clark, and W. S. Ostrander, *Energy Planning for Buildings,* The American Institute of Architects, 1979.

Smith, Hinchman & Grylls Associates, Inc., *Life Cycle Costing Workbook,* Washington, 1979. (ACEC/AIA Workshops handout.)

Tax Information on Depreciation, Internal Revenue Service Publication 534 (issued annually).

Terotechnology—An Introduction to the Management of Physical Resources, The National Terotechnology Centre, Cleeve Road, Leatherhead, Surrey KT227SA, United Kingdom, 1976.

UNIFORMAT: Automated Cost Control, General Services Administration, November 1975.

Williams, John E., "Life Cycle Costing: An Overview," Paper presented to the American Institute of Industrial Engineers and the American Association of Cost Engineers Joint Conference, Washington, Oct. 5–6, 1977.

ECONOMICS

Economic Analysis and Program Evaluation for Resource Management, Army Regulation No. 11-28, Headquarters, Dept. of the Army, Washington, Dec. 2, 1975.

Economic Analysis Handbook, Naval Facilities Engineering Command, Washington, July 1980. Page 442.

Engineering Economy, 2d ed., American Telephone and Telegraph Company, Engineering Department, 1975.

Grant, Eugene L., and W. Grant Ireson, *Principles of Engineering Economy,* The Ronald Press Company, New York, 1970.

Jelen, F. C. (ed.), *Cost and Optimization Engineering,* McGraw-Hill Book Company, New York, 1970.

Samuelson, Paul A., *Economics,* 9th ed., McGraw-Hill Book Company, New York, 1980.

Stone, P. A., *Building Design Evaluation: Costs in Use,* E. & F. N. Spon, London, 1975.

Stone, P. A., *Building Economy,* 2d ed., Pergamon Press, London, 1976.

VALUE ENGINEERING

Dell'Isola, A. J., *Value Engineering in the Construction Industry,* Van Nostrand Reinhold Company, New York 1975.

Fallon, Carlos, *Value Analysis to Improve Productivity,* John Wiley & Sons, Inc., 1971.

Handler, A. Benjamin, *Systems Approach to Architecture,* American Elsevier Publishing Company, New York, 1970.

Miles, Lawrence D., *Techniques of Value Analysis and Engineering,* 2d ed., McGraw-Hill Book Company, New York, 1972.

Parker, Donald, *Value Engineering Theory,* The Value Foundation, 986 National Press Building, Washington, DC 20045, 1977.

Whiting, Charles, *Creative Thinking,* Reinhold Publishing Corporation, New York, 1958.

ESTIMATING

ASHRAE 1977 Fundamentals, American Society of Heating, Refrigerating, and Air-Conditioning Engineers, Inc., New York, 1977.

ASHRAE Standard 90-75: Energy Conservation in New Building Design, American Society of Heating, Refrigerating, and Air-Conditioning Engineers, Inc., New York, 1975.

Automated Cost Control and Estimating System: Data Base, General Services Administration, Public Building Service, Washington, November 1975.

Building Cost File, Construction Publishing Company, Inc., New York, NY 10016. Published in Eastern, Southern, Central, and Western regional editions yearly.

Building Systems Cost Guide, Robert Snow Means Company, Inc., Kingston, Mass. (yearly).

Current Construction Costs, Lee Saylor, Inc., Walnut Creek, Calif. (yearly).

Dodge Construction Systems Costs, McGraw-Hill Book Company, New York, NY 10020 (yearly).

Dodge Guide to Public Works and Heavy Construction Costs, McGraw-Hill Book Company, New York, NY 10020 (yearly).

Dodge Manual for Building Construction Pricing and Scheduling, McGraw-Hill Book Company, New York, NY 10020 (yearly).

Dubin, Fred S., and Chalmers G. Long, Jr., *Energy Conservation Standards For Building Design, Construction, and Operation,* McGraw-Hill Book Company, New York, 1978.

Means Cost Data, R. S. Means Company, Kingston, Mass. (yearly).

Miller, C. William, *Estimating and Cost Control in Electrical Construction Design,* Van Nostrand Reinhold Company, New York, 1978.

Ostwald, P. F., *Cost Estimating for Engineering and Management,* Prentice-Hall, Inc., Englewood Cliffs, N.J., 1974.

Trane Air Conditioning Manual, Trane Co., La Crosse, Wis., 1977.

U.S. Air Force Manual 88-8, Engineering Weather Data, U.S. Air Force, Washington, 1975.

INDEX

About the Authors

Alphonse J. Dell'Isola is a Vice President and Director of the Value Management Division of Smith, Hinchman & Grylls Associates, Inc. (SH & G). A graduate of the Massachusetts Institute of Technology, he has been a consultant to the construction industry on cost-related services since 1966. In 1969 he was appointed construction consultant to the President's Advisory Council on Management Improvement. *Engineering News-Record* has cited him for outstanding achievement in value engineering, and he has received the Distinguished Service Award and the Fellowship Award from the American Society of Value Engineers. He is also the author of *Value Engineering in the Construction Industry*, and he is currently conducting seminars worldwide on cost and scheduling control.

Stephen J. Kirk is an Associate and Project Manager in the Value Management Division of SH & G. He holds bachelor's and master's degrees in architecture and is a registered architect in California. Mr. Kirk has developed various computer-based analytical techniques to aid architects and engineers in design decision making. He has presented papers on LCC to the National Science Foundation and the Society of American Value Engineers, and has written articles for such periodicals as *Architectural Record*, *Navy Civil Engineer*, and *Specifying Engineer*. A guest lecturer on the faculty of the American Institute of Architects, he is a member of that organization, as well as of the Society of American Value Engineers and the Society of American Military Engineers. Mr. Kirk was identified in "Portrait of a Young Architect" in the *Military Engineer* (1980) and has been selected for inclusion in *Who's Who in the East* (1981).

About the Authors

Alphonse J. Dell'Isola is a Vice President and Director of the Value Management Division of Smith, Hinchman & Grylls Associates, Inc. (SH & G). A graduate of the Massachusetts Institute of Technology, he has been a consultant to the construction industry on cost-related services since 1966. In 1969 he was appointed construction consultant to the President's Advisory Council on Management Improvement. *Engineering News-Record* has cited him for outstanding achievement in value engineering, and he has received the Distinguished Service Award and the Fellowship Award from the American Society of Value Engineers. He is also the author of *Value Engineering in the Construction Industry*, and he is currently conducting seminars worldwide on cost and scheduling control.

Stephen J. Kirk is an Associate and Project Manager in the Value Management Division of SH & G. He holds bachelor's and master's degrees in architecture and is a registered architect in California. Mr. Kirk has developed various computer-based analytical techniques to aid architects and engineers in design decision making. He has presented papers on LCC to the National Science Foundation and the Society of American Value Engineers, and has written articles for such periodicals as *Architectural Record*, *Navy Civil Engineer*, and *Specifying Engineer*. A guest lecturer on the faculty of the American Institute of Architects, he is a member of that organization, as well as of the Society of American Value Engineers and the Society of American Military Engineers. Mr. Kirk was identified in "Portrait of a Young Architect" in the *Military Engineer* (1980) and has been selected for inclusion in *Who's Who in the East* (1981).